"Many security leaders are traditionally in charge of correcting misconceptions just as much as they are in charge of building up solid security practices. We have plenty of resources on practices—but this book is the crucial guide to that essential myth busting."

—Phil Venables
gle Cloud

"I'm writing this on my phone, over Wi-Fi, in an airplane world's largest security conferences. The fact that I'm able to d e really learned about cybersecurity over the decades. Now it's all o share. Thank the wise authors, and most importantly: GET OFF T

—Wendy Nather
Head of Advisory CISOs, Cisco

"This book is astounding. A true tour de force—which I have never said about any other book. Inverting the viewpoint is a stroke of genius. This is going to be on my grabbable-at-any-time shelf. What I learned, recalled, and was refreshed on with technically astute agnosticism cannot be measured; just appreciated as a profound historical compilation of security practice and theory. Bravo!"

—Winn Schwartau
Founder and Chief Visionary Officer, The Security Awareness Company

"I am happy to endorse the central idea of this book—that cybersecurity is rife with myths that are themselves part of the problem. The brain wants to understand, the world grows ever more complicated, and the sum of the two is myth-making. As the authors say, even if some understanding is true at some time, with enough change what was true becomes a myth soon enough. As such, an acquired immunity to myths is a valuable skill for the cybersecurity practitioner if no other. The paramount goal of all security engineering is No Silent Failure, but myths perpetuate if not create silent failure. Why? Because a state of security is the absence of unmitigable surprise and you cannot mitigate what you don't know is going on. Myths blind us to reality. Ignorance of them is not bliss. This book is a vaccine."

—Dan Geer
CISO, In-Q-Tel

"This is a fun read for all levels. I like their rapid fire delivery and the general light they cast on so many diverse myths. This book will change the cybersecurity industry for the better."

—Michael Sikorski
Author of *Practical Malware Analysis* & CTO, Unit 42 at Palo Alto Networks

Cybersecurity Myths and Misconceptions

Cybersecurity Myths and Misconceptions

Avoiding the Hazards and Pitfalls that Derail Us

Eugene H. Spafford, Leigh Metcalf, and Josiah Dykstra

Illustrations by Pattie Spafford

Addison-Wesley

Boston • Columbus • New York • San Francisco • Amsterdam • Cape Town
Dubai • London • Madrid • Milan • Munich • Paris • Montreal • Toronto • Delhi • Mexico City
São Paulo • Sydney • Hong Kong • Seoul • Singapore • Taipei • Tokyo

For information about buying this title in bulk quantities, or for special sales opportunities (which may include electronic versions; custom cover designs; and content particular to your business, training goals, marketing focus, or branding interests), please contact our corporate sales department at corpsales@pearsoned.com or (800) 382-3419.

For government sales inquiries, please contact governmentsales@pearsoned.com.

For questions about sales outside the U.S., please contact intlcs@pearson.com.

Visit us on the Web: informit.com/aw

Library of Congress Control Number: 2022951313

ISBN-13: 978-0-13-792923-8
ISBN-10: 0-13-792923-4

2 2023

Pearson's Commitment to Diversity, Equity, and Inclusion

Pearson is dedicated to creating bias-free content that reflects the diversity of all learners. We embrace the many dimensions of diversity, including but not limited to race, ethnicity, gender, socioeconomic status, ability, age, sexual orientation, and religious or political beliefs.

Education is a powerful force for equity and change in our world. It has the potential to deliver opportunities that improve lives and enable economic mobility. As we work with authors to create content for every product and service, we acknowledge our responsibility to demonstrate inclusivity and incorporate diverse scholarship so that everyone can achieve their potential through learning. As the world's leading learning company, we have a duty to help drive change and live up to our purpose to help more people create a better life for themselves and to create a better world.

Our ambition is to purposefully contribute to a world where:

- Everyone has an equitable and lifelong opportunity to succeed through learning.
- Our educational products and services are inclusive and represent the rich diversity of learners.
- Our educational content accurately reflects the histories and experiences of the learners we serve.
- Our educational content prompts deeper discussions with learners and motivates them to expand their own learning (and worldview).

While we work hard to present unbiased content, we want to hear from you about any concerns or needs with this Pearson product so that we can investigate and address them.

- Please contact us with concerns about any potential bias at https://www.pearson.com/report-bias.html.

Contents at a Glance

Table of Contents

List of Figures and Illustrations

Foreword

When Gene ("Spaf") Spafford asked me to write a foreword to this book, I asked to see some of it first. First, I read the Table of Contents and was much taken and amused by the droll way in which the authors introduced the myths that mythguide us. Then I thought they should revise the title to *Cybersecurity Mythconceptions*. The introduction is wonderfully clear and plain spoken, with a certain self-deprecating and disarming style that helps readers accept the possibility that they may have been taken in by myths and mythunderstandings (OK, that can get old, I guess, but it is so tempting!).

All kidding aside this is an important book. Cybersecurity is often all about decisions and choices we make as to which software we use, which practices we adopt, and which safety beliefs we hold dear. The clarity with which the authors explain how we might be misled (see, I stifled my addiction to puns) aids in making the book so effective. As they uncover each myth about cybersecurity, they allow us to feel superior—"How ironic that some people believe this dumb idea!" You are made to feel as if you would never fall for this, and somehow this makes each case all the more memorable.

This is a style reminiscent of C.S. Lewis's famous *The Screwtape Letters*, in which a senior satanic tempter teaches his young protégé, Wormwood, about the ways in which humans can be steered away from goodness and rationalize their behavior to justify it. Safe networking is a serious matter. The Internet and the more general "cyberspace" of all programmable objects can be hazardous not only owing to deliberate, malicious behavior, but also because of mistakes programmers, network operators, and others make.

I have long believed that accountability and agency are key to safety in online, cyber-environments. It must be possible to identify bad actors and hold them accountable. That will require both the ability to penetrate the veil of pseudonymity and international cooperation because cyberspace, like the Internet, crosses international boundaries in the normal course of operation. Agency is vital. Participants in cyberspace must have the tools necessary for protection, including legal structures and agreements to track down those engaged in harmful or criminal behavior.

Among the most powerful of defensive tools is critical thinking. This book is all about understanding how to think more critically about risks in cyberspace. This takes work. It's not a free lunch. Bad actors prey upon our frailties as humans. Sadly, that includes our natural inclination to help those in need. So many scams exploit these and other positive social feelings. This book provides us with the ability to see through these ruses. It also arms us with safer practices such as two-factor or multifactor authentication, use of cryptography, backup, and redundancy. There are many ways in which things can go wrong in the complex cyberspaces of the 21st century. A combination of personal, business, and governmental practices is needed to defend against risks. As is often the case, forewarned is forearmed.

Read the book, laugh at the right places, and put your learning to work. You won't regret it.

—Vint Cerf, Internet Pioneer, August 2022

Introduction

Imagine a hypothetical company, GoodLife Bank. GoodLife is a mid-size regional bank with 12 brick-and-mortar branches, online services, and 325 employees. Terry, the Chief Information Security Officer (CISO), wants to implement user activity monitoring for bank employees. The Chief Executive Officer (CEO), Pat, balks at the proposal. "Our people are fine. They have never stolen money from us before, and we have never had this monitoring. We will be fine. That's a waste of money," Pat says.

As another hypothetical, imagine a government organization, the Department of Redundant Information Department (DRID), part of the Agency for Propagating Bureaucracy (APB). At a staff meeting, the new Chief Information Officer (CIO) asks the DRID department head, Chris, what they have as security beyond the Federal Information Security Management Act (FISMA) minimums. Chris replies, "We do not need anything else—we do not have anything anyone would want to steal. Plus, no one would want to steal whatever we have." (You can see why he is a valued employee at DRID.)

Both CISOs, Chris and Terry, have fallen for myths about cybersecurity. Throughout this book, we'll return to these fictitious (but representative) organizations and personnel. They represent common views and approaches that we hope to illustrate.

There is a lot to know to be successful in the profession and application of cybersecurity. Knowledge is passed along in many forms, including formal education and experiential learning. Defending a computer from digital threats requires insights into how the hardware and software work, how defenses can block some threats and not others, and how to recognize when something is incorrect. One potentially dangerous pitfall is perpetuating traditional practices or beliefs as truth without evidence. While cybersecurity is an evolving discipline, we still hear the refrain "that's the way it's done" when we question an approach. The human brain naturally resists change, so it will take effort to overcome old myths.

Many aspects of culture are passed down as proverbs and stories. History and traditions are core to the human story; however, those who relay wisdom about how we're supposed to act do not necessarily supply practical or reliable advice. Folk wisdom and folklore are sometimes used merely to justify what we already do or believe rather than as informed guidelines for action.

Why do you wear a hat when you go outside in the cold? Did someone tell you that you lose 90% of your body heat from your head and you do not want to catch a cold? Motivating, perhaps. Correct? Hardly.[1]

1. You lose body heat through anything uncovered. You would freeze faster, utterly naked, except for a hat, than if you were bundled up with a bare scalp. And being physically cold is not what gets you sick anyway. "Wear a coat, or you will catch a cold" is more folk wisdom that predates the medical knowledge that viruses cause colds, not cold weather. See, for instance, www.nytimes.com/2004/10/26/health/the-claim-you-lose-most-of-your-body-heat-through-your-head.html

Some myths are stickier than others. That is, some are more pervasive and persistent, thus making them difficult to change. In Chapter 8, for example, we will talk about whether "the user is the weakest link." Lots of people hold that view, but it is misleading.

We want cybersecurity to be effective, informed, and reasonable. In our experience, we have seen people make errors and suboptimal choices because they are influenced by bias or misunderstanding. In a few cases, people know the hazards and plow on anyway. There is also an important distinction between being uninformed and being misinformed. The primary goal of this book is not to teach technology concepts for the first time, though that is a desirable side effect. Instead, we will focus on areas where people *think* they are informed.

There's considerable confusion about good security practices, but there seems to be some agreement on bad security practices, such as reusing passwords. Those "bad" practices might not be uniformly poor but depend on other parameters and conditions. Many of the bad practices sound logical, especially to people new to the field of cybersecurity, and that means they get adopted and repeated despite not being correct. For instance, why is the user not the weakest link? We hope that this book helps you to think more clearly about cybersecurity.

Our goal is to tackle decades of accumulated folk wisdom head-on. We want our readers to make better decisions grounded in reality. No matter how cybersecurity folk wisdom started or how it's still being spread, we assume that people have good intentions and are not deliberately trying to misinform.[2] Myths are not lies or intentional falsehoods. Myths are stories that embody a belief regarding some fact or phenomenon. Our goal is to set things straight where persistent pitfalls exist.

We also want to address some of people's innate biases when confronting complicated or new situations. We all have some heuristics we employ to make decisions, and we have biases about the outcomes. Many of those are suitable for everyday situations; however, computing is complex, and some adversaries do not behave according to our typical mental models. Understanding where the biases might (mis)lead our decision-making is valuable.

The goal of this book is not to blame or accuse anyone of wrongdoing! We know that not everyone falls for every pitfall. You might even be shocked that there are people who believe a particular myth on our list. Some of the concepts we discuss might have even been (mostly) true once upon a time, but the field continually advances, and circumstances change. Too many people think that cybersecurity is only about technology, but it is about more than that. As an illustration, many computer science degree programs do not include required courses in psychology despite the important role that people have in cybersecurity.

You might have never been exposed to the logical fallacies and cognitive biases described in this book. When you hear myths in your everyday encounters, do not belittle anyone. Instead, consider our

2. Except those in marketing, perhaps. Clark Stanley knew exactly the fraud of his snake oil.

suggestions to help explain another view. We present this book with humility. We have been wrong before, and we will be wrong again.[3] We all learned new things writing this book!

Let's be clear that not everything we came to understand long ago about cybersecurity was a false belief or idea. For part of the 1990s, SSL/TLS was considered unnecessary and unimportant. This was not a myth: it was the reality of the time for many enterprises. Eventually, it became desirable and indispensable.

Cybersecurity Myths of the Past

A few decades ago, a common myth was that antivirus (AV) companies created and released malware so people would need their products. You can see the popular appeal of believing that a company manufactures artificial demand and its solution, but this is no more than a conspiracy theory. (It was also part of the plot of a science fiction novel, *When HARLIE Was One*, by David Gerrold, written in 1972.)

We do not hear this myth often anymore. Why not? It seems to be one that faded away on its own. Today, most people recognize that antivirus software is necessary for good cybersecurity. There is evidence of criminals, vandals, and nation-states creating malware, but no evidence suggesting that antivirus companies are doing so. . . or ever did.

How might this myth have been dispelled earlier, even in the 1990s during its height?

- **Looking for evidence or studies to support the myth would be the first step.** Some people did investigate. No evidence was found. Those findings did not make the myth completely disappear, but they did chip away at the claim's veracity. Looking for data is a common technique we suggest for other myths in this book.
- **Another technique is to consider alternative explanations and motivations, then apply Occam's Razor: give priority to the most straightforward and least-complicated explanation.** For antivirus companies to be writing viruses, they would have to swear all their employees to secrecy because it would destroy their business if the truth leaked. Also, they would occasionally have to miss viruses (or set them loose internally) so as not to appear to have too much insider information. Moreover, they would need to employ actors to attend conferences and post online about writing "their" viruses. Is that simpler and more likely than having rogue authors unaffiliated with the companies?

This book is about myth-busting, but there will never be a world free of myths. This is because humans tend to create myths to help explain our experiences. In particular, we have evolved to process information quickly, and when we cannot immediately explain something, we formulate an answer.

3. Well, at least two of the three of us may be.

Myths will likely become more common and more challenging to correct going forward. People have access to a growing wealth of information, including misinformation. We have seen the spread of ludicrous and sometimes destructive myths, including some about contrails, vaccines, and space beings infiltrating governments. For many people, it's increasingly challenging to determine what is authentic and credible. This is why we all need the skills to spot myths as soon as they emerge and the techniques to help correct them, whether in cybersecurity or elsewhere.

Who Is This Book For?

This book is primarily for cybersecurity professionals and amateurs, including students, designers, developers, analysts, and decision-makers. Existing infosec professionals gain by improving cybersecurity when myths are dispelled. Those new to the field will better understand folk wisdom in context and preempt mistakes. For experienced practitioners, it will shed new light on techniques and approaches they might apply and advise how they can avoid inadvertently falling into traps that undermine good cybersecurity. It also suggests how more experienced practitioners might help mentor others.

If you are not in the field of cybersecurity, this book might still be for you. Cyber defense is relevant for everyone who relies on technology. That undoubtedly includes you. In particular, decision-makers and business leaders also need an accurate understanding of cybersecurity: They often accept or manage risk, a key element of what we describe throughout the book.

We do not presume that our readers have particular titles, experiences, or deep technical knowledge in specific areas, only that they are discerning, open-minded, and are somewhat familiar with the topic area. We provide references throughout the book and a list of further reading at the end of each chapter that, we believe, might be helpful if a reader needs more information than we provide. Two characteristics of a professional are lifelong learning and the willingness to challenge current beliefs upon receipt of new information; unlike in the political arena, it is usually *positive* when someone evolves their viewpoint![4]

The three co-authors—who work in academia, industry, and government—have all studied and written about cybersecurity and computer science. Science can update, validate, and dispel cybersecurity myths by using standardized methods and producing valid evidence. Engineering can use science to create more robust, reliable artifacts. The authors have, combined, close to a century of experience in everything from cybersecurity design and research to incident response to forensics and beyond. We work in science and engineering. Throughout our careers, we have seen people in cybersecurity repeatedly make avoidable mistakes resulting from myths and misconceptions. Our intent with this book is to educate students and practitioners; we believe it is the first book to consolidate this information in one place.

4. Cf. https://doi.org/10.1016/j.tics.2022.02.004

The Myth and Legend of Hackers

Astute readers will notice that we are deliberate when using the term *hackers* in this book about cybersecurity. Despite its origins as a label for a skilled technology enthusiast, an unfortunate negative connotation has overloaded this term. Because we support the positive meaning of hacker, we use **adversary** or **attacker** to describe those persons with malicious purposes. We might use the phrase "malicious cyber actor," a term of art that arose in U.S. government publications around 2011. We also use the term "bad guy" as a term to mean a generic malicious cyber actor; this use is not intended to imply gender, and neither is "good guy."

Hacker is not the only negative connotation in cybersecurity. As we will see in our discussions of several upcoming myths, the term *user* is used with disrespect and contempt in too many discussions. We encourage people to be sensitive to this issue, seek other terms, or be clear in their usage.

The Origin of Myths

Before we explore and dispel any myths, it will be helpful to understand their origins and why they are so persistent. One reason is that technology and threats change, but education is slow to catch up. Unless people take continuing education seriously, it's easy to fall behind when old truths become modern myths. All too often, when workloads are high and things are moving quickly, education is given a lower priority.

Myths and misconceptions exist, to varying degrees, among all groups. No person or organization is immune, even cybersecurity experts. Here are three examples:

- In a 2017 Pew Research Center 13-question survey of American adults about cybersecurity topics, most could correctly answer only two of them. Only 54% were able to identify examples of phishing attacks.[5]
- In interviews with 25 students who had taken at least one course in cybersecurity, researchers identified four common themes: over-generalizations, conflated concepts, biases, and incorrect assumptions. For example, "Many students over-generalize and form misconceptions by assuming that encryption achieves additional properties beyond confidentiality: preventing manipulation, protecting against theft, and ensuring availability." The researchers attributed these errors to inexperience in the field of cybersecurity.[6]
- A study of 20 non-experts and cybersecurity staff at a university revealed cybersecurity misconceptions among both staff and employees. For example, "Some employees believed that links were more dangerous than attachments as clicking them automatically compromised the computer, while others argued that attachments were harmless if you did not allow them to install."[7]

5. www.pewresearch.org/internet/2017/03/22/what-the-public-knows-about-cybersecurity/
6. https://digitalcommons.kennesaw.edu/cgi/viewcontent.cgi?article=1030&context=jcerp
7. www.usenix.org/system/files/conference/soups2018/soups2018-nicholson.pdf

Are Myths Different From Superstitions?

A book about myths and misconceptions might make you wonder about their relationship with superstitions.

Superstitions have permeated every facet of human existence for all of recorded history, from sports to weather to medicine. Perhaps you have a lucky pair of socks or avoid the numbers 13 or 666. Maybe you believe in jinxes or curses. These are, in formal terms, examples of magical thinking.

Digital life is not immune from magical thinking. Today we might have a ritual to close all the background apps on our phone or reboot the computer to "optimize their performance."[a] According to Matthew Hutson, author of *The 7 Laws of Magical Thinking: How Irrational Beliefs Keep Us Happy, Healthy, and Sane*, magical thinking helps us make sense of an irrational world and gives us comfort, agency, and control. We will return to this topic of magical thinking in Chapter 3.

Myth and superstition are different. A myth is an incorrect fact or incorrect explanation of observation, while superstition is a belief based on the supernatural. It is a myth that goldfish have a 3-second memory. It is a superstition that knocking on wood wards off bad luck. To give a computing-related example, many kids in the 1980s believed that blowing on game cartridges would fix technical problems because dust might be causing issues. Removing the cartridge, blowing on it, and reinserting it often fixed the problem: a poor initial mechanical connection. The explanation that it was dust was a myth. If they believed the cartridge was infested with a poltergeist, removed it and performed an exorcism, then reinserted it, that would be superstition. Either way, the act of removal and reinsertion would fix the problem and reinforce the belief.

This book focuses on myths, not superstition. If you think sticking crystals to your laptop and deploying firewall rules based on your horoscope will keep your system safe, then this book is not for you; however, we advise you to have good backups and insurance.

Some readers might be thinking, "Wait, what about religion?" We are not going to opine on that in any way. We will observe that we have yet to see any peer-reviewed, replicable studies confirming that prayers affect downtime from security incidents. Furthermore, if you believe your computer center is being attacked by demons, this book will not help you—burn some sage and hire an exorcist but do not be surprised if neither helps!

a. For more peculiar technology behaviors, see Nova, Nicholas, Miyake, Katherine, Chiu, Walton, and Kwon, Nancy, *Curious Rituals: Gestural Interaction in the Digital Everyday* (2012); https://curiousrituals.files.wordpress.com/2012/09/curiousritualsbook.pdf

Overarching Themes

We have written this book based on our experience, studies, and conversations with peers. A few fundamental ideas underlie all of what we have written, and we would like you to consider them as organizing principles for your work in the field.

First, cybersecurity is not merely about protecting computers and networks. Cybersecurity is about protecting the technology and data that underpin society. Computing is not an independent area of academic study—it is a field of technology that enables and supports modern life. Computing is used to run banks, utility systems, commerce, schools, law enforcement agencies, medical care, entertainment, and more. Lives depend on the correct functioning of systems. Our ability to interact in civil society would disappear if computing stopped working, often in sudden and unexpected ways. Thus, when we talk about defeating attacks on computing or protecting computing, it is more than computers and networks: It is fundamentally about protecting society and civilized life.

Second, cybersecurity involves computers; however, cybersecurity is primarily about humans. People program computers. People design and build computers. People buy computers and deploy them. And yes, people abuse computers. We should not lose sight of the fact that computers are tools used by people, intended for people, and built by people. Addressing cybersecurity issues requires focusing on humans and human actions.

Third, sometimes computers malfunction. It is also the case that sometimes people make mistakes. Usually, computers malfunction because of errors or oversights by the humans who designed or run them; computer hardware has become increasingly reliable. We should not attempt to excuse the bad behavior of a computer system by blaming the computer, as in "The computer decided" or "The computer made a mistake." The issues are usually the fault of whoever wrote the software, entered the data, or operated the system. The same is true of systems using Artificial Intelligence (AI) and Machine Learning (ML)—the problem is how those systems were trained and who decided to depend on their output. In every case, it is people who bear the responsibility. When a car runs a traffic light, we can almost always assign responsibility to the driver, not the vehicle or the light.

Last, as you can gather from these themes, we see cybersecurity as human-centric. Our goal with this book (and much of our professional work) is to help people understand how to use computing better and more safely. We are not interested in assigning blame, but rather in identifying ways for people to improve the technology and processes. We believe cybersecurity experts should be viewed as enablers of good practice, as allies and educators—not as authoritarian arbiters of arcane rules who mete out punishment for transgressions.

One way to look at the human-centric fundamentals is to realize there is a misconception, often amplified by anthropomorphic terms, that computers somehow "think." Computers do not think—people do. As you read through the book, we hope you identify other cases where biases and misconceptions tilt toward blaming computers instead of people.

Roadmap for This Book

This book is divided into four parts—general issues, human issues, contextual issues, and data issues—where we present more than 175 myths, biases, and misconceptions. The chapters are organized and tied together by themes that group similar myths. The chapters can be read independently or back-to-back. The section titles within the chapters identify specific myths or themes. In each section, we explain a myth or misconception, give some examples of it in practice, and discuss how to avoid it. Some chapters are technical, such as those on vulnerabilities, malware, and forensics. Others describe how cybersecurity is influenced by our thinking and decision-making, such as the chapters on logical fallacies and communication.

The material we present contains only a few technology-specific security suggestions—most of the items we present go to people's perceptions, decisions, and actions. This is because, as we noted, most cybersecurity problems are caused by people.[8] Many books discuss how to architect and operate technological solutions, although those are usually about applying patches (often imperfectly) to the underlying problems. Our book is intended to help you make progress against some of those root causes.

Cybersecurity, and computing in general, are rife with acronyms. We have endeavored to expand every acronym we use the first time; however, we also realize that an unfamiliar acronym might no longer be remembered once you have read a few chapters. Thus, we provide a table of acronyms at the end of the book, so if you encounter one that is unfamiliar, you can find an expansion of the term. If that is still a mystery, we recommend using your favorite search engine to get some additional background information—but (of course) be careful which links you follow!

Also, at the end, we have provided a set of short explanations of some of the concepts and terms used in the text. Thus, if you are unfamiliar with (for example) a firewall or the `log4j` vulnerability, you can read a short explanation in the appendix. We will warn you that these explanations are not intended to be tutorials! The appendix is solely intended to help the reader understand the material enough to grasp the basic ideas. Thus, if you run across a term you do not immediately recognize, look for it in the appendix. We do not promise it will be there, but it might be.

At the end of almost every chapter, we have provided some references for further exploration: books, academic papers, reports, and standards documents. These lists are not intended to be exhaustive, so if we have missed some that you think are particularly important, let us know at <mail:myth-misconception@googlegroups.com>, and if there are subsequent editions of this book, we will consider them for addition. Our intent is to provide you with some helpful starting points for further exploration. As we note in Chapter 1, cybersecurity is a journey, not a destination!

The chapters are interspersed with original hand-drawn illustrations that offer a lighthearted view of various myths. These images showcase the essence of some of the myths, and we believe they will entertain as much as they explain. We hope that you find them a whimsical addition to the writing.

8. https://techxplore.com/news/2022-06-cyberattacks-human-error.html

Disclaimer

The views expressed in this book are those of the authors alone. Reference to any specific commercial product, process, or service by trade name, trademark, manufacturer, or otherwise, does not constitute or imply endorsement, recommendation, or favoring by the United States Government, the Department of Defense, or any other organization with which the authors may be affiliated.

Register your copy of *Cybersecurity Myths and Misconceptions* on the InformIT site for convenient access to updates and/or corrections as they become available. To start the registration process, go to informit.com/register and log in or create an account. Enter the product ISBN (9780137929238) and click Submit. Look on the Registered Products tab for an Access Bonus Content link next to this product, and follow that link to access any available bonus materials. If you would like to be notified of exclusive offers on new editions and updates, please check the box to receive email from us.

Acknowledgments

Though this book is based on many decades of first-hand experience, it is more complete and richer because of others' ideas, questions, and insights. We thank our many friends and colleagues who engaged in valuable conversations and contributed ideas of myths and misconceptions over the years. Thanks, in particular, to Mikhail Atallah, Becky Bace, Jon Biggs, Matt Bishop, Bob Courtney, Earl Crane, Will Dorman, Matthew Dunlop, Simson Garfinkel, Jeffrey Havrilla, Allen Householder, David Isacoff, Brent Laminack, Amir Manteghi, Gary McGraw, William Hugh Murray, Peter Neumann, Ken Olthoff, Brad Pittack, Damien Riehl, and Deana Shick.

Special thanks to the people who reviewed draft materials and provided valuable suggestions and feedback: Matt Bishop, Tom Longstaff, Kathryn Renae Metcalf, Wendy Nather, Megan Nyre-Yu, Thomas Schreck, Winn Schwartau, and Elizabeth K. Spafford; Andrew Grosso and Mark Rasch provided insightful comments on the law chapter. Additional thanks to Vint Cerf for writing the foreword to this book.

We are grateful to the entire team at Pearson, who expertly helped in this endeavor. Our thanks to copyeditor Jill E. Hobbs who made, sure, we; didn't—use: incorrectpunctuation and globs of wrongly letter thingies, er, words. Our executive editor was James Manly and our development editor was Chris Cleveland; both patiently navigated working with the three authors and the illustrator, even when it required doing something in a new or creative way.

About the Authors

Eugene H. Spafford is one of the most senior academics in the field of cybersecurity. During his 40-plus years in computing—including 35 years as a faculty member at Purdue University, where he founded CERIAS, the Center for Education and Research in Information Assurance and Security—Spaf (as he is widely known) has worked on issues in privacy, public policy, law enforcement, intelligence, software engineering, education, social networks, operating systems, and cybersecurity. He has developed fundamental technologies in intrusion detection, incident response, firewalls, integrity management, and forensic investigation.

Dr. Spafford is a Fellow of the American Academy of Arts and Sciences (AAA&S), the Association for the Advancement of Science (AAAS), the ACM, the IEEE, and the (ISC)2; a Distinguished Fellow of the ISSA; and a member of the Cyber Security Hall of Fame—the only person to ever hold all these distinctions. In 2012, he was named as one of Purdue's inaugural Morrill Professors—the university's highest award for the combination of scholarship, teaching, and service. In 2016, he received the State of Indiana's highest civilian honor by being named a Sagamore of the Wabash.

More information may be found at https://ceri.as/spaf-bio.

Leigh Metcalf is a Senior Network Security Research Analyst at the Carnegie Mellon University Software Engineering Institute's cybersecurity (CERT) division. CERT is composed of a diverse group of researchers, software engineers, and security analysts who are developing cutting-edge information and training to improve the practice of cybersecurity. Before joining CERT, Leigh spent more than 10 years in industry working as a systems engineer, architect, and security specialist.

Dr. Metcalf has presented research at numerous conferences. She is the co-author (with William Casey) of the book *Cybersecurity and Applied Mathematics* (Syngress, 2016) as well as the co-author (with Jonathan Spring) of the book *Using Science in Cybersecurity* (World Scientific, 2021). She is also the Co-Editor-in-Chief (with Arun Lakhotia) of the ACM journal *Digital Threats: Research and Practice* (DTRAP).

Josiah Dykstra is a seasoned cybersecurity practitioner, researcher, author, and speaker. He is a senior leader in the Cybersecurity Collaboration Center at the National Security Agency (NSA) and the owner of Designer Security, LLC. Dr. Dykstra holds a Ph.D. in computer science and previously served as a cyber operator and researcher. He is interested in cybersecurity science, especially where humans intersect with technology. He has studied stress in hacking, action bias in incident response, and the economics of knowing when sharing threat intelligence is more work than it is worth.

Dr. Dykstra is a frequent author and speaker, including Black Hat and RSA Conference. He received the CyberCorps® Scholarship for Service (SFS) fellowship and is one of six people in the SFS Hall of Fame. In 2017, he received the Presidential Early Career Award for Scientists and Engineers (PECASE) from then President Barack Obama. Dr. Dykstra is a Fellow of the American Academy of

Forensic Sciences and a Distinguished Member of the Association for Computing Machinery (ACM). He is the author of numerous research papers and the book *Essential Cybersecurity Science* (O'Reilly Media, 2016).

More information may be found at https://josiahdykstra.com.

Pattie Spafford is a freelance artist, writer, and equestrienne. She holds a Ph.D. in art education. This Dr. Spafford has over 25 years of experience in K–12, college education, and community and museum art programs. Her current major research project integrates geography, art, and horses. Pattie maintains an active studio practice with bead embroidery and ink drawing as her preferred media.

Pattie's programs have received awards from national, state, and local arts agencies throughout her career, including the National Endowment for the Arts, the Louisiana Board of Regents, a NAHRO National Award of Merit, and the Louisiana Art Education Association Art Educator of the Year.

PART I

General Issues

Chapter 1

What Is Cybersecurity?

A ship in harbor is safe, but that is not what ships are built for.

John A. Shedd

If you are reading this book, you are likely interested in cybersecurity. We present several ideas and lessons in this work that address more general topics in computing (and elsewhere). Still, the primary application area is cybersecurity. Whether you are a student, a practitioner, an executive, a regulator, or a criminal (tsk-tsk, unless you paid for a copy of this book, in which case simply tsk), the material we present has a bearing on what you do.

In this chapter, we will explore why the broad concept of cybersecurity is ripe with misconceptions, why the term is not defined well, and why we do not have any reasonable way to measure it.

Everyone Knows What "Cybersecurity" Means

In a book about myths in cybersecurity, there is no better place to start than with definitions. Sometimes this seems silly and trivial. Doesn't everyone know the definition of cybersecurity?

It might surprise you that even experts disagree about the meaning of "secure." The most salient reason is that there is no commonly accepted, precise definition of what cybersecurity *is*! For an area of such intense concern, and with nearly six decades of study, that seems inconceivable, but it's true!

Let's start with the term itself—cybersecurity. What does that mean? The immediate answer is "security of. . . cyber." We see many people throw around the prefix "cyber" to describe computing and networks, as well as "cyberspace," "cyberpunk," and "cyber crime." To start with, what the heck does "cyber" mean, exactly?

Most references we can find credit the mathematician Norbert Wiener for coining the term "cybernetics" in 1948 to describe the study of communications and control. "Cyber" in this context was likely derived from the Greek *kybernetes* meaning, roughly, to guide or govern. In 1982, William Gibson came up with the term "cyberspace" to refer to the virtual space of networks and computers experienced online. Before that use in science fiction, there was no cyber-X being bandied about to describe security or things online.

In the span 1960–1990, people mostly talked about "computer security," "communications security," "information security," "network security," and "data security." Those terms were fairly compact and descriptive, except when discussing a more comprehensive view of things was necessary. Then it became "computer and network and data security," which seems a tad unwieldy. Not only is that a lot to type every time someone wants to refer to the field, but it also does not have a good acronym as an alternative.

Perhaps that is why, in the late 1980s, when a U.S. Senate Committee held some hearings on the security of government systems, a staffer allegedly came up with the "cybersecurity" shorthand. This perhaps seemed exotic to the Senators, and maybe that is why it caught on—much to the dismay of many professionals who were working in the field at the time (and many since then).[1] That term found its way into some of the reporting and was picked up by the trade press. The term "cyber" is not that exact, and it is easy to lose sight of it meaning the data, processes, people, and policies in addition to the computers and networks. The novelty might be why it caught on, especially among marketing staff who wanted to gain customer attention. (In Chapter 8 we discuss why terminology is important.)

OK, so we kind of know what "cyber" means—computers, networks, data, communications, and let's be sure to include security of robotics, sensors and control systems, and AI[2] as well.

What does "security" mean in this context? First, security and its derivatives can be both a verb and an adjective: we take actions to secure (verb) a system to help the system be secure (adjective). Here again, we run into issues as there is no formal definition with which everyone agrees. For instance, the online Longman dictionary[3] defines cybersecurity as "things that are done to protect computer information and systems from crime." That omits issues of controlling access, detecting non-criminal misuse, and incident response, as well as protecting networks.

The National Institute of Standards and Technology (NIST) defines cybersecurity in a much more expansive fashion: "Prevention of damage to, protection of, and restoration of computers, electronic communications systems, electronic communications services, wire communication, and electronic communication, including information contained therein, to ensure its availability, integrity, authentication, confidentiality, and non-repudiation."[4] This is the same definition used in U.S. Department of Defense Policy 8500.1, although not all other U.S. Federal agencies use this definition. NIST uses at

1. One of us (Spafford) had a conversation about this with Senator Sam Nunn at the time, expressing reservations about the term. As the Senator's chief of staff at that time told Spaf, "It's you versus a senior U.S. Senator on this. You lose."
2. Philosophically, we are not fond of the terms "artificial intelligence" and "machine learning," either. Scholars do not have a good definition of intelligence and do not understand consciousness and learning. The terms have caught on as a shorthand for "Developing algorithms and systems enhanced by repeated exposure to inputs to operate in a manner suggesting directed selection." We fully admit that some systems seem brighter than, say, certain current members of Congress, but we would not label either as *intelligent*. Consult some psychologists, theologians, and philosophers if you want to explore the topic further.
3. https://www.ldoceonline.com/dictionary/cybersecurity. Reprinted by permission of Pearson, Longman Dictionary of Contemporary English, 2014.
4. https://csrc.nist.gov/glossary/term/cybersecurity

least three other definitions in their documents, further muddling the exact meaning. Here are some other definitions of security we have run across:

- "A system condition in which system resources are free from unauthorized access and unauthorized or accidental change, destruction, or loss. (Compare: safety.)"[5]
- "The process of protecting information by preventing, detecting, and responding to attacks."[6]
- "Protection of Internet-connected systems such as hardware, software, and data from cyberthreats."[7]
- "Technology, services, strategies, practices, policies designed to secure people, data and infrastructure from a wide range of cyber attacks."[8]

A more succinct definition was put forth by Rob Joyce of the National Security Agency (NSA) in 2019: "Cybersecurity is everything that results in protecting information and underlying technology from theft, manipulation, and disruption." That leaves a lot of things open to interpretation; however, it is closer to what most people think about when they think of cybersecurity. Even farther along that road is the 1990 definition from Garfinkel and Spafford[9]: "A computer is secure if you can depend on it and its software to behave as expected."

Everyone Agrees What "Hacked" Means

What do people mean when they say they were hacked? As we saw with the ambiguity of the word "cybersecurity," the term "hacked" also means vastly different things to different people. You might have seen friends or colleagues post on social media messages like "My account got hacked!" Some system administrators might even consider failed logins to be hacks.

In one study of self-reported victimization on Twitter, researchers found that 43% of these reports were related to social media accounts and 32% to online games.[a] The consequence was most often account loss (27%), followed by altered settings (18%) and spam (16%). So, people who say they are hacked generally cannot access their accounts. But is that always unauthorized access? If you shared your Netflix password with your sister and she changed the password, was that unauthorized, and were you "hacked"?

[a] Gratian, Margaret, et al., "'Help, I've Been Hacked!': Insights from a Corpus of User-Reported Cyber Victimization Cases on Twitter." *Proceedings of the Human Factors and Ergonomics Society Annual Meeting*. Vol. 63. No. 1; Los Angeles, CA: SAGE Publications, 2019.

5. https://datatracker.ietf.org/doc/html/rfc4949
6. https://csrc.nist.gov/glossary/term/cybersecurity
7. https://searchsecurity.techtarget.com/definition/cybersecurity
8. www.proofpoint.com/us/threat-reference/cybersecurity-network-security
9. Garfinkel, Simson and Spafford, Gene, *Practical Unix & Internet Security,* O'Reilly, 1990.

Cybersecurity professionals tend to use the words *incident*, *breach*, or *attack* instead of hack. These words generally describe issues after a bad thing has happened, such as when the attacker has gained unauthorized access or stolen data, rather than describing failed attempts.

As we will discuss in more depth throughout the book, not all incidents have the same consequences. This means that not all "hacks" are equally bad. Suppose an attacker guesses our coffee club password and gets away with your $20 account balance. That's quite a different loss than an Advanced Persistent Threat (APT) sending a company's confidential intellectual property to agents in another country or taking a university website offline.

Why is the definition important? In part, it is to be certain we are talking about the same concepts. It is also essential in defining metrics that allow us to gauge how effective some controls might be, compare them with each other, and judge the cost-effectiveness of those controls.

In summary, we do not have an agreed-upon definition. As a result, everything else is somewhat imprecise.

We Can Measure How Secure Our Systems Are

Cybersecurity professionals cringe at the question "how secure are we?"[10] The person asking probably thinks there is a nice straightforward answer, such as 90% secure or *very secure*. Professionals wince because this is not something they can meaningfully quantify. They wish the question could be asked more precisely.

People want a number. They want a value they can point to, saying, "This is how secure I am: I am a 5." It's something they can hang on to or publicize to make themselves feel better.

Without a good definition, however, we are left without good metrics. And, to scientists and engineers, metrics are important! As Lord Kelvin wrote, "I often say that when you can measure what you are speaking about, and express it in numbers, you know something about it; but when you cannot measure it, when you cannot express it in numbers, your knowledge is of a meagre and unsatisfactory kind."[11]

"Wait!" some people might say. "What about the traditional C-I-A measures?" In computer science textbooks and classes, we find references to confidentiality, integrity, and availability as the basic components of cybersecurity. But those are also poorly chosen. For instance, what is the dimension of integrity? How do I have two more units of confidentiality? Are three units of confidentiality more

10. For one lengthy example of this, see the responses to this question posted by @AccidentalCISO at https://twitter.com/AccidentalCISO/status/1379112763528769537

11. *Popular Lectures and Addresses*, "Electrical Units of Measurement," 1883.

important than two units of availability? Furthermore, those are not orthogonal properties: If data is overwritten (poor integrity controls), it is no longer available.

The shortcomings of the C-I-A model are not new realizations. Donn Parker developed his Hexad model[12] to add three more properties (Control, Correctness, Utility), and John McCumber developed his Cube model[13] to better focus controls on goals and whether data is at rest or in transit. Those are not the only models, either! None of those models fixed the underlying problems, which are rooted in not having a good definition of "secure."

All of this is complicated by two facts not reflected in most practice (and rarely in commercial advertising): (1) It is impossible to make an arbitrary system secure against all threats and still be usable, functional, and productive, and (2) all security is relative to a security policy. The first fact is relatively easy to illustrate. Think about protecting a PC against a planet-killing asteroid, against the combined cyber attack capabilities of North Atlantic Treaty Organization (NATO) forces, and an invasion of Unidentified Flying Objects (UFOs) carrying telepathic lizard people.[14] Those are all potential threats, and there is simply no current, complete defense against all of them—singly or combined. As to usability, consider the quote that opens this chapter.

The second fact is a bit more subtle and not as well understood as it should be. It is about defining what we are protecting and what we are protecting against. Situations and environments are different. If I am a grad student, I might not care about protecting my recipe for chocolate chip cookies on my home computer; if I am an elf running a baked goods empire from my hollow tree, I probably care a great deal about protecting my recipe! In both cases, it might be the same computing hardware, the same underlying Operating System (OS), and perhaps even the same recipe—but the risks and policies are definitely different! As Figure 1.1 illustrates, one size does *not* fit all.

This policy difference also shows up when comparing a home system versus a bank versus the computers used in the Situation Room at the White House. The differences are also interwoven with risk issues (How likely is the system to be attacked, and by whom?) and consequences (Is loss of my cookie recipe equal to compromise of the bank's balance sheets?) That, in turn, drives decisions about how much time, capital, and effort to spend on controls, countermeasures, and recovery mechanisms. We cannot afford to protect every system at the same level! Protecting a student's cookie recipe against potential theft by a team of elite cyber criminals is not likely to be a good use of funds and time, but the elves might view the tradeoffs differently.

---

12. Parker, Donn, *Fighting Computer Crime*, New York, NY: John Wiley & Sons, 1998.
13. McCumber, John, *Assessing and Managing Security Risk in IT Systems: A Structured Methodology*, Auerbach Publications, 2004.
14. The odds of them being hostile are small; see www.livescience.com/malicious-alien-civilizations-odds. However, if they dislike cat videos, we are toast.

FIGURE 1.1 Security must fit a myriad of users and situations.

This, too, has been understood for quite some time. Buried in a lesser-known Request for Comments (RFC) is a gem worth noting here. Internet Engineering Task Force (IETF) RFCs are individually numbered publications that include Internet standards, ideas, and occasional humor. For example, domain names and the Domain Name System (DNS) that underpin our Internet experiences are described in RFC 1034. The Internet Security Glossary is written in RFC 4949.[15] It is a fascinating and informative read. It defines terms such as "port scan" and "vulnerability." Within this document is an entry for *Courtney's Laws*, which Robert Courtney defined decades ago:

Courtney's Laws

> Principles for managing system security that were stated by Robert H. Courtney, Jr.
>
> - Courtney's first law: You cannot say anything interesting (i.e., significant) about the security of a system except in the context of a particular application and environment.
> - Courtney's second law: Never spend more money eliminating a security exposure than tolerating it will cost you.
>   - First corollary: Perfect security has infinite cost.
>   - Second corollary: There is no such thing as zero risk.

15. RFCs can be found by number at https://datatracker.ietf.org/doc

- `Courtney's third law: There are no technical solutions to management problems, but there are management solutions to technical problems.`

Bob Courtney was a pioneer in cybersecurity and well understood the limitations of what we can achieve. His three laws enrich the context of cybersecurity, and everybody who deals with cybersecurity should know them.

Trust and Risk

Notice that Bob referred to "risk." Those who have studied the field in depth generally prefer to talk about either trust, risk, or both rather than security. We try to measure how much we trust a system to address risk. One of the most influential documents in cybersecurity was the Trusted Computer System Evaluation Criteria (TCSEC), also known colloquially as "the Orange Book" because of the color of its cover. It was issued by the U.S. National Computer Security Center in 1983 and described how to build computers with increasing levels of trust.[16] We might say they were levels of security, but it was understood early on that it made more sense to speak about what we could do to increase our trust in a system to operate according to policy and minimize risk.

When Secure Rating Is Not Secure

Microsoft was proud when its then flagship server Windows NT was certified C2 from the Orange Book.[a] At the time, it was a significant rating for a non-military system. It meant that the system (in specific configurations) was suitable for environments that needed more trusted systems. Microsoft had even allowed special access to its proprietary source code to allow Windows NT to be certified. It was big news.

To Microsoft, C2 was the end goal; the company could brag about it in marketing materials, so celebrate! To the security experts, it was not.[b] A security expert demonstrated that unauthorized access to "secure" files on the NT system was still possible, even removing them. The label of *C2 secure* was not enough to make the system more secure. To be fair to the authors of the Orange Book, they did not claim C2 was *secure*. C2 was a level designating how trustable a system was, and several levels were above C2. That is why the experts did not view C2 as a big deal then; a toaster oven might have been certifiable to C2 if someone really tried.

[a] C2 was a trust level rating described in the TCSEC. See also the Appendix entry for "Orange Book" and www.itprotoday.com/ windows-78/microsoft-finally-gets-c2-rating-nt-4.

[b] https://gcn.com/1995/09/c2-rating-aside-nt-isnt-secure/307772/

Though related, trust is sometimes confused with security. Consider SSL/TLS[17] as an example. We have taught users to look for the lock icon in their browsers when visiting their bank's website.

16. More information on the Orange Book can be found in the Appendix.

17. SSL was the original protocol but was found to have deficiencies. TLS is the current protocol used.

Somewhere along the line, users also began to use this heuristic for safety to decide if the website was legitimate and not a phishing attempt; that is not necessarily correct, as Figure 1.2 illustrates.[18] Uh oh! TLS (usually) provides a secure connection, but this connection could still be with an untrustworthy attacker. This illustrates the difficulty in defining "secure": The network connection is secure (in a sense), but the actual session is not.

FIGURE 1.2 A lock icon does not necessarily mean there is no risk.

Importantly, as noted in the corollary to Courtney's Second Law, *there is no way to eliminate all the risk.* For instance, strong passwords lower the risk of attackers accessing our account, but all passwords can eventually be guessed with enough brute force. The first myth in this chapter acknowledges that it's difficult to quantify how much risk we face and how much cybersecurity lowers risk. The flip side is that cybersecurity can be so stringent that it degrades the ability to use technology effectively. Risk management is a spectrum from none to complete, where zero risk is unreachable.

Threats

When you read some of the definitions of security earlier in the chapter, did you notice that some of them referred to threats? That's yet another way to define security.

There is a vast difference between threat-based security and risk-based security. "Our firewall prevents network attacks" is vastly different from "our firewall lowers the risk of network attacks." Bruce Schneier summarized this difference in one of his Crypto-Grams: "Avoiding threats is black and white: either we avoid the threat, or we don't. Avoiding risk is continuous: there is some amount of risk we

18. More information on phishing can be found in the Appendix.

can accept, and some we cannot."[19] The end state of risk management is not risk elimination. We can lower our risk of injury or death while driving, but we cannot make it zero.

Despite popular lists of top 10 and best practices security advice, there is no accepted value for precisely how much risk is lowered by patching or firewalls or training. We know they help to an extent, but the remaining risk is still murky in the enormous range between less than 100% and greater than 0%. It would be nice if we could put a number to it, but we cannot.

Security Policy

We define the differences in security posture and risk tolerance in a *security policy*. The policy helps define assets, authorities, standards, and other issues necessary to build and operate the cybersecurity regime for an organization. Many large organizations have a structured, written policy.[20]

The relative nature of security policy is one factor that makes cybersecurity difficult. It is further complicated because few organizations have an overall security policy that can be directly applied to developing, procuring, and operating their computing ("cyber") resources. Most organizations simply have a policy of "no one should do anything to our systems we do not authorize" and depend on off-the-shelf components to enforce it; however, few consumer items are carefully specified and designed to support the full range of possible policies. After all, vendor businesses are focused on making a profit, not on spending unlimited amounts building in support for every possible policy and defense.

This parallels a situation described succinctly by one of our favorite observations from 1985: "A program that has not been specified cannot be incorrect; it can only be surprising."[21] Yes, the majority of security "bugs" and "weaknesses" are not flaws—they are *surprises* because they occur in systems never fully defined and specified against security policies. If we have no policy, and the software we are running was never explicitly specified and designed, how can there be a security flaw?

It is impossible to avoid yet more surprises given the difficulty vendors have in writing correct programs and the market-driven push to add new features and ever-more layers of complexity to legacy, broken code to drive new sales. Trends involving just-in-time, DevOps, and Agile code development often short-change design, too, leading to surprises. The philosophy is that the coders can quickly fix the problems, but quick fixes are not the same as inherent quality. Consider driving down the highway at 110 kilometers per hour.[22] Your car was built to go fast with a shiny exterior, and everything is fine until you need to exit. That's when you discover the car was built without brakes. Oops! Patching might make things better for the next iteration of the car model, but the situation will not end well for you or anyone else zipping down the road ahead of you. *Ease or speed of patching is **not** the same as good security!* Speed of code production is no substitute for considered, comprehensive design, either.

---

19. www.schneier.com/crypto-gram/archives/2000/0515.html
20. If your organization does not have one, you should. It's a good thing.
21. Young, W. D., Boebert, W. E., and Kain, R. Y., "Proving a Computer System Secure," *The Scientific Honeyweller*, Vol. 6, No. 2 (July 1985): 18–27.
22. We are scientists—we will use the metric system. You are welcome to use furlongs per microfortnight should you wish.

And So. . .

Thus, security is tightly intertwined with risk management, which is related to policy. We need protection because there is a potential danger, harm, or loss of things we value. We have locks on our houses to protect the people and items inside. If we care about the privacy of our cookie recipes and protecting the money in our bank accounts, then we need solid cybersecurity.

So, where does all this leave us? It brings us not to security per se, but rather to the process of building trust and assuring our systems. We want to trust (have confidence) that the mechanisms we have work the way we think they do, that we have backstops and preventive measures in place to add to our confidence in that operation according to policy, and we want to regularly examine everything to ensure there are no gaps or deficiencies. All of that must be within budget, using the lowest-cost software often written by people with minimal (or no) training in sound software engineering and based on architectures and hardware that might have been optimized for running spreadsheets and video games. It should not come as a surprise that the process is fraught with errors and frequent, spectacular failures.

Keep the introduction chapter in mind as you read through the rest of this book. Perhaps the biggest misconceptions in the field are that we know what cybersecurity is, that it is an achievable goal, and that existing technology is sufficient. (And we will not try to explain why safety, correctness, and privacy are also challenging to achieve, although the reasons are roughly similar.)

The Primary Goal of Cybersecurity Is Security

There is a perception, particularly among cybersecurity professionals, that people desire cybersecurity for its own sake. Once users feel safe, they say, all will be well! We must keep working until the users and systems are secure. Or at least feel secure. This goal sounds correct to many people, but it is misguided.

In reality, cybersecurity is not the primary goal; the goal of cybersecurity is to maximize and support what the user is trying to accomplish. People and organizations have goals that can be enabled and protected by security, but the *primary tasks* matter most. Users want to buy things online and share photos with their friends. Hospitals want to treat medical issues. Gamers want to play games. Elves want to make cookies. The users' primary goals are things like entertainment, healthcare, and sharing cat videos online. Security supports pursuing these goals by protecting the user and the activity against adversity and loss.

One reason that people ignore or circumvent their security is that it interferes with their primary goals. This is why people disable the antivirus software when the computer is running slowly and they simply want to play a game. When developers and engineers prioritize security at the expense of a primary goal, it often backfires and causes people to disable or work around that protection.

Consider automatic software updates. Because software is complex, created by fallible humans, and often built poorly, there is a need for continual bug fixes (and feature updates). At one time, users had to proactively check if updates were available and install them manually. Because that wasn't a priority for most people, users did not check or install updates. Vendors, including Microsoft, Apple, and Google, determined that systems were safer when the software automatically installed updates without user intervention, and users were (mostly) absolved of the effort. That also had the unintended effect of making some users think *all* of their software was self-updating, so they stopped checking everything else—oops!

To avoid the myth that security is the primary goal, cybersecurity professionals must better understand their users and context. Observe them doing their primary tasks in their natural environment. Then, as you consider cybersecurity measures, carefully consider the impact on users. Will it disrupt them every time they log in or browse the web? Is the cost worth the pain or inconvenience? In 2019, researchers examined the relationship between data breach remediation and hospital care quality. Because cybersecurity is often increased after a data breach, was there an increase, they wondered, in the time from a patient arriving in the emergency department to receiving an Electrocardiogram (EKG)? The data showed an increase of 0.5 to 2.7 additional minutes in the three years following the breach, suggesting that cybersecurity might have slowed the ability to access health records, and to order, review, and execute the EKG.[23] The longer the wait, the higher the mortality rate.

The takeaway is not to focus on maximizing *security*. We should focus on optimizing the protection of users' primary goals with an appropriate amount of security.

Cybersecurity Is About Obvious Risks

Imagine you are on a TV show similar to the American show *Family Feud*. In the usual setup, you are prompted: "We asked 100 cybersecurity professionals: What are the most common risks you deal with?" What would be your guesses for the top five most common answers? Malware? Password compromise? Whatever they are, the polled answers probably would not surprise you.

But cybersecurity is not always about the apparent risks. Cybersecurity is not always about the computers themselves. Other things impact the ultimate outcomes we care about.

Training is expensive and does not eliminate risk. Gartner, for instance, states that without phishing training, people click on phishing links 20% of the time, but yearly training yields rates still around 10%.[24] How many clicks are we willing to accept compared with the cost of training? (Of course, that assumes that every click has the same risk.)

We can get different protection levels at defined costs. Imagine an organization has invested in technology and processes to achieve 20-day patching as defined by its policy. If the business meets the goal and a vulnerability is exploited on day 21, that is a failure to achieve the promised security goal. If exploitation occurs on day 19, this is the result of a business decision.

---

23. Choi, Sung J., Johnson, M. Eric, and Lehmann, Christopher U., "Data Breach Remediation Efforts and Their Implications for Hospital Quality," *Health Services Research*, Vol. 54, No. 5 (2019): 971–980. https://doi.org/10.1111/1475-6773.13203
24. Proctor, Paul, "Outcome-Driven Metrics Optimize Cybersecurity Risk, Value and Cost," *Gartner Security & Risk Management Summit Americas*, 2021.

People often forget to consider a broader view than technology-specific security software and appliances. This happens for everyone from engineers to executives. Does the organization have a media disposal policy? When a computer dies, is the storage sanitized? Another issue is fatigue. Tired and frustrated users are prone to more accidents and mistakes. How does the security policy deal with that?

The "obvious" risks in cybersecurity are undoubtedly scary. In December 2021, for example, a severe new vulnerability was discovered in a snippet of code that was used by millions of websites and applications to record logs, known as `log4j`.[25] When someone clicks a link and gets a Page Not Found error, for example, this vulnerable software enables the web server to record the error in a log file for system administrators. Attackers immediately began trying to find and attack the websites and apps that used `log4j`. Many news articles were written about how scary it was; social media went wild about it. It was (and is) a genuinely worrisome event because of how easily an attacker could gain access through something as simple as a logging mechanism. Developers love logging mechanisms, because they help them debug and add auditing. Attackers now love them, too, because they're easy to exploit.

We should worry about any program that uses this code (`log4j`) and update it (or disable it) as soon as possible. Waiting for someone to take advantage of the vulnerability is definitely a grave mistake.

Many attacks do not originate outside the organization. We will spend a lot of time and effort cleaning up the `log4j` situation, but insiders do not need a Remote Code Execution (RCE) program: They are not remote; they are local. Depending on their position, they can do as much (or more) damage as the outsider. It might be inadvertent or deliberate, but an insider might easily take down the infrastructure or exfiltrate data and sell it. The external threat is the same as the "stranger danger" that kids are taught when they are young. Avoid the stranger and their malicious traffic to be safe.[26]

Jordan is a professional cybersecurity expert in a bustling Maryland suburb and an active volunteer in the community. At the invitation of the local Chamber of Commerce, Jordan developed a presentation for business owners titled "Ten Ways to Protect Yourself Online." Jordan's presentation started in a manner that was familiar to many people: a slide that showed a pixelated green image of someone in a hoodie hunched over a computer. Before even saying a word, the presentation took the tone to be afraid. Be afraid of the mysterious hooded figure![27]

A great many cybersecurity presentations begin by talking about cyber threats. How better, they think, than to educate (scare?) the audience into adopting better cybersecurity? "You better pick a better password, or attackers will steal all your money!" Fearmongering is a form of psychological manipulation playing on the (often-unsupported) threat of impending danger and doom. Advertisers have used this tactic to stimulate anxiety. Remember the "this is your brain on drugs" anti-narcotics television campaign showing an egg sizzling in a frying pan? For many people it was emotional and powerful. It was intentionally manipulative.

---

25. For more information on `log4j`, see the Appendix.
26. Meanwhile oblivious to the statistics that indicate most dangers come from friends and family, not strangers.
27. We do not understand the media's love affair with using hoodies to indicate malicious threat actors. When we put on our hoodies, it is to be warm rather than nefarious. Usually.

Cybersecurity often feels as though it is shaded by the negative. In academia and journalism, one is sometimes considered more serious if considered critical or negative. Positivity is associated with naiveté. It certainly sells better in some markets. We rarely hear about what is going well in cybersecurity!

Highlighting threats is done so often there's even an acronym to describe it: Fear, Uncertainty, and Doubt (FUD). There is an awful lot of FUD in cybersecurity because there is an awful lot of uncertainty. People use that to scare the audience into compliance or to convince them that the latest and greatest product will stop the FUD.

Does highlighting threats work, and even if it does, is it the right approach? "So in the last few years, we have been moving away from a fear-based approach to cybersecurity towards a pragmatic one where we are trying to enable people to get on top of the problem," says Ciaran Martin, the first CEO of the United Kingdom's National Cyber Security Centre.[28] Cybersecurity awareness is closely tied to empowerment and positive culture. If a workforce lives in constant fear of cyber threats or punishment for the wrong action, they will be unhappy, unproductive, and potentially paralyzed by fear. Blame-and-shame and other embarrassment tactics are unfortunately still used today. For example, the U.S. Department of Health and Human Services has a "wall of shame" for data breaches in healthcare.[29]

Yes, the world can be scary, but that does not have to be the primary approach to cybersecurity. We advise against dismissing warnings and stories as "simply FUD"—those warnings suggest there are things to think about. Instead of fear, consider focusing on messages and campaigns that encourage strength and stability, promote innovation and creativity, and empower people. People want to protect themselves and defend organizations they care about. It's a natural human instinct. There is no need to spend all our time talking about the threats.

Sharing More Cyber Threat Intel Will Make Things Better

Imagine an attacker sending a malicious PDF disguised as a fake invoice to Terry, the CISO at GoodLife Bank. Terry and Terry's staff are a talented group. After recognizing the potential phishing attempt, they analyze the file and create a signature to block it from the other bank employees. Their company is better protected, but what are the odds that the attacker used this malicious PDF against only one user at only one bank? How might GoodLife share this knowledge with other financial institutions or even everyone on the planet?

Cyber Threat Intelligence (CTI) is "evidence-based knowledge, including context, mechanisms, indicators, implications, and action-oriented advice about an existing or emerging menace or hazard to assets. This intelligence can inform decisions regarding the subject's response to that menace or hazard."[30] There are dozens and dozens of research papers and commercial products focused on sharing

28. www.zdnet.com/article/dont-let-cyber-security-be-driven-by-fear-warns-ncsc-chief/
29. https://ocrportal.hhs.gov/ocr/breach/breach_report.jsf
30. McMillan, Rob, "Definition: Threat Intelligence," www.gartner.com/en/documents/2487216 (2013).

CTI. We have services, mailing lists, and organizations to share threat information. The common refrain is that "more sharing is better." After all, how could more information *not* help cybersecurity?

CTI is knowledge, and knowing about a threat is different from using that knowledge to prevent or mitigate a threat. CTI has value when it is put into action. Knowing how to speak Greek, play chess, or that `bad.exe` is malware is not the end goal. Putting that knowledge into practice is how knowledge has value.

More sharing is not the answer. *Better* sharing is better. Threat intelligence takes many forms. On one end is a list of IP addressees, domains, or email addresses that one entity believes are malicious. This alone is generally unhelpful because the receiver does not know the time frame or any relevant details to put the CTI to use. Sometimes there is added context about the associated intrusion set or campaign that can help prioritize if this threat is relevant to us. Better, more sophisticated CTI describes malicious behavior. For instance, APT29, a known threat group, commonly uses legitimate credentials and PSExec to move around a network. That is specific knowledge to help a defender know which attacker behavior to look for and the *so what* if it is discovered.

Information sharing is not free. It takes time and people to produce and distribute useful threat information, even if they do not charge money for a subscription to their CTI. CTI also takes human and machine resources to ingest, deploy, and monitor the information. More sharing costs more. A company might be worse off with more CTI if the costs outweigh the benefits. As a result, better security comes from using only high-quality CTI that is timely, accurate, and actionable. Finding the gold is difficult if one has to deal with the overload of lots and lots of garbage. Security teams should start by tracking how CTI contributes today to business and security goals.

Blocklists are an example of CTI. People either sell them or provide them for free, and it's an easy way to block known-bad IP addresses, domains, or malware hashes. There are dozens of such lists. The problem is that research has shown that these lists are mostly distinct.[31] To use blocklists effectively, we need to collect all the lists. Yes, like Pokémon, gotta catch 'em all. That requires time, space, and processing.

Finally, information sharing requires trust among participants. There is a common refrain that organizations do not share threat information because they fear revealing their system weaknesses and the sources and methods of how they learned the information. One positive and growing avenue for trusted sharing is nonprofit, sector-based Information Sharing and Analysis Centers (ISACs). For example, in the Financial Services ISAC, more than 7,000 members in 70-plus countries collaborate and share confidential threat intelligence.[32]

Focus on quality CTI that produces effective security outcomes for your environment. In 2022, Mandiant released a CTI Analyst Core Competencies Framework. Among the competencies was that "CTI analysts should be able to understand and evaluate outcomes for threat intelligence in terms of demonstrable value to the business."[33] This skill will help temper the temptation to share for its own sake. If used effectively, CTI can help security teams avoid the pitfall of not defending against known threats. Still, we should be cautious about continually adding threat feeds and CTI tools without a

---

31. https://resources.sei.cmu.edu/library/asset-view.cfm?assetid=83438
32. See www.fsisac.com/who-we-are/. There are currently 25 ISACs that focus on different industry sectors.
33. www.mandiant.com/resources/cti-analyst-core-competencies-framework

thoughtful strategy. In Chapter 10, "Tool Myths and Misconceptions," we will discuss the pitfalls of applying too many tools. The volume of sharing should never be the end goal or measure of success. Continue to prioritize quality that leads to better outcomes.

What Matters to You Matters to Everyone Else

The first chapter of Todd Barnum's book, *The Cybersecurity Manager's Guide*, is entitled "The Odds are Against You." Barnum acknowledges that for managers in most environments, "nobody in the company, outside of your team, usually cares much about InfoSec." Even if senior leadership says they care, is that supported by money and other resources? We do not subscribe to the view that *nobody* cares about cybersecurity, but we should stop expecting our priorities to match those of other people.

People in cybersecurity are hired to help deliver cybersecurity. True story. These people are rewarded, personally and professionally, for ingenuity and performance in protecting networks. As with other professions, the more we specialize, the more narrow and specific our interests and care-abouts become. If our job is malware analysis, we are (reasonably) likely to believe that understanding malware is key to cybersecurity and advocate for more attention and resources. If we are cryptographers, malware analysis is nice, but crypto[34] is essential. When we extend this approach more broadly, we start to see a bigger picture and consider more perspectives. For the CEO of a wastewater treatment plant, cybersecurity generally is nice but not the primary objective—maybe not even in the top 10.

In a twist of irony, research shows that even people knowledgeable about cybersecurity sometimes behave more dangerously than expected. For example, "self-described experts reported less secure behaviors and had less knowledge about cyber hygiene than other participants."[35] So, even what seems to matter to someone based on expertise and experience might not manifest in their behavior! We are creatures of contradictions.

How do we avoid this myth? First, avoid assumptions. If we find ourselves saying things similar to "Obviously the CIO must care that we install these patches right away," seek clarification directly. There might be extenuating circumstances we could not possibly know about leading that person to hold different priorities. For instance, installing a patch that requires a reboot might interfere with the annual shareholders meeting or a big marketing event. We might find that installing that patch results in criticism rather than praise![36]

A key idea here is the need to consider "context." This relates to our mention of protecting our cookie recipe versus protecting a government system. What is true in one context may be nonsense (or a myth) in another! It is important to understand the context when planning and executing whatever strategies we may employ. Resources, goals, laws, personnel, values, and history are all part of the context

---

34. When we use the word *crypto*, we mean, generally, *cryptology*. We do **not** mean the various schemes around cryptocurrency.
35. Cain, Ashley A., Edwards, Morgan E., and Still, Jeremiah D., "An Exploratory Study of Cyber Hygiene Behaviors and Knowledge," *Journal of Information Security and Applications*, 42 (2018): 36–45.
36. See, for instance, https://www.zdnet.com/article/91-of-it-teams-have-felt-forced-to-trade-security-for-business-operations/

(among other things). We need to know our context, whether we are a CISO or a Chief Elf Officer (CEO). Note that this is true of many other things we talk about throughout this book!

Product X Will Make You Secure

Repeat after me: No single product will make me secure. That's not the reality of cyber threats, and it's not how cyber defense works. It's a lovely dream: find the magic product and ta-da! We are entirely secure; we have nothing to worry about!

People think (or vendors tell them to believe) that buying some product(s) will ultimately solve all of their cybersecurity problems. It does not matter what that product is—this statement will *never* be true. Cloud storage? No. Extended Detection and Response (XDR) platform? No. Next-Generation Firewall (NGFW)? No. Many individual solutions have value, but none alone is sufficient. This is not only because all products have vulnerabilities but because some problems have not been seen yet or resemble authorized use. Chapter 11, "Vulnerabilities," will discuss the more prevalent issues of passwords, patches, and configuration errors.

Some organizations buy lots and lots of products, believing more must be safer. Simply throw money and tools at the problem! This is a problem, especially for organizations that equate the amount they spend on security to a measurement of their security posture.[37] It leads to other adverse side effects, such as focusing too much on how our organization compares to other companies. Furthermore, piling on more tools might *reduce* our security.[38] Simply because the competition has a fancy new tool does not mean it's right for us. In Chapter 10, we will examine more myths about tools.

Too often, adding products is a reactive reflex after an incident. A company is attacked, and rather than consider the root cause of the problem, it throws money in an effort to prevent a repeat of that precise issue in the future. To use an old idiom, putting a lock on the barn after the horse has escaped is not a good approach to security. It leads to an overabundance of point solutions rather than broad strategies. Starting by considering the best way to keep the horse in the barn across various scenarios is a *much* better approach.

It's also important to consider what we are throwing our money at. If we build a new barn door with all the bells and whistles, yet the barn itself is falling down, we are not getting a good value for our money.

This is not a problem only for businesses and cybersecurity professionals. Ordinary people also think that a single piece of software should provide security. Further, they often accept the default program shipped with their computer and expect it to be free for life. Why is there not an *uber* security product? One endpoint protection program to rule them all? A modern device—smartphone, laptop, server, automobile—is complex, and the attack surface is enormous. No single cyber defense can ever protect against all the ways that an attacker might try to attack, affect, or extract data from that system—not to mention predict all new attacks that might come.[39]

---

37. www.gartner.com/en/newsroom/press-releases/2016-12-09-gartner-says-many-organizations-falsely-equate-it-security-spending-with-maturity
38. www.zdnet.com/article/the-more-cybersecurity-tools-an-enterprise-deploys-the-less-effective-their-defense-is/
39. We note that this suggests there are problems in overall design and complexity that should be addressed rather than adding more security apps, but the market does not seem to respond to this concept.

Avoiding this myth requires an appreciation for the complexity of technology and the diverse threats to it. No single security product can provide enough controls to lower all the risks present, especially in systems that are not designed well, are overly complex, and are poorly built.

Macs Are Safer Than PCs, Linux Is Safer Than Windows

The choice of computer platform is a specific instance of the myth that a particular product will make us secure.

Imagine that you are in the criminal business. Your tactic is to infect victims and run crypto mining malware.[40] The more computers you compromise, the more money you make. The malicious software you create must be developed separately for each platform. Malware for Windows does not work on Macs, so it's more work to go after both. Which is a better target for you: Macs or PCs?[41]

Setting aside potentially relevant factors such as the type of people who own Macs or PCs, consider the most relevant attribute: market share. As of June 2021, Microsoft dominated the desktop operating system market with 73%, with macOS next at 16%, followed by Linux at 3%.[42] People who run Linux believe that their computer is more secure.[43] While it might be, in practice, we would not expect attackers to spend their time on such a small market share. From a purely rational (though evil) perspective, criminals should target PCs running Windows because there are simply more potential victims.

In addition to market share, there was a time some decades ago when more care was put into the quality and security of some software systems. Looking at some measures of fault incidence, it might have seemed that one system would have an advantage over others; however, as we noted in the Introduction, things change and evolve. It is difficult to conclusively state that one particular system is more immune to common threats than another, especially considering various add-on defenses. The perception has remained, however.

Thus, Mac and iPhone enthusiasts have, from time to time, claimed that their devices are more secure than the competition. There is a lot of competition and loyalty in technology. Many people have strong opinions and allegiance to Apple products or, conversely, to Microsoft. You might remember the "Mac versus PC" television commercials in the 2000s suggesting that Macs were cool and PCs were bumbling.[44] You can be fiercely loyal, but do not let that blind you to the fact that all users and devices are vulnerable. Nobody is immune.

---

40. We suggest, somewhat tongue-in-cheek, that given its environmental impact, **all** crypto mining software is malware.
41. Attackers, similar to other humans, are lazy. See https://onlinelibrary.wiley.com/doi/10.1111/risa.13732?af=. Researchers have also studied how boring cyber crime can be. See https://academic.oup.com/bjc/article/61/5/1407/6226588.
42. www.statista.com/statistics/218089/global-market-share-of-windows-7/
43. There are many reasons they think this, including the ability to tweak more security settings to their liking and the fact that most software is open source. See the next myth for more about open source.
44. In 2021, Intel launched new ads in which the former "I'm a Mac" guy now prefers PCs. See www.theverge.com/2021/3/17/22335654/intel-mac-guy-new-ads-commercials-pc

Further, the market share of Macs continues to grow. If those users believe they are inherently more secure, they will be less cautious than they should be. Attackers will notice this and exploit the overconfidence bias. The truth is that both Macs and PCs have vulnerabilities. We have some risks whether we run Windows, macOS, Linux, or something else. In many social engineering attacks, such as tricking us into entering our password into a fake bank website, it does not matter what we are running. Users of all systems must be careful and diligent.

Open Source Software Is More Secure Than Closed Source Software

There is a belief that making source code available for all to see will result in fewer bugs. In a related manner, it is believed that closed source software, such as Microsoft Windows, means fewer people can audit, discover, and fix vulnerabilities. This has not made open source software immune from serious issues. Yet, the myth remains that open source products make us more secure.

In March 2012, a new feature was added to the hugely popular open source library, OpenSSL, which is used in most web servers and browsers. The implementation of RFC 6520 contained a flaw that went unnoticed for two years. In April 2014, Google discovered and privately reported the bug to the OpenSSL team, and a fix was released six days later. CVE 2014-0160 was better known as Heartbleed.

In May 2022, the Python library CTX was hijacked and modified so attackers could steal users' Amazon Web Services (AWS) keys.[45] CTX is not a library created to communicate with AWS servers. Instead, it's a library that manages a core feature of Python called dictionaries. The library was last updated by the developer in 2014, so most people probably considered it pretty stable and a useful library. Unfortunately, it was open to abuse, and someone modified it. At about the same time, it was discovered that a popular library used in PHP was also hijacked. In both cases, the code was open source and widely used. In both cases, the source was available for anyone to look over, but that did not prevent the attacks.

Some commercial, closed systems are developed by people paid to consider security and robust operations, whether they think it is a chore or not. The result might be code with fewer vulnerabilities than Open Source Software (OSS). Several systems evaluated at the highest levels under the TCSEC and successors, such as Scomp, GH INTEGRITY, and GEMSOS, are not OSS. They have been thoroughly examined and tested to provide very high assurance operation but are not free or open source.

Open source can mean faster security fixes, but not always. When a bug is discovered and fixed in OpenSSL, that fix does not automatically propagate to every software package. If our website uses the Apache Web Server, Apache needs to incorporate the new OpenSSL library, and then we need to update our installation of Apache. Three years after Heartbleed, for example, there were still more than 144,000 Internet-facing web servers unpatched to the bug.[46] In short, a patch is not the end of a security incident. It's simply the start of cleaning one up.

45. www.bleepingcomputer.com/news/security/popular-python-and-php-libraries-hijacked-to-steal-aws-keys/
46. https://securityledger.com/2017/07/heartbleeds-heartburn-why-a-5-year-old-vulnerability-continues-to-bite/

Open source indeed encourages transparency and community input; however, because it exists in the open does not necessarily mean that security experts are looking at it. There is evidence that the people who have access to open source are more active in creating new code and extensions than auditing existing code. One recent study showed that OSS developers spent less than 3% of their time working on improving security.[47] They described working on security as a "soul-withering chore and a subject best left for the lawyers and process freaks" and an "insufferably boring procedural hindrance." With some estimates that OSS makes up 70% of current software applications, these results should cause serious concern.

Avoiding this myth means accepting that open and closed source software are both vulnerable but that there might be more vulnerabilities in some OSS. Software development is difficult, and users must be motivated and diligent about patching.

Technology X Will Make You Secure

There is a well-known meme attributed to Internet pioneer Vint Cerf. It is a simple flowchart that starts with the decision point "Do I need a blockchain?" and points to a single endpoint: "No." Blockchain is not the answer to every problem (it might not be the answer to *any* significant problem), and it certainly is not the perfect answer to cybersecurity.

Cloud. Quantum computing. Open source intelligence. Blockchains. Artificial intelligence and machine learning. Even encryption! Innovation and technological evolution continue to drive progress in cybersecurity by lowering risk, and these technologies can be powerful enablers. Technology plays a prominent and important role in cyber defense—however, it is a myth that any technology alone will eliminate cyber risk. Beware the hype.

Jackie Fenn coined the term *hype cycle* at Gartner in 1995. She observed a predictable path of over-enthusiasm and disillusionment for new technologies before they eventually provide predictable value. The graphical representation covers five phases:

1. Technology Trigger
2. Peak of Inflated Expectations
3. Trough of Disillusionment
4. Slope of Enlightenment
5. Plateau of Productivity

The hype cycle acknowledges the value of technology but never espouses that any will solve all problems.

47. https://www.darkreading.com/application-security/open-source-developers-still-not-interested-in-secure-coding and https://www.techrepublic.com/article/open-source-developers-say-securing-their-code-is-a-soul-withering-waste-of-time/

The history of cybersecurity is full of examples of defenses we once thought were perfect. Address space layout randomization (ASLR) was created to prevent the exploitation of memory corruption vulnerabilities. So was Data Execution Prevention (DEP). They did have a positive impact and helped to cripple some malware. But ASLR and DEP did not stop attacks across the board. These technologies could not prevent phishing and other social engineering from affecting computers. Furthermore, attackers adapted and learned to bypass DEP and ASLR using Return-Oriented Programming (ROP).

This myth goes hand in hand with the myth that a single product will protect us. Nothing applies to all threats and all situations. Add into that the fact that these technologies and solutions often have their own vulnerabilities. Nothing is perfect in the cybersecurity world.

The key to avoiding the myth that any technology will solve cybersecurity is honesty about what it cannot do. Do not let that stop you from being excited about new technology. Evaluate, experiment, and deploy with open eyes, while acknowledging that it alone cannot save us. Also, be alert to any new vulnerabilities or exposures that might result from it!

Process X Will Make You Secure

DevSecOps.[48] Security Chaos Engineering.[49] SAFe Agile.[50] If products and technologies are not the answer to security, could a process or discipline be the solution? Let's see why not.

Modified security behavior intuitively feels promising. As an abstract concept, better processes supporting security can be applied to many situations. We achieve many benefits when we change our lifestyle by giving up smoking or starting to exercise.

Historically, some processes have been shown to reduce defects in code, but because of their overhead in time and personnel training, they have not been widely adopted. Code produced for (as an example) the Space Shuttle and nuclear power plant control were almost defect-free. The 1986 Capability Maturity Model (CMM) was a methodology to describe the formality and optimization of software development processes. Even though the People Capability Maturity Model was developed nine years later, it is much less known. Most code producers are interested in fast and cheap, and the processes shown to reduce defects are not known for those qualities. Unfortunately, the computing-using public and too many vendors have coalesced around the idea of "Yes, it's buggy and unsafe, but we get it quickly and cheaply!"

Improving our development and security processes is strongly encouraged! Well-validated methods are great, and we should consider them, especially in large corporate environments where the benefits accumulate with scale. But did you know that no formal research studies (to date) have proven definitively that Agile or DevSecOps or any other recent framework is measurably better than the alternatives? That does not mean we should not use them. It simply means we should understand their limitations. Many things influence security, so it is not easy to show that a particular process is the cause of

48. www.redhat.com/en/topics/devops/what-is-devsecops
49. www.techtarget.com/searchitoperations/definition/chaos-engineering
50. https://scaledagile.com/what-is-safe/

improvement. Sometimes, the simple act of enthusiastically doing something new will make it *seem* better. Robust processes are within our control as we develop and deploy systems. There are, unfortunately, a lot of things that influence security that are out of our control. We cannot control whether an attacker tries to launch a denial of service attack against our website. Amazing processes cannot eliminate supply chain attacks.

Remember that enterprises are the combination of infrastructure, personnel, threats, resources, time, and funding (at the least). Some approaches will work better than others for different mixes of these factors. Do not believe that a Harvard Business School study, popular book, or conference seminar about someone else's experience will translate seamlessly into your own!

One myth is that someone can buy a process solution from a vendor: That is not true. In the best case, there are open source tools available that can help in the practice of the discipline. Netflix, for example, has released Chaos Monkey (and many other tools) on GitHub to help support chaos engineering.[51] Further, it has published papers to help you measure the benefits and costs of chaos engineering.[52]

Færie Dust Can Make Old Ideas Magically Revolutionary

If the only way we learned about new technology was from vendors, we might have the misconception that one-of-a-kind, revolutionary solutions are appearing every day. Marketing, after all, is about promoting and selling products or services. Humans get pleasure at a biological level from novelty, even if it's the repackaging of old goods.[53] This is not an anti-vendor myth, although extravagant and intensive publicity or promotion—the definition of hype—are integral to some marketing. Given how few people practicing cybersecurity have ever bothered to study the field's history, this technique is particularly effective.

The myth here is that renaming, rebranding, or repackaging an existing or slightly evolved technology magically makes it more effective or desirable. There is no magic færie dust that gives existing technology special properties. If someone tries to rebrand and sell you firewall[54] technology as a new category of security products called Digital Sentinels, be skeptical.

Consider two contemporary examples: cloud computing and zero trust.[55] Both of these phrases are used with abandon because we have been convinced that they are novel and magical. In reality, both cloud computing and zero trust are, in their own ways, *old* technology with a bit of færie dust. Without a doubt, they offer value, but over-exaggeration has given some people a false sense of hope.

In modern cybersecurity, the momentum of adoption is too often confused with novelty and value. Momentum is not harmful per se, as long as consumers understand a technology's history. Jumping

51. https://github.com/Netflix/chaosmonkey
52. Tucker, Haley, Hochstein, Lorin, Jones, Nora, Basiri, Ali, and Rosenthal, Casey, "The Business Case for Chaos Engineering," *IEEE Cloud Computing*, Vol. 5, No. 3, (2018): 45–54. DOI: 10.1109/MCC.2018.032591616.
53. Swaminathan, Nikhil, "Our Brains on Marketing: Scans Show Why We Like New Things," *Scientific American*, June 26, 2008.
54. For more information on firewalls, see the Appendix.
55. For more information on these, see the Appendix.

on the bandwagon because everyone is talking about it is misguided, however. By the time average consumers hear about technology such as cloud computing, it has percolated and evolved, often for years. Pay-as-you-go computing services did not emerge suddenly in the 2000s when Amazon, Google, and others introduced their offerings. Time-sharing systems were commercially available in the 1960s and 1970s. Today's cloud services evolved from work done in the 1970s and 1980s on distributed computing. But it seems that overnight, everyone was talking about going to the cloud as if it was a revolutionary solution to all our needs!

Cloud computing is a form of resource-sharing, allowing users to use on-demand resources from a provider. If we store files online, we rent storage from a third party. These days we can hire vendors to do all sorts of online actions, including hosting databases and translating speech to text (think: Siri and Alexa). The self-service of commercial services also makes acquisition and adoption nearly seamless. But cloud services are not magic, and there are real disadvantages to consider. For instance, we have traded control and flexibility for convenience, vendor lock-in issues, and limits on transparency and control. There can still be downtime and breaches. Cloud computing might be the right choice in some cases, but think carefully before jumping on any bandwagons.

Zero trust is a modern description of the strategy of eliminating implicit trust, complete mediation, and compartmentalizing what is trusted rather than having a perimeter. Trust exists in many parts of the digital ecosystem, from the hardware of our devices to the networks that connect us to software and online services to other humans. Trust exploitation is the root of many types of cybersecurity compromises. Attackers target domain controllers because that's a server that member computers trust. Many system owners also assume that if someone logs in with a legitimate username and password, all of that person's actions can be trusted. When users log in to the GoodLife Bank app, they can deposit and withdraw money because they are trusted. An alternative is to validate every action, including the fact that a legitimate user might be using an untrustworthy device. If a user accesses GoodLife Bank from a new device or foreign country, maybe they should be scrutinized. The best practice is to limit trust, enforce least privilege, authorize all accesses, and compartmentalize that trust.[56]

But least privilege, complete mediation of access, and compartmentalization are old ideas dating back decades! Security professionals have been recommending these practices for many years. Modern implementations allow continuous analysis and adaptation that provide highly granular, real-time, least privileged access.[57] If you think about it, there is no such thing as fully *zero* trust because the systems need to trust whatever does the authentication and access control; a system based on truly *zero* trust would be inert. In the end, there is no færie dust that makes zero trust revolutionary. . . or a magic solution to security needs.

Passwords Should Be Changed Often

One topic on which almost everybody has experience and opinions is passwords. It is a reality that after more than 60 years, passwords—including words, phrases, and PINs—are still the dominant form of

56. For more on zero trust, see the Appendix.

57. For one example, see Google's BeyondCorps and BeyondProd. Osborn, Barclay, et al., "BeyondCorp: Design to Deployment at Google," *USENIX ;login* (2016).

authentication. This scheme seemed like a secret key that would protect our valuables. In reality, we have experienced the dangerous downsides of making users choose and remember many passwords. A brighter passwordless future has been promised for decades. In 2004, Bill Gates promised their demise because "they just don't meet the challenge for anything you really want to secure."[58]

The password to a computer is not like the key to a house. Nobody makes homeowners pick the teeth and notches on the blades of their house keys, and they do not need to reconstruct them every time they come home. Yet, we require users to self-generate and remember digital passwords (like the combination to a lock) or carry physical tokens. Multifactor authentication was introduced in the 1990s, dramatically improving security but inconveniencing users. "With all that said, it's difficult to see anything killing the password," said John Viega in his 2009 book *The Myths of Security*.

Despite the abuse heaped on passwords, they are unlikely to disappear anytime soon. The paradigm is understood by even novice users, requires no additional investment in hardware, and is still a reasonable mechanism when used appropriately. The key is using it with an understanding of the context and risks—a theme we will mention repeatedly. Poor password selection, password guessing, and interception/spoofing are all potential problems with passwords; however, there are circumstances where those are not significant threats or have mitigations. Effective authentication should be more than computational strength or resistance to every possible attack. To a cybersecurity professional, the priority for choosing an authentication scheme might be security, but we should also factor in the threat model, the cost, and user acceptance (at least). One approach will never fit every situation, as we noted in Figure 1.1.

As we know, 100-character passwords might be more secure than 10-character passwords but impossible to use in practice without assistance (such as a password manager). It is no myth that different authentication mechanisms have different cryptographic strength. That is, how much time and space are required to break the encryption? Experts note that the relative strength of passwords versus biometrics differs not only in the key but also in other considerations. For one, we cannot change our fingerprints if they are our authenticators and are compromised. And as with all things cybersecurity, bugs in implementing algorithms can happen even if the cryptographic protocol is fantastic.

This is not to say that many people have not worked on improving the password situation for users. Password meters nudge us to pick better passwords. Password managers remember strong passwords on our behalf. But it's challenging to shift the momentum of passwords and retool our systems for other options.

One myth is that nobody can guess our password if they do not know us well. Maybe our favorite sports team is Liverpool, or our dog's name is Charlie. If *liverpool* or *charlie* is our password, these are guessable in less than a second even if the attacker didn't have access to your memory board, as in Figure 1.3. Do not bank on the assumption that attackers need to know us personally with passwords such as those!

Another myth is that passwords should be changed frequently. Research shows frequent changes are counterproductive to good security because they lead to simple patterns or workarounds. Similarly, complexity requirements such as requiring symbols and numbers have resulted in worse passwords. That rule is no longer recommended.

58. www.cnet.com/tech/services-and-software/gates-predicts-death-of-the-password/

One authoritative source for password guidance is NIST 800-63B (Digital Identity Guidelines), last updated in June 2017. In particular, Appendix A describes how to think about the strength of memorized secrets. NIST recommends that users not be allowed to choose passwords from "previous breach corpuses, dictionary words, and specific words (such as the name of the service itself) that users are likely to choose."

In 2021, Microsoft announced that users could go passwordless for Microsoft accounts used to sign in to Microsoft Outlook and OneDrive.[59] To do so, users were invited to use an authenticator app, security key, or verification code. This might be the first of new authentication alternatives that are both strong and usable. Or not. Passwords might not be here forever but don't bet on it.

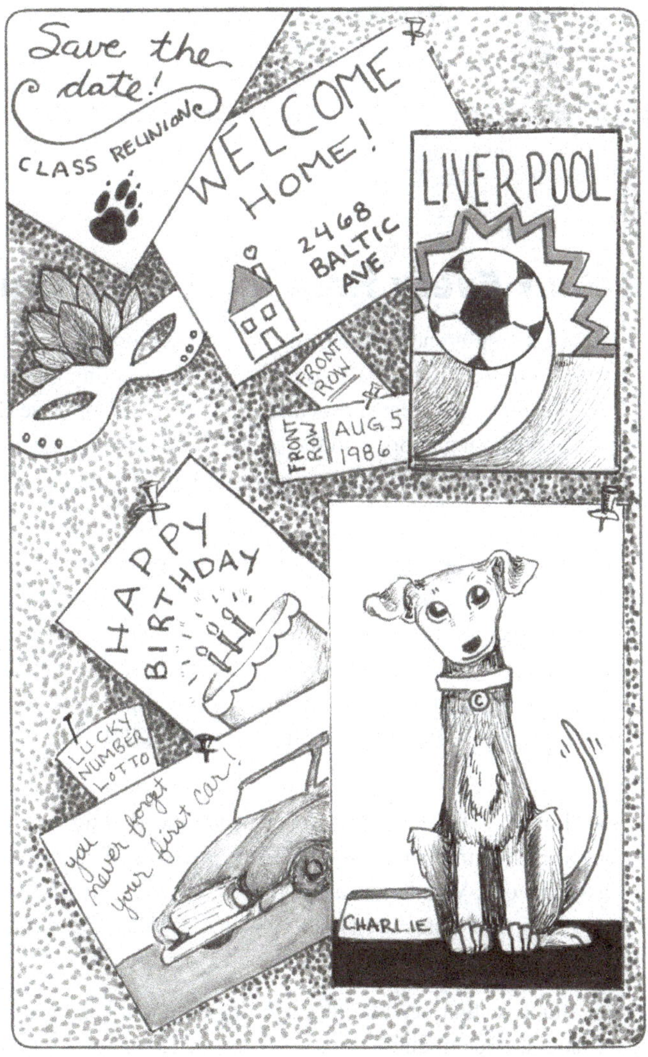

FIGURE 1.3 Strong passwords are difficult to generate and remember.

59. https://techcrunch.com/2021/09/15/microsoft-now-lets-you-sign-in-without-your-password/

Multifactor Authentication (MFA) Means Secure

MFA is a mechanism where we must not only know something (the password) but also have something. That something we must have could be a dongle, a smartphone, or something the system can use to double-check that it is us on the other side of the keyboard. It's an additional layer of security, so it must be secure, right?

If the something on the other side is SMS verification, it might not be secure. If the phone already has malware, it can intercept the messages and masquerade as the actual user. Not to mention, some places using this authentication use it to install malware.[a]

There's also the network that the SMS message traverses. That can be compromised as well.

a www.trendmicro.com/en_us/research/22/b/sms-pva-services-use-of-infected-android-phones-reveals-flaws-in-sms-verification.html

Believe and Fear Every Hacking Demo You See

DEF CON is an annual hacker conference known for new revelations and showy demos. In 2010, presenters demonstrated the hack of a car. In 2017, someone hacked a voting machine. In 2020, it was a satellite. These demonstrations make for great shows and stories, lots of applause (from other hackers), and widespread hype and fear (from the public and the press). It's like movies coming to life! They are amazing and scary, and who would not want to report on the fantastic things done outside of movie magic?

Cybersecurity professionals understand, appreciate, and admire new contributions to the field. Sometimes we even admire the skill of an attack or new offensive techniques. We can see the implications and severity of new vulnerabilities before they are understood or known by the general public. Vendors participating in bug bounty programs routinely ask for proof-of-concept code to demonstrate that a new bug can be exploited. Hackers also demand proof-of-concept examples to be taken seriously. One publication puts a fine point on this: *International Journal of Proof-of-Concept or Get the Fuck Out.*[60]

There is a misconception, however, that every demo or academic finding will result in widespread use. These demonstrations are revealing but often ignore the context and complexity of the real world. They often make *many* assumptions. Vote tallies are audited, as are ATMs. Physical protections might prevent an attacker from quickly or undetectably making a change. Hacking a voting machine or ATM is a different threat than undermining an election or financial system.

Rowhammer was a novel attack technique.[61] Cool, even. Researchers have created several proof-of-concept exploits. But we have no documented evidence (yet) of Rowhammer being used in the wild.

60. https://www.alchemistowl.org/pocorgtfo/
61. More information on Rowhammer can be found in the Appendix.

TCP Shrew is another novel attack technique for Distributed Denial of Service (DDoS). It's cool and awesome, but there is no documented evidence of it being used in the wild. The Exploit Prediction Scoring System (EPSS) is one model that uses threat information and real-world exploit data to calculate the probability that a vulnerability will be exploited. Hundreds of CVE are not a threat for most people. According to Kenna Security and Cyentia Institute, only around one-third of all CVEs are ever seen in live environments, and, of those, only 5% have known exploits.[62]

Simply because an attack can be demonstrated does not mean it will be used.

Cyber Offense Is Easier Than Defense

A great many respected voices in cybersecurity have said, "the defense has a disadvantage because they have to defend against all attacks, while the offense only needs a single way in." On the surface, this seems intuitively true. Defending many attack surfaces means resources are spread thinly. If all offensive resources are focused on a single attack at the time and method of the attacker's choosing, how could that not favor the offense?

This point of view makes one strong assumption: Cyber attack is easy. As Bruce Schneier wrote, "Contrary to popular belief, government cyberattacks are not bolts out of the blue, and the attack/defense balance is more. . . well. . . balanced."[63] While criminal attacks such as large-scale phishing attempts are not discriminatory, they still cost the attacker because of a low success rate. Furthermore, the phishing email is only one component for the criminal who needs functional malware, command and control infrastructure, and a way to monetize stolen data. These days, ransomware attackers even offer customer service and tech support for their victims.[64]

Believe Every Cyber Threat You Read About Online

The history of false and distorted information is ancient. Long before the Internet, lurid tales of danger were seen in newspapers and tabloids. But the Internet changed the game in the magnitude and speed of this phenomenon.

Cybersecurity is not immune from misinformation and disinformation. Misinformation is inaccurate or purposely misleading information, not intended to be harmful, but still able to cause damage. Disinformation is deliberately wrong, spreads false information as truth, and is designed to cause harm. In many places where free speech is highly valued, distributing false information is legal; in areas where free speech is viewed as a threat to the government, the government itself might be spreading false information. This can lead to problems, especially for the gullible or poorly informed.

62. www.kennasecurity.com/news/companies-can-safely-delay-patching-the-majority-of-their-vulnerabilities-kenna-security-report-finds/
63. www.schneier.com/blog/archives/2017/04/attack_vs_defen.html
64. www.wired.com/story/ransomware-gone-corporate-darkside-where-will-it-end/

Artificial intelligence is advanced enough to generate realistic but false cyber threat intelligence sufficient to fool professionals.[a] Here is one example of AI-generated cybersecurity misinformation:

> "APT33 is exploring physically disruptive cyber attacks on critical infrastructure. Attackers have injected a variety of vulnerabilities into web-based airline management interfaces. Once successful, attackers can intercept and extract sensitive data as well as gain unauthorized access to the Content Management System (CMS) utility."[b]

Everyone, including cybersecurity professionals, must be mindful and diligent, maintaining healthy skepticism for the information we consume. This is an excellent illustration of where *trust* is a paramount property!

[a] Ranade, Priyanka, Piplai, Aritran, Mittal, Sudip, Joshi, Anupam, and Finin, Tim, "Generating Fake Cyber Threat Intelligence Using Transformer-Based Models," *Proceedings of the 2021 International Joint Conference on Neural Networks (IJCNN)*, (June 2021): 1–9.

[b] https://theconversation.com/study-shows-ai-generated-fake-reports-fool-experts-160909

Professor Rebecca Slayton at Cornell University thinks it is premature to say that offense has the advantage.[65] First, she suggests reframing the conversation around relative utility or value. It is reasonable to associate high costs with defending high-value assets. Further, if the value of offense is relatively low, then the offense is not "favored." For example, consider Stuxnet:

> "This analysis suggests that the defense was likely less costly than the offense in the Stuxnet attack, contrary to dominant assumptions about cyber offense dominance. Perhaps most significantly, the value that the United States, Israel, and Iran all attach to Iran's nuclear program appears to be much greater than the cost of either cyber offense or cyber defense, making it unlikely that leaders were focused on costs."

This myth matters beyond simple misconception. It is unnecessarily discouraging for organizational leaders and cyber defenders who might feel they are always behind, chasing the attackers who have "easy" choices. Defenders need to try to understand the mind and behavior of an attacker. This is why some programs teach offensive techniques to students studying cybersecurity: Knowing the attacker mindset helps them defend better.[66]

The key to avoiding this pitfall is to be careful when opining that the offense has the upper hand. It's not simply about relative costs—defense costs should be appropriately matched with the protected

65. Slayton, Rebecca, "What Is the Cyber Offense-Defense Balance? Conceptions, Causes, and Assessment," *International Security*, Vol. 41, No. 3 (2016): 72–109.
66. This is not the reason many programs teach offense—offense seems more exciting and attracts students is the actual reason. To quote Bear Bryant, "Offense sells tickets, but defense wins championships." The pedagogy of a well-designed program requires a much more balanced and nuanced approach and is not as common as it should be.

value. (Remember Courtney's Laws from earlier: "We Can Measure How Secure Our Systems Are.") We need not lament how much we spend on security or how big of an attack surface we must defend.

Operational Technology (OT) Is Not Vulnerable

Most of us have a good sense of information technology (IT) because it's the hardware and software we see and use day to day: our phones, our tablets, our email, etc. This is not the only category of technology, however. Operational technology (OT) is hardware and software that controls industrial equipment, and it's more ubiquitous and essential than most people realize. For example, OT can open and close valves in a factory or control the elevators in a building. You might have heard references to subsegments of OT—namely Industrial Control Systems (ICS) and Supervisory Control And Data Acquisition (SCADA) systems.

There are notable differences between IT and OT that impact cybersecurity. A big one is that IT is user-centric and OT is machine-centric. Humans interact directly with their IT devices, such as by sending emails and writing books. OT systems are generally less interactive and more automated because they control things in the physical world, even though they are still programmed and monitored by human operators.

It might seem as if IT and OT are enough alike that the same kinds of vendors would build both, and the same types of skills and teams would operate both. This is increasingly true, but that is a recent change. IT and OT primarily evolved independently. Companies such as GE, Honeywell, and Siemens—which might not be familiar names to many IT users—produce OT platforms for power utilities and other needs using proprietary systems. These systems use communications and protocols that are "standard" for OT but different from IT. For instance, a smart meter might measure how much electricity your home uses and communicate that information to your electric company using the Open Smart Grid Protocol (OSGP). Similarly, the water show with more than a thousand fountains at the Bellagio Hotel in Las Vegas is controlled with the Modbus protocol.[67] Special protocols worked fine until people wanted to access and control their systems over the Internet. . . with all its many malicious users.

Security for OT systems was not originally a priority because threat models did not include it as necessary. OT networks were isolated initially. This "air gap" meant that data could not automatically move from the IT network to the OT network and was considered strong security. The reality is that there are business reasons for needing to transfer files between the IT and OT networks, such as to install software patches or move configuration files. When the networks are not connected, one solution is to copy data with USB drives. For many years, attackers (and security researchers) have found ways to jump the air gap. They might infect a machine on the IT network and the USB drive. They might even use sound or heat to communicate between disconnected networks.[68]

67. https://modbus.org/docs/MBNewsletter_Summer2010.pdf

68. For example, see Guri, Mordechai, et al., "Bitwhisper: Covert Signaling Channel Between Air-Gapped Computers Using Thermal Manipulations," *IEEE 28th Computer Security Foundations Symposium*, IEEE, 2015.

IT and OT are converging, which means both are vulnerable and require cybersecurity. It is a myth that OT systems are isolated or unknown to attackers, and that myth is receding every day.

Breaking Systems Is the Best Way to Establish Yourself

Egos are huge in cyber, and none more so than the egos driven by the perceived glory of a big hack. This is an unfortunate misconception. Finding flaws is sometimes an art, sometimes a science, and occasionally simple luck, but it is not usually the key to establishing oneself as an expert.

People who break things get temporary recognition and publicity, but that rarely showcases professional skill and expertise. There are a small number of exceptions, but *fixing* problems is the outcome most people desire, not a pile of broken code. Breaking things seems glamorous and fun, and it can occasionally be those things, but it alone is insufficient to build a career. It is not difficult for most people to break a crystal vase, but only some are qualified to make one. Houses can be broken into with minimal expertise; designing and building one takes considerable skill. Given the quality of most computer code, finding flaws is not a huge accomplishment; building systems that resist attacks is.

Generally speaking, breaking things is almost always easier than creating or fixing them, and the majority of cybersecurity careers are devoted to diagnosis and repair. We say that despite having extensive experience breaking systems ourselves.

Because You Can, You Should

There is an endless amount of cybersecurity-related activity and behavior that is legal and technically achievable, yet *inadvisable*. Simply because we can do something does not mean we should. We could run through the data center shouting the equivalent of "Fire,"[69] but we do not.

Let's start by reiterating that much of what we do in the field is based on "trust." That extends to the trust of people and the profession. Consider the generic and stereotypical reputation of used-car salespeople: It isn't always positive. That is perhaps unfair to most of those people, but the lack of candor by a few has tarnished the reputations of them all. The same can be said of politicians and, in some places, law enforcement personnel; unethical behavior by a few makes an entire class of people look bad and lessens trust. We'll return to this theme in several places in the book and highlight professional organizations' roles. Still, we want this concept to be central to these discussions: For cybersecurity to be successful and for cybersecurity professionals to be trusted, we (collectively) need to place a strong emphasis on behaving ethically—not simply doing things because of law or convenience, but because they are the *right* things to do. That also means encouraging others to do what is right and condemning improper behavior. A "nifty hack" that hurts an innocent party or endangers the public is unacceptable, no matter how clever it might be.

69. The database is down! There's an APT loose! The elves have lost their recipes!

Questionable Ethics

The University of Minnesota was banned from contributing to the Linux kernel. The story began with a research project.[a] The research was designed to see if it was possible to patch trivial bugs while simultaneously introducing stealthy, serious, new vulnerabilities. To demonstrate this attack, the researchers conducted it with their submissions to the actual Linux kernel. Thankfully, the demonstration included a safeguard to prevent the flawed code from being accepted and distributed.

The backlash from the cybersecurity and software development communities was severe. Many saw it as an experiment in human deception. The university argued that the research did not involve humans and was not subject to the review of an IRB.

This is a case study where something that can technically and legally be done does not mean it should be.

[a] "On the Feasibility of Stealthily Introducing Vulnerabilities in Open-Source Software via Hypocrite Commits"; www.theverge.com/2021/4/30/22410164/linux-kernel-university-of-minnesota-banned-opensource

Responsible disclosure of vulnerabilities, for instance, is not required by law in the United States.[70] A security team that discovers a critical vulnerability in a popular web browser could legally release it publicly without notifying the vendor, but doing so risks widespread exploitation and compromise. The researchers might not exploit it for their own gain, but they are leaving it open for others to do that. Leaving the door open for the robbers is almost as bad as joining them in their caper.

Morals and ethics are distinguishable and distinct from the law, but whether we *should* or *should not* is informed by both law and ethics. Many professions, professional organizations, and industries have codes of ethics and professional conduct. The Association for Computing Machinery (ACM) has a very good one.[71] The first sentence acknowledges the importance: "Computing professionals' actions change the world." This code speaks to the duties of computing professionals for the public good, care for society and human well-being, responsibility for ethical practice, and respect for privacy. The Forum of Incident Response and Security Teams (FIRST) also has a notable code of ethics.[72]

Many accredited academic computer science and engineering programs require a study of ethics. The Accreditation Board for Engineering and Technology (ABET) says that graduates will "Recognize professional responsibilities and make informed judgments in cybersecurity practice based on legal and ethical principles."[73]

70. The federal government has internal disclosure policies that apply to government agencies and departments, such as the Vulnerabilities Equity Program (VEP). https://archive.epic.org/privacy/cybersecurity/vep/
71. www.acm.org/code-of-ethics
72. https://ethicsfirst.org/
73. www.abet.org/accreditation/accreditation-criteria/criteria-for-accrediting-computing-programs-2020-2021/

In most research environments, an Institutional Review Board (IRB) reviews research proposals to protect the rights and welfare of human research subjects. If we want to study phishing by sending fake emails to people, an IRB will consider the potential harm to the participants.

Lastly, consider how other people will perceive our choices. We might get a lot of pushback and questions about the project or decision, even if we felt it was entirely right to do. Would we feel comfortable if the decision was front-page headlines in the news?[74]

Bottom line: If we find ourselves saying that something is *technically* feasible or *technically* legal, that situation should give us pause to reconsider the action.

Better Security Means Worse Privacy

If we ask people if privacy is important, we will undoubtedly get an enthusiastic "Yes!" It is explicitly mentioned in the United Nation's Declaration of Human Rights.[75] The consensus in law is that there is an implicit right to privacy embedded in the U.S. Constitution,[76] and an explicit recognition in several laws. Europe has enacted major laws around privacy, the best known of which is the General Data Protection Regulation (GDPR); however, similar to security, no formal definition of privacy is widely accepted. It is recognized as contextual within time and society—different cultures have defined it differently over time.

Technology has also played a role in defining privacy and the violation of privacy. The invention of the window, the camera, and the telephone are all examples of how technological changes have privacy implications. Computing and networking continue to push boundaries in this regard. Many venues associated with cybersecurity are labeled as about "security and privacy," making the association explicit.

The myth associated with this association is that increasing privacy protections reduces a system's security and vice versa. This is certainly not the case! If we think about it, one of the primary drivers of cybersecurity is to support privacy: We want to limit access to private information.

The myth comes about because there are cases where the most straightforward or cheapest solution to a security problem involves reducing privacy. For example, if we want to reduce the chance of phishing, we would examine and store copies of all emails coming into the enterprise. We have a better chance of catching phishing links at the expense of email privacy. This fails to acknowledge that there are other methods, including methods that allow us to use the power of computing to enhance security *and* preserve privacy. For example, we can automatically rewrite URLs in an email to neuter them without having to keep a record or have anyone read the contents.

74. A former CIA official described this colloquially as "*The Washington Post* test." See https://medium.com/@StratGleeson/the-washington-post-test-ffc184b510d9

75. Article 12; www.un.org/en/about-us/universal-declaration-of-human-rights

76. https://constitution.laws.com/right-to-privacy, although the recent decision by the U.S. Supreme Court in *Dobbs v. Jackson Women's Health Organization* has created some doubt about the scope of this implicit right.

There is not an automatic trade-off of privacy for better security. Adding logging or surveillance is not always the only way to address an issue, although it is often the cheapest and fastest way to do so. "Fast and cheap" often results in incrementally less privacy for the user community. Privacy is important. People should have the opportunity to give informed consent to when, how, *and if* their privacy is being reduced to use a system. Public pushback on cookies and online advertising are examples of growing awareness of these issues.

People who work in cybersecurity should protect privacy when they can, not reduce it. When presented with restrictions, such as those imposed by the GDPR, it should be a matter of professional duty to find ways to support them rather than circumvent them.

Further Reading

Anderson, Ross. *Security Engineering*, 3rd ed. Wiley, 2020.

Barnum, Todd. *The Cybersecurity Manager's Guide*. O'Reilly, 2021.

Bishop, Matt. *Computer Security: Art and Science*. Pearson, 2019.

Garfinkel, Simson, and Spafford, Eugene. *Web Security, Privacy, & Commerce*, 2nd ed. O'Reilly and Associates, 2002.

Hubbard, Douglas W., and Seiersen, Richard. *How to Measure Anything in Cybersecurity Risk*. Wiley, 2016.

Kaufman, Charlie. *Network Security: Private Communication in a Public World*, 2nd ed. (R. Perlman and M. Speciner, eds.). Pearson, 2002.

Lipner, Steven B. "The Birth and Death of the Orange Book," *IEEE Annals of the History of Computing*. Vol. 37, No. 2 (2015): 19–31; https://muse.jhu.edu/article/584410.

Loscocco, Peter A., Smalley, Stephen D., Muckelbauer, Patrick A., Taylor, Ruth C., Turner, Jeff S., and Farrell, John F. "The Inevitability of Failure: The Flawed Assumption of Security in Modern Computing Environments," *Proceedings of the 21st National Information Systems Security Conference*, 1998.

Miller, Alyssa. *Cybersecurity Career Guide*. Manning, 2022.

NIST Risk Management Framework. https://csrc.nist.gov/Projects/risk-management.

NIST Zero Trust Architecture. https://nvlpubs.nist.gov/nistpubs/SpecialPublications/NIST.SP.800-207.pdf.

Patton, Helen. *Navigating the Cyber Security Career Path*. Wiley, 2022.

Pfleeger, Charles P., et al. *Security in Computing*, 5th ed. Pearson, 2015.

Rasner, Gregory C. *Cybersecurity and Third-Party Risk*. Wiley, 2021.

Saydjari, O. Sami. *Engineering Trustworthy Systems: Get Cybersecurity Design Right the First Time*, 1st ed. McGraw-Hill Education, 2018.

Viega, John. *The Myths of Security: What the Computer Security Industry Doesn't Want You to Know.* O'Reilly, 2009.

Chapter 2

What Is the Internet?

We are in great haste to construct a magnetic telegraph from Maine to Texas; but Maine and Texas, it might be, have nothing important to communicate.

Henry David Thoreau

Forty years ago, a cybersecurity book would only be about the security of individual computers. There was no Internet. Since then, network technology has progressed and become ubiquitous to the point where, to recycle an old Scott McNeely quote, "The network is the computer." We have LANs, WANs, MANs, Wi-Fi, Bluetooth, NFC, and more connecting our systems—and our systems of systems. In a growing number of instances, our software and data are somewhere "out there" in the cloud, and our systems cannot function as we wish without working network access.

This book is not a treatise on networking, so we will not go into depth on networks and network security; however, several myths and misconceptions about the Internet and cloud computing exist. Let's start with what should perhaps be a simple concept: What is the Internet?

Everyone Knows What the "Internet" Means

At the most superficial and most general level, the Internet is the set of all computer systems that can communicate with each other using some network communications. We can have a network that is not connected to the Internet, which is often described as a "stand-alone" network. The Internet (and other networks) provide standardized services, including websites and email. Notably, the web is not synonymous with the Internet; it is only one part.

Computers on the Internet can communicate with each other because they use standardized protocols. These protocols define the rules and syntax for how information is exchanged. Many sources state that the network communications involved must use protocols in the Internet Protocol (IP) suite, such as Transmission Control Protocol (TCP), User Datagram Protocol (UDP), etc. This leaves out any systems that are still communicating using *only* protocols such as UUCP, Bitnet, DECNET, XNS, and X.25. . . if there are any. Systems can use IP and one or more of those protocols simultaneously and be on the same physical network (although that is uncommon).

The IP suite has addresses, ports, and protocols that define connections. An IP address is a point used to deliver packets. A computer (router, firewall, or smartphone) might have more than one address. With load balancers and firewalls, it is also possible that multiple systems might share the same address. IP addresses currently come in two forms: IPv4 addresses are 32 bits, and IPv6 addresses are 128 bits.[1] IPv4 and IPv6 are not interchangeable, although a system might use both, and both might be routed over the same physical networks.

A protocol defines how the bits in network packets are interpreted. Protocols might be nested so that the raw data in one packet (or set of packets) can be interpreted as another. For instance, an IPv4 transmission might contain a TCP packet that contains a Simple Mail Transfer Protocol (SMTP) mail message.

A port is a logical part of an address in some protocols and is a virtual place for packets to be delivered (or from which to originate). There are 65,536 (2^{16}) ports per address and protocol (UDP and TCP) (16-bit value). The triple address/port/protocol defines where a packet is to be delivered; two packets with the same destination and port but different protocols will not be confused by a standards-compliant system. If that is not clear, imagine an apartment complex where the IP address is the street address for the apartments, all of which have the same street address. The protocol can be thought of as a building number and delivery method. The port number is the apartment number. There might be two apartments with the same number and street address, but the building is different, so the full address is not ambiguous.

Most people are not good at remembering 32- or 128-bit numbers, but they do remember words. Thus, the IP protocol has a directory to map words (names) to IP addresses. This is the DNS. It uses a hierarchical, distributed database to map name requests to IP numbers. Other protocols hint at how to route packets from one place to the next based on the IP numbers and what to do when there are errors or delays.

If you, gentle reader, want more details, we suggest you consult some of the references listed at the end of this chapter.

With that as an abbreviated and abstract introduction, let's look at common misconceptions about the Internet and networks.

An IP Address Identifies a Unique Machine

People who do not understand Internet addressing and routing often believe that an IP address identifies a unique machine. We have heard people who assert, "Aha! We have their IP address, so we know where the message comes from!" That is not always the case. The IP address 1.1.1.1 (a popular public DNS server[2]), for instance, is not a single machine but a global network of servers, and hosts might interact with a different server every time they access that IP!

1. Yes, Virginia, there was an IPv5, but it was never standardized: www.lifewire.com/what-happened-to-ipv5-3971327. There also were protocols IPv7—IPv9. www.iana.org/assignments/version-numbers/version-numbers.xhtml.
2. https://blog.cloudflare.com/dns-resolver-1-1-1-1/

First, any individual host can have multiple connections (physical and virtual) to networks. Each of those connections has its own IP address, and they might not be closely related. A system on (for example) two distinct physical networks will have at least two addresses, one for each network.

Second, an address might map to multiple computers—even computers in different countries! This happens with load balancing. A packet will have an address, be routed to a balancer or concentrator, and then be readdressed and rerouted to a system determined to be "near" or least loaded. The reply will go back through the load balancer, adjusting the outgoing address to match the incoming address. For example, there is no single machine that answers everyone's requests to google.com. Instead, Google's infrastructure automatically redirects the query to the closest available server to minimize the time necessary to return an answer.[3]

Third, some form of proxy, firewall, or Network Address Translation (NAT) gateway might be in use. If someone uses NAT, it is highly likely that if all of the devices in their home visited the same website, the server would think they all came from the same IP address. Yes, each device has a different private IP address inside the network, but the outgoing packets are rewritten with a different Internet-routable IP address than the actual sending machine. Return packets are sorted and re-sent by the gateway based on a cache, so connections are maintained. Many organizations and some whole countries are behind such gateways. Some privacy-preserving proxies such as The Onion Router (TOR) hide sources under layers of forwarding addresses.

And fourth, there is no requirement in the protocols that the actual sending address is included in any IP packet. If the sender does not care about getting any response, any value can be put in the sender IP field. This can be used to spoof the sender or to perpetrate attacks such as the Smurf DDoS attack.[4] Although Internet Service Providers (ISPs) can detect and block some spoofed source IP addresses, there is an overhead to doing so, which slows down network speeds.

These four possibilities are not mutually exclusive, either. It is possible that all four could even be combined in multiple ways! So, although we might be able to see an IP address in the sender field of an IP packet, it does not mean that we can match it against any particular machine (or organization) with certainty.

So, what good is knowing an IP address? One benefit is the ability to block it. If attacks are coming from an IP address, wherever it is, the network can refuse to accept traffic originating from that IP address. Another use is as a lead in an investigation. Even without 100% accuracy, it might be valuable to know that activity—an email, a web request, or malicious command and control—appears to be coming from a particular company or country. In legal investigations, it is common to ask an ISP, "What logs do you have about the activity of this IP address during the time in question?" It is not foolproof but can produce new leads to keep tracking the attack.

---

3. Geography matters because of latency. Like a busy highway, Internet traffic traverses many different network segments, or hops, and each additional intersection incurs delays and possible delays. For more, see https://cloud.google.com/load-balancing/docs/load-balancing-overview.

4. https://www.cloudflare.com/learning/ddos/smurf-ddos-attack/

The Internet Is Managed and Controlled by a Central Body

Wherever you are sitting right now, point to the Internet. Did you point to your device? To the sky? To a wire leading into your wall? The Internet is not an abstraction. It exists in physical form, including an unfathomable quantity of computers, wires, fiber optic cables, and a nontrivial amount of radio waves. It even includes some satellites. It exists on all seven continents, on (and under) the oceans, and beyond the Earth: Some robots on other planets and the International Space Station communicate using IP protocols! A great deal of the Internet travels on wires and fiber optic cables underground or undersea. When websites go "down," that commonly means that a wire was cut or a network configuration made the server inaccessible. It can also mean that a solar storm is interfering with some of that radio communication or an earthquake has disrupted a connection.[5]

The Internet is complex. We know it has more than a billion active IP addresses. We have all those addresses, protocols, routing, and other issues working 24/7, supporting government, academia, entertainment, and commerce. It must be a huge job to control all that, right? Well, no. No entity controls the Internet.

The Internet functions because the various telecommunications companies providing the major long-haul networks cooperate using the same protocols. It is an example of cooperation and interconnection of shared interests, not control. If one major network provider decided not to follow the shared protocols, its peers would cease to interoperate with it (either by choice or as a consequence of failures). That would mean its customers would not be able to communicate with everyone else. That certainly provides an incentive to cooperate!

This also means that laws governing network usage are local, not global. If country X passes a law that states certain things will not appear on the Internet, it is up to the companies doing business in country X to filter those things from their traffic. There is no central authority to dictate what will and will not be shared, who can connect, and what standards for content might be observed globally. (See also Chapter 9, "Legal Issues.")

So, for example, it is against the law in several countries, such as Thailand, to insult the country's leader (this is known as lèse-majesté). The authorities in Thailand can enforce that law inside their country. In a few countries where it is illegal to insult foreign heads of state (e.g., Iceland, Switzerland), it would also be against the law to insult the king of Thailand in a public forum. That is the extent of regulation, and there is no central authority to which a complaint can be made if, for example, a blogger in Kansas posts insulting content about the royal family in Thailand or the president of the Italian Republic, although that blogger should perhaps be cautious about traveling to those countries in the future.

It is this same lack of control that makes the pursuit and punishment of criminal behavior particularly difficult. One well-known example is that of Russian ransomware gangs. They attack sites in other countries, notably the United States, and commit acts of vandalism, theft, and extortion. In many cases, the perpetrators are known by name, and law enforcement even has their addresses and pictures;

5. https://netblocks.org/reports/eastern-turkey-earthquake-knocks-out-telecommunication-networks-gBLRMp84

however, the Russian government will not extradite those individuals to stand trial.[6] (It is suspected that the Russian government sometimes tasks those criminals with its own unsavory business, so they are protected as a reward.)

The lack of control does provide some benefit, however. It is not required that any site on the Internet accept all traffic from any particular source. Sites that do not have business relationships with parties in other countries might use geolocation data or blocklists to stop inbound network traffic from those countries to help protect against threats. Commonly blocked traffic sources include Russia (because of that lawless behavior) and the People's Republic of China (for similar reasons). The consequence of this blocking, however, allows some governments to prohibit their residents from accessing information available in other countries; this can be viewed as political censorship or maintaining public order, depending on one's views.

To summarize the discussion: Your view of the Internet differs from everyone else's and changes with time and location. In particular, unless you go looking for it, you might not realize how many different languages are used online. Of particular note to readers in the United States, the First Amendment applies only to the U.S. government: No other country or private company is required to accept and publish any statements you make.[7] We do not all see the same traffic or the same attacks. Differences in law and culture are significant when we discuss cybersecurity, and there is no central authority to which we can appeal for help.

The Internet Is Largely Static

The origins of the Internet are different from how things look today. Today, the Internet is so fast that data can travel around the globe more quickly than you can finish reading this sentence. That certainly was not true in the beginning, in the age of the 110-baud modem and 56kb leased line connections!

Back in the original days of the Internet, registering a domain was a process that could take a long time. The registrar would accept a request and set up the domain, and then everyone would wait, and wait, and wait. It would take time for the domain information to be propagated to all the nameservers. It was not the (nearly) instant process as it is today. Today, someone can register a domain and use it immediately. Back then, depending on the day and the nameservers, it could take several days.

Domain names can be used and discarded in minutes, not days. A bad guy can register the domain, use it to send spam, and immediately drop it.[8] By the time we realize it should be blocked (or it gets added to a shared blocklist), the domain is no longer in use. This was unthinkable in the late 1990s, but it is commonplace today. One expert on domain name use, Paul Vixie, has suggested that if we block all new domains for 24 hours after they are created, the amount of spam we see will drop significantly.

Attacks have evolved as well. The original ransomware attack was delivered by hand on a floppy disk at a conference.[9] Today, it's often transmitted by email. That's a major change in delivery that affects

6. https://learningenglish.voanews.com/a/how-ransomware-criminals-are-protected-in-russia/5858722.html
7. See "That Violates My First Amendment Rights!" in Chapter 9.
8. Using the statistics from https://siteefy.com/how-many-domains-are-there, there was, on average, a new domain registered every 5 seconds in the fourth quarter of 2021.
9. That was the AIDS computer virus in 1990. See "https://en.wikipedia.org/wiki/AIDS_(computer_virus)"

how we deal with ransomware. If we were stuck in the past, we would be blocking people from putting floppies in their computers and thinking that was all we needed to do. We would still be victims of ransomware via email, but we stopped the floppy delivery channel.

If a researcher assumed that all ransomware was delivered by floppies and did a study on that in 2022, then their result would be that no, it is not. It is such an obvious result that it would essentially be ignored, as is almost everything still involving floppy disks. But, in this basic example, we know that that result is important. It tells us that things have changed. We need to know the changes so that we can defend appropriately. Defending against ransomware by only blocking floppies is an excellent way to be a victim of ransomware.

The original threats were focused on servers. The Internet was relatively flat, and personal computers were not a thing yet, so the targets were those server computers. Webpages were primarily static, cell phones were the size of large bricks and cost a small fortune, and email was text-based only.

Today, the smartphone in your pocket has more power than the supercomputers of three decades ago. The personal computer and the cell phone are where attacks are directed. Servers are still under attack—that has not changed—but the spread of attacks has. And increasingly, Internet-enabled appliances will be the targets: your dishwasher, doorbell, and automobile.

It goes beyond these simple examples. Terms have changed meaning over time. Threats have evolved. If we do not know the changes, we risk missing the new threats entirely by focusing on the outdated ones.

That evolution is continuing as well. The defense that works today might not work tomorrow. That is why security is not a set of things you do and then forget about them; instead, cybersecurity is a continuing activity that needs to adapt and change with time and circumstances.

Your Network Is Static

It is common for an organization to have a "map" of its network. These exist as Visio diagrams, Excel spreadsheets, and even paper printouts. How accurate do you think *your* map is at this moment? Whatever you think the answer is, there is a nontrivial chance that your map is incorrect. There are many reasons, and a big one is that networks are seldom static.

Imagine a network diagram as an old-fashioned paper map of Los Angeles.[10] The map allowed people to find and navigate the city, but it was only as good as the snapshot in time when it was printed. New roads and buildings come and go, as do temporary closures and disruptions. Before GPS and digital maps, police and fire response were slower and less efficient. Likewise, a network map is a snapshot in time and might be inaccurate moments later. Pretty much every network these days has a wireless component. The network diagram might show the access points, but the actual devices connected change all the time. People move around with their phones and tablets, go to lunch, or move between buildings, all the while disconnecting from the network and rejoining it again. Virtual machines are

10. For younger readers who only know online maps, use a search engine to find some pictures.

started or stopped, each appearing as an entity on the network, and Virtual Private Networks (VPNs) create virtual tunnels to remote outposts.[11]

Modern cloud environments are also dynamic by design: This is one of the key features. As workloads increase, virtual machines and other resources are added; when demand goes down, those resources can go away. This is a powerful and useful feature, but the result is that the network map is constantly changing. It can also be a challenge for security if not managed carefully.

There are implications to erroneously believing that your network is static. The biggest is that it leads to a false sense of understanding about risk. Think you have all the network communications safely routed through your firewall? What happens when employees tether their work laptops to their personal hotspots for an hour? The carefully crafted firewall rules and policies you thought were protecting the computer are missing.

It is possible to instrument a network to detect and respond to changes. The network requires users and devices to authenticate in some settings, such as using a database of approved certificates or Media Access Control (MAC) addresses. Every other user and device is blocked or given strictly limited access. Alternatively, if someone operates a coffee shop such as the one shown in Figure 2.1 and has users who come and go from the network dynamically, they presumably understand the risks and appropriate mitigations.

FIGURE 2.1 Modern networks are dynamic.

11. See the Appendix for more information on VPNs.

You Know Your Crown Jewels and Where They Are

In 2016, a hacker stood on stage and said, "We put the time in to know that network. We put the time in to know it better than the people who designed it and the people who are securing it." Later, he continued, ". . . you know the technologies you intended to use in that network. We know the technologies that are actually in use in that network. Subtle difference. Did you catch that? You know what you intended to use; we know what's actually in use inside."[12] This was not just any hacker. At the time, Rob Joyce was the head of NSA's elite hacking office, Tailored Access Operations.

In both static and dynamic networks, even network owners might not know the critical servers or vital network links! This happens over time for many reasons. One is network complexity, especially as the network grows over time. We might forget what each computer is for and only realize after shutting it down that it served some critical function. It's a crown jewel we didn't know we had.

Good security requires substantial documentation, constant network mapping, and regular monitoring of the protocols in use. We should not be in a situation where potential attackers know more accurate information about our network than we do!

Email Is Private

Experts in cybersecurity like to remind the public that email is not secure. After all, traditional email is transmitted in plaintext that anyone could read if they had access to the email in transit. We do not know how often this violation of privacy occurs in reality, but we know that some employers and service providers read our emails. Sometimes this is for debugging, sometimes for legal reasons, and sometimes because they are nosy. So, why is there a myth that email is private?

The general public commonly has an expectation of privacy in their email. Or, at the least, they are willing to accept the risk of potential privacy violations. Perhaps this is because they have a sense of privacy in their paper mail and because email has "mail" in its name. In the United States, this behavior seems to be at odds with the third-party legal doctrine.[13] Under this precedent, when someone voluntarily gives information to third parties, they forfeit any reasonable expectation of privacy. It applies when they hand over an email to their ISP. Still, we send messages and files over email that are private or sensitive that we would not say out loud in a restaurant.

Even those who do recognize the vulnerability of email misunderstand the solutions. For instance, in the United States, people think the Health Insurance Portability and Accountability Act (HIPAA) regulations protect the privacy of their email containing medical information. In reality, HIPAA requires "reasonable safeguards" when *healthcare providers* communicate with patients.[14] HIPAA does not forbid email and does not explicitly require encryption. Some providers ask patients to sign a consent

12. www.usenix.org/sites/default/files/conference/protected-files/engima2016_transcript_joyce_v2.pdf
13. See the 1979 case of *Smith v. Maryland* where the Supreme Court said that "this Court consistently has held that a person has no legitimate expectation of privacy in information he voluntarily turns over to third parties."
14. The regulations specifically define what a covered entity is and it's more than only physicians. See 45 CFR § 160.103.

form acknowledging that the patient understands the risks of communicating by email. Whether patients actually understand what this means, most sign off for the convenience; however, some health providers also seek solutions for "secure email." Encrypted email remains cumbersome and is highly unusual in healthcare.[15] More often, doctors have adopted patient web portals. These websites allow doctors and patients to share records and messages where traffic can be encrypted over the Internet using web encryption protocols.

These days, email is more and more secure in transit and commonly sent over encrypted links between mail servers and clients. The traditional Internet Message Access Protocol (IMAP) and Post Office Protocol (POP) protocols are now usually protected in transit using Secure Socket Layer (SSL) or Transport Layer Security (TLS). Whether we should trust all the mail servers handling our mail is a different question and not one we will address here.

We would be remiss if we did not mention that the transfer of email is not the only cause for concern. If access credentials are compromised, or the operator of an ISP is malicious, email might be read while "at rest" on the mail server rather than "in transit" across the Internet. There are restrictions on such access according to the Electronic Communications Privacy Act (ECPA) but those are neither guarantees nor are they applicable outside the United States.

The bottom line is that statements such as "email is not secure" and "email is secure" are both overgeneralizations and open to misinterpretation. First, there have been few reports about the level of risk and threats to privacy from email as it moves over the Internet. We do know, however, that ISPs and nation-states have the ability and motivation to look at traffic as it moves over the Internet. Second, email service providers present a much more potent threat to email privacy than random strangers. With few exceptions, these providers can read our email. This is true of Google and Microsoft and the organizations for which we work. Legal or contractual reasons might limit if and when they look at the email, but we might never know if those are respected 100% of the time.

Cryptocurrency Is Untraceable

Over the last decade, there has been increasing interest in mechanisms representing and exchanging value over the Internet. Some of the mechanisms that have been developed use cryptography as a basis for defining and protecting these transactions. Collectively, these are referred to as *cryptocurrency*. Currently, many people shorten this to "crypto," often to the annoyance of those who refer to cryptography that way.

Cryptocurrency has gathered advocates because most forms allow the exchange of value independent of government interference and oversight, often with some level of anonymity. Some privacy advocates and most cyber criminals view this as a plus. The lack of government backing, however, also means a lack of protection, and there have been many spectacular frauds, thefts, and losses as various cryptocurrency

15. An important result from 1999 about encryption challenges is still relevant today. See Whitten, Alma, and Tygar, J. Doug, "Why Johnny cannot Encrypt: A Usability Evaluation of PGP 5.0," *USENIX Security Symposium*, Vol. 348 (1999).

schemes have failed. Despite the losses, and the caution by some experts that cryptocurrencies are unsustainable,[16] they have nonetheless grown in popularity. In particular, the misperceived lack of visibility and control by governments has made cryptocurrency the preferred medium for extortion in ransomware cases.

Thirty days after a ransomware attack halted all the operations of Colonial Pipeline, the U.S. Department of Justice announced that it had recovered the ransom payment of 63.7 bitcoins (approximately $2.3 million at that time). The government did not disclose how it obtained the private key necessary. Bitcoin is pseudo-anonymous, but it is definitely traceable.

Anonymity and traceability are related but distinct attributes. With Bitcoin, for example, it is trivial to trace an action back to a specific identity even if we cannot name that identity. In addition, an identity could be public but untraceable when using an anonymizing network such as TOR. Anonymous systems are sometimes untraceable as a side effect, but the reverse is not true. We cannot be anonymous if someone can trace our identity back to us.

It is true that with Bitcoin, a crypto address can be created without revealing anything about identity; however, every Bitcoin transaction is traceable by design. A key feature of a blockchain is that it is a public ledger. The ledger of transactions is also permanent. Every transaction would be public if addresses were ever connected to people. If you thought Bitcoin was anonymous, simply visit the company's website, which states, "All Bitcoin transactions are public, traceable, and permanently stored in the Bitcoin network."[17]

What about other cryptocurrencies that promise anonymity?

Enter exchanges. Most people convert traditional currency into cryptocurrency through an exchange, and vice versa. These companies almost always require some kind of proof of identity. This is a know-your-customer (KYC) protocol, common in financial laws around the world. When law enforcement wants to track a crypto transaction, it can use legal processes such as subpoenas to get information from the exchange.

Online privacy is a function not only of technology but also Operational Security (OPSEC). That is, the things others can see someone say and do play a role in their security and privacy. This is true not only for cryptocurrency but across the board. It is generally the case that people—and criminals in particular—are not as good at OPSEC as they think.

16. See https://blog.dshr.org/2022/02/ee380-talk.html and https://onezero.medium.com/the-inevitability-of-trusted-third-parties-a51cbcffc4e2 for some lucid explanations of this view. Many experts counsel caution, such as the ones endorsing this letter: https://concerned.tech. Consider that for any cryptocurrency system to work as expected requires that a body of complex code must be written and operate flawlessly under all conditions; we are not sanguine that this is achievable.

17. https://bitcoin.org/en/protect-your-privacy

Everything Can Be Fixed with Blockchain

This myth is a variation of the myth that "Technology X will make you secure," discussed previously in Chapter 1, "What Is Cybersecurity?" This myth, however, has become such a fad in distributed systems that we will address it here.

Blockchains are a form of distributed ledger system that depends on cryptography. Additions to the ledger require some form of consensus and proof. Entries can never be removed. Generally, blockchains are supposed to be decentralized and supported by a community. Blockchains are used to support most cryptocurrencies.

As scientists, we appreciate some of the theories underlying blockchains. We have seen some clever theoretical papers on the use of blockchains; however, we are also appalled at the zealotry with which they are promoted for use. They are one of the worst cases of a buzz phrase in recent memory. A centralized database with change tracking (audit) and access control will be faster, less complicated to maintain, and more easily managed than a blockchain implementation in almost every use case. Blockchains are ideal for environments where multiple, independent participants do not trust each other or any central authority, and there is a need for a visible, immutable record of writes. That is a minuscule set of cases.

Furthermore, the computation involved in extending and verifying blockchains makes them expensive to compute and bad for the environment (because of the vast amounts of energy expended). Errors and stale data will accumulate over time, with no reasonable way to trim them (blockchains are forever). A good database (DB) will have locking, auditing of changes, controlled visibility, and the ability to trim and correct entries as needed. If operated within a closed environment or by a trusted (by reputation, statute, or contract) party, the DB will serve as a verifiable record. A DB using a Merkel tree of hashes can also be used for integrity without the overhead of a distributed consensus calculation.

We suspect blockchains have garnered such great interest partly because of their novelty and use in some cryptocurrency mechanisms. Their use in cryptocurrency, however, is also a poor idea because of, among other reasons, their environmental impact and use in various criminal pursuits. They also lead to nonsense such as Non-fungible Tokens (NFTs) (and no, we are not going to go into depth on why those are beyond silly and into the realm of Ponzi schemes). We suggest, again, that you read the documents cited in footnote 16.

The Internet Is Like an Iceberg

There is considerable misinformation and confusion about the dark web and the deep web. Media and marketers sometimes draw illustrations of the Internet as an iceberg, with sites such as Google and Netflix above the water. The image intends to show that these are websites anyone can see and access online. If someone visits google.com in a browser, they get their webpage. Sites such as this are part of the visible web: the part of the iceberg above water.

The massive portion of the Internet under the water is better described as the *deep web*. There is certainly a lot of Internet-connected content that is not directly indexed and not directly accessible by a casual user (or web crawler). For example, bank account information is likely on the network, but to access it requires knowledge of the account number and password (at least). Thus, this content is invisible to casual users, but it is there if someone has the correct information. The deep web is not all that interesting, other than the fact that it exists. It is not more dangerous than the visible web in the way that the submerged portion of an iceberg is dangerous.

The *dark web* is a small subcomponent of the deep web and has even more aura of mystery. While it is connected to the Internet, special software is needed to connect and access dark web content. Without this type of software, there is no way for someone to access its content. TOR is one such dark web network. Most estimates are that the size of the dark web is tiny compared to the total size of the Internet, perhaps 0.01% or far less.

Drawing or describing the Internet as an iceberg is misleading. This description implies that because the information is not directly accessible, it is dangerous or a threat. Perhaps 90% or more of the data on the Internet might be hidden from public view, but that's largely good for security and privacy.

The Dark Web Is Only for Criminal Activity

The dark web is perhaps best described as a "shady" neighborhood. It's not illegal to live or visit, but illegal activity does happen there. Many legitimate companies also have a presence on the dark web to support security and privacy. ProPublica, *The New York Times*, and Facebook all have websites on the dark web. Instead of facebook.com, Facebook's dark web address is facebookwkhpilnemxj7asaniu7vnjjbiltxjqhye3mhbshg7kx5tfyd.onion. That link will not work unless the browser is connected via TOR. Why would Facebook have a site there? It supports access by users who might otherwise get in trouble if they were seen accessing the site. For example, users in politically oppressive regimes or government whistle-blowers might want to communicate with a journalist without being discovered.

TOR is both a network and software for accessing the dark web it supports. TOR encrypts traffic so that users and websites are mixed and scrambled among different servers to shield the identification of the hosts and IP addresses. These features are useful to criminals, legitimate journalists conducting sensitive investigations, and citizens in oppressive countries. The TOR Project, a nonprofit that works on software used on the dark web, is partly funded by the U.S. State Department[18] to promote democracy and human rights in oppressive regimes.

Activity on the Dark Web Is Untraceable

The TOR network includes a concept called *hidden services*. A TOR website can exist, for instance, somewhere on the network without revealing its IP address. As a result, it is difficult to know if the physical server hosting the content is in Detroit, Dubai, or anywhere else.

---

18. www.torproject.org/about/sponsors/

Note, though, that the TOR Project website has a notice that "Generally it is impossible to have perfect anonymity, even with TOR."[19] Why is this so?

A hidden server on its own might be challenging to find, but human and technological activity is what generally betrays anonymity. This is OPSEC, discussed earlier in this chapter. For example, the government took down the underground marketplace on TOR known as AlphaBay, and its creator was arrested.[20] This has been explained as the result of an OPSEC failure.

First, TOR runs on top of regular Internet networks and links. When someone browses over TOR, there are still (encrypted) packets that leave their computer and connect to other computers on the Internet. The TOR network sends the traffic to several servers to help scramble it before it eventually arrives at the intended destination. Some or all of these links and connections could be monitored, however, and an observer could theoretically use metadata to trace the traffic to a dark website. It's simply impossible for a computer to communicate without the potential of leaving a trail of evidence. As with security, anonymity is a spectrum in which we can never achieve perfection.

Another way activity could be traceable is from leaky plugins and applications on the computer. In 2011, researchers collected 10,000 IP addresses over 23 days of TOR users accessing BitTorrent.[21]

Lastly, users' behavior can undermine their anonymity. Users who voluntarily post personal information such as their name or credit card number trivially undermine the privacy provided by TOR. This is poor OPSEC.

So far, no one been able to quantify the amount of security and privacy afforded by the dark web.[22] Given that some of the organizations most interested in finding ways to pierce anonymity are unlikely to disclose their successes, a reliable metric is unlikely to emerge any time soon.

A VPN Makes You Anonymous

There is only one dark web, but many VPN tools and providers exist. As with TOR, people use VPNs to circumvent censorship and geo-restricted content. Both anonymize the client's IP address and encrypt the traffic.

VPNs are common for two primary reasons. One is to establish an encrypted connection to an organizational network remotely. Many employees do this when working from home, for example. The other use is adding security in untrusted networks or networks with unknown properties (such as public Wi-Fi) and avoiding monitoring by an ISP. This is useful if someone connects while away from home, such as in an airport coffee shop. In both cases, the VPN establishes a virtual tunnel to a server.

19. https://support.torproject.org/faq/staying-anonymous/
20. www.fbi.gov/news/stories/alphabay-takedown
21. https://static.usenix.org/events/leet11/tech/full_papers/LeBlond.pdf
22. Nor has anyone quantified any threats from the dark web.

A VPN is one mitigation for untrusted networks. An untrusted network could violate privacy or security, or both. It's not a stretch to think that private equals anonymous in the phrase "virtual private network." In the best case, a VPN hides the originating IP address. Depending on the online activity, and the capabilities of an adversary, that alone does not guarantee anonymity.

Imagine that the admins of CyberMyths.net look at their server logs. If you accessed the website from a VPN, the log entries show requests from the VPN provider, not your computer. Astute investigators and law enforcement could request logs from the VPN provider, however, to piece together that you accessed the VPN at the same time that a user visited CyberMyths.net—assuming the provider kept such logs. Many providers claim that they do not, specifically to protect privacy.

The VPN makes it more difficult for an observer or website admin to figure out that you were the visitor. That assumes you are also careful with your OPSEC. Realistically, the information you send over the VPN might reveal your identity at the endpoint or the pattern of sites you visit using the VPN. A determined investigator with access to enough of the correct data might be able to make an extremely accurate guess about who is connected.

It is difficult to quantify how much more anonymous a VPN connection might be, but it should not be assumed it is fully anonymous by default. One free VPN accidentally left more than 18 GB of logs accessible to the public, exposing the users who used it.[23] We advise against believing that any VPN will keep you fully anonymous, although functional ones should help protect your content from eavesdropping and manipulation.

A Firewall Is Enough

I have a firewall, so my network is protected. That was the misconception more than a decade ago, but sadly, it is still believed by some managers. Firewalls are an important—almost always necessary—component in a network security scheme, but they do not obviate other security measures.

A firewall is hardware or software in the middle of a communications path, such as between a computer and the Internet. The firewall watches the network traffic, allowing or blocking data based on security rules. Cable modems and home routers usually also have firewall capabilities enabled (whether configured or not). Your computer probably has firewall software built into the operating system. Companies often have a dedicated device that does nothing except act as a firewall. Complex networks also use firewalls internally, such as to control traffic to the file server or employee database.

Suppose you are designing security for a remote office building. You could put up an electrified fence to keep burglars and vandals out; however, you are poorly defended if that is your only security mechanism. What happens if someone finds a spot to tunnel under the fence? What about when someone with a key to the gate forgets to lock it after coming in or leaves it open on purpose for a confederate to enter? What about that person delivering food to the building? They need to get in somehow, or at least

23. https://cybernews.com/security/25-million-free-vpn-user-records-exposed/

have the food get in. What happens when your power goes out as a result of a thunderstorm or random squirrel activity—the 1 and 2 causes of power failures?[24] There are many paths through, over, or under any wall you might have, as shown in Figure 2.2—including, perhaps, your firewall!

Bill Cheswick, one of the pioneers in firewall design, once described firewalls as "crunchy on the outside with a soft, chewy center." That is, they are tough to get through but offer no protection on the inside. Flaws, misconfigurations, mistakes, malicious insiders, supply chain insertion, phishing, and other avenues of attack can result in malicious activity inside the perimeter that a firewall will not stop. Appropriate protections must be present *inside* the firewall to detect and prevent untoward activity. This includes intrusion detection, integrity monitoring, malware detection, and encryption of sensitive information. This is the genesis of the current buzz phrase *zero trust*.[25]

Reliance on firewalls is related to the often-mistaken belief that there is a defensible perimeter. The virtual boundary is permeable to email, network services, and user-initiated traffic, and it is often also regularly transited by user VPNs and wireless connections.

Most networks above a certain size no longer have a defined perimeter to defend because of wireless connections and portable hosts. Does this mean that firewalls are useless? Not at all! It means firewalls are still helpful in regulating and monitoring traffic, but all the various forms of traffic must be routed through the firewall.

Also, a related misconception is that only one firewall is needed. This is often false, especially in more extensive networks. A security architecture involving an "inside" network with a firewall separation from the "outside" is perhaps better structured as a set of independent "island" or "walled garden" networks separated from the rest by their own firewalls. Each of these islands has its own access control rules, independent monitoring, and differentiated access control (no universal passwords for all "islands"). Each of these subsets of the network is configured and controlled according to policies optimized for local use. Thus, the accounting department is separate from the shipping department, which is separate from development. Each has an appropriate set of policies and independent controls; compromising one island does not enable a cascade of failures into all the rest.

But even in the best cases, it is crucial to understand that a firewall is only one layer of defense, similar to how a fence is only one layer of protection around a building. It can help keep "outside" from getting "inside" but does not offer protection beyond that.

24. https://blog.nature.org/science/2019/10/29/fear-the-squirrel-how-wildlife-causes-major-power-outages/
25. For more on zero trust, see the Appendix and "Færie Dust Can Make Old Ideas Magically Revolutionary" in Chapter 1.

FIGURE 2.2 Breaching the firewall.

Further Reading

Blum, Andrew. *Tubes: A Journey to the Center of the Internet*. Ecco, 2012.

Cheswick, Bill, Bellovin, Steve, et al. *Firewalls and Internet Security: Repelling the Wily Hacker*, 2nd ed. Addison-Wesley, 2003.

Comer, Douglas. *Internetworking with TCP/IP Volume 1*, 6th ed. Pearson, 2013.

Fall, Kevin, and Stevens, W. Richard. *TCP/IP Illustrated, Volume 1: The Protocols*. Addison-Wesley, 2011.

Garfinkel, Simson, and Spafford, Eugene. *Web Security, Privacy, & Commerce*. O'Reilly, 2002.

Garfinkel, Simson, Spafford, Eugene, and Schwartz, Alan. *Practical Unix & Internet*, 3rd ed. O'Reilly, 2003.

Kurose, James F., and Ross, Keith. *Computer Networking*, 8th ed. Pearson, 2021.

Stallings, William. *Network Security Essentials: Applications and Standards*, 6th ed. Pearson, 2016.

Zwicky, Elizabeth, Cooper, Simon, and Chapman, D. Brent. *Building Internet Firewalls: Internet and Web Security*. O'Reilly, 2000.

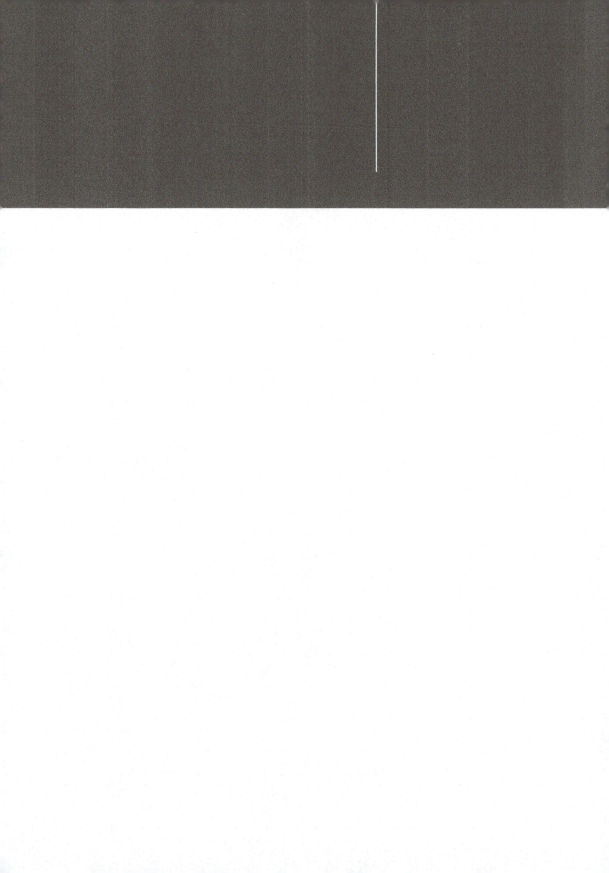

PART II

Human Issues

Chapter 3

Faulty Assumptions and Magical Thinking

> The most damaging phrase in the language is "We have always done it this way!"
>
> *Grace Hopper*

Many musicals and movie fairy tales begin with an "I Want" or an "I Wish" song where the main character sings about hopes and desires that launch a happy story. "I wanna be where the people are," sings Ariel in Disney's *The Little Mermaid*. "I wish to go to the festival," sings Cinderella in Stephen Sondheim's *Into the Woods*. In these stories, the beauty and satisfaction of the magic are in realizing the characters' dreams.

Dreams and goals are a foundation and motivation for people and their creations. Curiosity for pushing the boundaries of the possible attracted many of us to fields of technology. *I wish we had an automated way to share information among scientists*, Tim Berners-Lee might have said before creating the World-Wide Web (WWW).

Dreams are motivational, but fantasies can be dangerous. In cybersecurity, wishful thinking leads developers and researchers astray and produces unsuccessful outcomes when we make assumptions about the real world. Web developers cannot assume that every user has Firefox. If they do, it is possible that their website will not look or function as intended on other browsers. Data and evidence must be used to make informed decisions that lead to more successful outcomes.

This chapter is about 18 errors people make in cybersecurity based on poor or incorrect assumptions that usually lack evidentiary support. For example, simply wishing users know how to identify phishing emails does not make it a reality. That's magical thinking.[1] A faulty assumption is an error in the basis for a decision. Biases are errors in the argument itself and are covered in Chapter 5, "Cognitive Biases."

1. See www.britannica.com/science/magical-thinking and our discussion in the Introduction.

We cannot cover every faulty assumption in cybersecurity, so you will need to take some care to avoid the ones we have not included. We hope what follows gives you some insight into how to do that.

Humans Will Behave Rationally, So Blame the User!

The discipline of behavioral economics is devoted to reassessing what classical economists got wrong: People are complex and do not always behave rationally. Rational behavior refers to making a decision that maximizes benefit given the costs. Rational users would never pick 123456 as their email password because the benefit of protecting their email with a stronger password outweighs the burden (cost) of choosing and using that better password.[2]

There are many different human roles in cybersecurity. There are developers and engineers; there are network administrators and security staff; there are educators; there are incident responders; there are human adversaries. There are, of course, end users. Even this group has diversity in its goals, needs, and security understanding. A scientist might value open collaboration, while a Human Resources (HR) specialist deals with confidential, personally identifiable information.

There are many theories in psychology about what drives human behavior that are beyond the scope of this book. Indeed, most people are not random in their behavior. An excellent place to start if you want more background in this area is Daniel Kahneman's book *Thinking, Fast and Slow*. Kahneman and many others have found evidence that people, for various reasons, do not pick the "best" choice. This causes no end of frustration for cybersecurity professionals. Why do people keep clicking links in email even when they know it's dangerous? Humans evolved to avoid physical world danger, but identifying danger online is more complicated and difficult. If phishing had existed during the Renaissance, it might resemble Figure 3.1!

A corollary to the myth of rational users is that we like to assign blame. This is particularly commonplace in cybersecurity events. Many events start with a user clicking on a link, opening an attachment, or choosing a poor password. Those simple actions can start a chain of events that can cost a company a lot of money in lost data and work. Therefore, blame the user! It's all their fault! This would not have happened except for their actions. Or, as they used to say in the *Scooby-Doo* cartoon, this would all have worked if it weren't for those meddling kids! Of course, blaming that user for doing things does not prevent anyone else from doing the same thing. There are always meddling kids around.

Blame does not help achieve cybersecurity goals. First, tracking down someone to blame does nothing for cleaning up the event. It might make management feel better to point to Robin in Accounting as the source for this problem, but still, we have a problem. Pointing to the tiger in the room and saying "Robin let the tiger in" may be accurate, but we still have a tiger in the room, as illustrated in Figure 3.2, and getting rid of it should be our priority.

---

2. Technically, this is only irrational if the user understands the risk. If the user is unaware, then it might be a rational decision.

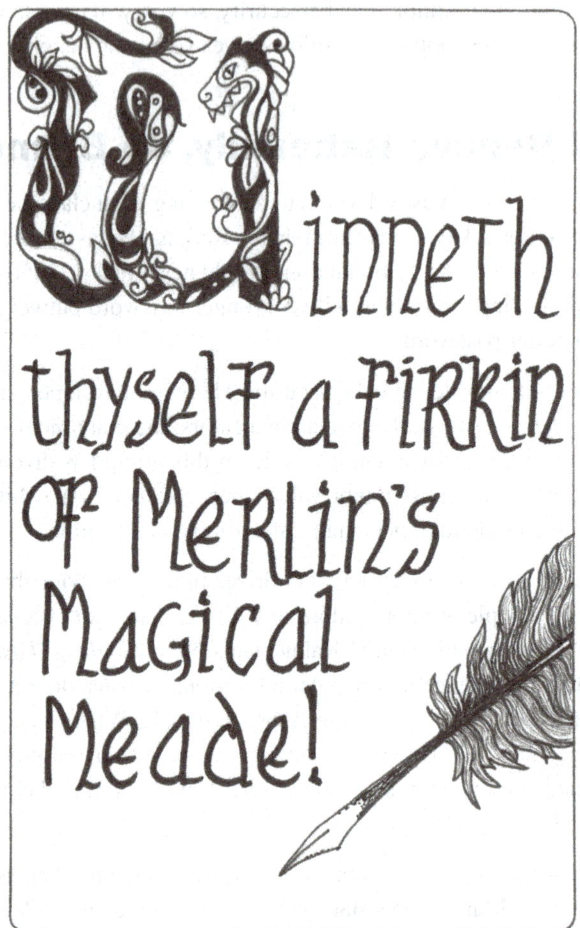

FIGURE 3.1 What phishing could have looked like during the Renaissance.

Don't Blame the Intern

There is a human tendency to assign blame for bad events. "One throat to choke," as some say morbidly. Cybersecurity is about preventing harm, so it's common to seek someone or something to blame when incidents inevitably occur. For example, shortly after the SolarWinds incident[a] in 2021, an executive publicly blamed an intern for choosing a weak password.[b] This was neither helpful nor appropriate and quite possibly inaccurate.

More to the point, even if it was an intern, why was the intern not given better mentoring and supervision when put into a position to make such decisions? Not only does this cast some severe shade on the management processes, but it also is not likely to aid in recruiting in the future.

---

[a] See the Appendix for more information about the incident.

[b] https://techcrunch.com/2021/03/13/why-blaming-the-intern-wont-save-startups-from-cybersecurity-liability/

FIGURE 3.2 Blaming the user while the threat is still in the room.

Second, we should consider what part of our environment allowed the action. If the user chose a poor password, why was that password allowed? Users are subject to the constraints imposed by the security systems in place. They do not randomly select a poor password; they choose it because the system allowed them to and (presumably) because they did not understand the potential consequences. If the user's password is "password," that should never have been allowed. It's a failure of the systems in place that allowed it to happen. Yes, the user should have chosen a better password. They should have known to choose a better password. We cannot assume they know why they should choose strong passwords without education. We also cannot assume that they will choose a strong password, even with education. Poor passwords are easy to remember. And there is still the fact that the system allowed them to choose the poor password.

Blame the Programmer!

Programmers write code, and code has vulnerabilities; ergo, the programmers are to blame. That's a nice logic chain that gives us someone to blame when something goes wrong; however, that might not be correct.

This is not a mystery novel by Agatha Christie or the murder mystery game of Clue, where the murder can be tied to one person and weapon. Software developers do not work in a vacuum; they work with tools. A C programmer works with a C compiler; a Python developer works with a Python interpreter. They don't (usually) create their compiler; they work with the standard compilers or interpreters available.

Code can inherit vulnerability from a compiler.[a] The programmer can do everything right and still have a vulnerability baked into the code. It's nothing they did, it's nothing they caused, but still there is a vulnerability. Some versions of Java had a vulnerability where it would accept even a blank certificate as valid.[b] A program could tell it, "This is the certificate you are looking for," and it would blithely go along with it, and we would never know something was wrong.

Ken Thompson, one of the original designers of the UNIX operating system, showed how easy it was to stealthily alter the C compiler to look for "login" commands and alter them to accept any password.[c] Any program compiled with this compiler would have this feature, and the programmer would not have the slightest idea. He even coded it so that it would hide the changes in the compiler from examination.

Placing blame perhaps makes one feel better but does not fix the fundamental problem and might well be misplaced.

That does not mean that a programmer might not have made a mistake. The appropriate approach is not to blame, but rather to find root causes and put measures in place to prevent them (and their ilk) from occurring again. Is it a lack of training? Poor specifications? Faulty libraries? Too aggressive a production schedule? Lack of appropriate validation and verification processes? It could be all of these things, plus more! Rather than pin the blame on someone who was probably trying to complete their tasks, investigate the root causes and seek to fix them. Even if it is traceable to incompetence, that suggests something to fix—the screening and hiring process, at a minimum.

---

[a] www.redhat.com/en/blog/security-flaws-caused-compiler-optimizations

[b] https://neilmadden.blog/2022/04/19/psychic-signatures-in-java/

[c] https://doi.org/10.1145/358198.358210

Perhaps the user clicked on a phishing link or downloaded a malicious document. Blaming users is, again, the easy way out. Do we educate our users on what to look for? Are systems in place for them to report malicious documents? Users have been known to say, "Yes, I knew it could be malicious, but I had to make sure." If the systems are in place, and they still click on the link or download the document, it might be time to educate the users.

Companies often send out documents from third parties, use them for vendors, or send out emails that, quite frankly, look like phishing. Even if we educate the users well, we might find they do not do what they need to do, or they are confused because education says, "Don't open that attachment!"—and yet, at the same time, we are implicitly telling them, "Yup, open that attachment."

Also, we should note that not everyone has the same knowledge base. Thus, people might behave rationally, but it is rational only relative to their understanding. As experts, cybersecurity professionals have the curse of knowledge that makes it a challenge to put themselves in the shoes of ordinary people.

Blaming the users is easy, but it does not solve anything and only highlights that there are issues to be addressed. This could mean education or considering the constraints of the systems that allowed the users to act contrary to proper procedure.

The advice for avoiding this myth is straightforward: Never assume that people will know or make the best choice. Furthermore, it is unfair to blame them for this. It's human nature. Repeat after us: *I will not automatically blame the user.*

Note that we said "automatically." This is because there are situations where it *is* appropriate to blame someone or hold someone responsible. Forgiveness is not likely the proper response if someone is incompetent, flouting the rules, showing up to work intoxicated, committing crimes, or wasting organizational resources (as examples). In some cases, it may benefit the organization (and the people involved) to make some effort to help the person responsible: training, counseling, assigning a mentor, etc. It is a matter of context and resources. For example, some organizations have a "three strikes" rule for some behaviors: warning on the first occasion, retraining on the second violation, and job termination on the third violation. Remember that everyone makes mistakes and has bad days. Titrate policies accordingly.

Pros and Cons of the Wisdom of Crowds in Cybersecurity

In discussing the myth that humans will behave rationally, we took the perspective of primarily individual decisions. What about the wisdom of crowds?

Imagine two common questions in the workplace: (1) Is this file malware? and (2) What programming language should we use for the new project? One shows the benefit of consensus, and the other shows the opposite.

In 2004, James Surowiecki wrote a well-known book titled *The Wisdom of Crowds: Why the Many Are Smarter Than the Few and How Collective Wisdom Shapes Business, Economies, Societies and Nations.*[a] He described how large groups show more intelligence in some situations than individuals or smaller groups. This idea dates back thousands of years to Aristotle. It is also related to the concept of democracy.

[a] Surowiecki, James, *The Wisdom of Crowds*, Anchor, 2005.

In judgment problems, such as deciding if a file is malware, collective wisdom does better than individuals. A typical example in cybersecurity is malware identification. If 5,000 people download a file and nothing terrible happens, that provides us higher confidence in its reputation than observations on one or two machines. Antivirus companies take precisely this approach, using data points from the "crowd" of computers and looking for consensus. This approach is also being applied to evaluating the reputation of domain names and URLs.

On the contrary, picking a programming language for a new project is *not* a judgment problem. The typical program manager will ask "What languages do our programmers know?" or "What is the most popular programming language?" The wisdom of crowds does not offer any benefit for addressing such questions. C++ or Java might be more well-known than Rust or Go, but that does not mean the so-called crowd is leading to the best choice. Please don't pick a language because it's the latest and coolest invention. Instead, choose the one that is best for solving the problem.

Also, refer to the social proof discussion bias in the chapter "Cognitive Biases." The wisdom of crowds should guide fact-based decisions but should never replace deliberate, informed thinking.

Curiously, too often, we make an incorrect assumption about rational adversaries. With every attack—every single one—there are people behind it, at least indirectly. Packets do not simply show up magically for no reason. They have authors with motives. We should not presume that adversaries will think like us, hold the same values, or make what seems to us to be logical decisions.

We often make decisions based on what we would do because we consider ourselves to be rational people. Other people have their reasons for doing things, some of which might seem irrational to us but are entirely reasonable to them. Keeping this perspective in mind helps.

We Know Everything We Need to Know About Cybersecurity Problems

To quote the great Arthur C. Clarke: "Two possibilities exist: either we are alone in the Universe, or we are not. Both are equally terrifying."

Errors are caused by both lack of information and the limited ability of humans to process information.

We do not know how much malware exists or what kinds of malware exist. We only know what people have found and dubbed "malware." Other than that, we do not know. Malware has often slid under the radar because if we do not know about it, we cannot detect it. For example, consider APTs. There are cases of them being present on a system for years before they are discovered. And that's only the ones we have found!

In short, there is a lot of missing information about malware. The same is true for flaws. We do not know about all the defects and interactions in software, including some that are not written yet. It's true across all fields in cybersecurity: We are missing information because the bad guys are up to their tricks, they certainly are not going to call us to tell us what they are up to, and we are working with computing artifacts that might be flawed. We only know what we find. To channel Donald Rumsfeld, there are known unknowns and unknown unknowns in cybersecurity.

Ransomware, for example, makes itself known when it is triggered. It's not like a stealth APT; it's a noisy attack that lets the victim know that they were hit so they can pay the ransom. Unless every victim speaks up and hands over the malware used against them, however, we are still in a realm of uncertainty when it comes to ransomware. We do not know what we do not know about ransomware, and we are not even sure about what we do know.

We are fumbling in the dark if we are trying to estimate how much money an APT could cost an organization. We are assuming we know how long the APT was lodged in the system, how many instances there are, and what information it stole (or could have stolen). Best-case scenario: It was there for 10 minutes before we caught it, stole nothing, and was only one instance. Worst-case scenario: It was there for years, invaded the entire network, and compromised everything it could access, including all our backups. Of course, in business-speak, we always want to know where to put the cost. Do we put it on the APT budget line? Which department pays for it, and how much of their budget should be designated for this?

In other words, there is a wide range in which to make that estimate. It could be anywhere from zero to the total value of the information in the company. Given that wide range, how do we pick the best estimate?

The best solution is to seek additional data and not *assume*. If we need to guess, sometimes it is better to err on the side of the worst case rather than the best case; pleasant surprises are better than rude shocks.

Compliance Equals (Complete) Security

Compliance is one approach used to help ensure the protection of information. Compliance rules are created to set minimum standards for security that can be measured and enforced, sometimes with penalties for noncompliance. HIPAA is a compliance standard for healthcare information in the United States. GDPR is a legal framework for personal information about people who live in the European Union. Payment Card Industry Data Security Standard (PCI DSS) is a compliance standard for credit card processing sites. Compliance with these standards ranges from outside audits to self-reporting, and in the case of self-reporting, nothing says it can't be an inaccurate report.

Compliance with one of these frameworks will be an improvement if a company has *weak or no* security, if not for compliance requirements. Unfortunately, compliance is not equivalent to adequate protection if, after people do the minimum required, they assume they are secure enough. At best, when an organization is fully compliant, compliance attests that the minimum standards of one set of rules have been met. There are many examples of organizations that were in full compliance with some set of rules but were still not secure enough and became victims of a cyber attack. Compliance simply raises the bar a little bit.

Consider the analogy of driving on the highway. Suppose we meet the compliance rules of having insurance, having a valid license, fastening our seat belts, and observing the speed limit. In that case, we are less likely to have an injurious accident than driving 50 kph too fast with no seat belt buckled. However, none of those things—either separately or together—shields us from being hurt in an accident.

Cybersecurity compliance is not that different. The teleconferencing program Zoom for Government has been compliant since 2019 with the U.S. Federal Risk and Authorization Management Program (FedRAMP).[3] The vendor followed and was certified in compliance with a set of government-defined security controls for cloud-based services. In 2020, the use and sales of Zoom soared to unprecedented levels during the coronavirus pandemic. Hackers and security researchers also took notice and found previously unknown security vulnerabilities in Zoom, such as CitizenLab's discovery that Zoom's cryptographic strength was less than advertised.[4]

In one research study, experts audited compliance standards for federal tax information, credit card transactions, and the electric grid.[5] They identified 148 issues of varying severity, including unenforceable controls and data vulnerabilities that the standards would miss. For example, CIP 007-6 states that administrators should "[h]ave a method(s) to enforce authentication of interactive user access, where technically feasible."[6] "Technically feasible" is ill-defined, so a compliant entity might be compliant without having secure, authenticated access. "Compliance might be helpful (even required) to achieving the end goal of protecting an individual or organization's goals and assets, but it is not sufficient," summarized the study's authors.[7] "We recommend that all organizations audit the compliance standards they follow to identify gaps that are relevant to their specific requirements and develop mitigating strategies accordingly."

In the aside "When Secure Rating Is Not Secure" in Chapter 1, we discussed how Microsoft had achieved a C2 security rating of its Windows NT system, while at the same time, security researchers showed it was unsecure. The security rating was a base set of "It met this standard," not a pronouncement that it was secure. Misunderstanding a difference such as that gives a false sense of security that can be quickly replaced with the dread that a security incident brings. Compliance is not a guarantee, and taking it as one is wrong.

We heard Joel S. Birnbaum, when he was senior vice president of Hewlett-Packard, opine that "Standards are where we stand to innovate. They are not goals in and of themselves." This is especially true of security compliance standards.

3. https://marketplace.fedramp.gov/#!/product/zoom-for-government
4. Zoom took notice and subsequently made relevant updates.
5. www.ndss-symposium.org/wp-content/uploads/2020/02/24003-paper.pdf
6. www.nerc.com/pa/Stand/Reliability%20Standards/CIP-007-6.pdf
7. Stevens, Rock, et al., "It Lurks Within: A Look at the Unexpected Security Implications of Compliance Programs," *IEEE Security & Privacy*; Vol. 18, No. 6 (2020): 51–58.

Authentication Provides Confidentiality

Almost all colleges, dining establishments, libraries, and other facilities offer wireless networking connectivity. A faculty member at one university recently raised a concern with the school's IT security team. Students, faculty, and staff were required to enter a username and password to access the Wi-Fi, but the wireless network was not encrypted. Users assumed that their authentication was not only for access control but also for network security. As a result, they acted as though their browsing was secure, even though it was not. The faculty member demonstrated to the head of IT that he could easily eavesdrop on conversations and financial transactions of students in the dining area. Oops!

Logging into a wireless network commonly requires a password. This security act feels to users as though subsequent actions should be protected and private. They feel safe inside their house when they use a key to enter, thus proving that they are authorized to be there. But authentication—doors and keys—are entirely distinct from confidentiality. Authentication is more akin to a bouncer at the gate of a private party at an outdoor beer garden: We can still see what people are doing inside.

Assuming that authentication means confidentiality is conflating two concepts. One is access; the other is privacy. Authentication is not confidentiality. Authentication and confidentiality can be provided simultaneously, but it does not have to be the case. This situation is where using a VPN makes great sense if we are unsure of what is provided.

This might also be a good place to mention that authentication is not the same as either identification or authorization. Authentication is simply gaining sufficient confidence that the claimed identity matches the entity claiming it. Authorization is giving some privileges based on the authenticated identity.[8]

I Can Never Be Secure, So Why Bother?

Some people acknowledge the reality of cyber risk but think that it cannot be managed. "The bad guys and nation-state actors will always be one step ahead of me," they lament. "I can never win the security game, so why bother trying?" We can understand how people fall into this cynical trap. The misconception affects average users who might not understand the positive benefits of security. It also affects experts who know a lot about what they are up against. The more we understand the extent of the situation, the more hopeless it might feel. In psychology, this is known as *learned helplessness*, which is exhibited after enduring repeated adverse events beyond our control, including constant cyber incidents.[9] The bad guys will keep trying to attack forever because we have valuables they want. Threats are continuous.

Still, security is not hopeless. It's true that we have to be persistent and diligent. But we can effectively reduce the risk from the impact of attacks. Security is not a binary all-or-nothing proposition, as we have discussed. Risk management is a spectrum, remember? Every time we walk down the street, we risk

---

8. For a more complete description, see www.acm.org/binaries/content/assets/public-policy/usacm/privacy-and-security/privacy-and-security/usacm-identity.pdf.
9. Bada, Maria, and Nurse, Jason R.C., "The Social and Psychological Impact of Cyberattacks," *Emerging Cyber Threats and Cognitive Vulnerabilities,* Academic Press, 2020, 73–92.

tripping on the sidewalk or being hit by a bus, so pedestrians must exercise appropriate caution every time. We can never be entirely safe on the sidewalk, but that does not mean we should be careless or reckless.

In 1965, American politician and consumer advocate Ralph Nader published the book *Unsafe at Any Speed: The Designed-In Dangers of the American Automobile*, which helped bring about the modern era of seat belts, airbags, and anti-lock brakes. Crashes are inevitable, Nader pointed out, but fatalities are not. The analogy is apt: Cyber threats are unavoidable, but compromise is not.

In 2021, four zero-days[10] were discovered in Microsoft Exchange Servers. According to Microsoft, more than 250,000 servers worldwide have been victimized by Hafnium, a Chinese APT. What is a security team to do? Patch! As quickly as possible! Will patching make our mail servers invincible? Of course not. But the patched server will be less vulnerable to a now-known vulnerability. Patches are not perfect, but they can close a hole an exploit would use. Recall from "Everyone Knows What 'Cybersecurity' Means" in Chapter 1 that depending on the definition of secure, the premise of this myth is true: We might never be secure. That does not mean we should not bother trying, though. Defeatism is not the answer. If we take appropriate precautions, we might not be entirely secure, but we also might not be a victim. That's a victory.

If you still think it's hopeless, skip ahead and read the last chapter!

I Am Too Small/Insignificant to Be a Target

A widely held misconception is that "I'm too small or insignificant to be a victim." This is so common that we include three variations of it in this section. In a 2016 study about where users get security advice, participants felt their risk was low.[11] One participant said that he did not have a password on his phone because "I just don't feel I have that much interesting stuff on there."

This naive optimism springs from two fundamental errors. First, it assumes that individuals and small companies have nothing of value. A company of any size has assets, from its online reputation to its computers or servers. If the company cares about its data or systems, an attacker could destroy them or hold them for ransom, resulting in losses to the company. Any company with an online presence can be used as a springboard for more attacks. The same is true for people. Cybersecurity helps manage those risks.

Remember that the asset might have a different value to an attacker than it does to us. To a poacher, the horn of a rare white rhino is worth much more than the replacement value of the rhino to the zoo (sadly).[12] Malicious actors are usually motivated differently than their victims. We are not all valuable targets for espionage, but we are all valuable targets for attackers' financial gain. Even the 2017

10. We define and describe zero-days in "Zero-Day Vulnerabilities Are Most Important" in Chapter 11, "Vulnerabilities."
11. Redmiles, Elissa M., Malone, Amelia R., and Mazurek, Michelle L., "I Think They Are Trying to Tell Me Something: Advice Sources and Selection for Digital Security," *Symposium on Security and Privacy*, IEEE, 2016.
12. www.npr.org/sections/thetwo-way/2017/03/07/519009851/poachers-break-into-french-zoo-kill-white-rhino-and-steal-his-horn

WannaCry ransomware[13] outbreak was an opportunistic attack, self-replicating to randomly generated IP addresses across the Internet.[14]

Second, this attitude assumes that the attacker knows and cares how big we are. Targeted attacks, where the attacker selects and tailors their crime to a person or organization, are relatively rare compared to broad, nontargeted campaigns. Targeting is time- and labor-intensive for criminals, so many instead choose to use "spray and pray" techniques, such as indiscriminately sending phishing emails to millions of addresses and hoping that some victims will open them. As a result, the size of the business is largely irrelevant to the probability of attack, and we face similar risks as everyone else.

Third, we'll note that in some circumstances, someone can be held liable for damage caused by resources they control. If their dog bites a passerby, if a tree in their yard falls on a neighbor's house in a storm, or if their computer is used to attack a third party, they might find themselves in a position of defending their (in)actions to authorities and needing an attorney to defend against a lawsuit. Claiming that they didn't think they would be a victim themselves isn't likely to be a valid defense!

Denial is a significant impediment to cyber defense. Many victims, large and small, once said, "I'm not important enough, big enough, or valuable enough to be targeted."

It makes sense that ride-hailing company Uber was a victim of a ransomware attack. It is big, everywhere, and worth billions of dollars.[15] Going after Uber for money is reasonable (to a criminal). In contrast, small nonprofits have also been the victim of ransomware attacks. A small nonprofit running a single homeless shelter was the victim of one such attack.[16] It did not matter to the malicious actors—the homeless shelter got hit by a ransomware attack the same as the giant company.

A related misconception is that "I have nothing an attacker wants, so I'm never going to be a victim." Again, this statement is built on an incorrect assumption that an attacker is targeting you specifically. There is a strong chance that the attacker knows nothing about you other than they can reach you and profit from your loss. For example, a botnet owner is always looking for victim computers to add to their botnet. That criminal does not care about any attribute about you other than you have a computer that can be compromised to join the botnet. The victim is a means to an end.

The next related misconception is that "nothing bad has ever happened, so nothing ever will." Similar to the *Gambler's Fallacy* (see Chapter 4, "Fallacies and Misunderstandings"), this misconception plays to our misunderstanding of probabilities. It's essentially the converse of Murphy's law (If anything can go wrong, it will). This is the sort of denial that attackers are counting on. It's also related to the *Optimism Bias*. This refers to the human tendency to overestimate the likelihood of positive events and underestimate our likelihood of adverse events. People who underestimate their risk put inadequate protections in place and become easy prey.

---

13. See the Appendix for more information on WannaCry.
14. https://blog.malwarebytes.com/threat-analysis/2017/05/the-worm-that-spreads-wanacrypt0r/
15. www.datastore365.co.uk/an-uber-disaster-how-the-worlds-largest-taxi-firm-pays-hackers-to-hide-ransomware-attack/
16. www.govtech.com/security/massachusetts-nonprofit-shelter-targeted-by-ransomware.html

Outrunning the Bear

A mistaken belief in cybersecurity is related to an old joke. In the joke, a pair of hikers surprise a bear, and one stops to put on running shoes. The other says, "Why are you doing that? You can't outrun the bear!" The first hiker replies, "I don't need to be faster than the bear—I only need to be faster than you!" The implication is that the slower hiker will fall victim, and the speedier hiker will thus escape. In cybersecurity, the associated idea is that your security does not need to be perfect, only better than that of others somehow near you; the attackers will avoid you and attack the "weaker" target instead.

There are problems with the reasoning behind the joke. For instance, if the bear's attention is focused on the first hiker for some reason, it does not matter how quickly that person tries to get away. It also suggests a certain level of psychopathy to wish for a colleague's demise to save oneself. It's also possible the hiker with the running shoes will run right into a different bear. Plus, do the hikers truly know how fast they are compared to each other? And, once the bear is done with the first hiker, it may well come after the second! All of these issues map onto cybersecurity as well.

It is not sufficient to simply augment your defenses to be better than your peers in hopes of not being a victim. In the words of Wendy Nather: "There are more than enough bears to go around!"

Lastly, there is the related misconception "I know I have never been the victim of an attack." Absence of evidence is not evidence of absence. Cyber attacks are not always obvious or evident to victims. A victim might never realize that their computer is part of a botnet. Users do not always know about the warning signs of a compromised device or think it is always signaled by running slowly. They might ignore or fail to notice the warning signs (if there are any), writing them off as technology being inherently buggy.

Assuming we know that attackers will not bother with us because we have nothing is assuming they bother with finding everything there is to know about us. It's much easier and faster for the attacker to simply hit the button and see what happens.

There is code on GitHub to send phishing emails so someone does not need to write their own.[17] All they need is a fake site to collect login credentials, an email list, and voilà, they have all they need to phish. If our email ends up on that list, we will get phished, and there isn't much work for the attacker. Furthermore, they do not need to do much work building the website or obtaining the email list—those are often for sale if one knows where to look.

Now compare that with the amount of research an attacker needs on a company, especially if the company is global and well protected. It's quite a difference in effort. If the attacker has a goal they can achieve only by attacking the big company, that's one thing. A low-effort approach will be much

17. https://github.com/BiZken/PhishMailer. We provide this as illustration, not as a suggestion for your own use!

more attractive if they are interested only in the easiest way to make money or cause havoc. They do not necessarily know more than that.

Everybody Is Out to Get Me

Thomas is an acquaintance of ours. He has a strong sense of privacy and a vivid imagination. He is not a criminal, but Thomas believes that the government is listening to his conversations, the police are following him, his neighbors are watching him, and his family is trying to take his money. He has a laptop with encrypted email, no smartphone, and no social media. Although he thinks this distrust is warranted, most of his friends believe Thomas is unduly paranoid.

In the previous section, we described one extreme assumption that risk is nonexistent. Some people make an irrationally low assessment of risk. Unsurprisingly, the bell curve of people's risk perception also includes some who believe the risks are so prevalent that they take extreme measures for protection. They assume that if there is a knock at the door or the computer is running slowly, it must be malicious.

People seem to mistake unpredictability and lack of reliability for malice. Computers misbehave all the time for reasons ranging from software bugs to solar flares. Sometimes, these sporadic issues are not attacks but rather instances of fragile and unreliable tech. Our devices are reliable enough to keep, but they are not perfect. There are real cyber threats, to be sure, but sometimes we misattribute the cause of an error.

We do not have good actuarial numbers to describe the probability that a computer will get attacked today. It's certainly greater than 0% but also less than 100%. Companies that sell cyber insurance would like to understand these likelihoods better. In 2019, the RAND Corporation looked at how underwriters price cyber risk in insurance policies.[18] One of the policies included a calculation of premiums using a frequency of 0.20% for a "computer attack" event. Given the market's infancy, RAND also pointed out that other research had shown the probability of a cyber incident across the top 10 most risky industries as around 0.6%.

Every individual and organization will struggle to evaluate their cybersecurity risk. We acknowledge that this is a difficult task. As we have said throughout this book, there is a limit to how much cybersecurity should be used to protect users' primary tasks. Even in environments where security is a high priority, such as financial institutions, there are limits to the amount of cybersecurity needed to accomplish the work.

18. Romanosky, Sasha, et al., "Content Analysis of Cyber Insurance Policies: How Do Carriers Price Cyber Risk?" *Journal of Cybersecurity*, Vol. 5, No. 1 (2019).

Is Cyber Insurance a Myth?

During the dot-com bubble of the 1990s, cyber liability insurance first emerged for the purpose of covering errors in data processing. As the approach to cyber coverage evolved in the 2000s, policies began covering unauthorized access and data loss.[a] In addition, insurers expanded policies to include coverage that extended to business interruption and extortion. Since 2010, we have seen a massive increase in cyber attacks caused by phishing, ransomware, and malware. As more and more businesses become heavily reliant on technology, these attacks continue to evolve. Because of these exposures, cyber liability insurance companies are being enticed to develop new policies that are broad enough to cover a variety of attacks while providing certain protections against business interruption risks rather than only data breach exposure.[b] The market is changing as new data is accumulated. For instance, insurers are excluding risks they cannot manage, such as attacks by nation-states.[c]

The biggest factors in calculating cyber insurance costs are generally:

- Risk class of the insured (e.g., do you keep credit card numbers)
- Coverage amount/limits sought
- Deductible
- Revenue
- Number of unique Personally Identifiable Information (PII) or Protected Health Information (PHI) records stored or maintained on the insured's systems.

Curiously, it is uncommon for an insurance company to ask about the level of cybersecurity or how often a client patches its systems. Homeowners and renters insurance providers, however, do ask questions about risk-mitigating circumstances, including whether the building has a sprinkler and an alarm system.

We think it will be clear the market is maturing when insurers regularly offer differential premiums that reflect risk and awareness. For instance, a firm with a firewall gets a 5% discount. An up-to-date incident response plan might merit a 10% premium reduction. Evidence that everyone in the company has purchased and read a copy of this book might warrant a 15% decrease in premiums. And so on.

---

[a] Lee, A., "Why Traditional Insurance Policies Are Not Enough: The Nature of Potential E-Commerce Losses & Liabilities," *Vanderbilt Journal of Entertainment Law & Practice*, Vol. 3, No. 1 (2001): 84–94.

[b] *U.S. Cyber Market Outlook*, Risk Placement Services, 2021; www.rpsins.com/learn/2021/oct/us-cyber-market-outlook/

[c] https://therecord.media/lloyds-to-forbid-insurers-from-covering-losses-due-to-state-backed-hacks/.

I Engage Only with Trusted Websites, So My Data Is Safe from a Breach

Imagine that you need milk and plan a trip to your local supermarket. You like and trust this store and have been there many times before. Think, however, about the various aspects that require your safety and trust in the transaction. You need safe transportation to get there, whether a trustworthy automobile, a convenient bus ride, or even a safe neighborhood for walking. You need to trust the employees or self-checkout machines not to steal your credit card number. You must trust the store's contractors, from physical maintenance to hired security officers. You also need to trust every step that took the milk from the cow to the store. An untrustworthy cow could have tainted that supply chain.

You might feel comfortable with all these things, but your risk is still greater than zero. Highly trusted and secure businesses are still victims of criminal activity every day.

We have come a long way in securing online shopping, including the number of websites adopting secure protocols and teaching users to recognize the need. Hypertext Transfer Protocol Secure (HTTPS) is often the first line of defense in establishing online trust. Sadly, it is sometimes the only line of defense, leaving users with hollow security.

When consumers buy things online, as they often do, their risk calculus often includes only a few factors: Is this a company I trust, and is the website secure? HTTPS offers security through encryption between their browser and a website. This is valuable and necessary security but not sufficient on its own. Data moving over the Internet seems the most at risk, but sensitive information can be exposed elsewhere in the transaction.

Unfortunately, trust can be breached at many points in an online transaction. First, even reputable companies get attacked. Most people think of Target as a trustworthy and reputable company, and it had a significant breach in 2013. Marriott did in 2018. Macy's did in 2018. The list goes on and on.[19] No company is immune. Second, pretty much no modern website is self-contained. The vendor's website might appear to be the only site the user sees in the transaction, but behind the scenes, it uses external services to process their credit card, show ads, etc. Finally, the victim's own device might be the culprit. If their system has spyware or malware, it can spy or steal data even as they access an otherwise secure website.

What can consumers do? Avoid making purchases on a public computer, which could expose their password or payment information to prying eyes. Use a different password on every website so that their other passwords are protected even if one is compromised. Use a virtual one-time credit card number[20] to limit the impact if the credit card number is stolen. In general, do not let down your guard and understand that some risk, however minor, always lurks online even when using trusted websites.

---

19. https://www.safesmartliving.com/recent-data-breaches
20. Several major credit card companies offer this service. You should check if any of your cards are covered.

Security by Obscurity Is Reasonably Secure

Many years ago, the City of Atlanta had an emergency announcement line. In a time of grave public danger, one of the city leaders could call an unpublished phone number and speak an announcement, which would be broadcast on all the local radio and television stations. Note: No passcode was required—security by obscurity at its finest. If nobody knows the number, nobody will call it.[21]

Enter stage left the first generation of robocallers. As the robocall program was marching through its list of numbers, dutifully calling every combination, it hit the emergency line. Yes, all the radio and TV stations informed people that they would win a $500 vacation package. All they had to do to claim it was to call 404 xxx yyyy. These were analog days, and the last digit of the announced phone number was broadcast slightly garbled. Multitudes called, overloading the robocaller's switchboard and the landlines going to it. Collateral damage was the childcare provider whose phone number was one digit different, as it was the closest some people could make out of the garbled last digit. They were inundated with irate callers trying to claim their free vacation.

The cybersecurity version of this myth is "If there is a vulnerability in the system and no one knows about it, is it still a vulnerability?" However, this is not a philosophical question because the answer is still "Yes!"

As with the unlisted Atlanta emergency announcement phone number, Internet-connected hosts and services will be found. Shodan,[22] for example, crawls the entire Internet collecting and indexing service banners. If someone launches a secret web server and tells nobody about it, Shodan will *still* find it in under a week.

"Security through obscurity" is a common mantra and concept that has been around for a while.[23] As in, there are examples through history of various people trying the "If you do not know about it, you cannot exploit it" tactic. The key to this myth is to entirely avoid obscurity as the *sole* means of protection. Obscurity is a weak secret and is likely to be uncovered. Depending solely on secrecy for defense is a surefire way for security to fail. Figure 3.3 illustrates that some things may not be hidden as well as you think!

Where is security through obscurity still practiced if it is so well-known to be weak? Security through obscurity is used when obfuscating source code, hard-coding passwords or cryptography keys, installing backdoors into systems for corporate use, and proprietary cryptography. So, for example, the customer has a problem? Use the magic backdoor key and fix it. The problem with those backdoors is they are only secure if no one else knows about them. Once someone finds out, they are no longer secure. The vendor might think, "It's our secret; no one will ever find out about it!" Insiders know about it, however. An insider who needs money could sell that knowledge. The customers probably know about it once it has been used—even if they do not know how to access it, they know the backdoor exists. Once someone knows that it exists, finding it is only a matter of time. They do not even have to know it exists to stumble across it. It's on the Internet—the magic of the backdoor key will not stop someone from locating it.

---

21. The story was recounted to us by Brent Laminack, a senior computer expert in Atlanta who experienced it.
22. www.shodan.io/
23. One of the first cybersecurity texts to mention this by name was: Garfinkel, Simson, and Spafford, Eugene, *Practical Unix Security*, 1st ed., O'Reilly & Associates, 1990.

For example, Borland's Interbase SQL database server had a backdoor superuser account. And, of course, as it happens, the password got out.[24] Atlassian's Confluence had a hard-coded password for an internal app that was leaked on Twitter.[25]

These problems also occur when developers do not understand how something, such as a database or website, actually works. For example, a reporter for a St. Louis newspaper discovered that teachers' Social Security numbers were included in the source code of a public website even though they were not visible to casual website visitors.[26] The people who coded the website did not know (or did not care) that the sensitive data would be included in the webpage. If they did, they thought it was safe if no one knew it was there.

FIGURE 3.3 Security through obscurity is like believing a moose behind the floor lamp will never be found!

24. www.kb.cert.org/vuls/id/247371
25. https://arstechnica.com/information-technology/2022/07/atlassian-warns-hardcoded-password-flaw-is-likely-to-be-exploited-in-the-wild/
26. www.rollingstone.com/politics/politics-news/missouri-governor-teacher-data-hacking-1242493/

The History of "Security Through Obscurity"

In 1851, Dutch cryptographer Auguste Kerckhoffs formulated a basic principle, since named after him, that the security of any cryptographic algorithm should depend only on the secrecy of the key. Subsequently, Claude Shannon stated his version, which is to assume that your enemy knows the details of the system in use.

Cryptographers widely embrace this general principle. Any attempt to claim that a new encryption algorithm is secure because it is secret is greeted with derision.

This principle might be the progenitor of the "No security through obscurity" catchphrase. It certainly shares the same vibe!

Keeping information secret can help protect the information. But if the only defense is "It's a secret! Don't tell!" then, once that obscurity is breached, it's no longer secure.

To be fair, adding obscurity might add to security. An unpublished bit of information might be found through effort or luck, but it requires something extra on the attacker's part. Sometimes, imposing that additional cost is enough to make a system less attractive than another or to keep an automated attack from working. So long as it is not the only or primary defense, it might have some value.

The Illusions of Visibility and Control

In contrast to the assumption that something hidden is more secure is the belief that the more we see, the better we understand (and control) security.

A network visualization that illustrates the state of the network at any time can be a lovely thing. Imagine a screen where we have the IP addresses of our system on the bottom and the ports on the left side, and we can watch as traffic hits the various ports on our network. It's real-time and impressive: Now we know what's happening in our network, as in Figure 3.4. Some products specialize in pretty graphics that might not actually represent what is going on in the system but look great in sales presentations. (Some people refer to this as the "blinkenlights effect.")

Except, we do not get an accurate picture. It looks pretty, but not every connection from a bad guy will last long enough for someone watching the visualization to notice. Or our corporate trade secrets are being exfiltrated on a normal-looking web connection. That one pixel that flashes red for 1/60th of a second then went back to normal—did you see that? We think we know what's going on, but in reality, the truth is hidden from us.[27] If the network is large enough, we might imagine seeing patterns when none exist. It's certainly pretty enough to watch, but so are holiday lights synchronized to music, and they might have equal value in protecting our system.

27. Researchers continue to study how to make visualizations that are helpful for humans. Unfortunately, humans are awful at signal detection and vigilance tasks. See Sawyer, Ben D., and Hancock, Peter A., "Hacking the Human: The Prevalence Paradox in Cybersecurity," *Human Factors*, Vol. 60, No. 5 (2018): 597–609.

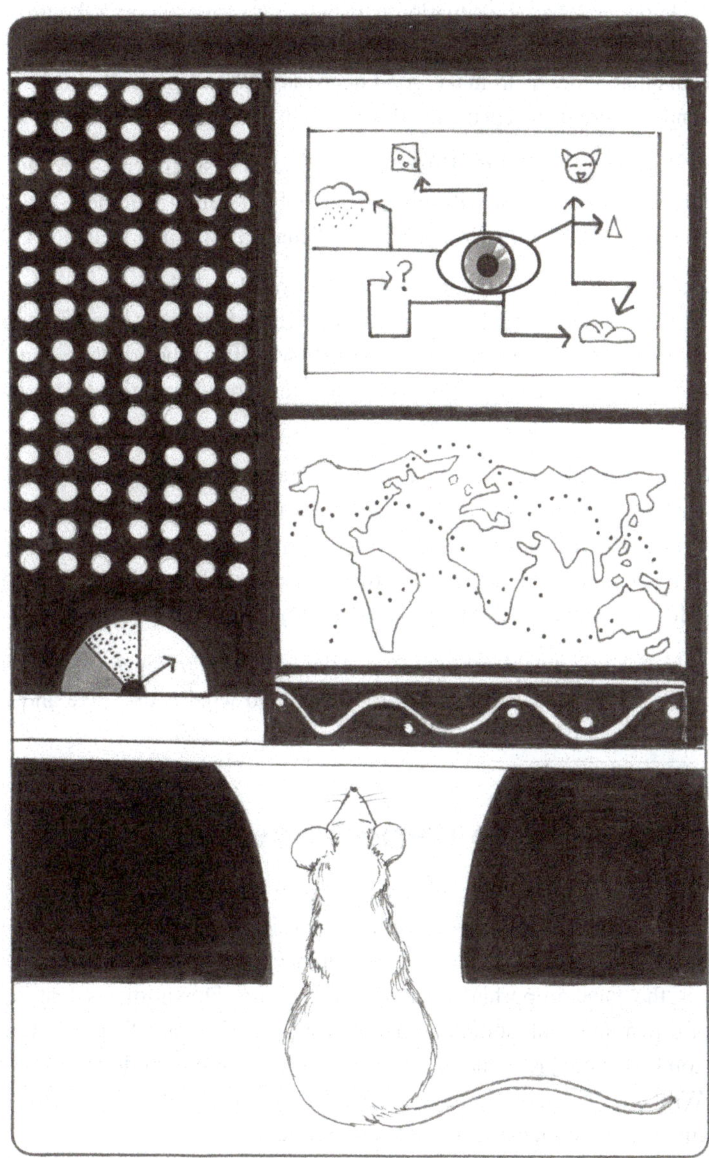

FIGURE 3.4 Blinkenlights! The illusion of visibility and control.

The truth is out there, but it is not in that visualization. That visualization gives us an illusion of visibility into our network. The magician's hat, though, still has the rabbit hidden inside it. In other words, we are missing that important attack stealing our data.

For another example, suppose we are using a traffic light system to monitor the state of the network. Everything is perfect if the light is green; if the light is red, there is a problem. Except that obfuscates things again. Do we know how bad the situation is if the light is yellow, or is the light simply a way of letting people know there might be a problem? It's an abstraction of what could be going on, but it does not provide full details that allow us to make good decisions. We are given the illusion of visibility, but there is nothing behind the curtain except a wizard who might, or might not be, a wizard. . . or *your* wizard.

Do not fall for the illusion of visibility. Effective and useful visualizations are difficult to achieve. Thinking that a colorful map or graph will inherently "help" is often simplistic and shortsighted. We will return to this theme in Chapter 15, "Illustrations, Visualizations, and Delusions."

Along with the illusion of visibility is the illusion of control. People incorrectly think they can predict or control events, similar to believing they can roll the dice so they get a specific number they desire. Or, if they deal the cards, it will be the ones that will win them the game (assuming they are not cheating). Sometimes things randomly align with our intent, resulting in the idea that we controlled what happened.

It's an illusion that we can fully control what the adversary is doing. The adversary has their own aims, objectives, and motivations. Our desires alone are not going to control them fully. We might use honeypots[28] to try to distract them or nudge them into a low-threat environment, but there are no guarantees this will be successful. If we roll the dice, we can still lose the game. If we have security mechanisms and policies, we can still lose by the adversary achieving their goals.

The illusions of visibility and control are tempting. They are often mirages that hide the actual events behind the pretty front end. It takes some effort to understand what is effective and what is theater—and it is worth investing that effort.

Five 9's Is the Key to Cybersecurity

Businesses that rely on critical systems often strive for five 9's availability. That is, they desire 99.999% uptime from their servers. This is commonly called a Service Level Objective (SLO) and defines the target range of service.[29] Businesses that can make money only if their systems are available might think that uptime is the most important attribute of security. Downtime is lost revenue, and 5.26 minutes per year of downtime is all some companies wish to risk. Four 9's is 52.60 minutes. In 2020, for example, Amazon had annual revenue of $386 billion, so 1 minute of downtime would have been a loss of $734,398. Why does Amazon S3 have availability of *only* 99.99%? It could be that the cost of ensuring another nine is more expensive than the downtime.

Availability is one of the three tenets of the C-I-A triad, along with confidentiality and integrity. As we noted in Chapter 1, these attributes are often viewed as the heart of information security. Cybersecurity is intended to help deliver all three, including the availability of data and systems necessary to users and businesses. To some cyber professionals, the three are often considered equal priorities. That might not be the reality of their actual needs. Availability might be the most important in their environment, but it will never be the *only* thing that matters.

---

28. See the Appendix for a definition.
29. This should not be confused with a Service Level Agreement (SLA), which is a commitment between providers and customers with terms such as refunds. For more, see https://sre.google/sre-book/service-level-objectives/.

FIGURE 3.5 The magic of five 9's is also an illusion in cybersecurity.

Availability is not a guarantee of reliability or resilience. There is a common misconception that if the organization has 99.999% uptime, it mitigates the need for effective incident response. They might have stellar availability for highly vulnerable, unpatched servers. That's not great. Five 9's is not the only thing that matters in cybersecurity.

To avoid this trap, consider availability appropriately in the entire cybersecurity portfolio. Leadership might have tunnel vision that revenue is correlated neatly to uptime alone. They might want nine 9's! Broaden this perspective by showing how other threats and mitigations influence the bottom line, perhaps with a better return on investment.

Everybody Has Top-of-the-Line Technology

People who work in cybersecurity are often technophiles and early adopters. After all, we work on the bleeding edge of cyber. As a result, there is a common presumption that other people share the reality of a high-tech existence. This leads to a misconception that if *we* have the newest iPhone, then *everyone* must have a modern iPhone. And everyone must have high-speed Internet by now, right?

Consider phones as one example. According to the Pew Research Center, 97% of Americans own a smartphone. But, that distribution is not uniform across all populations. Among Americans 65 and older, only 61% own a smartphone. If someone builds a website that is to be used by older people, such as for COVID vaccination appointments or airplane boarding passes, it would be a mistake to assume everyone has a smartphone.

These assumptions lead to poor design choices, unusable systems, and increased risk. Consider cryptography for the Internet of Things (IoT). Small sensors are resource constrained, and encryption algorithms are computationally intensive and power hungry. Since 2015, NIST has pursued lightweight cryptography that respects such limitations.

There are many reasons why people do not have the most current technology. Sometimes, security-specific tech is optional, such as a Trusted Platform Module (TPM), and cost-conscious consumers do not opt to buy it.[30] Microsoft initially insisted that computers needed TPM 2.0 hardware to run Windows 11. This confused consumers who had an older, more common TPM 1.2 module and led Microsoft to relax the requirement, noting that users assume a risk by doing so. In some circumstances, the most current software updates break business-critical software. For example, the software system most commonly used in the healthcare industry is notoriously brittle to Windows updates.

Sometimes, it's the "If it ain't broke, don't fix it" syndrome. Fixing nonbroken software often leads to broken software, so why touch the software that works perfectly fine? That takes money and time, and it could make the situation worse, so companies find themselves still using old software. The old programming language COBOL is still used in financial operations for this reason.[31] Swapping in new software could cost more money than maintaining the ancient code.

30. A TPM chip is a secure chip designed to enable hardware-based cryptography. https://docs.microsoft.com/en-us/windows/security/information-protection/tpm/trusted-platform-module-overview

31. There are an estimated 800 billion lines of COBOL still in use. www.techradar.com/news/this-ancient-programming-language-is-way-more-common-than-we-all-thought

Is High-Tech Better than Low-Tech?

It feels like a trick question, doesn't it?[a]

Imagine you went to your job tomorrow and a new policy had been enacted: No phone; leave it in your car. Nothing changes, and you still have to do your job for the next eight hours. Could you do it?

Many of us have this experience flying in airplanes, even though we can commonly connect to the Internet with Wi-Fi. Most people, however, do not fly all day, every day. Even in environments where quiet is preferred, such as a movie theater, your phone is still in your pocket.

There is another environment with no phones, even in 2022: rooms and buildings where classified work is performed. At the Pentagon, for example, everyone leaves their phone outside the room before entering a classified meeting. The entire Central Intelligence Agency (CIA) campus is classified, and employees cannot have personal devices. In meetings, presentations are done from wired computers, and participants take notes in paper notebooks.

These are risk management decisions. The U.S. government decided that smartphones are too great of a threat to classified information, and thus they are not allowed. While the threat from the cameras and microphones incorporated into those devices is lowered, it comes with costs. It is more challenging to reach family members inside the building. Productivity in meetings might be lower; however, in some of these environments, employees report being less stressed and more productive. The opportunity cost could outweigh the security benefits, but this would be known only by measuring both.

[a] See the Arthur C. Clarke short story "Superiority" for a fictional version of this.

The implications of this myth are clear: Experiences are fragile when they do not consider the full range of users and devices. This is more than a trivial consequence of not having access to Netflix for entertainment or the ability to play virtual reality games online. Applicants might be unable to get jobs or sign up for healthcare without access to the Internet. It has been said that teens must have access to social media if they want to have modern social lives.[32] There are significant negative consequences—especially for children—who are unable to access good technology.[33]

Avoid this pitfall by being aware of real-world technology adoption *and mastery*. One source is the insights from Gartner and Pew Research studies.[34] In addition, be as inclusive as possible. Test your solution with new and old technology and slow and spotty Internet coverage. Conduct user studies across demographics. Not everybody has top-of-the-line technology.

32. www.pewresearch.org/internet/2018/05/31/teens-social-media-technology-2018/
33. See the aside titled "The Digital Divide" in this chapter.
34. www.pewresearch.org/topic/internet-technology/technology-adoption/

The Digital Divide

The availability of advanced technology is not universal. It is similar to William Gibson's statement, "The future is already here—it's just not evenly distributed." Inequities of access to technology result from economic, social, and spatial differences. We might be accustomed to using Wi-Fi at a local coffee shop. People living in rural areas or on remote Native American lands not only do not have a coffee shop nearby, but also do not even have a wired network connection—it is too expensive for ISPs to run lines to where they live. During the COVID lockdown of 2020–2021, some children had to sit outside fast-food restaurants to access Wi-Fi to do their school assignments; their families could not afford to have Internet at home.

The problem with divides such as this one is that the people who are the "have-nots" are increasingly disadvantaged. As advanced technology becomes more prevalent, they are falling behind in educational, employment, and civic opportunities. The result is that the divide is perpetuated and sometimes widened in their neighborhoods and families.

This divide also has important cybersecurity implications. We should not assume that our user population has been programming since third grade and knows all about malware and firewalls. We should not assume that every potential customer uses recent hardware with the latest software releases. We should not believe that our end users have the resources or know-how to research what they do not know.

Think about how to provide appropriate information and access without being condescending. This goes with our overall theme that computing can be an enabler for good. The only divides we advocate are ones with the bad guys on the other side!

We Can Predict Future Threats

People generally dislike surprises. Unpredictability is scary, whether they care about stocks or weather. While some people look to the *Farmers' Almanac*'s 16 months of weather predictions, most scientific accuracy analyses have shown the predictions are only around 50% correct. Weather *forecasting*, however, is seriously different from weather *prediction*. Forecasting uses temporal information, such as current atmospheric pressure and temperature, historical information, and extensive computational modeling to arrive at forecasts.

Every year, experts try to predict trends and the year ahead in cyber threats. These are educated guesses, at best, based on trends and momentum.[35] This is why these are always labeled as *predictions* and not *forecasts*.

There is an interesting and potentially helpful area of exploration about whether we can forecast cyber attacks and victimization. As with the weather, forecasts are a likelihood based on data. For example, how similar is a newly discovered bug to ones that went wild historically? Do they share common attributes that provide accurate insights into possible future events? Similarly, victims might exhibit

35. We cannot verify if they used a crystal ball. It's entirely possible.

behavior that in the past has been followed by a user falling victim to a cyber attack. The evidence so far is mixed, and a combination of variables matters. Not every driver younger than age 25 gets in an automobile accident, but enough do that most insurance rates for that demographic are higher.[36] Maybe people younger than age 25 also fall for phishing more (or less) often. We imagine that predictive analytics will play a prominent role in the future of cybersecurity, given its use of historical data and statistics in predicting future threats.

Can we abstractly predict the most significant cyber threat for the next 12 months? Not likely. Similarly, we cannot anticipate technology's creative and devious new uses in the coming year.

Suppose we want to predict the future of DNS abuse. At its core, DNS translates domain names to IP addresses. Beyond that, it is an incredibly flexible method of transmitting information across the Internet. We can query things other than domain names, such as the time or weather.[37] At one point, someone even used it to create a game. We could use DNS queries to pick up (virtual) swords, kill (virtual) trolls, and explore a medieval fantasy area. As it is so flexible, it is also ripe for misuse. We have seen DNS used for botnets' communication, data exfiltration, and even DDoS attacks.

Considering there is a googol (not google)[38] of possible domains out there, it's magical thinking to believe that the three methods listed here are the only ways DNS is being misused or has been misused. People are clever and creative. There will always be a new method or variant on an old method—perhaps even one involving a vorpal sword!

We cannot predict all the future uses and misuses of technology because humans are endlessly inventive, especially when they do not want to get caught. (We might, perhaps, have an easier time detecting and defeating attacks by the unimaginative, who tend to outnumber the imaginative.)

Security People Control Security Outcomes

One thing humans desire is control. In psychology, control is conceptualized as internal (you control what happens) and external (outside forces control you). People in cybersecurity quite often exhibit a desire for internal control over security outcomes. They set the policies. They configure the access control. They implement the logging. They monitor for anomalies. Don't all of these things determine the security outcomes?

Our actions in cybersecurity *do* matter and allow us to demonstrate some control. If our efforts do not matter, we should all quit our jobs. A physician, for example, makes diagnoses, manages and treats health conditions, collaborates to optimize care, educates, and advocates for patients. Despite all of these efforts, a physician does not have complete control over healthcare outcomes. Likewise, there are *many* factors that we cannot control that impact an enterprise's cybersecurity.

36. Numerous variables matter to vehicle safety, including age and gender. For more, see www.cdc.gov/transportationsafety/teen_ drivers/teendrivers_factsheet.html.

37. www.dns.toys

38. A googol is 1 followed by 100 zeros or 10^{100}.

Consider two examples. First, the security staff has little control over unknown bugs in software. They trust that vendors are performing due diligence and that patches will be available, but the security team mostly cannot control if, when, or how other people discover bugs. Second, the security staff cannot entirely control who, when, or how attackers will target a victim. Defenders can be proactive and have robust incident response plans but are also at the mercy of adapting to unforeseen attacks.

If a CEO believes this myth, they will naturally hold the security staff 100% accountable for the enterprise's security. This is a mistake. Security teams can make good, thoughtful choices, yet incidents might still occur. Furthermore, it can be stressful for security staff members if they hold themselves to an impossible standard of believing they can fully control security outcomes.

It is a misconception that security people have complete control over security. To avoid this myth, be sure everyone appreciates the things that security people can and cannot control.

All Bad Outcomes Are the Result of a Bad Decision

In the aftermath of a cyber incident, it is human nature to ask: What poor decision(s) led to this bad outcome? *We followed our approved process and chose not to fix that bug before releasing the software, but it got exploited before we could patch it.* The bad outcome of exploitation resulted from a poor decision to release early. . . right?

In a famous experiment by Tversky and Kahneman, participants were offered a choice between a sure thing with a certain outcome (such as getting $10) and a risky option with a variable result (such as a 50% chance of winning $20).[39] Most people displayed a strong preference for the sure thing. In this case, both provide the same expected value. But let's say that you picked the risky option and, by chance, lost the bet and received nothing. Poor outcome but reasonable decision!

The human psyche gets pleasure from the resolution of unanswered questions. The tension and suspense of an unresolved cyber incident share a lot in common with a suspenseful movie.

Returning to the software release example, imagine being responsible for authorizing releases. Do we wait until all the bugs are fixed, or release now and patch later? More than one manager has said, "I would rather have it wrong than have it late."[40] A software vendor might have a deliberate process for accepting a certain number of known issues given the perceived likelihood and risk of their discovery and the value to be gained from release. This trade-off is the basis of opportunity cost (see the aside "Optimizing Decisions: Opportunity Cost and Cybersecurity").

39. Kahneman, Daniel, and Tversky, Amos, "Prospect Theory: An Analysis of Decision Under Risk," *Handbook of the Fundamentals of Financial Decision-Making, Part I* (2013): 99–127.

40. Arora, Ashish, Caulkins, Jonathan P., and Telang, Rahul, "Research Note—Sell First, Fix Later: Impact of Patching on Software Quality," *Management Science*, Vol. 52, No. 3 (2006): 465–471.

Optimizing Decisions: Opportunity Cost and Cybersecurity

Opportunity cost is the loss of potential gain from other alternatives when one alternative is chosen. For example, if we spend time installing software patches, that time cannot be used to conduct user training. In principle, we should pick the choice that offers the most value to us (probably installing updates!).

Decisions also intersect with accountability. Joint Force Headquarters–Department of Defense Information Network (JFHQ–DODIN), a component command of U.S. Cyber Command, is responsible for securing, operating, and defending the Department of Defense's complex network with roughly 3 million users.[a] It has to decide how much money/effort can be spent on tactical patching versus strategic Plans of Action and Milestones (POAM). Furthermore, who is held responsible for the operational and financial impacts of being compromised? If a ship runs aground, the captain is removed. That is not the case with an IT captain. Should it be? Is that the only way for this to be taken seriously? Or will it result in the removal of every IT captain that is selected for the position?

Most people neglect to consider other options at all. They see one or two choices and pick the best of those. Unfortunately, there might be a better choice, including the option to save time and money and do nothing! Knowing any given selection's "cost" and "value" is also challenging.

Sadly, neglecting opportunity cost leads to a lot of suboptimal decisions. The development team wants to patch all the bugs before releasing software, even if it's better to release now and patch later. The forensic analyst wants to find every detail of the case and every artifact, even if enough is known and it's more valuable to move on to the next case. People obviously cannot consider alternatives forever without being paralyzed by the decision.

Can opportunity cost ever be positive? It can, according to U.S. Cyber Command, which routinely discusses the goal of "imposing cost" on adversaries. Honeypots are one example of this because they consume an attacker's time and effort without causing real damage.

Opportunity cost should be an integral aspect of cybersecurity in every decision.

[a] www.disa.mil/-/media/Files/DISA/Fact-Sheets/DISA-Capabilities.ashx

Taking this idea further, not all bad outcomes result from a *bad person* doing a bad thing. Think back to our hypothetical company, GoodLife Bank, which has 12 branches. Imagine that a local system administrator changes the password on their branch server, which prevents corporate admins at headquarters from accessing the system. The local admin isn't bad and was trying to do the right thing for cybersecurity. From the headquarters perspective, this might be a bad outcome—even a security incident!

The mental error in decision-making here is one that psychologists call *Outcome Bias*. When evaluating others' actions, most people focus more on the outcome of decisions rather than on the intention. The intention of releasing software is to maximize the developer's profits and the user's utility. There was a deliberate decision that bugs would be fixed later. Outcome bias can be costly to organizations if it causes people to be blamed for adverse outcomes despite having good intentions and using a thoughtful decision-making process.

More Security Is Always Better

It should come as no surprise that cybersecurity professionals advocate for cybersecurity. After all, they are intimately familiar with the risks and understand how effective various mitigations can be. We rarely hear a cybersecurity professional say, "Mission accomplished—we are secure!"

This is quite shocking considering the cost of cybersecurity. It was estimated that global cybersecurity spending in 2022 was $170.4 billion.[41] That is not the total cost, however! We often forget that cost has many more meanings than financial, most notably time. Consider several scenarios.

The first scenario, and pitfall, is the One Automation Framework to Rule Them All fallacy. This is the dark side of automation. Ambitious development or quality assurance teams might look for efficiencies and thoroughness when testing code for bugs. But, they might sacrifice a good-enough manual solution to seek a perfect automated solution. Despite years of development, it still has not produced a solution.

The second scenario is knowing when to stop a security task. Malware analysts, for example, would often prefer to keep analyzing malware until every last detail of the code is understood completely. More analysis is more security knowledge for understanding the threat and defending against it. Their bosses, however, might want to know only if the malware is a significant threat. No? Forget about that one and move on to the next malware sample.

Third, imagine an organization that develops open source software. The code and the workforce are low risks. Yet, the organization imposes strict oversight and monitoring, limiting Internet access, and defending the development environment against nation-state attacks. These choices add security, but are they appropriate and necessary?

Knowing when enough security is enough is an uncommon skill. There is such a thing as too much security. An economist would point out that cybersecurity has an opportunity cost: What value do we *give up* by picking cybersecurity over something else? This might include productivity, employee happiness, and even savings.

We should continually evaluate the costs and benefits of doing nothing to avoid this myth. Imagine we do not require a reset of passwords every month for our organization along with maintaining two-factor authentication. What is the worst loss that might happen? What is potentially gained?

---

41. https://cybersecurityventures.com/cybersecurity-market-report/

Best Practices Are Always Best

Best practices are intended to be general guidelines developed and refined over time. They are generally accepted as the optimal way of doing things and boil down to *always* and *never* statements. Here are two examples: "Always clean the kitchen counters after cooking" and "Never mix bleach and ammonia when cleaning."[42]

Where do best practices come from? Some emerge over time based on the experiences of practitioners who talk together or from repeated research findings. Others become codified in government regulations or compliance standards. There is no authoritative source of best practices and no central body that reviews or updates them.

Best practices are generic. They are designed to fit every situation, not each precise situation. What's best for someone else might not be best for you (except see our footnote about cleaning products). Not everything should be one-size-fits-all—some recommendations might be unnecessary, impractical, or suboptimal.

One common best practice is to keep software up to date; however, operating system updates could break the functionality of a hospital with special medical hardware, causing catastrophic consequences. That's not the best.

Best practice rules are also relatively static. A best practice is not a fluctuating rule of thumb; it's a fixed statement. As a result, best practices maintain the status quo. To adopt a new technique or approach might violate a so-called *best* practice.

Best cybersecurity practices are equally generic. Unfortunately, rather than being regarded as rules of thumb designed to guide the process of making good decisions, they are often used in place of careful, deliberate decisions. Remember, the *Titanic* was built with best practices. It was the best-engineered ship of its time and ran into an iceberg that had other opinions on best practices. In other words, it said, "Nope, not today"—and there went the ship.

Most cybersecurity shops have local best practices. The really good ones use them as suggestions rather than rules. For example, it used to be that best practice with passwords was to change them often and incorporate some non-alphabetic characters. This has since been shown to be ineffectual. The person who wrote one of the better-known forms of this "best practice," Bill Burr, has since said he was wrong and that it's a poor idea.[43]

This is not to say best practices are entirely useless; they can serve a purpose. But people should not base their entire cybersecurity posture on mindless, static, generic rules. Flexibility is required, and the adversary often changes the rules of the game.

---

42. Cleaning counters is good practice, but it is unlikely to cause serious harm if you do not. You might get food poisoning from your next meal, or your guests might be grossed out at the mess, but those are not horrendous. Mixing ammonia and bleach, however, will produce a gas that can kill you and anyone around you. **Never** mix bleach or ammonia with any other cleaner or chemical, or with each other. This is an example where a best practice is really, truly, absolutely the right thing to do.
43. www.wsj.com/articles/the-man-who-wrote-those-password-rules-has-a-new-tip-n3v-r-m1-d-1502124118

Because It Is Online It Must Be True/Correct

Often, when people are unsure of an answer to something, they turn to a search engine to find the answer. After all, we have this global repository of knowledge. Let's use it!

A potential problem with this approach is that sometimes the people searching for an answer do not have the appropriate background to evaluate the information they find. They might also be unable to tell the difference between an official site and one set up to scam people out of their money.

History of Online Myths

Online myths are not new. Some of the earliest ones started as jokes, and occasionally people failed to learn they were jokes—or misinterpreted the stories into something else that they thought was real.

One of the classic cases of this was the KremVAX April 1 announcement on Usenet[a] (https://godfatherof.nl/kremvax.html). Piet Beertema, in the Netherlands, faked a posting that appeared to come from the USSR.[b] The posting also suggested that the site was hosted on a DEC VAX[c], which was banned for export to the USSR. Much hilarity ensued, but more than a few people thought it was real, even months after the joke was revealed.

[a] For the younger readers, Usenet was a precursor of the Internet in many ways, primarily connected over telephone lines.

[b] For the younger readers, once upon a time, there was a confederation of countries led by Russia known as the Union of Soviet Socialist Republics. There were also two Germanies, and the eastern one was associated with the USSR.

[c] For the younger readers, at that time one of the largest computer companies in the world was Digital Equipment Corporation (DEC), and one of its premier systems was named the VAX.

If we look online, we can find bogus but professional-looking sites run by prestigious-sounding organizations and with content citing people with impressive-sounding titles. If we are not discriminating, we will be fooled with false information. Those sites are generally linked to other sites with reinforcing fake information (often run by the same people, although that is not obvious).

Fake information and rumors presented as news are big business. Unfortunately, too many people fall victim to those ruses regularly. On the milder end, it could be marketing hype by a company that selectively quotes reviews (or makes them up) to make its product look better. At the worst end, it could be disinformation placed by a foreign country to encourage people to distrust real authorities and harm others.

If you look online, you can find slick-looking sites that are promoting bogus health cures using crystals, propaganda against vaccines, tales of conspiracies about how the moon landings were fake, "proof" of how the Earth is flat, descriptions of how lizard people are surreptitiously running the government, and even statements that birds are not real.[44] We could write a whole book about this topic alone!

44. This last one was set up to show how conspiracy theories get spread. See www.nytimes.com/2021/12/09/technology/birds-arent-real-gen-z-misinformation.html.

In cybersecurity, we can find websites that will present convincing-looking stories of how, for example, shadowy government agencies are spying on all our emails and that cryptocurrencies and NFTs are fantastic financial investments. This is disinformation, and some people are interested in manufacturing more: to make money, to cause unrest, or to cause confusion for the lulz.

Our advice is to carefully check information against known, trusted sources—especially if the information source appears to have some political bias or is from a source trying to sell something. Judiciously apply Occam's Razor: Prioritize the simplest and least-complicated explanation for the phenomena in question.

Further Reading

Ariely, Dan. *Predictably Irrational, Revised and Expanded Edition: The Hidden Forces That Shape Our Decisions*. Harper Perennial, 2010.

Gladwell, Malcolm. *Blink: The Power of Thinking Without Thinking*. Back Bay Books, 2005.

Kahneman, Daniel. *Thinking, Fast and Slow*. Farrar, Straus and Giroux, 2013.

Tetlock, Philip E., and Gardner, Dan. *Superforecasting: The Art and Science of Prediction*. Crown, 2016.

Chapter 4

Fallacies and Misunderstandings

> Think left and think right and think low and think high.
> Oh, the thinks you can think up if only you try!
>
> *Dr. Seuss*

The development and practice of cybersecurity require regular argumentation and debate. We mean this in the constructive sense of respectful persuasion, not to encourage fighting or heated disagreement. To be effective in cybersecurity, we must avoid flawed reasoning and rhetorical errors. Vendors and other professionals are also continually trying to convince us of their claims, such as that AI,[1] blockchain, and cloud computing will solve every problem, or that quantum computers will doom cybersecurity.

As this chapter's opening quote suggests, humans are a creative and imaginative species. Technology reveals this clearly in our invention of computers and the Internet.[2] Progress does not happen spontaneously, however. Someone with a new idea for an IoT gadget must convince investors that it has value. Likewise, we might need to persuade users to be careful when opening files or convince the CISO to take time to rehearse the ransomware playbook. These activities require careful thought, precise words, and effective rhetoric. These requirements are difficult for many tech experts, who default to persuasion based on technical attributes or comparisons. They quickly learn that effectively arguing for technical solutions requires more than a fact sheet that Option A has twice as much RAM as Option B. It also requires solid reasoning and communication.

1. We are not fans of the terms "AI" and "ML" for several reasons, not least of which is that we do not understand what consciousness and intelligence are. We recommend reading the thoughtful positions presented in https://medium.com/center-on-privacy-technology/artifice-and-intelligence%C2%B9-f00da128d3cd and https://garymarcus.substack.com/p/nonsense-on-stilts
2. A close second is the invention of chocolate lava cake.

A ***logical fallacy*** is an error in reasoning within an argument when trying to explain something or persuade someone. Fallacies make arguments less effective and compelling. Logic has been studied and taught for millennia, and most fallacies are thus well understood. As a result, some have fancy Latin names, such as the *ad hominem* fallacy. Others are better known by more colloquial names, such as *The Gambler's Fallacy*. Many of these fallacies result from not comprehending underlying probabilities or logic. People use some fallacies to win arguments. They might even know what they present is fallacious but use the argument unethically. Understanding these mental pitfalls—and avoiding them—can help make us better professionals, better communicators, and better critics.

The fact that humans are susceptible to these mental errors might seem like a human design flaw. The complex and information-rich environment around us has changed more quickly than our biology has evolved. A mental shortcut that worked historically in "most circumstances" might fall short in today's world.[3]

Humans also sometimes misunderstand concepts. We have opportunities to learn, either through instruction or self-study. In that process, we might be taught incorrect material (recall the "you lose the most heat through your head" trope in the Introduction), or we might not have the foundation to grasp the nuances. There are also occasions when we are exposed to false information presented as truth, and we learn the wrong facts! There might also be things we simply do not know about. The result is we might make future decisions based on an incorrect understanding of the world.

This chapter presents 14 common logical fallacies and misunderstandings in cybersecurity, from correlation and causation to the sunk cost fallacy. While there are dozens of others, this discussion will help you recognize some specific pitfalls and perhaps understand logical fallacies more generally. See the Further Reading resources at the end of the chapter to learn about others.

The False Cause Fallacy: Correlation Is Causation

Correlation is a statistical artifact between numbers often assumed to mean more than "only a number." However, this relationship is often nothing more than a coincidental, statistical artifact without intrinsic meaning. Further, in-depth explanation of this fallacy is presented in Chapter 14, "Lies, Damn Lies, and Statistics" in the "Correlation Implies Causation" section.

Imagine that an alert triggers for a cloud-based server, and the SIEM shows the logs in Table 4.1. What happened? A novice infosec professional could tell this appears to be a password guessing attack. There were multiple failed logins in a short time originating from the same source and then a successful login. Password guessing attacks do generate logs like this. It could have been a password guessing attack, or it could have been a frustrated user who accidentally left the caps lock on and kept trying until they realized that.

---

3. For more, see Haselton, Martie G., Nettle, Daniel, and Murray, Damian R., "The Evolution of Cognitive Bias," *The Handbook of Evolutionary Psychology* (2015): 1–20.

TABLE 4.1 Sample login logs showing correlation.

Date	User	Host	Login Status	Source Address
5/1/2022, 7:01:30 AM	user01	vm01	Failure	203.0.113.6
5/1/2022, 7:01:31 AM	user01	vm01	Failure	203.0.113.6
5/1/2022, 7:01:32 AM	user01	vm01	Failure	203.0.113.6
5/1/2022, 7:01:33 AM	user01	vm01	Failure	203.0.113.6
5/1/2022, 7:01:34 AM	user01	vm01	Failure	203.0.113.6
5/1/2022, 7:01:35 AM	user01	vm01	Failure	203.0.113.6
5/1/2022, 7:01:36 AM	user01	vm01	Failure	203.0.113.6
5/1/2022, 7:01:37 AM	user01	vm01	Failure	203.0.113.6
5/1/2022, 7:01:38 AM	user01	vm01	Success	203.0.113.6

Importantly, a log such as this does *not* alone tell us the cause of the events, only that they occurred.[4] There are plausible alternatives for the cause of these login failures. It could have been the legitimate user making mistakes. Uncertainty does not mean the logs are useless; they might be the key indicator of a compromised account. Regardless, we should be honest that the logs *suggest* a password guessing attack, and we cannot say for sure (without other data) that it was. In the end, such logs offer a helpful hint, not a definitive cause.

The False Cause Fallacy is not new. In ancient Rome, sacred chickens were consulted about major undertakings. A widely known story was how Publius Claudius Pulcher (consul, 249 BC) consulted the chickens before a planned naval battle in the First Punic War. The chickens were not eating their feed, which was viewed as a bad omen. Claudius, enraged, said something (in Latin, undoubtedly) along the lines of "If they will not eat, let them drink!" and had them thrown into the sea. The battle went badly for Rome, resulting in the loss of the fleet. People of the time saw the correlation and assumed causation was involved: Pulcher narrowly escaped with his life. Few people today base major decisions on chickens.[5]

Correlation does not mean causation, but it can give a nudge that the items should be examined more closely to see if there is a functional relationship.

4. Somtimes, logs do include causation, such as the event that triggered an error.
5. Though some chickens have made better decisions than people. https://money.cnn.com/1996/09/27/personalfinance/yomo_ worst/

FIGURE 4.1 Killing chickens will not cause the battle to go better.

The "Magic Bullet" and Other Errors in Cause and Effect

The concept of a *magic bullet* (sometimes *silver bullet*) creeps into cybersecurity now and then. It suggests a highly effective—even perfect—single solution to a specific problem. The phrase is commonly "there is no magic bullet in cybersecurity." But that's not the end of the story.[a]

As we will continue to discuss, cybersecurity is complex, and no single tool or solution exists that can fully mitigate security challenges or deliver perfect outcomes. In that sense, people generally understand that there is no single security appliance or piece of software for complete cybersecurity.

A related pitfall exists in the investigation and causation of cyber incidents. How did the breach happen, for example? Humans seem to be wired to latch on to simple explanations. "The breach resulted from a password guessing attack," we say. That's a direct and understandable cause.

It gets worse. Once we spot the simple cause that feels right, we stop looking for other reasons. Breaches can have *many* causes, including insufficient policies, lack of multifactor authentication, allowing too many password attempts, misconfigured system configurations, and on and on. There can be many causes, not only the first one that sticks firmly in our minds. Furthermore, attackers increasingly use exploit chains where multiple vulnerabilities are combined to achieve the desired outcome. So, it's no longer one cause but many.

Finally, be aware of a related bias known as the *fundamental attribution error*. This error surfaces when evaluating a situation where a human is involved. Research shows that we tend to over-emphasize personality-based explanations—Morgan clicked on the phishing link because of laziness—rather than situational and environmental factors. Maybe Morgan is super busy or undertrained, or the spam detector is broken. Again, be careful about tunnel vision and losing sight of other causes.

We will talk a lot more about troubles with other analogies in Chapter 8, "Pitfalls of Analogies and Abstractions."

---

[a] To the best of our knowledge, silver bullets are needed only against werewolves. Our advice is to avoid investing in precious metal ammunition. If you find you are being attacked by lycanthropes, summon the Long Ranger as an outside consultant before the next full moon. Also, contact the authors: We have questions.

Absence of Evidence Is Evidence of Absence

If someone does not see an intruder in their apartment, does that mean one is not hiding there? If their doctor has not told them that they have cancer, does that mean that they definitely do not have cancer? If their security tools do not tell them there is an attacker, does that mean there isn't an attacker present?

Unfortunately, the answer to each of these questions is "no." An attacker might be using a method that the security appliance does not detect. It's possible that the attacker was in place before the appliance was installed and was not detected. It's possible that the appliance itself is defective or has a faulty configuration. It's possible that the attacker is clever and knows how to fool the appliance. It might even be the case that the attacker got in, did something nefarious, and left before the appliance could detect anything. Those are not all the possibilities of what could happen, but the same underlying reality is that because there is no evidence that it's happening does not mean it is not happening (or happened).

Even with all of these considerations, if the appliance indicates there is a problem, most likely there is a problem. There is evidence that the problem might exist (although false alarms happen). No evidence of a problem does not mean there is no problem.

This fallacy shows up in many aspects of our lives. Only 65% of the people infected with the original SARS-CoV-2 (the COVID-19 virus) had symptoms. The asymptomatic 35% had no evidence of infection, but that did not mean they were not infected. It simply meant that the virus did not result in symptoms in those people.[6]

The same is true with computer viruses. If human-created tools do not detect malware, that does not mean there is not any malware present! It simply means that those tools did not find any. Tools generally detect only known threats. Someone or something has to identify the threat for it to be appropriately detected later by a signature-based tool. A new, novel threat could easily slip by a tool, and we would never know until it was too late.

Retrospective Security and Infinite Storage

When a new attack or malware is discovered, security researchers now commonly have historical data available, allowing them to look back in time to reveal where and how long that attack was being used before it was discovered.

For example, on January 6, 2021, Volexity first identified a new attack against Microsoft Exchange mail servers. Looking at historical data, it was later determined that attacks were occurring as early as January 3.[a] Such discoveries can identify new victims and better understand the origins of the attack.

This powerful capability is made possible by retaining logs and other historical data. It allows an investigator to reveal activity that seemed benign or unremarkable in the past but can now be seen as related to an incident.

There is a related misconception that everyone can indefinitely store unlimited data volumes, given the practically unlimited storage options today. A counterexample is Netflix. It has stated that "at some point in our business growth, storing device and server logs did not scale because the increasing volume of log data caused our storage cost to balloon and query times to increase."[b] So now the company filters logs and selectively stores the ones it needs.

While we gain better insights about attacks and attackers from retrospective analysis, we should not rely on it to remedy the absence of evidence fallacy. If queries do not find any activity, it is more accurate to say that we *did not find any evidence in the dataset* than to say that *none exists*. There could have been activity that the sensors did not observe or did not record.

[a] www.volexity.com/blog/2021/03/02/active-exploitation-of-microsoft-exchange-zero-day-vulnerabilities/

[b] https://netflixtechblog.com/lessons-from-building-observability-tools-at-netflix-7cfafed6ab17

6. https://epi.ufl.edu/articles/35-percent-of-all-covid-19-infections-never-show-symptoms.html

A related fallacy shows up in many real-world cases in another form. That is when there is a challenge to prove a negative. It is often quite simple to prove the existence of something, as in "Prove that gravity exists." If someone asks us that, we can simply drop a microphone in front of them and watch it fall. So, it would seem natural that if we can prove something exists, we should be able to prove the opposite. This is impossible outside some restricted domains because of the limits of experience and observation. If we do not have an example of something, is that because it does not exist or because we have not looked for it in the right places yet? (This is related to Black Swan events, further described in the section "Ignorance of Black Swans.") This has implications in many domains, from philosophy to physics. It is also used, sometimes unscrupulously, in politics ("Prove the election was not compromised—you cannot, so it was."), religion ("Prove Cthulu does not exist—you cannot, so it does"), relationships ("Prove you are not cheating on me"), and so on. Beware of anyone trying to win an argument with this approach!

Vendors have exploited this fallacy to set up "contests" around their products. They offer a reward to anyone who can defeat the product under some restricted circumstances.[7] Then, after no one succeeds (or even bothers to try), they advertise that their product is "unhackable by everyone on the Internet." It means no such thing; the absence of evidence to the contrary does not mean it is true.

Another example devised from an assignment one of us has presented to students: Prove to us there are no unicorns. There is no way to prove this negative, so it would be wrong for us to claim thereby that unicorns must exist because the students failed to show proof they did not! If that is not obvious to you, then we have a special offer: For $3 million, we will sell you a monitoring package guaranteed to keep your systems from ever being attacked by evil, rampaging unicorns. No one can prove it is not 100% effective, so send us the money!

The Straw Hacker Fallacy

Let's presume we know our network, our systems, and the worst thing a hacker could do to all of it. If we were the hacker going after our network, that high-value asset would be the first thing we would go after. In this thought exercise, the attacker would use the new and improved SomeWare rootkit. This is an interesting attack that is almost impossible to defeat once lodged in a system. Thus, that must be the attack that would be used.

In this scenario, we imagine that the attacker would only make the attack that we would make. We are reducing the list of possible attacks to only a few and assuming that's all we need to defend against or where we should apply the bulk of our defense resources.

Attackers, unfortunately, seldom think as we do. They will use the tools and knowledge they have at hand. They will attack the resources they believe are interesting or whatever is immediately available. The SomeWare malware might be fascinating to us, but if a social engineering phone call or simple phish gets attackers what they want, they will use that and not bother with the malware.

7. This is not the same as setting up a bug bounty program.

Attackers can be clever and unpredictable. An attacker might use techniques that we consider too simple to be practical. It's also possible that they might use attacks we have not even considered (see the discussion of Black Swans later in the chapter). If it works for them, it does not matter how simple it is. They get to achieve their goal, and that's all they want.

Defenders often try to imagine the attacker's techniques, but we should not restrict ourselves to our imagination. Attackers have goals and might use any means to achieve them. Simply defending against known techniques and behaviors is not enough. As the saying goes, truth is stranger than fiction. The many people surprised by the SolarWinds attack should be able to vouch for that![8]

Ad Hominem Fallacy

Internet trolls often skip discussing the argument and go straight to calling the other party names. They effectively admit they have no facts to argue with, so name-calling it is. (Some trolls simply prefer slinging metaphorical poo and do not even care if they win the argument. That is not new: "Never wrestle with a pig. You just get dirty, and the pig enjoys it." predates the Internet.[9]) This tendency is called the *ad hominem fallacy*. It skips the logic of the argument and goes straight to a personal attack. It's effectively attacking the messenger instead of evaluating the message.

For example, suppose HR is interviewing a candidate for the Security Operations Center (SOC) team. Chris has a great resume, and is invited to an in-person interview. Chris shows up and has a prominent facial tattoo and a bluegreen mohawk. HR cuts the interview short because Chris clearly cannot be a serious candidate looking like that. Or the security team has an employee, Bobbie, who is known to have a recent problem with alcohol and was charged last week with driving under the influence. Bobbie's manager gets a text message from Bobbie at 2:00 am that North Korea has compromised the system. The webpage is still up, so the manager assumes Bobbie is drunk and will file a report with HR in the morning. In both cases, people have fallen prey to *ad hominem*. Chris might be a rising star in the field, and Bobbie might be raising a valid alarm. In both cases, the company loses out because the decisions were based on factors that were not central to the issue but on personal biases.

As Figure 4.2 illustrates, it often feels as if the sky is falling. In cybersecurity, attacks come from everywhere and are varied: ransomware, DDoS, phishing, and more. Similarly, the origin of the episodes can vary widely, from script kiddies to crime syndicates to nation-states and more. Often, we do not know precisely where an attack originated. Some attackers will mask their attacks to look like they came from somewhere else. At other times it might require out-of-band information to determine the exact origin and nature of an attack.

If we restrict our thinking to a particular source or automatically label "good guys" and "bad guys," we are not focusing on the attack itself but on its origin. We are committing the *ad hominem* fallacy. In some texts, we have seen this referred to as the *genetic fallacy*. We are not paying attention to the

8. See the Appendix for more information on the SolarWinds incident.

9. https://quoteinvestigator.com/2017/07/08/pig/

attack; we are blaming a potential attack source. Concentrating on that feature does not stop the attack. It might make us feel better, and management feels better, but we will still be the victim of a myriad of attacks. Our response might be impaired because we have already jumped to certain conclusions.

FIGURE 4.2 There are threats everywhere, and the sky is falling!

Hasty Generalization Fallacy

Systems administrators often blame users (or interns) for everything that goes wrong with their systems. The trope that "humans are the weakest link" has long dominated cybersecurity. It's the user's fault. It cannot be old hardware; it cannot be an attack from a sophisticated outside source; it cannot be a configuration error—it must be the user.[10]

A similar generalization is when companies assume that every attack on them began with an extensive reconnaissance. The attacker had to do some in-depth research on them before starting an attack. We blame the service provider because an attack happened, but the recon should have been spotted and stopped. This fallacy is reinforced through naive acceptance of hacking methodologies and commonly taught life cycles, where reconnaissance is the first step, scanning is next, and so forth.[11] Attackers are not bound to such rigorous thinking.

10. Otherwise, it's the admin's error, and we cannot believe that.

11. For example, the Cyber Kill Chain framework. Reconnaissance has also been called footprinting, such as in the first edition of *Hacking Exposed: Network Security Secrets and Solutions* (1999).

It's a quick generalization. Sometimes, it's even correct.

Except, often, it is not. Not every attack starts with the attacker wanting to learn about their targets. There are different types of attackers with different motivations, skills, and characteristics. Sometimes, the attacker has a hammer, and every possible system looks like a nail: They simply want to hit it to see what happens. In Chapter 3, "Faulty Assumptions and Magical Thinking," we described a related myth that you are specifically the target.

Some people quickly generalize from one or two problem users to all the users. It's easy. Furthermore, it might be correct a few (or many) times, thus reinforcing the habit; however, deeper consideration is warranted rather than simply blaming the users.[12] Have they been adequately trained and incentivized? Are the policies clear and comprehensive? Are the interfaces to commands clear and user-friendly? It's easy to blame the "crowd of users" when there is a problem, but they are likely trying their best to do their work with what is available. Not every user is lazy or a problem. Yes, there are problem users, but to assume that "every user is a problem" ignores the fact that users represent a wide range of capabilities and behaviors. Some people are problems. Some are not. Some people simply want to watch the world burn, some see the fire and break out some s'mores ingredients, and some want to help put the fire out. Do not be too quick to assign blame!

Also, be sure if we assign blame that the target of that blame had some opportunity to avoid the problem. That is, do not use people as scapegoats. About 30 years ago, one of us[13] articulated Spaf's First Law of System Administration in an interview: "If your position in an organization includes responsibility for security, but does not include corresponding authority, then your role in the organization is to take the blame when something happens. You should make sure your resume is up-to-date."[14] Here's a key way to think about the issue—if you would not credit someone for taking actions that would have prevented something from happening, be hesitant to blame that person if it does happen.

Regression Fallacy

As an illustration, imagine Jie is the CEO of a medium-sized company. Every month Jie studies the CISO's report of aggregated statistics on data loss, malware, phishing, attacks, and downtime. The situation is the same from month to month.

Then, **BOOM**! Two months in a row, data loss is at an all-time high. Attacks are increasing. The CISO cannot explain why and swears nothing has changed internally. Well, *something* is different. So, Jie fires the CISO (see also Spaf's First Law of System Administration). The following month is a little better, but still not good. Clearly, that CISO mucked up the system. It's time for drastic action. The staff is directed to buy the latest and greatest network whizbang security appliance Jie heard about during the last CEO golf tournament. Also, a new CISO is hired. It's costly, but something needs to be done!

12. Also see the section "Blame the User" in Chapter 3.
13. Three guesses.
14. https://spaf.cerias.purdue.edu/quotes.html

In the following months, with the new security appliance and CISO, the systems seem back to normal. The company is experiencing fewer losses per month! Jie smiles inwardly at the result of decisive management decisions and anticipates a bonus from the board of directors.

Unbeknownst to anyone, however, the new whizbang appliance does nothing different from what was already installed other than slow the network by 20%. Articles are beginning to appear in trade journals that it is poorly designed—and the company spent a bundle on a three-year license! Oh, and not only is the new CISO incompetent, but they are also covertly selling company trade secret data on the dark web. Meanwhile, the former CISO was recently hired by a competitor and has cut their cybersecurity expenses in half.

What went wrong? Jie fell for the fallacy of regression to the mean. Unusual and extreme cyber events are likely to be followed by more typical ones. The company experienced a few months with events away from the norm—the average behavior over time. To understand that, consider throwing two dice repeatedly. The most common roll of two fair dice is seven. But if someone throws them long enough, they will hit a run of snake eyes (1 and 1) multiple times in a row. That does not mean the dice have suddenly become broken. It means that, when looking at averages over time, we will occasionally encounter some series of values away from the norm.

So why did things seem to improve after making changes? That happens because the process returns to the mean after a while. In the company's case, the misuse cases returned to their average, so it *seemed* as if the changes made a difference. In this example, it's resulted in wasting money and creating a significant security problem.[15]

There is a similar problem with viewing a sudden decrease in events compared to average as the result of something we did. We need to probe more deeply to understand cause and effect.

How do people avoid this fallacy? Understand what the underlying processes are that drive the reports being examined. If a deviation from a long-term baseline is identified, carefully investigate the causes before assigning credit or blame.

Base Rate Fallacy

The *base rate fallacy* is the tendency to assign greater value to specific data and ignore prior probabilities or prevalence (the base rate).

Understanding concepts related to "accuracy" and "precision" is essential when facing claims about how well something works. These are rooted in some basic ideas in probability. We will give you a crash course in the highlights and more detail in Chapter 14, "Lies, Damn Lies, and Statistics."[16]

Suppose we make a bet with you that we can provide you with a program that runs in constant time and correctly identifies the presence of malware 100% of the time. Having heard some passing references

15. The board still awards a bonus to Jie because they haven't read this book, and hey—it isn't their money, and that is what boards do too often.
16. A slightly more expansive overview can be found at https://towardsdatascience.com/taking-the-confusion-out-of-confusion-matrices-c1ce054b3d3e.

about proofs of undecidability and Turing machines,[17] you take the bet with confidence. Thereafter, we supply you with a program that labels *every* program as malware as soon as it is run. You lose. (Contact us for our Venmo and Patreon accounts.) What went wrong? You neglected to consider the specificity of our prediction—does it have false positives?

Formally, we talk about Type I and Type II errors in classification. Type I is false positives, and Type II is false negatives. The overall *accuracy* is how often the system gets both correct. The *precision* is the percentage of true positives identified, and the *specificity* is the percentage of true negatives identified. Ideally, we would like 100% accuracy, but that is not always possible.

Let's look at an example to illustrate why these concepts are important in cybersecurity. Suppose someone comes to us and tells us that they have a method that is 99% accurate in identifying websites as malicious or benign.[18] Out of every 100 bad sites, the method correctly tags 99 of them as malicious. This is great, right? Now 99% of the malicious websites will be tagged that way and avoided—there's only 1% that will be missed. This result sounds great—not having users go to malicious websites would significantly reduce the number of malware incidents we must deal with each month.

In reality, malicious websites are not that common compared with the set of all websites. Let's pretend that out of 10,000 randomly picked websites on the Internet, only one is malicious. This keeps the math nice and pretty (you can do it using numbers such as 87,343, should you choose to do so). If we scan those sites at 99% accuracy, we expect to get 100 incorrect. That could be 100 benign sites classified as malicious, or 99 benign sites classed as malicious and the one bad site labeled as good. All those false positives are not a good result.

The more general problem is that in a sea of data in cybersecurity, only a tiny amount of it is malicious. In math terms, the base rate of maliciousness is low. Therefore, unless we have high-specificity (rejection of false positives) tools for malware and intrusion detection, we will be overwhelmed with erroneous results. This excessive "noise" makes the defender's job difficult. If our tools cannot help us sort/filter information, they are not necessarily helping in time-sensitive, resource-constrained environments with a history of burnout.

If the dataset has 5,000 good sites and 5,000 bad sites, then we should expect a mix of misclassified sites, totaling 100 (on average). That's not good, either.

Think of it: A busy network can create a terabyte of network data daily. A connection to a malicious website can be as small as 64 bytes or even smaller. That's a tiny base rate of occurrence. Any method that claims to find those 64 bytes even 99.99% of the time means that it will miss many thousands[19] and generate a massive number of false reports.

The false positive rate of any tool is important. How often does the tool tell us something is wrong when it is not? The false negative rate of a tool is important as well. If a tool often misses maliciousness, it is not a good tool. Understanding these values is key to avoiding the base rate fallacy.

17. More to come on this in Chapter 7, "Problems and Solutions."

18. Many people use the words *benign* and *safe* interchangeably; however, security professionals use "malicious or benign" as their comparisons of choice. *Safe* feels a bit too strong.

19. To be more exact, assuming we do not examine overlapping 64-byte sequences, on average, we would misclassify 1,717,987 instances in a terabyte (TB) of data.

Gambler's Fallacy

When someone flips a coin, each flip is independent and does not influence any other flip. The first flip does not affect the second, the second does not affect the third, and so on. The events are not affected by each other at all. Same with rolling dice. These events are called *independent events* because they do not affect each other. (Note that we make no claims about these being fair dice or coins—do not confuse "fair" with "independent.")

Gamblers, though, often believe otherwise. They will make statements like "I'm due" or "It will happen for me!" The dice roll is not going to listen to them. It's going to be unaffected by anything else. Believing that independent events affect each other is called the *Gambler's Fallacy*. Gamblers want to believe that they are due to win, that the dice will eventually see it their way.

Unfortunately, dice are inanimate objects and have no opinion on the matter. If someone visits Las Vegas (or Reno or Macao or Monaco, et al.), minimal observation of the surroundings should tell them that the casinos are not losing money to lucky bettors, on average. Somehow, most gamblers do not seem to make this observation.

It's a typical thought process to put meaning in a random series of events. It even has a name, *apophenia*. We tend to think unrelated things have a meaning or connection. Flipping a coin repeatedly is a series of unrelated actions, but because it's flipping the same coin we want those actions to be related. They are not, though. Each flip of the coin does not affect any other coin flip.

Cyber attacks have been studied and can be modeled as independent events. That means we cannot say, "It's been a while. . . I'm due for an attack" or "This attack happening means others will not happen for a while." One attack does not necessarily mean another will or will not happen, the same as a lack of attacks in the past does not mean we will not be attacked in the future.

The Gambler's Fallacy also impacts the Base Rate Fallacy from the previous section (and all the others). If users click on every dangerous link in email and indiscriminately open every attachment, the infection rate will be high, and we should expect the user to continue clicking.

Fallacies of Anomalies

Cybersecurity is often about finding an anomaly. Find the weird traffic, the abnormal DNS query, and the software behaving oddly. It's the oddities that excite security professionals. They uncover an unexpected piece of software, so it must be malware, or they found a large email sent to a new email address that has never received any email. It must be data exfiltration. Congratulate the professionals for their excellent work. As discussed in Chapter 5, "Cognitive Biases," infosec professionals might presume that these anomalies are malicious, and confirmation bias is a powerful force. This is also related to the Base Rate Fallacy.

Except, it might not be a real problem. Xio in Accounting might be sending a large email to a new customer for the first time, not exfiltrating sensitive data. Or a new supplier requires a large contract to be signed and emailed, which could be anomalous but is not malicious.

The WannaCry ransomware[20] worked by trying to resolve a nonexistent domain. Once that domain existed, the ransomware stopped working.[21] Is it anomalous when systems start trying to resolve a name that does not exist? Yes and no. People make errors. It's possible to mistype a domain name repeatedly, for the domain owner to forget to re-register, or for a new company to neglect to register the domain it wants to use. People make mistakes, and mistakes can cause anomalies. Attackers also know that we are sensitive to anomalies, so they try to hide their trail or use trickier methods to do damage.

Anomalous is not a synonym for malicious, the same as correlation does not mean causation. It can mean "You should pay attention to the man behind the curtain," but it does not mean "The man behind the curtain is stealing all of your data," or even "There are a man and a curtain."

Ignorance of Black Swans

Before Australia was explored, it was believed that swans came in only one color: white. There were no other color swans—it was impossible to believe otherwise. Then Australia said, "Hold my beer,"[22] and the Black Swan was discovered (Figure 4.3). The inconceivable was conceived.

FIGURE 4.3 "Hold my beer!" said Australia to those who thought all swans were white.

20. See the Appendix for more information on WannaCry.
21. A domain can exist when someone registers it in the global DNS system. System and network administrators can also make local DNS records so that their computer thinks the name is registered, even though it does not exist globally. This technique, known as a sinkhole, is common and was used by some organizations to defend against WannaCry.
22. That beer was likely a VB, Carlton, or Tooheys. We recommend field research.

A *Black Swan event* occurs outside the realm of imagined possibility. It's an event that's so weird, so out there, that it's impossible to imagine it will happen. Speaking mathematically, these events are so odd that we do not even think to include them in models of what could happen because they are not supposed to happen.

We only know they are a Black Swan event after the event. We could not have said finding a Black Swan would be a Black Swan event; the known truth at the time was that swans are white, not black.

We could make guesses of what the next Black Swan event could be, but those would only be guesses, and we might not even know the existence of the elements of that event. We would have better luck picking a random science-fiction book off the shelf and assuming it describes what will occur next.

To give some examples of things that could definitely ruin your day that few people have considered in their threat models, search online and read about the Carrington Event and the possibility of a Cumbre Vieja tsunami. We'll wait.

Pretty gnarly, eh? If we had not told you about them, and they happened, you would call them Black Swan events—if you survived them. Now you can simply add them to your list of things that keep you awake at night.

Back to computers. In the 1990s, during the Internet bubble, the Denial of Service attack was commonly used by various ne'er-do-wells. They would take over a system and flood their target with packets. This was not difficult to deal with because the attacks either lasted a short time or, as only one IP address was attacking, it was easy to block. These events were annoying, but it was not anything we did not already know how to address.

Then came the Distributed Denial of Service (DDoS) attack: a complete paradigm shift in the attack. No longer was it "Oh, just block, go about your day," but you were flooded with packets from many IP addresses and had no way of blocking them all. An entire industry needed to be built around surviving the DDoS. It was a paradigm shift in the possible attacks an organization would have to address.

Another example is Stuxnet. Approximations of the idea had been put forth in movies, television shows, and books. Still, Stuxnet was a novel cyber weapon created, used, and exposed to the world.[23] It was spread by USB and attacked centrifuges. Rather than trying to steal data or money, the worm did its best to destroy a military complex. The stuff of movies was not fictional anymore, and the world had changed.

This also means that planning for Black Swan events is nearly impossible. How do we plan for an event that we cannot predict? Plan for catastrophic, generic effects on resources rather than base all of our planning on events we cannot anticipate. Suppose we consider preserving all our data against catastrophes such as fires, explosions, and floods. In that case, we likely will also have some protection against volcanic eruptions, meteor strikes (small, not an extinction event), tsunamis, and some invasions by little green people in UFOs. . . armed with black swans.

23. It is tempting to label it as the *first* nation-level cyber weapon, but we have no information to know if that is the case.

Conjunction and Disjunction Fallacies

Probability has laws, and as with countries with their laws, it's essential to follow them. People will not go to jail if they break the laws of probability, but they could completely misunderstand a situation. While not throwing away the keys, it can lead to throwing away money, time, and security.

Let's start with a simple example. It can be sunny outside, and it can be rainy outside. Both events can and do often happen on their own. It's much rarer, though, for it to be both sunny and raining.

For a cybersecurity example, let's consider a vulnerability. Suppose we have 100 different servers, but only one is critical to operation because it runs the finance database. A vulnerability is announced that affects 80% of the servers and must be patched. The probability of a server being critical *and* having the vulnerability is smaller than the probability of *any* server having the vulnerability (0.8% and 80%, respectively). The probability of two events cooccurring is less than the probability of either event.[24] This holds true all around and is one of the laws of probability mentioned earlier.

There's a fallacy called the *conjunction fallacy*, where people convince themselves otherwise. They think that the probability of the two events co-occurring is more than the probability of one of the events. An example is the amount of ransomware increasing and bitcoin increasing in value simultaneously. People can convince themselves that the combination of the two is more likely to happen than simply the amount of ransomware increasing.

More formally, if the probabilities of two independent events are P and Q, then the probability of both occurring is $P \times Q$. If the likelihood of each event is 50%, the joint probability is only 25%.[25] Remember the laws of probability. Any other result would be breaking those laws.

The conjunction fallacy is related to the *and* of two concepts: rain and sun, or critical server and vulnerability. A related fallacy, the *disjunction fallacy*, is related to the *or* of two concepts.

Or is inclusive, not exclusive when we use it in probability. If we say it is raining or it is sunny, we are not saying if it is raining then it is not sunny. We are saying that at least one of those two statements is true. It's also possible that both are true because both being true would fit the *at least one* qualification.

Suppose a user installs software and says, "Either it's a game or it's malware." Does that mean that if the software is a game, it is not malware? It does not. Malicious actors created a fake version of *Angry Birds in Space* that was malware.[26] It was both a game and malware.

It's a typical thought process, though. In this case, it is breaking not only a law of probability but also a law of logic. It's a common mistake to make. The *or* of two events does not mean, by default, either the first or the second, as we often use it in ordinary speech. It means, in terms of the laws of logic, at least one of the two events occurred.

---

24. Well, for the pedants in the audience, the chance of both is equal if the likelihood of each is 100%.
25. If the two are *not* independent, it gets more complicated—we need to bring in Bayes' Theorem, at least. Consult a good book or expert on probability if you need more information.
26. www.cnn.com/2012/04/12/tech/gaming-gadgets/angry-birds-virus-android/index.html

To cast this more formally, given the same P and Q previously mentioned, the joint probability is $1 - ((1 - P) \times (1 - Q))$: The probability is the inverse of both P and Q not happening. Thus, if they are both 50%, the probability of at least one happening is 75%.

Falling for this fallacy can lead to poor outcomes. If we consider the software to be a game that could not be malware, we are opening ourselves to a malware infection. (One could argue that a case of *any* version of *Angry Birds* might also be a problem, but we will leave that to you to decide, gentle reader.)

In summary, obey the laws of probability and logic. There are no actual penalties for breaking the laws unless we count spending more money and time than we should as a penalty. Feelings have no place in probability because math does not care if anyone likes the results. It might feel as if it's raining every day you have off, but until you count the occurrences over a long period, you do not know if that's true. The math might prove you are right that it rains every day, or it might not. Either way, math is like a honey badger: It does not care what your feelings on the matter are.

Valence Effect

Reasonable people want good things to happen. We want our defenses in cybersecurity always to succeed, we want the adversaries to leave us alone, and if they do not, we want the cleanup to be painless. It's a common characteristic to assume that good things will happen and that bad things will not. In probabilistic terms, we think that good things are more likely to happen, and bad things are less likely to happen. The *Valence Effect* is this tendency to overestimate the likelihood of good things happening rather than bad things.

For example, in one survey of companies, 25% had no process to identify insider threats. Insider attacks often cause more expensive damage than external attacks. Insiders have inherent access to exfiltrate data and steal from the company, and it's harder to stop when the threat is an employee. We trust our employees; otherwise, we would not continue to employ them.

If an organization has no insider threat program, it is saying it believes that no matter what, employees will never do anything to damage the company. People change, though. The lure of money can override their loyalty to the organization, and pretending that it will not is pretending nothing bad will happen. Employees can be compromised, too, and might misbehave as a result of extortion or extreme duress. Also, employees transition from "gruntled" to "disgruntled" more often than some employers believe.

Bad things happen. It's best to be prepared for that. As the old Russian proverb goes (in English) "Trust, but verify."

Endowment Effect

Research has repeatedly found that people put more value on something they own than what the market might tell them it's worth. This is called the *Endowment Effect* and has interesting implications in cybersecurity.

For example, people can perceive a company as more trustworthy if they own a product from the company, even if it has been known to have significant privacy and security breaches. This is sometimes known as the *Fanboy Effect*. Well, not really, but the fanboy effect results from it. A fan is more likely to excuse a flaw within their favored company. Privacy breaches, zero-day vulnerabilities—it does not matter. Fans put more faith in that company because they own its products. Ever get in the middle of an Android versus iPhone slapdown?

People also believe in their abilities, including their unique password creation algorithms. Users endow special meaning to their passwords and will not change them even if there's a security issue. The password is important to the user, and because it's theirs, they will put more value on it.

This is also seen when we detect a problem emanating from someone else's domain. We contact admins there and tell them, "You need to look at your machine X.Y.com—I think it has been compromised." The admins consult their logs and see nothing and thus dismiss our alert because of trust in their own (compromised) software above our report. Law enforcement agents encounter this kind of response far too often from victims, thus delaying useful action.

Three things can help us avoid the endowment effect. The first relates to us as consumers. Vendors love giving free trials because people can evaluate the product and because it creates a sense of psychological ownership. Simply because we get to try a product does *not* make it inherently better than the other options. The second caution is to us as vendors. We might feel that people should pay top dollar for our pride-and-joy product. But, the price might be too high for the market that does not have our pride of authorship. The third thing we can do is to be conscious of the effect. Avoid being quick to excuse faults in our system (or team or political party) without careful evaluation.

Sunk Cost Fallacy

A similar fallacy to the endowment effect is the *Sunk Cost Fallacy*. People think that the time, money, and effort they put into a project gives that project special meaning when it might be best to walk away instead.

GoodLife Bank has an Intrusion Detection System (IDS) in place. Over the years, Terry's staff has carefully tuned it to ignore internally produced software and some one-off behaviors. They have also had contractors build custom reporting software to use the logs of the scanner for everything from threat assessment to employee education. Every six months, the subscription price increases 2% because the vendor says that is the cost of issuing updates for new threats.

Terry has been looking at ways to cut costs and has identified a new IDS that could be deployed. A competitor's software is available at one-third the annual cost. Reviews and independent tests show it is more reliable than the software GoodLife has now; however, to make the switch would require throwing out all the customization and exception lists.

FIGURE 4.4 Trying to keep balancing the things that might be better to let go.

When Terry pitches this replacement idea to the CEO, Pat vetoes the purchase on the grounds that GoodLife cannot replace the current software because it has only recently finished paying off the contractors to make all the customizations. The bank is not going to "toss all that expensive software away."

The change alone would pay for itself in a few years. Plus, by being more effective, it might prevent more losses.

The CEO has fallen victim to the sunk cost fallacy (and probably should not be a CEO).

What should Pat and Terry do? Terry should consider a side-by-side comparison or pilot evaluation to compare the costs and results of the promising alternative with the existing solution. During a review of the security budget, Pat should focus investments on the future, not the past, and not stick with a solution or a particular strategy simply because money was spent on it. It is important to focus on what *can* be done instead of on feelings of loss or guilt from an earlier choice. The sunk cost fallacy is reduced if one can make decisions that are not influenced by emotions.

Bonus Fallacies

There have been scores of fallacies identified in research and practice. The ones we presented in the previous sections are ones we have seen in a cybersecurity setting but that is hardly the whole set! What follows are some other fallacies, informally presented, that might show up in discussions, debates, and arguments. These all skew thinking away from useful analysis, so they should be recognized and avoided when possible. Formal studies in logic and rhetoric can more thoroughly address these (and more) if you are so inclined.

External Appeals

In the Introduction of this book, our friend Chris at DRID argues against hiring a new security expert to supervise him. He states, "No other agency has a position like this. Furthermore, the Secretary has not recommended it." These are not arguments on the merits—they are appeals to external arguments. The first is an appeal to popularity, and the second is an appeal to authority. Both might be true, but they do not address the facts of the matter under discussion.

Two other fallacious appeals are an appeal to "nature" (it is not natural, and we do not see it happen in the real world) and an appeal to emotion (it will make me feel bad, and you will regret it, so you should not do it).

A fifth form of appeal is the appeal to purity, sometimes referred to as "the true Scotsman" fallacy. This seeks to counter examples that would refute an argument. For instance, Blair might argue that no true Scottish person would click on a suspicious phishing link advertising haggis. Skye identifies as Scottish and avers to have once clicked on such a link. Blair exclaims that Skye must therefore **not** be of true Scots heritage.

All five of these can also be argued in the reverse—for example, "Every other agency is doing it" and "It's recommended in the book."[27]

Questionable Evidence

Several fallacies involve citing questionable evidence. One of the most notable is known as *begging the question*: including the assumption that the argument is true when making the argument. For instance, if Sarki claims, "Perl is the best programming language because it has the most Perl-like features," that is begging the question.

Two other questionable evidence forms are personal anecdotes and cherry-picking evidence to support an argument. As we saw with the Black Swan fallacy, it is possible to pick examples—including those from personal experience—that might not reflect the overall truth of a situation. In general, examples do not prove issues, although they can be a counter-example (disprove) to an argument.

---

27. Admittedly, if it is in **this** book, it is undoubtedly correct, but it is still an appeal to authority rather than based on intrinsic merit.

Related to the personal anecdote fallacy is one of incredulity. "I simply cannot believe that our system might have been compromised given all that we have spent to secure it!" It denies the assertion based on belief, not evidence.

Yet another questionable evidence fallacy is improperly generalizing a fact based on an example or condition. For example, "The two best software engineers we know both got their degrees[28] from the University of Southern North Dakota at Hoople. All their graduates must be similarly outstanding."

The Loaded Question

Pat and Chris meet at a bar with Seong after work. Both have a romantic interest in Seong. Pat asks Chris so that Seong can hear, "Are you still under investigation for insider trading and wire fraud?" This is a loaded question, which, no matter how Chris answers, is intended to create a poor impression of Chris with Seong—unless Seong has read this book and forms a negative impression of Pat instead. This is the classic "Do you still beat your spouse?" type of question.

False Choices

When we have some significant contention, a party might seek some "middle ground" to reach a conclusion that does not seem to take sides. When one of the "sides" is based on facts, however, this approach might well result in a poor decision because it will result in a conclusion that is not entirely grounded in reality. We see this a great deal in some news media[29] where there is a "both sides" approach, even though one side is based on scientific fact and historical events. In contrast, the other side is pure political posturing.

Another form of false choice is to limit the possible answers to an arbitrarily small set of choices that might not capture the full nuance of a correct answer. For example, Terry has explained to Pat that GoodLife Bank's firewall gear is increasingly unreliable. Pat states, "We cannot afford to replace all our network gear, so you will have to make do." Terry was not presenting "replace everything" as a choice, but Pat reduced it to an all/none choice. This is often used in arguments where the demand is for only a "yes or no" response, but the correct answer is "sometimes" or "it depends."

Tu Quoque

A classic fallacy is engaging in *tu quoque* (Latin for "you also"): accusing the other side of something similar to the issue under discussion, but that is unrelated. This often happens in political and familial arguments (and should definitely be avoided). For example, "You are blaming me for not installing the patch on the file server? How about the fact that you use the same password for all your accounts?"

---

28. In music history, no doubt.
29. Only *some* media. Many news organizations strive to produce unbiased and accurate reporting. We have found the material at https: //adfontesmedia.com, among others, to be helpful when evaluating some stories. Keep the *ad hominem* fallacy in mind, though—occasionally, even the most biased report might have some truth to it!

This is a form of deflection that can escalate to the point where the original item is forgotten, and a minor disagreement can turn into a huge argument.

Overloading the Question

There are several ways that an issue under discussion can be extended or refined to make the question something other than what it is about.

- **Slippery Slope**: Asserting that if a decision is made a particular way, it will lead to additional, undesirable results and, therefore, should not be made. This might be a valid observation, but it can also be used to cloud the issue. One example is "If we allow people to print from their work laptops at home, they will print out all the company secrets, and we will go out of business."
- **Ambiguity or Equivocation**: Defining terms and conditions ambiguously or imprecisely implies that a decision impacts more (or less) than what is at issue. Imagine an argument that states "our two-factor logins add only 10 seconds to authentication" but fails to acknowledge that users of the system authenticate 25 times per day, not once.
- **Moving the Goalpost**: A claim is made and refuted by an example, so the person making a claim refines the question to add additional conditions and exceptions. For instance, GoodLife Bank is considering behavioral analytics to detect insider threats. The CISO argues against it by claiming they would not know if an employee copied the client list, but the staff points out that logging could reveal it. So, the CISO moves the goalpost by saying, "But what if the insider also installed malware to clean the logs?"

Further Reading

Gula, Robert J., *Nonsense: Red Herrings, Straw Men and Sacred Cows: How We Abuse Logic in Our Everyday Language*. Axios Press, 2018.

Kahneman, Daniel, Sunstein, Cass R., and Sibony, Olivier. *Noise: A Flaw In Human Judgment*. Little Brown, 2021.

McInerny, Dennis Q. *Being Logical: A Guide to Good Thinking*. Random House Trade Paperbacks, 2005.

Taleb, Nassim Nicholas. *Fooled by Randomness: The Hidden Role of Chance in Life and in the Markets*. Random House, 2005.

Chapter 5

Cognitive Biases

You will find that many of the truths we cling to depend greatly on our own point of view.

Obi-Wan Kenobi

The world we experience online and offline is a firehose of data. If our brains had to pay attention to every stimulus, we would quickly become overwhelmed and paralyzed. Instead, humans use heuristics. Gerd Gigerenzer, a psychologist at the Max Planck Institute for Human Development, describes heuristics as "a strategy that ignores part of the information, with the goal of making decisions more quickly, frugally, and accurately than more complex methods."[1] Among behavioral scientists, there is considerable contention about whether heuristics are good or bad.

Heuristics allow us to be efficient with our time and energy. We can tie our shoes, drive to work, cook our favorite dishes, and check our email without thinking about each step. Heuristics are also used in our thinking and our technology for cybersecurity. We do not need to analyze every piece of malware inside and out. For instance, heuristics can look for suspicious properties or behavior. Close enough is good enough in many situations.

Heuristics can also be a problem. "Heuristics are highly economical and usually effective," wrote Daniel Kahneman and his research partner, Amos Tversky, "but they lead to systematic and predictable errors."[2] Tversky and Kahneman extensively studied judgment and decision-making and identified scores of cognitive biases. These arise when we engage in fast, instinctive, and emotional thinking (called System 1) rather than slower, more deliberative, and more logical thought (System 2). Cognitive bias occurs when our heuristics go wrong.

Remember that there are many human roles in technology, including designers, developers, users, administrators, and adversaries. Biases affect everyone. Attackers exploit human bias in social

1. Gigerenzer, Gerd, and Gaissmaier, Wolfgang, "Heuristic Decision-Making," *Annual Review of Psychology*, Vol. 62 (2011): 451–82.
2. Tversky, Amos, and Kahneman, Daniel, "Judgment Under Uncertainty: Heuristics and Biases," *Science*, Vol. 185 (1974): 1124–1131.

engineering. Those same attackers are vulnerable to confirmation bias and loss aversion.[3] We might need to use bias offensively against adversaries (such as with honeypots) while simultaneously seeking to manage bias in defense.

In this chapter, we present 11 biases that are common and dangerous to cybersecurity. Most people will exhibit cognitive biases of some kind, and there are no *cures*. As we make security-related decisions and empower others to make their own, we should be aware of the existence and impact of cognitive bias. In each section, we will suggest things you can do to reduce the chances of these hazards. We follow that up with a baker's dozen bonus biases you might encounter, but that we do not think are quite as common in cybersecurity.

What If We Do Not All Agree on Good and Bad?

There are many professional judgments in cybersecurity. Is this file good or bad? Is this incident important? Is this zero-day a high priority to us? Is this account real or fake?

After studying bias for many years, Daniel Kahneman turned his attention to a related topic: noise. He describes noise as unwanted variability in human judgments. The summary of this work is "Where there is judgment, there is noise—and usually more of it than you think."[a]

While bias is a predictable error in the same direction, such as always being overconfident about how soon one can complete a project, noise is error in many directions. For example, if we ask 100 malware experts to judge whether a file is malicious, they should generally agree. If 25 say it is dangerous, 25 say moderately dangerous, and 50 say benign. . . that is noisy and indicates a problem.

The most extreme countermeasure for noise is to use formal rules—algorithms—instead of human judgment. Algorithms produce consistent results. Algorithms are not simple or practical in all cases, and replacing human judgment is painful for some people. Equally important is that humans must determine how to translate an algorithm's output into action.

Kahneman recommends a noise audit. Look at the variance in the outputs across your organization or field, even if you do not know what the "right" answer might be. Imagine we have conducted a vulnerability analysis of a public-facing application server and discovered a blind SQL injection. The private records of 100,000 users are in the database. What is the value of the potential loss if the vulnerability is exploited? If we ask 10 experts, they should roughly agree. If they do not, a senior executive will make an uninformed and potentially costly error in their decision about what to do: "That is a critical system. The CISO will have to accept the risk and keep the system up."

In his book *How to Measure Anything in Cybersecurity Risk*, Douglas Hubbard advocates for teaching calibrated probabilities. People can learn to make reasonable estimates for specific events, such as "the probability of losing more than $10 million caused by an insider threat in 2022 is 6%" (this is an illustration, not necessarily a reasonable estimate).

a Kahneman, Daniel, Sunstein, Cass R., and Sibony, Olivier, *Noise: A Flaw in Human Judgment*, Little Brown, 2021.

3. Johnson, Chelsea K., Gutzwiller, Robert S., Gervais, Joseph, and Ferguson-Walter, Kimberly J., "Decision-Making Biases and Cyber Attackers," *2021 Workshop on Human Centric Software Engineering and Cyber Security.*

Action Bias

On Monday, November 24, 2014, employees of Sony Pictures Entertainment came to work and saw an image on their screens of a skull and crossbones, including the message, "If you do not obey us, we will release data shown below to the world." Attackers backed by North Korea had stolen personal information about employees, corporate emails, unreleased films, and scripts. On November 25, Sony shut down its entire network. "There's no playbook for this. . . ," said Sony CEO Michael Lynton. "Sony Pictures Entertainment could not have been fully prepared for a massive hack that hit the company. . . ," said Kevin Mandia, whose company FireEye was hired to investigate the attack.

When a crisis inevitably occurs, people naturally want to gain control. We obviously want to extinguish the flames when the house is on fire. We want to do something to stop the burning. In the wake of cyber incidents—from the SolarWinds supply chain incident to ransomware attacks—people in cybersecurity feel compelled to do something. . . anything! Without preparation, our decision-making in the heat of the moment is compromised. The danger is over- or under-spending based on faulty risk assessment and possibly taking actions that increase the loss.

Sometimes, the best thing to do is nothing. Once we have covered the grease fire, the best action is to wait. Watchful waiting can be a deliberate choice, even though it looks and feels like inaction and paralysis. The best thing to do might be to get out of the way and let the professionals do their work.

The action bias is where we prefer action to inaction, even when it is counterproductive. It is the urge to do something, anything, when sometimes the best thing to do is nothing. Action bias is more likely to occur when there is perceived urgency to take action. The crisis could be a breach or a phishing email claiming a password has expired. People succumb to action bias because they think it shows leadership in gaining some control over a chaotic situation. They do not realize that better leadership is in preparation and practice.

Action bias is not unique to the world of cyber. The original study on action bias looked at goalkeepers in soccer games.[4] When a kick was aimed at the goal, the goalkeeper decided that the best course of action was to move. They would jump to the left or the right, even though statistically, the best way to stop the most kicks was to stay right where they were.

Doctors do this as well. Rather than taking a wait-and-see approach, they (and their patients) want to do something, even if that something is useless. Doctors feel that if they are only monitoring the symptoms, they are not doctoring; therefore, they must do something.

Companies often buy blocklists to stop their users from going to suspicious domains or IP addresses. These lists are also used to block spam—ergo, the name. The lists stop people from getting things from bad places or going to those bad places. The temptation is to buy the list and immediately put it into play. After all, it was bought to stop the bad guys. Except, sometimes, non-malicious domains end up on malicious domain lists. For example, Twitter has been used for command and control of

4. Bar-Eli, Michael, et al., "Action Bias Among Elite Soccer Goalkeepers: The Case of Penalty Kicks," *Journal of Economic Psychology*, Vol. 28, No. 5 (2007): 606–621.

botnets. That means twitter.com often ends up on blocklists because command and control are bad and blocking them is good; however, as social media are so prevalent and used legitimately, blocking that domain might be a wrong move. Without analyzing the list before using it, we risk blocking an important domain. Domains end up on blocklists for all sorts of reasons, so we could block an important customer from sending us email if we jump to action. We want to block the bad domains because that is likely protective, but it is a poor idea to block everything without actually looking at what we are blocking. Jumping to action without analysis looks proactive but can cause more trouble than it is worth.

A key to avoiding action bias is to slow down. We do not mean to act slowly in a crisis but instead take time before a crisis to carefully plan and practice how we would act if the incident occurred. Many people have incident response playbooks. Good companies conduct red team and tabletop exercises to rehearse the plans. Even if a situation arises that is not in the book, as with what happened at Sony, we will still have reasoned about our most critical assets and business functions. "Plans are worthless, but planning is everything," said former President Dwight Eisenhower. Finally, communicate with executives and shareholders so that they know that the experts are making calculated decisions and are not paralyzed in front of the goal.

Omission Bias

To quote Yoda, "Do, or do not. There is no try."

Suppose that a vulnerability is found in a product. It's a bad vulnerability that can allow an attacker to take over a computer. If it gets out, it will cost the company a lot of money, time, and reputation. If the company buries it and pretends it does not exist—that is, it does nothing about the vulnerability and hopes no one finds it–it is committing the *omission bias*: the tendency to favor inaction (omission) over action. In particular, people judge painful action as worse than equally (or more) harmful inaction. People would rather do nothing than do something because doing nothing is less risky than doing something. What has happened is they have judged it less risky to do nothing. They might well be incorrect.

In 2015, security researchers discovered a flaw in the transponder chips found in key fobs for cars.[5] If the transponder is not near the car, then the vehicle is not supposed to start so as to protect against hot-wiring or unauthorized keys. The researchers found a bug that allowed them to recover the secret in less than 30 minutes and bypass the system. They did the responsible thing and notified the company that made the chip.

Then after a sufficient time (nine months, long enough for the transponder to have a baby), the researchers notified Volkswagen and told them they were taking this information to a conference. Volkswagen used the chips, so it was more than responsible to let the company know what was happening.

5. https://www.computerworld.com/article/2971826/hack-to-steal-cars-with-keyless-ignition-volkswagen-spent-2-years-hiding-flaw.html

Rather than notifying the public and trying to determine how to get new key fobs to everyone, Volkswagen decided on a different approach. It sued the researchers. The company decided it was less risky to do nothing about the vulnerability (aside from suing some security researchers) than actually to address the problem.

This, needless to say, was not the correct response. It took two years of negotiations before the case was settled. This was not about stealing virtual information; it was about stealing cars. According to some reports, the vulnerability was exploited by thieves. Instead of doing the right thing and addressing the problem, Volkswagen omitted action (and prohibited others from doing so), thus making the situation even worse.

Hiding the problem (even behind lawyers) does not make a problem go away. Ignoring the problem also does not make it go away.

To illustrate this further, let's examine passwords. Passwords are a problem. Every site has its requirements, so the more sites we have accounts on, the more passwords we need to remember. To add to that, changing passwords often has traditionally been viewed as a good thing. Remembering all the passwords, especially once they have changed, is difficult. According to DashLane (which makes a password manager), in 2017, the average American user had 150 online accounts, each with potentially its own password.[6]

That's a lot of randomness to keep up with, especially with widely varying password requirements. One place requires passwords containing special characters; another place requires that they do not contain special characters. The definition of special characters varies widely from place to place. The intelligent thing to do is to change the password and write it down where only you have access. For example, put it on a card in your wallet. If your wallet is stolen, immediately change all the passwords.[7]

Instead of doing that, people will refrain from changing passwords. It is easier to do nothing with the passwords, even though it's riskier security. The user sees it as less risky because they will not forget the passwords, but they are ignoring the risk to the password itself. Inaction, not changing passwords, is seen as less risky than the action.

A key to avoiding omission bias is to consider the consequences of inaction. Omission bias has a moral component when given two bad options—feeling more guilt from taking a harmful action rather than the inaction of it happening anyway can seem overwhelming and add to inaction. This is often presented as the trolley problem (see the aside). Be sure to correctly capture the consequences of inaction. Think about the implications of inaction rather than thinking of it as inconsequential.

---

6. https://blog.dashlane.com/world-password-day/
7. You did keep a copy of the card in your safe deposit box, right? This is a form of *key escrow*. We should be sure we have some protected, alternate copy of critical information in case we lose our current list or suffer a bout of amnesia—or our system admin, who has all the passwords memorized, wins the lottery and abruptly quits to live on the beach, refusing to answer our increasingly desperate calls.

The Trolley Problem

In its history and description of the trolley problem, Merriam-Webster attributes it to English philosopher Philippa Foot.[a] It is a thought experiment to discuss ethics and choice.

The canonical example of the problem is to envision a streetcar (trolley) speeding down the tracks, out of control. If allowed to proceed, it will strike and kill a crew of multiple workers on the track; however, you are standing at a switch lever, and if you act, you can divert the car to a siding to miss the work crew. Unfortunately, there is an unsuspecting person on that track, and shifting the streetcar will strike and kill that one person. There is no other choice.[b] What do you do?

There are many variations on this problem, many of which currently bear on autonomous vehicle controls. It is also indicative of how the omission bias might work in reality. Without explicit thought, many people would simply "not want to be involved." It illustrates that not making a decision is making a decision, even if all the potential choices have unfortunate results.

---

[a] www.merriam-webster.com/words-at-play/trolley-problem-moral-philosophy-ethics

[b] There is likely an additional choice if the trolley is named the Kobayashi Maru, but only if your name is Kirk.

Survivorship Bias

Survivorship bias can best be illustrated with the canonical example from World War II. Planes returning to England after their bombing runs were decorated with bullet holes. It seems people object to having bombs dropped on them, so the defenders shot at the planes—a not unexpected reaction.

The Allies wanted more bombers to return, so they studied those planes. As they had been shot at, there were holes in them. The engineers' first guess: "Let's add more armor where all the holes are! Then the returning planes will have fewer holes!" This conclusion was incorrect and an example of *survivorship bias*. They were restricting themselves to the survivors of the bombing raids. The real question was, "What about those planes that did not return? They did not survive the raids, and the Allies wanted those planes to survive the raids, so why didn't they survive?"

The proper solution was to reinforce the parts of the planes that *did not* have the same bullet holes as the survivors. If we only look at the survivors, we overlook an important piece of information. We are ignoring the question, "For those that did not survive, why?" The vulnerable parts of the plane needed more reinforcement because that is why those planes did not return.

Survivorship bias happens when there is a selection process that only some things pass. We tend only to examine the things that make it through the process, such as the planes returning from the bombing runs. It is often the items that do not get examined that are the most interesting.

An antivirus process that identifies malware is another such process. The malware that "survives," that is tagged by the process, is what we often study. We consider which malware was discovered by an antivirus program, but we are ignoring the rest of the malware that could be there, unreported. We examine only the survivors, when the important pieces of malware are really the ones that are missed. The ones that are caught are not a threat; the ones that are not caught are the threat.

We do this because we lack visibility into the entire issue. We do not know what malware we are not catching with that antivirus software; if we do not know, we cannot study it. But it is important. That's the dangerous malware. Malware that we catch is not hazardous to the system. The malware that we do not detect is the danger.

We should consider survivor processes, as the Allies did for the returning planes. What are we missing, and why are we missing it?

Confirmation Bias

In television shows about detectives, there is often a plot line where the maverick detective informs everyone around that they know who the murderer is, no matter what the evidence suggests. The detective will ignore the experts, will dismiss the evidence, and at the end of the show, will be proven right. After all, that is what mavericks do!

The detective has decided the outcome before doing the research. The detective is also so sure about being correct that any research done by others is ignored. The detective has been caught up in *confirmation bias*. Luckily for everyone involved (except the victim and the criminal), the script ensures justice triumphs in the end. In real life, confirmation bias can lead to catastrophe.

The same as that fictional detective, people often fall victim to myth. They get so hung up on what the answer should be that they are willing to ignore experts, evidence, and anything that could prove them wrong. *That* result is accurate, and it does not matter; they are going to believe those results. If they are correct, then no more work needs to be done. They do not need to examine anything further, their hypothesis is correct, and the bad guy is stopped. Similar to the detective catching the murderer, everyone is happy, and congratulations are all around.

Except. . . they could be wrong. They did not confirm their hypothesis; they assumed they were correct and went merrily on their way. This was not scripted to guarantee a good outcome.

Suppose Chris decided that the only security needed at DRID is a firewall. Chris is assuming that a firewall will stop every attack and because DRID spends a lot of money on it, that is all that is needed because it is that good. Not only does Chris know the firewall is excellent, but every review and all the marketing literature describes how it stops every threat. Chris has made a great choice.

Let's make a brief list of what Chris is ignoring: phishing, insider threats, website defacement, malicious media, malicious documents, supply chain attacks, and much more. Chris is assuming that the firewall will stop everything, but email has to get through, the insiders are on the other side of the firewall and can easily steal anything they want, and the website has to be accessible. Software needs to be updated. Backups need to be stored somewhere. A firewall does not address the full range of threats.

A firewall can protect against something akin to the SQL Slammer worm by blocking off the port that it uses, but it cannot protect against email that contains malware embedded in a spreadsheet. Plus, firewalls often have vulnerabilities. What if one is found in the firewall, such as CVE-2021-26088?[8] That vulnerability allowed attackers to bypass firewall rules by using a UDP packet that was crafted in a particular way. If someone buys a firewall and assumes that that is all they need to do, they are leaving their organization open to other attacks.

An investigation is always necessary. Our first idea might be correct, but we should look further into the issue to ensure that we are right. We also need to be sure we are considering all the evidence, not only the evidence that supports our theory.

Choice Affirmation Bias

A bias related to confirmation bias and the sunk cost fallacy is the bias of *choice affirmation*. This occurs when we have previously made some choice, and the current situation relates to that choice. Rather than make a (correct) decision that casts our previous choice in a negative light, we make the incorrect decision.

For example, Pat has executed a significant acquisition of security monitoring software for GoodLife Bank from FBN (Fly By Night) Software. Terry is concerned that FBN's firewall does not seem fully effective and wants to license another firewall to run alongside the FBN firewall. Pat vetoes the acquisition because Pat says that FBN is a full-service solution. Pat is biased because Pat made the selection and will therefore minimize any criticism of FBN, even if the evidence presented is to the contrary. (As we have mentioned, Pat is not an effective CEO.)

It is desirable—not only in cybersecurity but also in other fields—to be willing to reconsider past choices in light of new evidence. We need to be willing to admit to making incorrect choices and be ready to fix them; obstinacy and haughtiness are viewed as unattractive and are disadvantageous qualities.

Hindsight Bias

After an incident, we look at what caused it and what we can learn from it for the future. It is always a good thing to do; we do not want to make the same mistakes again. To quote Winston Churchill, "Those who fail to learn from history are condemned to repeat it."[9]

8. https://nvd.nist.gov/vuln/detail/CVE-2021-26088
9. Churchill was misquoting George Satyana.

The problem is that people often look for something, or someone, to blame. The team member working at the time of the incident should have seen it. Or the software should have caught it. Or I would have found it if I had been working at the time. They would have seen it because it was obvious to anyone, right? Anyone who paid attention should have seen it!

The reality is that it wasn't noticed. The alarms did not sound. The team members failed to detect it. Looking at it now, with the knowledge of what happened, might cause a distorted view of what happened—and what was possible at the time. This is known as *hindsight bias*. Hindsight bias is the belief that an event was more predictable after it occurs rather than before. We want to believe the event was foreseeable. We want to think that someone missed the cues, and if we had been more involved, we would have seen it.

If the world were orderly and predictable, then we would be able to predict these events. Everything would be foreseeable, and we would not have to worry about missing things. But it is not—it is messy and chaotic and unpredictable. Hindsight bias is our attempt to make the world orderly and predictable when it most certainly is not.

One notable instance of hindsight bias is the *nobody ever listens to me* argument. Rather than saying "if only we had known," the lament is instead "I have been saying this for years! Nobody listened, so of course, bad things happened." This only matches the bias if the warnings have actually *not* been made for years in any notable and specific manner. Some of us have been warning about cybersecurity issues for decades but have been ignored, and (surprise) what we warned about continues to happen. In this case, it is not a bias but a symptom of frustration as a descendant of Cassandra.[10] In either case, the focus should be on the future and how to prevent future problems.

In the wake of an incident, humans also want someone (else) to blame. Hindsight bias lets us think we would have seen the cues, so the person who did not see them is the person to blame. The person in the SOC who missed the one successful remote login in a sea of unsuccessful login messages is clearly the person at fault in the incident. The problem could not possibly have been that the system did not highlight the occurrence of this event—it must be the fault of the SOC operator, who was probably goofing off as well as incompetent. What a pity *I* was not on duty then.

Part of learning from the past is not blaming someone, but determining what happened, so we will not repeat it. The Internet is a wild place, and new threats continually appear that look nothing like the old threats. We depend on our instrumentation to find anomalies; sometimes, those anomalies are not caught. That's especially likely if the attack is new and the attackers prefer not to be detected, which is usually the case (except for ransomware).

Rather than blaming people and telling everyone how we would have caught it, the better thing is to take the information and use it, so the same event will not reoccur.

10. Cassandra was a priestess in ancient Troy who bore a terrible curse placed upon her by the god Apollo: She could accurately foretell the future but no one would ever believe her.

Availability Bias

How likely is it that your computer will get compromised today? Soon after you read that question, a heuristic fired in your brain, giving you a quick answer. The answer was likely based on the number of cases of compromise immediately coming to mind. If you could not think of many people who were attacked recently, your answer might have been low. If you worked the help desk all day, you might say your chances of compromise are high. *Availability bias* is the tendency to be influenced by the things that come to mind quickly, which we have often heard about recently. As in Figure 5.1, if we focus too intently on what we saw most recently, we may miss the next incident!

FIGURE 5.1 Thinking the mouse must be in the last place it was seen.

Part of this pitfall is that we give weight to things that come to mind quickly, so we consider them more important, more frequent, and more probable than others. We overestimate the probability of similar things happening again. This frequently occurs when a company or government spends a lot of money on mitigating a recent incident, such as a data breach. It is at the top of everyone's mind, even if it is unlikely to happen again soon.

The more we see and hear about something, the more rapidly it comes to mind. If people do not know anybody who has been the victim of identity theft, they will probably make riskier decisions, such as not shredding credit card applications that come in the mail. Advertisers know this, too. The more we see ads for fast-food tacos, the more they will come to mind when we are hungry. This is even more insidious in the age of online ads, as ad companies target expressed and implied interests. Did someone search for the "best antivirus" or click on a news story about new wireless headphones? Chances are they will see a lot more ads about those things now.

Availability bias presents itself most often when thinking about the prevalence or likelihood of something. We can avoid mistakes with this heuristic by slowing down our thinking. We can remind ourselves that vivid facts and exciting stories are more memorable, but they are not necessarily the average. Whatever comes to mind first, we can ask ourselves, "Is this the most likely answer or simply the one I thought of first?" Instead of thinking of specific instances, think about how big the total population is. When something comes to mind, we should remind ourselves to consider the base rate (also covered in Chapter 4, "Fallacies and Misunderstandings"). Suppose we recently saw reports of one or even 100 hospitals impacted by ransomware. In that case, it does not necessarily mean that the likelihood for other hospitals is high (there are more than 6,000 hospitals in the United States).

We do not suggest anyone try to forget or discount what people think of first as a countermeasure. This heuristic can be helpful but requires caution. Maybe the answer that came to mind is an outlier. We all like to think that we have excellent memories, but human memory is quite fallible. For important questions, consider starting to keep track of information you might need to make a future decision.

Bad Things Always Happen on Friday

If you work in cybersecurity, you probably remember a Friday afternoon when things went south. Maybe it was a new critical vulnerability that had to be patched ASAP.

Remembering the Fridays is an example of an availability bias. There are plenty of serious vulnerabilities that were made public on other days. The EternalBlue details (CVE-2017-0144) were disclosed on a Tuesday. Heartbleed (CVE-2014-0160) was also on a Tuesday. If these two examples cause people to wonder if Tuesday is unusually common, that would be wrong, too. Even though Microsoft, Adobe, and Oracle have long released regular software patches on Tuesdays, there is only anecdotal evidence about why this day was chosen.[a]

[a] According to the Patch Tuesday entry on Wikipedia, "Tuesday was chosen as the optimal day of the week to distribute software patches. This is done to maximize the amount of time available before the upcoming weekend to correct any issues that might arise with those patches while leaving Monday free to address other unexpected issues that might have arisen over the preceding weekend." No citation is given.

The following figure was created by Jay Jacobs and shows the percentage of Common Vulnerability Enumerations (CVEs) by their published date grouped by the day of the week. In some cases, exploits are released before CVEs are made public (ShadowBrokers released its EternalBlue exploit on Friday, April 14, 2017, and the CVE came on a Tuesday, 32 days later). Most work for cyber defenders comes when patches are released, which more often correlates with CVEs.

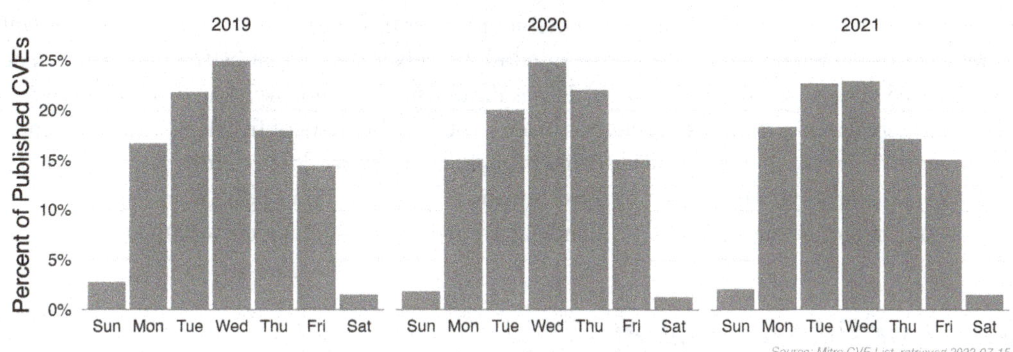

The timing of CVE releases could be a product of the workflows from CVE Numbering Authorities.

Interestingly, disclosure of data breaches *does* happen more frequently on Fridays, at least according to one source.[b] This is probably related to a desire to downplay attention to them over the weekend.

[b] https://privacyrights.org/data-breaches

Social Proof

Parker is a team player. Like many other people, when confronted with a new and uncertain situation, Parker tends to look at how other people act in similar situations and copy that behavior. Many of us go with the crowd about what products to buy and what behavior is "normal." For example, Parker's company, GoodLife Bank, is trying to decide if it should do simulated phishing campaigns. How might the bank determine what choice to make? Should Parker ask colleagues in other companies if they are doing phishing simulations?

This phenomenon is known as *social proof*, sometimes referred to as the *bandwagon effect* or *conformity bias*. In his 1984 book *Influence: Science and Practice*, Robert Cialdini presented his list of six principles of influence, one of which is social proof.[11] It is one way to reduce uncertainty when we lack confidence about a decision. If we do not know whether we should do phishing tests, but our peers are doing it, we are more likely to copy their behavior. Popularity makes something attractive to us.

11. The others are reciprocity, commitment/consistency, authority, liking, and scarcity.

Social proof can be used for good. Imagine someone gets a pop-up that says: "Nine out of 10 people in the United States have automatic updates turned on. You are currently in the small minority of people who have them disabled."[12] Social proof would suggest that this message will convince some people to go with the crowd and enable updates.

Unfortunately, social proof can also be a pitfall. First, the choice that others make might be wrong for us. We might come to a reasoned, sound conclusion and then discover that everyone else has made a different choice. If that alone is enough to change our minds, we fall victim to the conformity bias. Be aware of groupthink and how our circumstances might differ from others'—we might have more information involved in the decision. Second, be mindful that advertisers might be trying to manipulate us into a choice we might not otherwise make. This is the classic "I did not even know I needed this!" situation. The more it seems that the majority has made a choice ("Four out of five dentists recommend..."), the greater the pressure to conform. This could be an issue of the wisdom of crowds[13] but it could also simply be manipulation. This is one of those situations where it might be wise to listen, seek more information, and refine our position—or stand our ground. Facts are not a matter of majority vote!

Overconfidence Bias

Overconfidence bias is the tendency to exaggerate our ability to achieve goals. People often overestimate their abilities. They believe they are better than average. They believe they can get more done in a unit of time than they really can.

For example, your boss asks whether you can complete a new project in three months. What happens might be that (a) you estimate that the project will take only three weeks (in the best case), so you agree; then (b) you forget about the project for two months because you believe you have time, then discover that it will take six more weeks.

Two-thirds of all drivers believe they are better drivers than the average driver. The average driver is in the middle,[14] better than half of all drivers, and a worse driver than the other half. Two-thirds of all drivers can't be better than half of all drivers! People can believe it, though, and that is the overconfidence bias.

People overestimate their ability to detect phishing scams, but people still get phished. Even those who believe they would never fall for such a thing click on the link. Clicks happen. Assuming that we will not fall victim to a scam is not the same as not falling victim to it.

In *Star Trek*, Scotty always gave Captain Kirk time estimates to fix the engines; then he always looked like a miracle worker because he fixed things so much faster than the estimate. In *Star Trek: The Next Generation*, we learned that Scotty's trick for looking like a miracle worker was to multiply all

12. This is a variation of a real message sent by the Behavioural Insights Team in the United Kingdom, which said, "Nine out of ten people pay their tax on time. You are in the minority that does not pay their tax on time."
13. See the "Pros and Cons of the Wisdom of Crowds in Cybersecurity" aside in Chapter 3.
14. Assuming a normal distribution, for the statistically inclined.

estimates by four.[15] That way, he had plenty of time, and if he got it finished early, he was the miracle-working engineer. Scotty was confident he could get the engine working in time but gave himself extra. We recall one method for estimating software development time as "double, add 1, and promote to the next unit of measure." Thus, an estimate of two hours would be quoted to management as five days; our experience has shown this is often a reasonable estimate.

Too often, we see software engineers who assure us, "It will only take a day to do that!" (it actually takes six weeks at least), or we encounter a salesperson who says, "It will work in an hour!" (it actually takes 10 days). They are overconfident in their estimations of time. It is another way the overconfidence bias affects people: They are overconfident in their abilities—not only the ability to do something but also the time it will take (minimizing distractions).

It is good to be confident in our abilities and knowledge. It is a pitfall to be overly confident, as overeating ice cream is bad. A scoop is good, two cartons at once might be unpleasant for most people, and being forced to consume 10 gallons at one sitting would be a harrowing experience.

Dunning–Kruger Effect

We would be remiss if we did not mention the Dunning–Kruger effect, named for two researchers who studied it. There is some debate about this, but basically, it holds that the people who know the least about something are the most confident in their answers. That might be partly because most topics have a great deal of nuance that is not immediately obvious to those who have not studied those topics. It is also tied to the tendency of people to want tidy, closed-form answers.

Consistent with the Dunning–Kruger effect, our own experience has been that real experts tend to be more likely to give answers of "Not in every case" and "I do not know" more often than less experienced people. We are also especially cautious about colleagues who say, "I know a shortcut no one else knows!"

Zero Risk Bias

Malicious documents are a common source of malware these days. One study says they were the source of 41% of all malware downloads in the third quarter of 2020.[16] People email documents constantly, so it is not unusual to receive a document, download it, and open it. This leads to malware and danger.

Macros have historically been a common cause of trouble with malicious documents. The easy way to reduce the risk from malicious documents is to disable macros for everyone. That way, there will be no bad behavior from malicious documents, and the risk has been reduced to zero. Well done, team!

In reality, that is not the only way malicious documents cause trouble. Some use remote templates. Some have URLs embedded in them to download malware. Some download images or contain images

15. Season 6, Episode 4.
16. www.hackread.com/malicious-office-documents-malware-downloads/

that do bad things. There are many ways malicious documents can cause trouble that are not directly tied to macros. Focusing on one element that removes risk without considering all the other possibilities is falling victim to the *Zero Risk Bias*.

Banning macros did remove some risk, but it did not remove all the threats. It is incorrect to think we have completely solved the problem by fixing that one fixable area. It is like standing in the middle of a forest fire and declaring that everything is okay because we doused the burning sapling in front of the house.

Another example of this is the length of a cryptographic key. Longer keys are usually better because they are harder to guess. If we choose a long enough key, it will take millennia of computing power to guess the key using a brute-force search. Therefore, we are safe, and there is nothing to worry about; we removed that critical risk.

Let's look at this from an attacker's perspective, though. Why should they use all the resources they can get their hands on to break a key when there are much simpler attacks that work? Phishing is a simple attack that only requires the adversary to send an email—they do not need to use any extraordinary resources to break cryptography if a simple phishing attack gets them the access they want. Alternatively, they can insert a keystroke logger in the cable from the keyboard or spyware via a supply chain attack to read the key. Or they can kidnap the user's family and threaten them until the key is revealed.

While we have removed the risk that a poorly chosen cryptographic key can cause, we have ignored the real risk of an attack that avoids the entire question of cryptography. We have also ignored the insider threat. Insiders might be in the position to steal data without worrying about our 19,301-bit cryptographic key.

Removing the easy risk is tempting but not always the best solution. Reframing the problem to ensure the best solution is a better way to look at it. For example, cryptography is important but does not stop all attacks. Rather than focusing on the easy "pick a longer key," consider how attackers could compromise the organization and the risks to sensitive information, both in transit and at rest. Cryptography might be a part of the answer, but it might not be the most important part.

Frequency Bias

People have sometimes noticed that when they get a new car, they start to see vehicles like it everywhere they go. Or, after reading a chapter on bias, did you begin to notice biases in cybersecurity?

Frequency bias, also known as the Baader–Meinhof phenomenon, is the tendency to notice something more often after seeing it one time. This might lead a person to the illusion that the event or item occurs more frequently than before. It seems to appear everywhere! (This is somewhat related to the Availability Bias discussed earlier, but it is not the same thing.)

In reality, the things were there all along, but we simply did not notice them. Our brains are wired to look for patterns. We are keenly aware of coincidences even when they are meaningless.

There is a potential pitfall if our newfound focus tricks us into thinking that thing is more frequent. Have you recently learned about an obscure cyber attack? You might think you see it everywhere, even though it is rare. Is the press talking a lot about ransomware? This might make it seem like a more prevalent problem than the data suggest.

Finally, frequency bias can be weaponized by advertising. Seeing repeated ads for a particular company or security widget leads to an assumption that it's popular or desirable. We cannot always control the onslaught of advertisements around us, so we must carefully check our frequency bias when deciding on purchases.

Bonus Biases

There are scores of other biases that have been identified. We have applied our own biases and chosen the ones that we have seen to occur most often, as described in this chapter. Here are a few more that we will briefly mention.

Outcome Bias

This is when we evaluate the outcome of something without taking into account the intent and context of the original decision. We discussed this on page 83.

Discounting Bias

Vendor X promises a 10% reduction in phishing over the next six months if its product is installed now. Vendor Y promises a 30% reduction in phishing over the next two years, but it will take a six-month training period before it can be used. The products cost the same. If someone chooses X because it will give something right away, then they are falling victim to the discounting bias. The better choice is the one that gives the more significant reduction over time, even if there is a delay in getting it.

A similar bias has an impact on scheduling and expenditures. Being able to postpone something, even if the cost will be higher, is often chosen because there is the bias that time and cost *now* are somehow different and more valuable.

Locality Bias

The *locality bias* affects our reaction towards local versus remote. It occurs when we believe our staff is better or different than the staff elsewhere or that what happens elsewhere could not happen here, simply because we are somehow better. This contributes to the insider abuse problem (although it is not the only factor). The further removed the "other" is, the larger the perceived difference appears, especially if the one making the comparison does not have first-hand experience with the "other."

This applies to many other contexts, too. A flood in our basement is much worse than a monsoon in another country. And tell a grandmother that her grandchildren are not that special compared to others at your peril!

Denomination Bias

This bias shows up in purchasing and when ordering from a menu at a restaurant. The menu will have a budget version and an "all bells-and-whistles" version. A moderate version will be somewhere in between (explicitly, or if you ask). That is the option the vendor wants to sell and might have a more inflated profit margin than the other two. The bias comes into play because few people have the budget to go all-out on the most expensive item, and the budget item seems inferior to the other choices. Cybersecurity vendors sometimes price their goods and services to take advantage of this bias—the platinum plan is very expensive, but the gold plan looks reasonable in comparison.

Denial or Ostrich Bias

We have seen this bias more in government than in industry. It is not as common currently as it used to be, but it occasionally shows up. The *denial bias*, also called the *ostrich bias*, occurs when someone in authority would rather be ignorant of risks and problems than be forced to take action on them. For example, the auditors require that an IDS be installed, but the admins do not enable it—if it was enabled, they would need to respond to the alerts, and who wants that?

Aura or Halo Bias

We get a fantastic firewall from vendor Fly By Night (FBN). It does everything we want, has no bugs, and exhibits rock-solid performance. So, when FBN offers us its new IDS system, we assume it must be outstanding. Furthermore, the news stories we have been hearing about how FBN's CEO and CIO were indicted for insider trading—they were clearly set up by jealous competitors. These are examples of the *aura bias*: There is something we like and trust, so everything associated with it in some way must be equally outstanding.

One Upmanship

Oh, woe betide the CISO whose CEO suffers this bias and hears about another company adopting a new infrastructure! The biased CEO will want to get something even more flashy and expensive simply to brag about it at the next golf outing, whether it is needed or not. Thankfully, this exact scenario seldom occurs, but we see it sometimes at the level of personnel: One analyst gets a new machine to replace one that failed, and someone else senior demands the same *plus* some extra storage and a higher-resolution screen, even though they were content with what they had before.

Anchoring Bias

When exposed to (relatively) new information, we might form what we hear first as an anchor point. After that, we judge further information based on how it relates to that anchor. If someone tells us that they repel 15 attacks a day, we do not know if that is a lot or a little, but what we hear next will be judged relative to that. It is important to realize that what we hear first might be an outlier, and not give it undue weight.

Priming

Priming is somewhat related to the availability bias. If we are presented with a concept unrelated to what we are doing, we are more likely to choose something related to that concept later on. For instance, suppose we go to lunch and have a nice souvlaki sandwich with a side of briami. That afternoon, we find someone trying to break into our domain controller, and we assume it is a malicious attacker from Greece. This might seem ridiculous, but the effect has been repeatedly demonstrated (although not with souvlaki, to our knowledge).

Knowledge Bias

By finishing this book, you will have a deeper insight into biases and misconceptions; however, do not assume anyone else you meet has read the book and has similar knowledge. Similarly, do not assume that people you are talking to have the same depth of knowledge you might have on any other topic. When everyone involved must be operating from the same assumptions, it is wise to explore what is understood in common.

Beware here, though—it is possible to be viewed as condescending if one regularly explains things to others who already know them. Even more egregious is if it appears one is assuming that someone else does not know as much on a topic because of something superficial—as happens in, for example, mansplaining! The best way to determine the level of understanding is to ask gentle questions, while keeping in mind that the conformist bias might come into play in a group, and some people will not want to be seen as admitting to not knowing something that others seem to understand.

Status Quo Bias

Many people do not like change. The more significant the proposed change, the more they push back. This is unrelated to the actual merits of the proposed change. This bias can be quite extreme in some people, and they will find (or manufacture) reasons to avoid or minimize the proposed changes. Whether the change is to switch vendors, go to a new programming language, or move to a new office, they might push back. "We have always done it this way!" is the rallying cry. Understanding this bias helps to counter it, but it is deeply ingrained in some people. Using the Socratic method to help them admit to the advantages of the change is often a helpful technique to overcome this bias.

"Ism" Biases

Do you know someone sure they will have all their data wiped by ransomware in the next month? Or maybe someone who believes they will never be a target? Both might be suffering from "ism" biases: pessimism and optimism, respectively. With "ism" biases, the determination of something is based not on evidence or analysis but on a general personal outlook. Understanding where we fall in this range is valuable, so we know how to temper our reaction to things that happen.

Self-Serving Bias

Beware of people who tend to exhibit this bias. If something good happens, it is clearly their accomplishment. Of course, if something terrible happens, it is clearly the fault of others. Not only are people like this toxic in a group environment, but they also can become disgruntled if they believe they are not getting a fair share of credit/blame. Unhappy employees are dangerous to an enterprise; try to keep everyone gruntled.

Further Reading

Cialdini, Robert. *Influence: Science and Practice*. Allyn and Bacon, 2008.

Hubbard, Douglas. *How to Measure Anything in Cybersecurity Risk*. Wiley, 2016.

Johnson, Chelsea K., Gutzwiller, Robert S., Ferguson-Walter, Kimberly J., and Fugate, Sunny J. *A Cyber-Relevant Table of Decision-Making Biases and Their Definitions*. Technical Report, 2020. DOI: 10.13140/RG.2.2.14891.87846.

Kahneman, Daniel. *Thinking, Fast and Slow*. Macmillan, 2013.

Matthews, Luke J., Parker, Andrew M., Carman, Katherine Grace, Kerber, Rose, and Kavanagh, Jennifer. *Individual Differences in Resistance to Truth Decay: Exploring the Role of Reasoning and Cognitive Biases*. www.rand. org/pubs/research_reports/RRA112-17.html.

Thaler, Richard, and Sunstein, Cass. *Nudge: The Final Edition*. Penguin, 2021.

Chapter 6

Perverse Incentives and the Cobra Effect

> The best-laid plans of mice and men often go awry. (The original wording in Scots-English was "The best-laid schemes o' mice an' men Gang aft agley")
>
> *Robert Burns*

Terry, the CISO for GoodLife Bank, sends a memo to the security team: "I want you to prevent users from pasting text into the password field when people log in to their accounts. We do not want to make it easy for attackers to enter passwords."

This is a well-intentioned policy that is going to backfire. It is built on a fallacy, in which the fundamental problem will get *worse* than before the change. When legitimate users have to type in their long, strong passwords rather than copy them from a password manager, users will likely create shorter, weaker passwords. The resulting user behavior is the opposite of what we want.

This phenomenon is known as the *cobra effect*. It is named for something that happened when the British ruled India. The officials of the Raj wanted to decrease the number of cobras. So, leadership offered a bounty for every dead cobra. At first, it worked, and the population of cobras decreased. But, unsurprisingly, in retrospect, people began to breed cobras, knowing they could get rewards. Once the British found out this was happening, they canceled the bounty. The people breeding the cobras no longer had any incentive to keep breeding them, so many of them simply released all their cobras into the wild. The result was an *increase* in the number of cobras from before the bounty program existed!

The cobra effect is one type of *perverse incentive*, which are unintended and undesirable outcomes contrary to their creator's intentions. Unfortunately, multiple cases of this phenomenon can be found in cybersecurity as well. In this chapter, we will look at some examples, specific ways to avoid them, and some unintended consequences.

Uncovering perverse incentives is sometimes difficult. In cybersecurity, we often want to motivate more secure behavior. Perverse incentives also encourage behavior, but for the wrong reasons.

Compliance standards, for instance, could lead an organization to adopt minimum security simply to meet the requirements rather than doing more to manage its risk appropriately. HIPAA, for example, does not require multifactor authentication, but that does not mean that healthcare clinics should avoid it. The U.S. FISMA standard relating to federal agencies' cybersecurity also has been notorious for weak controls, yet has been used as an excuse for not doing more. Standards should be viewed as the *minimum* practices that should be considered, not the actual blueprint.

Unintended consequences and perverse incentives are particularly insidious when financial incentives are involved. In the Introduction, we described an old myth that antivirus companies created malware to create an artificial demand for their products. If a company paid bonuses for the number of closed help desk tickets, someone might create many needless tickets simply to close them and reap the reward. Another example is planned obsolescence: Vendors that make cheap products with short lifetimes cause consumers to need to buy a replacement. This benefits the vendor to the detriment of consumers. So, let's start with a myth about cybersecurity companies and profits.

The Goal of a Security Vendor Is to Keep You Secure

The social responsibility of a business is to increase its profits. So said Milton Friedman in 1970 in a *New York Times* column.[1] Friedman would have said that this principle applies to cat food companies and software vendors alike.

Do not be fooled: The primary goal of cybersecurity vendors is to increase profits. Yes, they are selling security products and services, and we might counter that people will not buy hardware and software if they are not safe or secure. Experience has shown, however, that some products in the marketplace do not work as well as advertised and sometimes do not work at all. This happens more than we might expect. . . or want.

Vendors and service providers need to persuade us that the cost of their offerings is justified, and that task should be simpler (over the long term) if they provide quality products. After all, reputation does help in sales; however, the goal of marketing is to influence us, and it is more about psychology than facts, as evidenced by the emergence of fad products (e.g., NFTs). Advertisers have gotten quite good at selling us products that might not be everything they are claimed to be.

It is this push toward profits that influences much of the marketplace. For instance, many software subscriptions auto-renew, a feature much more valuable to the vendor than the convenience is to the client. Another example is the cycle of new releases, often with new features of dubious utility. The releases come about because the vendor needs a steady income stream. Thus, there might be less care put into any particular release because improved efficiency and security of future releases can be used in marketing those new versions. Plus, even in security, some companies might have the attitude, "Eh, so what if there are flaws—we will address them in a patch."[2]

1. www.nytimes.com/1970/09/13/archives/a-friedman-doctrine-the-social-responsibility-of-business-is-to.html
2. It's not a bug, it's a feature!

Another by-product of vendors putting business first is that they sometimes give us what we want, not what we need. That trade-off can compromise safety and security. If an Endpoint Detection and Response (EDR) vendor learns or thinks that customers want machine learning features, it might add some even if those additions are ineffective. The goal, after all, is to sell more units. This creates a feedback loop, too—if the vendor adds some largely useless features that result in more sales, it encourages the company (and others in the market) to continue to add those features. Hence, "Now with machine learning, quantum-based threat intelligence in the cloud, and blockchain-enabled distributed enterprise visualization" becomes required even though it adds complexity and cost with minimal (or possibly negative) benefit.

Tangentially, vendors we patronize that are not in the security business might not care about security, and thus, the safety of their products may be far below our acceptable standards. Think about your gym or fitness center. Do they have strong passwords or lock their screen so your personal details are hidden from nosy viewers? That business might accept more risk than you would or more than you know about. We know of one firm that saves $5 million per year, knowing that it might have a $10 million cyber-related loss once every five years. It is less secure but comes out $15 million ahead overall. If the firm loses our information, it is not a major loss—to *them*.

Even if vendors have motives that do not put our security first, there are still things we can do. First, we should never assume that anyone else has our best interest in mind. Take precautions that you can control. For example, use a password manager to pick a unique password for the fitness club so that even if the club fails to protect your account adequately, a compromised password does not threaten your other accounts. Do not trust a company not to sell your email address. Use a secondary email. Are you worried about the security of your credit card number? Credit card companies such as Capital One and Citibank can generate virtual card numbers for you. Vendors offering lots of shiny new features? Evaluate the products to see if (a) they work and (b) they are helpful to you.

Your Cybersecurity Decisions Affect Only You

Drew and Cameron do not patch their computer. They don't want to and don't want anyone telling them what to do. So, they disabled automatic updates. Windows XP still works fine for them, thank you very much. If their computer gets compromised, the only people who suffer are them, they believe, and they will deal with it.

Their ISP might take a different stance. Some Internet service providers quarantine infected machines, an approach known as a walled garden.[3] The reason for this action is that attacks spread. Attackers with access to one machine routinely scan for other machines on the network to infect. Drew and Cameron's poor security puts others at risk.

3. www.ndss-symposium.org/wp-content/uploads/2019/02/ndss2019_02B-2_Cetin_paper.pdf

Consider another example: email. Cameron and Drew incorrectly believe that they can pick weak passwords, and it is their risk alone to bear. Unfortunately, attackers could break those weak passwords and use the compromised accounts to victimize Cameron and Drew's friends and clients by sending phishing emails from their accounts. Cameron and Drew are adding risk for other people by not understanding what the risks really might be.

Companies make decisions in their private interest. The security of individuals affects the security of others. Few security decisions take the whole into account.

Individuals who do not understand the threat are also a hazard to the rest of us, whether they are subjecting us to second-hand smoke, dumping chemicals in our rivers, or failing to get vaccinated for a contagious disease. Worse are the individuals who simply do not care about the public good. They often impose extra expense on the rest of us to protect against the primary threat **and** the selfish.

Don't be like Drew and Cameron.

The Common Good?

The Cobra Effect occurs when some rational parties are incentivized to work against what would seem to be the common good. Some circumstances encourage *all* the rational parties to actively work against the collective security! Consider the Tragedy of the Commons.[a] This is often described in a parable. Imagine a town with a "commons"—a shared park. No one and everyone owns the park. Some of the town residents see that the commons has lush grassy fields, so they turn out their flock of sheep into the commons. The sheep graze and grow fat, with quality wool. The neighbors see this and decide to turn their sheep out into the commons, too. Before long, the commons is full of sheep, and they have eaten and trampled all the vegetation and covered everything in sheep poop. There is no longer a place for people to picnic and play Frisbee golf, as illustrated in Figure 6.1.

The unfortunate consequences are apparent to everyone. The problems could be solved by everyone resisting the temptation to move their herds; however, this would mean voluntarily putting themselves at an economic disadvantage compared to those who graze their sheep in the commons.

You should see clear correspondence with the Internet and security culture, among other things.

[a] Term coined by Garrett Hardin, derived from earlier work by William Forster Lloyd.

FIGURE 6.1 Tragedy of the Commons.

Another way our decisions affect others is via *third-party risk*. We might have a brilliant risk management program, but we do not control all the variables of risk. That's because we are consumers of someone else's goods and services. How everyone else manages risk affects us: That is a third-party risk.

Imagine that your company does business with a credit card processor. You share risk with this firm by sharing customer credit card information. It has been reliable and trustworthy for many years. The processor advertises that it complies with payment card standards. Unbeknownst to you, however, it neglects to install a critical security update that attackers quickly exploit to steal your customers' sensitive data. As a result, your company shares in the fallout of the vendor's security incident.

Always keep in mind that our security is affected not only by our actions but by the actions of others. Vendors, employees, and customers can all impact our security posture.

Bug Bounties Eliminate Bugs from the Offensive Market

Santiago Lopez was 19 when he surpassed more than $1 million in bug bounties. He bought two cars and a beach house.[4] Bug hunting is his full-time job, and he has discovered and been paid for reporting

4. www.hackerone.com/press-release/teen-becomes-worlds-first-1-million-bug-bounty-hacker-hackerone

over 1,600 flaws in software programs large and small. Lopez is an extreme case of the productivity of a single individual, but paying people to disclose vulnerabilities responsibly is big business. HackerOne, which orchestrates bug bounty programs for fixing software, has partnered with over 1,200 companies to find over 100,000 bugs and awarded over $100 million. Other companies offer bounties for flaws that might be used offensively. In early 2022, exploit vendor Zerodium was offering up to $2.5 million for exploits defined as "Android Full Chain with Persistence Zero Click" and up to $1 million for zero-click Windows remote code execution bugs.[5]

Most flaws submitted to bug bounty programs are worth much less than a million dollars. Viewed as a pyramid, the number of low-value, easier-to-find bugs is at the bottom, and the rare, sophisticated, high-value flaws are at the top. If anything, the commercialization of hiring poorly trained developers has created *more* vulnerabilities on the scene.

HackerOne is far from the only entity that coordinates bounties on bugs. An unknown number of international brokers, exploit vendors, and governments are interested in profiting financially or otherwise. What's to stop an attacker from selling the information to an exploit vendor and later cashing in a bug bounty? Sometimes ethics and contracts prohibit this behavior, which might be problematic.

There are numerous business models in the exploit market. According to one report, "some gray-market players lease, rent, contract, or license their exploits, so they retain all intellectual property."[6] Even once a vulnerability is sold to an exploit broker, the broker could sell it to multiple buyers at their discretion.

What about laws? It is legal to buy and sell zero-day exploits in the United States. In most cases, the act of *exploiting* a computer with the flaw is the point at which laws are broken. Possession and use are different, and there is a spectrum of policies around discovery. As of 2022, no U.S. laws require the disclosure of vulnerabilities, but in China, all vulnerabilities must be reported to the Chinese government.[7]

Think of it from vendors' perspective: Why should they capitalize a high-assurance software engineering team if they can spend one-tenth that amount on bug bounties? If anything, bug bounty programs might lead some vendors to skimp on assurance, design, and testing.

Bug bounties might help encourage responsible disclosure and more secure software, but experience to date has shown it is incorrect to think that bounties make the exploit market smaller or that they result in fewer flaws being incorporated into software.

Cyber Insurance Causes People to Take Less Risk

Imagine that a startup buys a cyber insurance policy to cover the expenses related to a data breach. It pays $1,500 per year for $1 million in coverage, with a $10,000 deductible. What is the incentive to

5. https://zerodium.com/program.html
6. www.rand.org/content/dam/rand/pubs/research_reports/RR1700/RR1751/RAND_RR1751.pdf
7. https://therecord.media/chinese-government-lays-out-new-vulnerability-disclosure-rules/

maintain reasonable security and prevent a breach, especially if cybersecurity costs more than $10,000? Why not simply gamble that an incident will not happen and pay the deductible if it does?

This is an example of *moral hazard*, where someone is incentivized to accept the risk because that person does not bear the full costs of the risk. It is not new, nor is it unique to cyber. Insurance carriers traditionally deal with moral hazards by setting sufficiently high deductibles and capping maximum payouts. They encourage good behavior by lowering premiums for solid cybersecurity. More and more, they also consider how risky applicants are to insure. Insurance company Chubb, for example, recently asked applicants whether they conduct penetration tests on an annual basis and whether they store sensitive data on web servers.[8] Companies might also refuse to pay claims if they can show that the insured failed to continue to meet the terms of the policy.

In reality, people with cyber insurance transfer risk to a third party. If insurance carriers do not have a way to evaluate the risk of applicants, and many people buy insurance instead of doing good cybersecurity, there is a teetering tower of systemic risk. A widespread cyber attack against many insured victims would be catastrophic to insurers.

Note that risk transfer is a *financial* issue. Risks to reputation cannot be transferred to a third party, nor can operational risks. Insurance might cover some losses, but the intangible aspects of operation might not be set right by any financial compensation.

Cyber insurance today is evolving. Insurers should offer incentives for security practices that reduce the likelihood of a claim in a manner similar to how they incentivize clients to quit smoking in return for lower life insurance premiums. Understanding which investments effectively reduce risk requires more research. (We suggest buying at least one copy of this book for everyone working at a company should qualify the firm for some downward adjustment in premium!)

Fines and Penalties Cause People to Take Less Risk

From the enforcement of safe driving behavior to proper cybersecurity, punishment for noncompliance is used as a deterrent and penalty for undesirable behavior. Fines for HIPAA violations, for instance, range from $100 to $50,000 per violation, depending on the level of negligence and other aggravating and mitigating factors. As of 2022, there was a maximum cap of $1.5 million per year. There are, of course, additional financial costs that are incurred after an incident, including remediation.

In 2018, shipping company UPS paid $33.8 million in fines for parking tickets incurred while delivering packages in New York City.[9] To UPS this wasn't a punishment. "UPS pays for parking tickets that result as a cost of doing business to support the flow of critical commerce," said a spokesperson. Similarly, a research study found that when a daycare began charging a small fee to parents who were late picking up their children, the number of late pickups went *up*.[10] Parents simply saw the fine as a price for longer daycare.

8. www.rand.org/pubs/external_publications/EP67850.html
9. www.freightwaves.com/news/todayspickup/ups-fedex-parking-fines
10. Gneezy, Uri, and Rustichini, Aldo, "A Fine is a Price," *Journal of Legal Studies*, Vol. 29, No. 1 (2000): 1–17.

One might ask why businesses follow the rules if they can afford to simply pay the impacts or penalties as a cost of doing business. According to one analysis, "If it is true that on average, businesses lose 5% of their annual revenue to fraud, and that the cost of a cyber event represents only 0.4% of firm revenues, then one might conclude that these hacks, attacks, and careless behaviors represent a small fraction of the costs that firms face, and therefore only a small portion of the cost of doing business."[11]

Some businesses cannot afford the costs of a fine, which is strong motivation to follow the rules. A $1 million fine might put them out of business. One cancer care provider filed for bankruptcy following a $2.3 million fine to settle potential HIPAA penalties.[12] For companies such as those, files and penalties might be effective in motivating lower cybersecurity risk. But big businesses can afford fines. Numerous researchers have examined how data breaches impact the stock prices of publicly traded companies.[13] Despite evidence that unfavorable events can lower stock prices, companies rarely go out of business. After the 2017 Equifax data breach, that firm's stock took a hit but then recovered despite Equifax paying up to $700 million to settle with the government and victims.[14]

The bottom line is that penalties and fines do not always have the effect regulators and policymakers intend and can lead to a perverse incentive to accept cyber risk.

Attacking Back Would Help Stop Cyber Crime

"The hacked are itching to hack back." That was how a 2014 news article began.[15] Banks and other victims of cybercrime were—and continue to be—tired of their losses and waiting for law enforcement to do something. In the United States, it is likely illegal under the Computer Fraud and Abuse Act for private-sector businesses to *hack back*; that is, a victim may not launch a counterattack against their perpetrator. Many other countries have similar laws.

It is easy to empathize with the frustration of victims who want justice. Some want to recover stolen data. Some want to neutralize the threat. Some simply want retaliation. Compounding the situation, law enforcement does not have the resources to investigate and prosecute every crime, whether ransomware or car theft. Given the overall lack of enough talented people in the field, it might well be the case that the companies have much better (and faster) capabilities than law enforcement, adding to the temptation to take private action.

Attacking back, even if legal, would have significant unintended consequences and risks. As we discuss in Chapters 12, "Malware" and 13, "Digital Forensics and Incident Response," attribution is extremely difficult. What would be the threshold to prove that the hacked-back entity was the true criminal and a

11. Romanosky, Sasha, "Examining the Costs and causes of Cyber Incidents," *Journal of Cybersecurity*, Vol. 2, No. 2 (2016): 121–135.
12. www.paubox.com/blog/hipaa-violations-can-bankrupt-business-learning-21cos-2-3m-fine/
13. Ali, Syed Emad Azhar, et al., "Stock Market Reactions to Favorable and Unfavorable Information Security Events: A Systematic Literature Review," *Computers & Security*, No. 110 (2021).
14. www.ftc.gov/news-events/news/press-releases/2019/07/equifax-pay-575-million-part-settlement-ftc-cfpb-states-related-2017-data-breach
15. www.latimes.com/business/la-fi-hacking-retaliation-20141230-story.html

legitimate target? What are the boundaries of the "property" someone has the right to defend or attack? What laws would apply, and who would enforce them against errors and recklessness? If someone attacks back and accidentally damages an innocent third party, they now might face both financial *and* criminal liability.

Consider when the target of the hack-back is an element of a foreign country. In some cases, attacking it might be the only way to get any sense of retribution.[16] This could backfire, however, and increase the risk of becoming a target of increased levels of attack from that country's intelligence and military services. Suppose that country has an extradition treaty with your country, or you are not careful with your international travel. In that case, you might find yourself arrested and on trial (or worse) in a foreign land. It might also be disrupting a covert intelligence or law enforcement action that you would otherwise wish to support, which is not going to win you any friends in high places.

This also has its tie-in to the cobra effect. If companies and individuals started attacking back, it would prompt adversaries to attack more sites to act as proxies for their primary attacks, thus involving more third parties as victims. Total attacks might well go up!

Innovation Increases Security and Privacy Incidents

This book has described the importance of thinking about cybersecurity as risk management. Vulnerabilities and threats pose a risk to our data and our privacy. Technical and nontechnical mitigations help lower risk. Some people offload risk with insurance.

What about environments where risk is welcome or even encouraged? Startup companies routinely take risks head-on, like developing new code that could have bugs. Academic institutions are similarly innovative environments where openness and collaboration are valued, sometimes over tight cybersecurity controls. This raises the question: Is there a tension between innovation and cybersecurity incidents? Should we expect a certain level of security and privacy incidents in innovative environments?

Similar arguments were made in developing nuclear weapons during the 20th century. The urgency of World War II and the Cold War led to a relentless pressure to innovate, shortcuts were taken, and bad things happened. This included some deaths from radiation exposure and environmental contamination. Scientists working with genetic engineering also sometimes chafe under rules restricting what they can do. We contend that responsible science and engineering are performed with appropriate considerations given to risks and that capitalization of safeguards should be part of the process. After all, the community no longer defends the concept that releasing malware into the Internet is a valid means of "experiment"—if we ever did.

16. See, for instance, www.wired.com/story/north-korea-hacker-internet-outage/

Ethics and Professional Conduct

In our discussion of moral hazard, we described how a person or company might allow an incident or breach because the cost of paying an insurance deductible was cheaper than preventing the breach. This is an economic decision, and not one generally endorsed. We suggest that ethical behavior towards the common good is worthwhile, although it does not always generate a line item in the P&L statement.

All of the major professional organizations for computing and cybersecurity have codes of conduct or ethics. For instance, the Information Systems Security Association (ISSA), (ISC)², Institute of Electrical and Electronics Engineers (IEEE), and ACM all have such codes. We would direct the reader to those, especially the ACM Code of Professional Ethics,[a] which has "Avoid Harm" as a major precept.

---

[a] www.acm.org/code-of-ethics

It is possible that certain positive things we want, such as innovation, might increase risk. Maybe mistakes are even an inevitable consequence. Research is needed to evaluate this claim.

Blaming innovation as the root cause of cyber incidents is facile but incorrect. Many variables in every environment contribute to risk, from the budget to the experience of the workforce. It is difficult to attribute more or fewer cyber attacks to innovation as opposed to those other variables. Plus, over time, innovation might well reduce overall risk.

We should not lose sight of the fact that the primary cause of serious cybersecurity incidents is people acting out of greed or malicious intent. Blame should always go to the perpetrators, first.

Finally, we must consider reverse causality. Imagine that one of your competitors has a major data breach from an unpatched third-party vendor. As a result, you invest heavily into ensuring your systems are patched. Even while your patch status might be better, you might still be more likely to be a victim of a cyber threat simply because of other factors. Clearly, patching did not *increase* your risk. Nevertheless, your business or sector might be statistically more likely to be attacked despite your attention to patching. Reverse causation occurs when a heightened risk of victimization leads people to make cybersecurity changes to reduce that risk, but those changes were either too little or too late.

Further Reading

Barreto, Carlos, and Cárdenas, Alvaro A. "Perverse Incentives in Security Contracts: A Case Study in the Colombian Power Grid," *Annual Workshop on the Economics of Information Security* (WEIS), 2016.

Blum, Dan. *Rational Cybersecurity for Business: The Security Leaders' Guide to Business Alignment.* Apress, 2020.

Freakonomics Radio. "The Cobra Effect," Episode 96, October 11, 2012. https://freakonomics.com/podcast/the-cobra-effect-2/.

Wu, Tim. *The Attention Merchants: The Epic Scramble to Get Inside Our Heads.* Knopf, 2016.

Chapter 7

Problems and Solutions

People do not want to buy a quarter-inch drill. They want a quarter-inch hole!

Theodore Levitt

Computing is about solving problems: How can we efficiently store, process, and receive data? How can we increase the speed of important calculations? How can we store and allow access to cat videos? What is a way to produce better results that customers will pay to get? At its core, cybersecurity is also about solving problems. A user accidentally clicked on a phishing link, our website was the victim of a DDoS attack, or ransomware has infected our core servers. These are problems found in cybersecurity that need solutions. The field is full of solutions created for problems, and new issues emerge daily that need resolution. It's a never-ending cycle: Solve a problem, a new problem crops up, or the old problem finds a way around the solution, and we are back to the beginning.

Cybersecurity is different from mathematics. Once someone finds a solution, the math problem is no longer a problem.[1] Finding the derivative of (most) functions is relatively straightforward. How many apples can I buy with $14 when they are $1 each? That is simple algebra.

Some cybersecurity problems require extra insight or domain knowledge to solve. One example from an oft-used meme is the difficulty of herding cats. Cats are notoriously prone to ignoring direction; however, one key insight can be used to solve the problem: move their food. With some domain knowledge and a can of tuna, the solution to the problem is straightforward!

Cybersecurity is often not straightforward at all. It's a delightful (or vexing) mix of technology and humans that can often have one, many, or no solutions. There are numerous myths and misconceptions about both problems and solutions in this field, and this chapter covers a few.

1. Yes, we know that mathematics sometimes has advanced as more elegant solutions are found, but generally a solution means a problem is finished.

Failure Is Not an Option in Cybersecurity

If we are concerned about security, we do not like to think about being unsuccessful. Failures suggest that something bad has happened, but failures can also be instructive. If we learn from failures, we can avoid them.[2] These can be important lessons. For instance, `telnet` is not a safe protocol for connecting to a remote system. We did not know or appreciate the dangers of unencrypted communications when that protocol was created, but we learned it through trial and error and using it on the Internet. Nor was DNS the first method ever used to map host names to IP addresses; only later did it replace the original solution of using a `hosts.txt` file.[3]

These examples are about building things and illustrate that today's design choices and implementations might be considered unsecure, inefficient, or inappropriate—even failures—in the future. We seldom get it perfect the first time. Naturally, there are starts and stops when building something new. Rome was not built in a day, and when it was constructed, some buildings were fine and some were torn down (or collapsed). It was not a case where a magic wand was waved, and an entire city showed up perfectly constructed from the start; instead, it was a case where the Romans learned as they went along.

In the day-to-day operations of cybersecurity, there will also be adverse events. This is not building something new, but rather dealing with the current situation. For example, our antivirus software did not stop the latest malware, or the user clicked on a link they should not have. Those are adverse events that can cause problems in an organization.

Assigning blame when those things happen is tempting, but blaming someone is not constructive. The better idea is to learn from the experiences and consider them to be *negative results*, not failures. In science, negative results are findings that do not support the hypothesis. For example, we hypothesized that phishing training would lower the number of phishing incidents in the company, but after trying it, the number of incidents did not decrease. This is a negative result because we rejected our hypothesis, but what we learned from trying is a valuable bit of knowledge.[4]

These results seem like failures of the system, but they are not. The system works as designed, but it did not find the problem because cybersecurity is never static. Change is the only constant in cybersecurity. There is always a new attack around the corner. In business, it is often the case that past performance is used to predict future performance. We predict how much this year's budget should be based on last year's. We predict how much money we should make based on the previous year's revenue. Following this same logic, we should theoretically have a chance to predict the next attacks based on previous attacks. Yet, this isn't so.

Recall from the section "We Can Predict Future Threats" in Chapter 3, "Faulty Assumptions and Magical Thinking," that we are bad at predicting future threats. The adversaries are not likely to keep using the same attacks forever. They learn that the current attack is known and will be caught, so they

2. The pessimist would add, "And thus spend our time failing in new ways."
3. https://nap.nationalacademies.org/read/11258/chapter/4
4. Cybersecurity generally does a poor job of documenting and sharing negative results. We almost always see presentations and papers talking about *positive results*. We should also be sharing things we tried that did not work so that others can learn from our attempts.

want to find a new attack that will not be caught. They might reuse their current methods. Then again, they might not. Basing our entire analysis of the future on the current state-of-the-art can keep us from catching the new, nasty attacks.

While it seems like a failure of the system not to catch these new attacks, it is like asking people to forecast the Black Swan event[5] or to predict the creation of the Internet in 1900. It is not possible, except in fiction. Science fiction is terrific for guessing what could happen, but we cannot make decisions based on that. Businesses are based on data and making money, not reading science fiction and making somewhat-uninformed guesses.

In sum, negative results in cybersecurity often tell us that something new and unexpected is here, and it is time to adjust and adapt. We should learn from those results, not consider them failures of the system or incontrovertible proof that the system does not (or will not) work.

Every Problem Has a Solution

Cybersecurity professionals are problem-solvers by nature. We like to take things apart, see how they work, improve them, and solve problems. That mentality can be helpful; however, the complexity and ambiguity of cybersecurity mean that not every situation has a complete solution or mitigation. For example, antivirus software might catch only 50% of malware; it is still helpful, and we need it, but it is not the complete solution to the malware threat.

Let's take a step back and consider a simple application. The software developers of this application knew what they wanted it to do when they created it, the documentation authors knew what they believed it was supposed to do when they wrote the documentation, and the users knew what they wanted it to do when they used it. (We will make no claims that all three groups agree.)

Does that mean we know all possible behaviors of the program? Collectively, the software developers, the technical writers, and the users should know everything the software will do. In some limited circumstances, we might. If the software was developed using rigorous formal methods, exhaustively tested, and run only with libraries and an operating system developed using the same techniques, then we can have high confidence about how the program behaves. Unless something in the hardware develops an error, or less trusted software is loaded into the system, or the operator makes an error, or. . . . Little software is developed with such formal methods. Even then, the software is subject to human error. For other software that is not as carefully constrained, we cannot, in the general case, determine what it will do, especially if it was created by someone else and given to us. See the aside "Cybersecurity and the Halting Problem."

Now consider malware. Malware is defined by its behavior. It does something that is against the security policy. If we cannot determine all the possible actions of a computer program, how can we

5. See the discussion on "Ignorance of Black Swans" in Chapter 4.

know if the activities of any random program, possibly including malware, will be harmful? Because of this, there is no way to definitively identify all malware without additional knowledge.[6]

It's a similar problem for finding all the vulnerabilities in a program. Vulnerabilities arise when the software behaves in a way that allows someone to exploit that behavior contrary to policy. That word *behave* is there again. In general, we cannot enumerate every behavior for all input, so there is no way to list all the possible vulnerabilities in arbitrary software programmatically.

These two problems have no complete solutions. We would like to think that we can take a piece of software, throw it in a black box, and have a red light illuminate if it is malware. Or that we could make a black box that would take that piece of software and print out every vulnerability found in it. Either of those would solve countless problems. Those black boxes do not exist and cannot exist, in general. (Again, see the aside, "Cybersecurity and the Halting Problem.") There are no simple solutions to the difficult problems of "Is this malware?" or "What vulnerability does this software have?" outside of some narrowly defined circumstances. We get approximations of solutions to these problems, but there is no exact solution. We are always going to miss things.

Cybersecurity and the Halting Problem

There is a famous problem in computing called "The Halting Problem." It started with a question, "For an arbitrary program and input, can a computer determine if the program will complete or will continue running forever?"

This is an example of an *undecidable problem* for which there is no algorithm that will always give a correct true or false decision for every input value. The proofs imply that it is impossible to determine by examination if *any* arbitrary program will exhibit a particular behavior if allowed to execute indefinitely.[a] We might be able to run a particular program against all inputs, but in general, we do not have the time or resources to execute our programs indefinitely. It's a bit of a brain-bender to think about.

Why does this theory of computing matter to everyday applied cybersecurity? Malware detection is a noteworthy example, as we discussed previously. We should appreciate that theory shows we can never build a malware detection system to perfectly label an arbitrary file. Still, malware detection isn't hopeless, and we can and should employ cybersecurity solutions that are as effective as possible in real life, even if they aren't perfect. Theory is an essential grounding in cybersecurity, and so, too is the practical reality of our implementations.

a The first formal proof of this for computer viruses was by Fred Cohen in "Computer Viruses: Theory and Experiments," *Computers & Security,* Vol. 6 (1987): 22–35.

6. We are glossing over some details here, but this is the basic idea. Also, note that if we do not have a security policy, there is nothing against which to evaluate the behavior.

Let's look at another problem. Is it possible to enumerate every attack that was tried against our system? Again, the answer is "No." We might have the best-engineered defense solution available that will capture and log every possible attack, but we will still miss things. We will miss them and not even be aware that we missed them. The system can catch only things it knows about, but if a brand-new attack is created, we will not know about it. We might get lucky and catch traces, but we will not see everything. In addition, if there is a successful attack against our logging system, any trace of it might have been removed before we perform our review! Sometimes we miss unsuccessful attacks, but that does not sound so scary, right? It did not work; yay, who cares if we missed it? But that highlights holes in our logging. We did not see the attackers try, but what if they tried something slightly different? We might miss that successful attempt as well.

We Can Solve All Our Problems with Big Data

At the core of cybersecurity is data. The chief function and design of the Internet is to move data around. We might call it pictures, movies, music, or text, but at its heart, it is all data that moves from computer to computer. Cybersecurity studies how this data is misused and altered, by malware, vulnerabilities, malicious websites, or any other badness. As a result, we should be able to solve all our security problems by throwing data at them.

Believing that we can solve all our problems with data is wishful thinking with a side of hope. It also is the (false) claim made by people pushing machine learning and AI solutions.[7]

After 9/11, investigators discovered that there was information about the hijackers in the myriad of information collected by various government departments.[8] It was sometimes known in a narrowly constrained system and sometimes lost in the noise, but in both cases, it failed to attract the attention of analysts. Likewise, after a cybersecurity incident, we often find traces of evidence we should have paid attention to in the logs or other data collections but we missed it for some reason. For example, in one case, investigators found that a file was world-writable when it should not have been, and that allowed the attacker access.[9] The data existed, but nobody noticed or acted until it was too late.

There is so much potential cybersecurity data available at our disposal. Even a small organization can create a terabyte of network traffic daily, assuming everything is captured. Any method designed to look for a tiny amount of maliciousness will find more false positives than not.[10] That's assuming we are collecting the correct data, or that we can even collect the data we need while rejecting noise.

Context is also often missing from the data we collect. Suppose we suspect that a particular IP address is the origin of an attack. The data suggests that "Attacks came from here." Does that mean that the IP address points to only the system it originated from? Unfortunately, no. Because of NATs and VPNs, there could be one computer at that IP address—or thousands. It's also possible that a computer at the IP address is being used as a proxy relay. We simply do not know.

7. Cf. footnote 1 in Chapter 4.
8. https://govinfo.library.unt.edu/911/report/911Report_Exec.htm
9. https://xmcyber.com/blog/did-you-just-create-a-paradise-for-hackers/
10. See "Base Rate Fallacy" in Chapter 4 for why that is true.

FIGURE 7.1 We can solve all problems with data. Moar data!

We do not mean to suggest that data is useless, only to highlight that more and more data alone cannot solve all problems. In recent history, we have labeled these large collections as *big data*. Big data is often characterized by V-letter words, such as volume, velocity, variety, and veracity. Data with these attributes are not inherently good or bad; however, as we have discussed, the misconception persists among some data scientists that more data is the answer to all problems.

Cybersecurity professionals want to find the dangerous items. We want to stop the attackers, but the amount of data can be overwhelming and incomplete. Think carefully about what big data can tell us and where there are limitations and challenges.

There Is One, and Only One, Correct Solution

The Perl programming language has a motto: "There is more than one way to do it," or "TIMTOWTDI," pronounced "Tim Toady." The point of the motto is that the language was designed to be flexible, not to assign one, and only one, solution that works.

Another way to put it is "If it is stupid, and it works, it is not that stupid." We would like to design sleek and streamlined solutions, but sometimes packing crates and duct tape are sufficient; there is something oddly appealing about a Rube Goldberg piecemeal solution for a simple task.[11]

Engineers sometimes cannot help themselves. They want to solve a problem, and they will solve it in a way that makes sense to them. That means every problem might have multiple solutions, but not every solution is a perfect fit for *your* version of the problem.

Consider managing patches for software. Managing software patches to a major system for a hospital is much different than managing them for an ISP. For a hospital, we need to consider things such as "Will doing this upgrade mean we have to take down a system we need for patient support for a minimum of 24 hours?" For an ISP, we are likely concerned with whether the update will disconnect our connected customers. An update done at the wrong time to the wrong system can potentially cause trouble. The hospital wants to keep people alive, and the ISP wants to keep connections alive. Two different goals with the same result: Vulnerable software gets patched, but maybe not immediately.

It's not like finding a way through a maze. There is a beginning, and an end, and we can usually use the right-hand rule to find our way out.[12] Cybersecurity is more like a maze with 10 entrances, 12 exits, and many paths. The goal is to start at some entrance and make it to some exit in one piece. The goal is not to find the one, and only one, way through it because there might not be only one—if one even exists. Oh, and did we mention the Minotaur living in the maze?

Flexibility is required in cybersecurity. Holding on to the idea that *there is a correct solution out there and only one will fit* is an excellent way to either spend too much money, waste time, or create an inflexible solution that might not work well.

---

11. Donald Knuth stated, "The root of all evil is premature optimization." While we suspect that is not true of every evil, it does apply to a great deal of computing. Spending valuable time and effort to optimize a solution used only a few times while other important tasks are pending should be avoided.

12. The right-hand rule says that when you enter a maze, put your right hand on the wall and then continue to follow the right wall, which will eventually lead you to the exit. We can also use the left-hand rule, but not both together.

Everyone Should Solve a Given Cybersecurity Problem in the Same Way

The Coordinated Vulnerability Disclosure (CVD) process manages the disclosure of vulnerabilities, particularly faults (bugs), that apply to products from multiple vendors. The CVE for the Heartbleed vulnerability (CVE-2014-0160), for instance, lists nine different companies with products known to be vulnerable to the bug. Those nine were certainly not the complete list of affected products, but it was a significant subset. The list covered various vendors, from established companies to open source projects.

The point is that each of those vendors had a different method for handling vulnerabilities. Large companies generally have a different process than open source projects An open source project relies on volunteers for the most part. A large company has software developers available to develop patches, while a small company might have to hire a contractor or move someone from another project.

They all have a different process for fixing a vulnerability, which means they all have a different time frame to make a patch available. Assuming that "Everyone can get it done within 5 days!" is wrong. It's still incorrect if we change 5 to 7 or even to 45. The CVD process attempts to manage this discrepancy, but it is still consistent with the proverbial saying of "Different strokes for different folks."

Every organization has its particular requirements and needs. For an extreme example, a hospital has different requirements than a home. The software that will protect a home user's laptop is quite different from protecting, for example, a Magnetic Resonance Imaging (MRI) machine. A laptop is easily updated, while an MRI system is not. Any security policy needs to accommodate the special differences of the application environment.

Anecdotes Are Good Leads for Cybersecurity Solutions

Our personal experiences and first-hand knowledge can be trustworthy sources of facts. Have you tried a new feature for automatically detecting misconfigurations and found it helpful? Great! Also valuable is knowledge, which is the careful, thorough, and thoughtful evaluation of facts by multiple people. The body of scientific knowledge is an example. Overall, this evidence is a good source when evaluating how to address a cybersecurity challenge.

Anecdotal evidence is based on someone's stories and observations. It's a personal account without independent and objective data to back it up. If a colleague reports that kicking the computer always fixes it, should that anecdote convince us to do it, too?

Some anecdotes are hearsay, simply repeated based on a story the person heard. But, as we know from the game of telephone, reports can be misheard, misunderstood, or changed in the retelling. There is potential danger in phrases like "My friend Shawn says. . . " or "I know a case where. . . " These experiences might not be average. Anecdotes are more likely to be repeated if they are sensational or unusual. This is how myths get started.

For many years, there was a widely held belief among cybersecurity professionals about lost USB flash drives. The anecdote went that users were susceptible to picking up and plugging in flash drives that they found lying in parking lots and that such behavior would cause them to be victims of cyber attacks. This story lacked evidence, but in 2016 a team of researchers took on the myth and confirmed in a controlled experiment that users would fall for this type of attack.[13] The story is no longer an anecdote.

The key to avoiding the myth that anecdotes are reliable is to have a healthy skepticism and evaluate whether the story can be validated. In particular, be wary of single examples that might be atypical of the average case. Investigate citations and documentation. If necessary, conduct your own trials to verify or refute what you hear.

Detecting More "Bad Stuff" Means the New Thing Is an Improvement

Imagine that you work at a tech startup. You are working on an exciting new product that is starting to get a lot of press attention. Because your company is growing, you have upgraded from free desktop security software to cutting-edge defenses on everyone's machine to ensure your intellectual property is well protected. Soon after, you get a flood of alerts about suspicious activity. Does that mean the new system uses a better approach to finding bad things than the old one? Not necessarily. Your company was in the news (for a good reason), and attackers might have read that and thought, "Hey, new target! Let's see how hard it is to get in" and deployed their tricks. It's not necessarily an incredible jump forward in technology simply because you see more alerts; it might only be a factor of publicity. Attackers read news articles, too.

This was an unfortunate side effect of the COVID-19 pandemic. As companies and individuals began to work from home, the uptick in video conferencing was swift and significant. In a message to users, the CEO of Zoom reported that the average number of daily meeting participants had exploded from 10 million to 200 million![14] It is little surprise that the number of teleconferencing attacks and hijackings increased at the same time.[15]

More attacks detected does not mean a novel detection method was suddenly created. Their increase could be because of publicity and popularity, as in the case of Zoom. It could be that the attackers have a new tool in their toolbox and are trying it out on everyone. Any number of reasons could be at play.

Another example of this myth is seen with malware. Malware researchers are regularly creating new methods to detect malware efficiently, and many like to declare that their new method is the best and the most novel because it finds the most malware. Possibly, it is; however, as we have noted elsewhere,

---

13. Tischer, Matthew, et al., "Users Really Do Plug in USB Drives They Find," *IEEE Symposium on Security and Privacy*, IEEE, 2016.
14. https://blog.zoom.us/a-message-to-our-users/
15. www.fbi.gov/contact-us/field-offices/boston/news/press-releases/fbi-warns-of-teleconferencing-and-online-classroom-hijacking-during-covid-19-pandemic

a simple malware detector that finds the most malware is one that declares *every* piece of software it examines to be malware. Therefore, it finds more malware than anyone else! It also mislabels most things, but no one said that information was important to report (they should and often do not). This is not a novel malware detector, though. We could call it novel because it finds more but is not. Suppose our new system suddenly finds a lot of malware where the previous system did not. That does not necessarily mean the new system is an incredibly novel way of examining software. It could mean that our company made the news and malware attackers decided, "Hey, that looks like a nice target!" or "They are in the news, and so they must have money. Show me the money!" Or it might be that an older attack method has been rediscovered by attackers who are unfamiliar with history and are trying it against our system.

That issue is not one confined to the attackers, either. Far too often, defenders will reinvent some defensive technique that they think is new because they are unfamiliar with the field's history. They will make a big deal about their "new" method. It might increase the efficacy of their existing systems by adding some new features. That does not mean the method is new and novel. It also does not mean the defenders have invented something valuable. Experts in the field have many stories of "new, military-grade, proprietary, unbreakable" cryptography systems that employed ideas hundreds of years old—and broken. (See also our discussion of Færie Dust in Chapter 1, "What Is Cybersecurity?")

Every Security Process Should Be Automated

Some fast-food chains are adopting automation in their stores. Instead of talking to a cashier to place their order, customers stand at a kiosk. Using a touch screen, they pick out the food, pay for it, then wait for their number to be called; no human interaction is involved until the customer picks up their meal.

There is a trend in cybersecurity toward ruthless automation. It's part of a drive for ever-better productivity and efficiency. The thinking is that fewer people involved means lower cost, fewer errors, faster response, and fewer bad guys. We will have AI systems trained on petabytes of intrusion data that can flag each problem automatically, say advocates. Imagine an entire security defense as a touch screen the user can customize for the network. Then the user can sit back and play games until it's time to pick up the report on the attempt to attack the network. Oh, and it will work perfectly and without error, right?

Let's talk in terms of the fast-food restaurant for a moment. We can only order what's on the menu at these kiosks. We cannot suddenly decide we want a strawberry-rhubarb milkshake and have it magically appear if it is not on the menu. It will not work. We can only get the chocolate or vanilla milkshake, not the other flavor.

Automation is suited to routine problems but it is not a good fit for novel situations. To a programmer, this is a simple algorithm: If Event A happens, then do Action B.[16] The same holds if we suddenly had a magic first-level cybersecurity screen. It would not know about new attacks, only the ones that existed when it was created. If a new attack took advantage of a new vulnerability in our web browser, our system would not know how to block it because it would not know it existed. It could not recognize the attack unless it was updated.

This is still true if the magic first-level cybersecurity screen uses ML. ML is not a panacea—what it learns is based on current knowledge. If a brand-new attack that is not like the others shows up, an ML-based system will not automatically recognize and learn it. It cannot. It's similar to learning algebra and expecting that, based on that, we can suddenly understand differential calculus! They are related in that they are both math. And yes, differential calculus uses some algebra, but they are worlds apart in terms of complexity and knowledge.

Ransomware first appeared in 1989, but it was not until Bitcoin was invented in 2008 that it became a thing.[17] The ransoms could no longer be easily traced, so launching ransomware attacks without getting caught was suddenly feasible. In 2012, 30,000 different samples of ransomware were found. In 2021, it was estimated there was a new ransomware victim every 11 seconds.

Now imagine a magic first-level cybersecurity screen in 2009. It might recognize Bitcoin, but ransomware was not common enough to be part of its knowledge.[18] Ransomware is a shift in attack; rather than stealing data, suddenly, the data is still there but unusable.

A person can say, "That's funny. . . ," but a computer cannot.[19] The computer cannot see the shift and think, "That is weird and should be investigated further," but a human can. A person can be completely flummoxed by the new attack but still handle it. A magic first-level cybersecurity ML screen will either ignore it or get confused, depending on how the code was written.

Lastly, there is an opportunity cost to creating and maintaining automation. The upfront cost might save time and money in the long term, but this is not always true. Researchers, for instance, have explored the costs and value of automated software testing compared with manual testing.[20] In particular, they propose shifting the perspective from minimizing cost to maximizing value. This is an important insight as a common motivation for automation is cost saving.

Overall, this is a partial myth. That is, it depends on context. Automation is never a complete solution, however.

---

16. This is extremely common in computer science. It also spawned a commercial company named *IFTTT* (If This Then That), where users can automate actions based on triggers, such as the weather, an email, or their location.
17. For a deep dive on ransomware, see *Ransomware: Defending Against Digital Extortion* by Allan Liska and Timothy Gallo (O'Reilly, 2016).
18. By recognition, we mean part of its training set. ML is trained on data, and there was not enough in 2009 to train it on ransomware.
19. "The most exciting phrase to hear in science, the one that heralds new discoveries, is not 'Eureka' but 'That's funny. . . ' " (Isaac Asimov)
20. Ramler, Rudolf, and Wolfmaier, Klaus, "Economic Perspectives in Test Automation: Balancing Automated and Manual Testing with Opportunity Cost," *Proceedings of the 2006 International Workshop on Automation of Software Test.*

Professional Certifications Are Useless

We know that people like to use labels to organize their view of the world. Sometimes the labels are simply for grouping—those fruits are red, and these are blue. Other times, the labels are used to rank or order items in some way, such as blanco, reposado, and añejo for tequila. In this way, we signal others to help them make informed choices. Other kinds of signals might be something like having an Underwriters' Laboratory seal, an award from J.D. Power, or a degree from Purdue University, all to signal a high level of quality.

Computing, and especially cybersecurity, is a relatively new field—the knowledge required to form a coherent body of study culminated in formal degree programs only recently. The first formal degree-granting program in computer science was started in October 1962 at (surprise) Purdue,[21] and the first cybersecurity degree was initiated in 2000 at. . . wait for it. . . Purdue University. Compared to chemistry, psychology, and mathematics, these are new fields! Cybersecurity, as an area of formal study, is less than a human generation old (a human generation generally being viewed as 30 years).

With a strong need for personnel to work in these increasingly complex areas, employers unfamiliar with the composition of the field look for signals indicating knowledge, mastery, and excellence. Traditionally, degrees from accredited colleges and universities have been one way of doing this, with academic awards and references adding to the signal strength. Another mechanism for signaling is professional certification, where someone is certified by a recognized body as having some level of experience and mastery. A third is a work history in the field at a known employer. There are other signals, too.

There are problems with these signals, though. Not every academic program is rigorous or covers all the material some employers expect. Not all certification programs are rigorous, either, with some having a reputation for certifying nearly everyone who pays the fee. When an employer sets hurdles for people to be employed based solely on one of these degrees or certifications, qualified individuals may be excluded. It also makes it difficult for some potentially qualified individuals to get a start and build their experience, especially those who cannot afford the fees for the classes and exams despite having the requisite skills and knowledge.

What follows are several myths/misconceptions about employee qualifications.

To Work in Cybersecurity Does (Not) Require a College Degree in Computing

Not every organization has or even needs a staff of cybersecurity professionals. Others cannot afford experienced security employees even if they wanted them. Our relatives certainly do not pay us for our tech support, despite their desperate calls, and sometimes they get what they pay for. But for those in the position to hire cybersecurity talent, knowing who to select is a thorny issue. What knowledge or skills are required, and how does one know if an applicant or contractor has them?

21. www.cs.purdue.edu/history/.

One study analyzed the required and desired qualifications for 11,938 entry-level cybersecurity jobs. Most (60%) required a college degree in a related field. A full 29% required certification of some kind. Degrees and certificates are supposed to give employers confidence about the level of knowledge among applicants who, at a minimum, passed a test and paid their bills. For many, they are a personal accomplishment and a source of pride.

This is a dual-edged myth. Some people believe a college degree is necessary to succeed in cybersecurity (and computing in general). Others believe it is unnecessary and might even "get in the way." Both of these positions, if believed exclusively, are myths.

As we continue to note throughout the book, people are different. People have different outlooks, strengths, weaknesses, and styles of working. This is one of the reasons having a diverse team is so valuable. When facing problems—especially gnarly new problems—having multiple points of view and skills is beneficial.

It is also the case that there are a variety of cybersecurity roles, from reverse-engineering to law and policy. The current National Initiative for Cybersecurity Education (NICE) framework from NIST[22] outlines 33 specializations in seven general areas, and it can be argued that it is not complete!

Some cybersecurity roles require deep technical expertise in one or more areas. Some of these areas require college study or a college degree. Others might not *require* a degree, but having obtained a degree in an accredited program might result in a better range of knowledge and skills. Some might not need a degree but require in-depth self-study and practice that might or might not be something a particular individual can achieve.

For example, someone who decides to practice cybersecurity law will generally need an undergraduate degree and J.D. and will need to pass one or more bar exams. Someone who teaches cybersecurity at a Tier 1 university will require a Ph.D. or equivalent. In contrast, someone who is going to be doing reverse-engineering or work in a SOC might well be able to master the skills independently with no college degree.

In general, a *good* college program in a major related to one's career path will not only provide general knowledge but also strengthen ancillary skills such as technical writing and public speaking. The degree should also provide practice in solving problems, working in teams, and foundational concepts. Depending on the type of degree and program, it might emphasize hands-on use of current tools (e.g., community colleges and polytechnic programs), fundamental concepts and theory (e.g., university programs in computer science), or a mix.

As we previously noted, the first cybersecurity degree was created in 2000 at the graduate level. There are not enough formal cybersecurity programs (as of 2022) to require a degree with cybersecurity as the major without unnecessarily excluding potentially qualified personnel. In the coming years, this might change as cybersecurity programs at the undergraduate level become more common. For instance, we expect an increasing number of undergraduate programs structured according to the Cybersecurity

22. www.nist.gov/itl/applied-cybersecurity/nice/nice-framework-resource-center/workforce-framework-cybersecurity-nice

Curriculum Guidelines[23] from ACM, IEEE, AIS, and IFIP TC-11. There are also highly talented technical staff with no formal degrees. Nowadays, a growing number of "nontraditional" outlets are available where people might learn and grow cyber skills. Capture-the-flag competitions, open source software contributions, and hackathons require participants to demonstrate some skills and initiative, which might or might not be good indicators of success in a particular position. The opportunity to work in cybersecurity need not be limited to people with the means to obtain a high-priced education. Someone immersed in self-study, perhaps including military training or industry internships, with significant motivation and talent, might also have a deep skillset. The skills such individuals bring might be more profound than those of someone with a college degree, although they might also be less broad. For some current positions, this might be more desirable than a degree.

Most current college curricula related to cybersecurity focus on computer science, computer engineering, or information systems. Some cybersecurity coverage is superficial because there are not enough trained experts to teach, and few vendors are willing to provide tools affordably for instructional use. Other programs have been in operation for decades, are taught and advised by industry leaders, and produce some of the best in the field. As with many academic programs, the rigor and coverage vary and depend on the available resources (including faculty).

We expect the situation to change as time goes on. Not too long ago, someone could become a lawyer by shadowing a practicing attorney and reading law books. Someone could become a doctor by shadowing a doctor and reading medical literature. That is no longer the case. We think the trend might well be that having a degree will differentiate between a hobbyist and a professional in cybersecurity, although that is still some years away. It is the trend of every major profession, though, from law enforcement to medicine to even some higher-end auto mechanics.

This can go too far. The practice of overly narrowing the qualifications for a cybersecurity job is known as *gatekeeping*. The excessive requirements might take the form of years of experience or certifications that are unrealistic and unnecessary for the role. This exclusivity prevents people from getting jobs that would be a good fit, especially early in their careers. Furthermore, it tends to exclude candidates who could bring a diversity of thought and experience—something that is highly valuable when dealing with people and new issues. Having a highly homogeneous, senior workforce might seem like a good idea, but it will likely lead to groupthink and lockstep errors in many environments. In sum, when seeking someone for a position in cybersecurity, carefully evaluate what an applicant can do, what kind of willingness there is to learn, and the job's complexity. Do not require a degree unless one is really needed—that might be excluding someone ideal. Also, do not assume that a college degree in an apparently unrelated subject (e.g., psychology or music theory) is not useful, as those students have undoubtedly acquired valuable skills and worked with computers, too. Finally, do not assume that a college degree in a related area is necessarily useful unless you know the program. Even some well-known schools offer iffy degrees; remember, too, that 50% of the students in every program graduate in the bottom half of their class!

Thus, we conclude that the myth of needing a degree is only partly true.

23. http://cybered.acm.org

About That Resume

We would not be security people if we did not also mention that sometimes applicants misrepresent their experience and qualifications—or make them up entirely.

We know of one case where someone listed former positions as "Data entry and customer relations" and "Troubleshooting and patch management." These looked good until a reference check revealed them to be positions operating a cash register at a fast-food restaurant and as a mechanic at a tire store. Those were not automatically disqualifying, although the hiring manager felt it was not appropriately truthful. (As we recall, he did not get the job as a SOC analyst but was hired into a position in marketing.)

In another case, someone was applying for a senior executive position. He had a string of prior senior positions, an MBA from a major university, and a set of relevant skills; however, he had a three-year gap in employment that he explained as "time off to study and reflect on my experiences." Self-aware and experienced—good hire, right? Well, except those three years were spent in federal detention for a fraud conviction. Oops!

Currently, North Koreans with fake credentials are seeking remote work positions with major U.S. companies, particularly cryptocurrency and cybersecurity firms. Hiring them can result in significant legal penalties; if that connection is not discovered, what they might do from a position of a trusted insider could be far worse.

Always verify references and claimed qualifications for anyone hired into a position of trust!

Cybersecurity Certifications Are (Not) Valuable

This pair of myths is related to the previous ones about degrees. We see debates in various fora about the value of different professional certifications. Are they worth the money? Do they test for something worthwhile? We might have candidates with alphabet soup after their names on resumes, but what are those, really?

Some certifications attest to basic knowledge for junior or new entries to the field. In that regard, they are valuable and help differentiate individuals. For some certificates, the person needs to read in depth in the area and possibly master some hands-on skills. Unfortunately, there are also some certifications that are given to the top 110% of those who pay the fee. Not all certificates are alike, and not all attest to worthwhile skills.

It is also the case that people with more experience in the field, with proven expertise, probably do not benefit as much from some certifications. Instead, those people should be evaluated by their records and recommendations, not by the set of letters after their names in their resumes. There may be some value, however, in senior people maintaining some certifications because that indicates continuing education and involvement in the field.

Some certifications do not match some job specializations (see our previous discussion about degrees). An SSCP, IAPP, or CISM certification will not provide much context for someone seeking a position as a reverse malware engineer, for example. Some specializations do not have a corresponding certificate (yet) worth having; some commercial concerns might offer certifications, but they are more about making money for the instructors than enhancing the students' skills.

When filling a position, think carefully about what certification means.[24] Research the detailed requirements for any certification and whether it really will serve a purpose to require it. One thought exercise: If the certification is that important, is the organization willing to subsidize an otherwise-qualified hire to get it? It's the same reason many employers will subsidize a graduate degree for good employees rather than require it at the outset. If there is no interest in helping an otherwise-qualified employee get the certification, perhaps the certificate is unnecessary.

Continuing education cannot be overlooked in a field where technology and threats change continually. A hiring manager is interviewing someone who got a relevant degree or certification a decade ago. Great, are they still current with the field? For example, a vulnerability researcher who was great 10 years ago but does not know now about how speculative execution attacks such as Spectre and Meltdown work has not kept up with the field. Many certifications require ongoing education and thus attest to at least some level of current knowledge. Even people without certifications benefit from improving their skills—as do the organizations for which they work. One study[25] found that more than half of personnel surveyed indicated they considered changing jobs because of lack of opportunity to improve their skills. Thus, there are both direct and indirect benefits from continuing education.

For practitioners in the field, certifications might have value to show seniority, the scope of knowledge, or when seeking new employment. We also suggest that *appropriate* certifications help add to the image of professionalism of the field and help support organizations that are seeking to build standards. Senior members with certificates and designations serve as role models and examples for junior people in the area. The role of certifications should not be to pay a fee and pass a test. Instead, it should designate competence and professionalism.

Similarly, the same is true for advanced member grades in nonprofit organizations such as ACM (senior member, distinguished member, fellow) and ISSA (senior member, fellow, and distinguished fellow). Participating in these organizations brings value by advancing the profession, recognizing excellence, and promoting shared values, whether one continues to hold a certification. Recognizing the senior achievers is a way to represent the field to those outside it and have those advanced members serve as role models for junior members.

As a myth, we suggest certifications have value for some, but not all, so it is partially true.

There Is a Shortage of Cybersecurity Talent

There are around 65,000 new college graduates with computer science degrees yearly in the United States. The numbers in China and India are substantially higher, approximately 185,000 and 215,000,

24. American National Standards Institute (ANSI) has a standard process for certifications: ANSI ISO/IEC Standard 17024. This is also an International Standards Organization (ISO) standard. Substantive certifications meet this standard.
25. https://securityboulevard.com/2022/08/upskilling-is-critical-to-closing-cybersecurity-skills-gaps/

respectively.[26] Only a tiny fraction of these graduates go into cybersecurity, although graduates with other majors—and non-graduates—also go into cybersecurity. There is a reasonable supply. Yet, cyber incidents continue, and many organizations would love to hire more people.

Most businesses are looking for experienced cybersecurity professionals. "Instead of hiring for potential, we are demanding people have years of experience working in security when they can't get a foot in the door," says CISO Helen Patton.[27] The result is that there might be too few people with experience, even though those newer to the field could also lighten the load.

It's a chicken and egg problem. If we only hire experienced cybersecurity professionals, how do we create experienced cybersecurity professionals?

We have heard some executives say they do not want to hire people with no experience and then train them because they will then seek jobs elsewhere. We suggest that in such cases, perhaps they should be asking what they are doing to retain qualified personnel rather than have them leave. We have heard of some companies that bring in new personnel, train them well, and then give them benefits and responsibilities commensurate with their new skills. Not only do many of them stay, but they also tend to excel.

If we want to attract talent, two of the characteristics of successful cyber practitioners are curiosity and competitiveness. This population needs advancement and challenging problems (but not to the point of overload) to stay satisfied. There will always be money-chasers, but how much more retention could be achieved if we appreciated the other facets of people who excel in this line of work?

Related to this is the issue of how we train computing personnel more generally. Too often, we teach people how to write computer code and operate computers, but we fail to teach them basic security and privacy. Fundamentally, the problem is they are taught how to make things *work* but not how to *work safely*. We then worry about producing cybersecurity specialists to clean up after them. To use a variation of one of our (Spafford's) analogies from several years ago: Instead of worrying about how to produce more firefighters, perhaps we should put some effort into reducing the construction of buildings from gasoline-soaked balsa wood.

There Is a Disconnect Between Study and Practice

If we talk to enough people in different venues, a theme might well pop up: People in academia have no idea what the "real world" is like, while practitioners are ignorant of the deeper issues in the field. This is reinforced through various misconceptions, such as these:

- There are practitioner conferences ("cons") and academic conferences, with minuscule overlap of participants.
- There are refereed journals that discuss theory and systems that will never be used in practice.

26. Loyalka, Prashant, Liu, Ou Lydia, Li, Guirong, Chirikov, Igor, Kardanova, Elena, Gu, Lin, et al., "Computer Science Skills Across China, India, Russia, and the United States," *Proceedings of the National Academy of Sciences*, Vol. 116, No. 14 (2019): 6732–6736.
27. https://hpatton.medium.com/once-upon-a-time-in-security-a51fc933d98c

- Prestigious awards in the field (e.g., the ACM A.M. Turing Award) go only to professors and scientists who publish in those scholarly journals.
- Certifications such as CISM, SSCP, and Security+ do not count for anything in academia.
- "Have you ever talked with one of *them*? They have no clue about the big news *we* just heard about!"

As with any generalization, there is some truth to these statements, but they are not always or universally true:

- Some researchers attend (and speak at) cons,[28] and there are academic events that welcome (and feature) nonacademics.[29]
- A number of the "academic" journals regularly publish items about current events and practice, and some professional organizations (e.g., ACM, ISSA) have journals and magazines primarily about practice. One example is ACM's *Digital Threats: Research and Practice*.
- Prestigious awards (e.g., Fellow of ACM or ISSA, the ISACA Joseph J. Wasserman Award) have been given to both researchers and practitioners.[30]
- Some academic programs do evaluate certifications as part of the admissions process, and some encourage students to sit for certifications after graduation.
- There is definitely awareness and cross-participation, especially on social media.

The reality is that research does contribute to practical solutions. Researchers at Google Research and Microsoft Research not only sit with their respective product and production teams, but the researchers and practitioners also collaborate and field new features. Sometimes, it is difficult to see how a basic research study ended up changing the way to do cybersecurity in practice, but the thread is there. Researchers often have to explain why their work matters to get funding or approval. One of the widely used Heilmeier questions for the proposed research is "Who cares? If you are successful, what difference will it make?"[31]

It is also the case that many—if not most—technologies in computing have come from basic research labs.[32] For instance, the research that led to cloud computing started in the 1960s. Sometimes, it takes years to get from those labs to practice, but some of today's blue sky research will eventually impact practice. We should all recognize that continuum.

There is a gap, however. Many practitioners do not know the history of the field and do not appreciate the value of advanced study and research; that often leads to a lack of awareness of what is already known. Many academics do not understand the real problems—and, more importantly, the

28. The three authors of this book have done so.
29. One example is an ongoing set of talks by members of the full range of the community, archived at https://ceri.as/secsem.
30. The members of ACM self-describe as "researcher" and "practitioner" in almost equal numbers. www.acm.org/binaries/content/ assets/about/annual-reports/acmarfy21.pdf
31. www.darpa.mil/work-with-us/heilmeier-catechism
32. Cf. www.nationalacademies.org/our-work/depicting-innovation-in-information-technology.

true *scale* of the issues—faced in practice because it is outside their personal experience. A great deal of this disconnect comes from the relative youth of the field: We need more experience and mixing. The problem is exacerbated by academic institutions' inability to afford (and thus present to students and use in research) current, common technologies. Commercial and government organizations are reluctant to share data and logs with academia and research because of disclosure concerns. Therefore, experiments and teaching need to be performed with made-up, often trivial, data sets.

So, it is a myth that there is a vast divide, but there are some disconnects. The best way to bridge this is to recognize value across the spectrum of experience and practice. Do not practice gatekeeping. Do not think that labels capture the totality of someone's knowledge and potential. And perhaps we should broaden our study of material in the field. (We suggest encouraging others to read this book is an excellent example of how to do that!)

Further Reading

Doerr, John. *Measure What Matters: How Google, Bono, and the Gates Foundation Rock the World with OKRs*. Penguin, 2018.

Kruchten, Philippe, Nord, Robert, and Ozkaya, Ipek. *Managing Technical Debt: Reducing Friction in Software Development*. Addison-Wesley, 2019.

Miller, Alyssa. *Cybersecurity Career Guide*. Manning, 2022.

O'Neil, Cathy. *Weapons of Math Destruction: How Big Data Increases Inequality and Threatens Democracy*. Broadway Books, 2016.

Patton, Helen E. *Navigating the Cybersecurity Career Path*. Wiley, 2021.

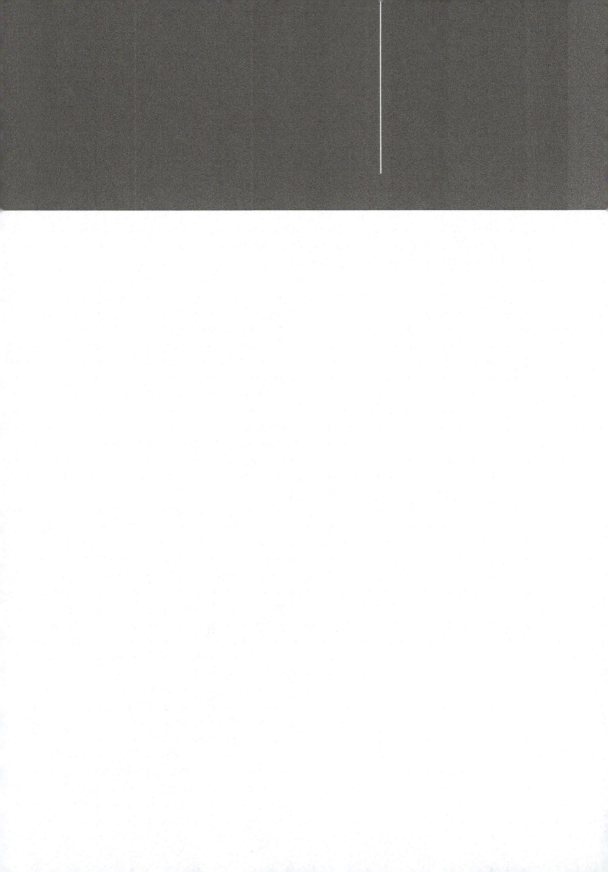

PART III

Contextual Issues

Chapter 8

Pitfalls of Analogies and Abstractions

Words have no power to impress the mind without the exquisite horror of their reality.

Edgar Allan Poe

In 2006, former Alaskan Senator Ted Stevens said of the Internet: "It's a series of tubes." Many people still chuckle at the highly simplified analogy. While Stevens may not have understood or tailored his analogy intentionally, presenting it to someone with little knowledge of technology is perhaps not a bad starting point. Good analogies depend on context and the level of awareness of the recipient.

Cybersecurity is rich with analogies, from keys and locks to Trojan horses. We look for the "needle in the haystack" and "evict malware resident on our systems." We debate "baked-in" versus "bolted-on" security. We do not mean all of these things literally, of course. The language and analogies we use in this field are borrowed from many different domains, as we will explore in this chapter. "Firewall," for instance, was a term in building construction for 100 years before it was applied to cybersecurity.[1]

Cyber attacks and defenses are often compared with the biological world. We use common terminology such as "virus" and "infected" to describe and communicate digital threats. Using analogies such as these can feel helpful but can also be incomplete or worse.

Human communication is an underrated skill in cybersecurity. We might prefer to build, create, and tinker alone, but cybersecurity is difficult to achieve if we cannot communicate with others. Technology, in general, is described by analogy to help teach and explain complex topics to our peers and lay audiences. For example, email might be compared to sending a postcard, where the content is visible to anyone who sees it. Cybersecurity is also often compared to the physical defenses of a castle,

1. The term was debated at the National Fire Protection Association Annual Meeting in 1920. See https://buildingcoderesourcelibrary. com/Fire-Protection-History-Part-194.00.pdf

where a strong boundary protects people and their property. These ways of thinking form heuristics, mainly to help communicate and translate abstract cybersecurity concepts into more familiar domains for non-experts. An analogy might help users form a mental model about what is happening with their device or how they should make a decision.

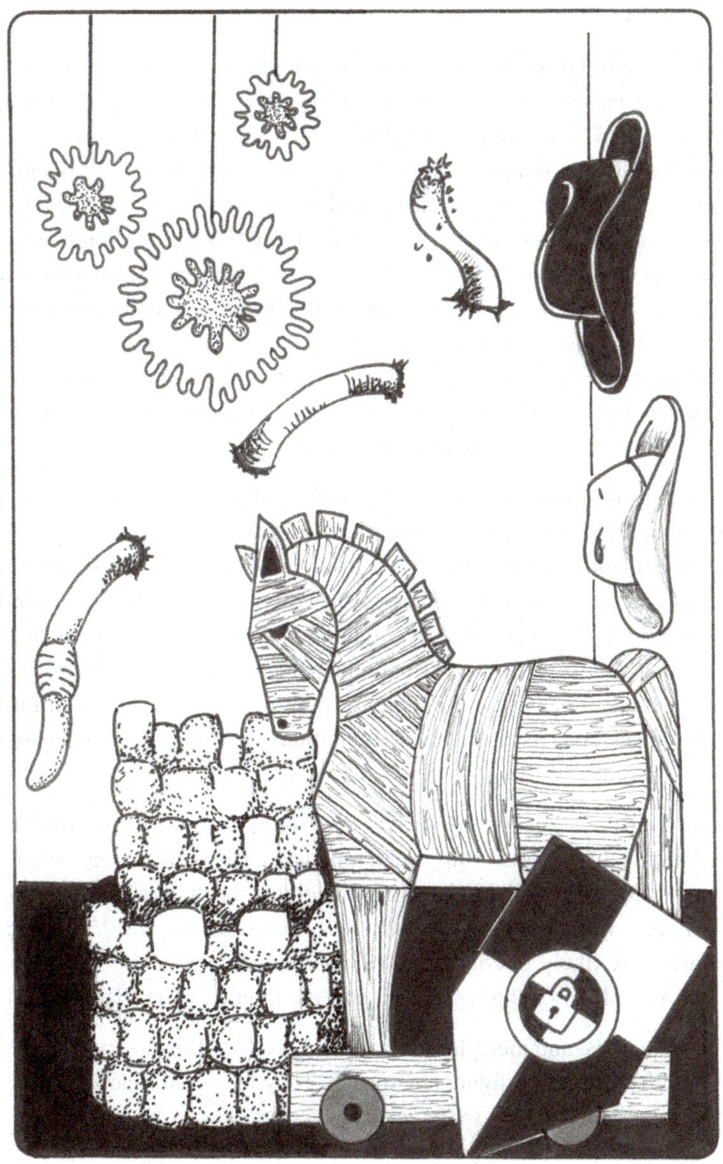

FIGURE 8.1 The attic of cyber analogies.

Analogies are also prevalent because of our limited attention spans. Short, snappy headlines draw more clicks and advertising dollars. They appeal to fear more than clear communication. "SolarWinds backdoor infects tech giants" and "Ransomware attack hits JBS, shutting down operations" are headlines built around analogies. The pundits do not have the technical insight to explain the nuance of their analogy, even when some words (such as *backdoor* or *infect*) have specific technical meanings to the cybersecurity community.

Analogies can help explain basic cybersecurity concepts, but too often they omit or overgeneralize important details. They can mislead, sometimes deliberately, because the experience they purport to connect might be out of proportion. No cyber weapons, for example, have caused the physical destruction of modern kinetic weapons (yet). As discussed in Chapter 5, "Cognitive Biases," the shortcuts of using analogies have consequences similar to heuristics. Sometimes we use abstractions, a description with some details and special cases removed. Drawings of clouds were used to hide the details of a telephone or computer network long before *cloud* became synonymous with online services. In Chapter 2, "What Is the Internet?" we referenced the Open Systems Interconnection (OSI) model of networks, which is almost always illustrated as seven layers stacked similar to a cake, one on top of another, and called the *protocol stack*. Everyone in computing learns networking with this model. The model is an abstraction that has helped students understand modern networking for decades, allowing us to present the general idea but leave out many details.

Those details, however, must also be presented to fully understand the nuances. A protocol stack is not perfect; it is an imprecise analogy, no matter how useful. The directionality of "up" and "down" in the stack must be explained because these are not intuitive. Directions can be equally problematic in engineering designs and network diagrams when we talk about information moving "north and south" versus "east and west."[2] These phrases might be understood by technical audiences but not by non-experts. Even experts must learn to remember the names of all the OSI layers. Among the relevant mnemonics: Please Do Not Teach Stupid People Acronyms.[3] Abstraction is helpful in understanding broad concepts, but unless one is clear about limitations, it can be misunderstood as a complete explanation.

Statistics has a well-known aphorism: "All models are wrong, but some are useful." The same might be said of analogies. Despite their shortcoming and imprecision, using an analogy or an abstraction might be helpful in appropriate situations. In all communications, written or spoken to any audience, ask yourself, *"To whom am I speaking?"* and *"What do I want to accomplish?"* If we carefully consider the audience, we are more likely to communicate clearly and achieve the best outcome. Remember, nontechnical people are unlikely to know domain-specific jargon and probably do not want to learn it.

Using analogies, abstractions, and metaphors shapes technology's development, practice, and policies. The analogies are more than simple figures of speech. They have a normative dimension; sometimes, they can be used to help the imaginary shape reality.

---

2. In a network diagram, north (or upstream) often refers to data moving toward the Internet. East–west movement (lateral or downstream) means communications among hosts inside a private network.
3. The words correspond to the OSI layers: physical, data link, network, transport, session, presentation, application.

This chapter explores the use and misuse of analogies and abstractions across cybersecurity. We consider analogies from the physical world, medicine and biology, war and military, and law before discussing tips for avoiding pitfalls in using analogies and metaphors.

Cybersecurity Is Like the Physical World

The digital world is composed of computers and networks that exist in the physical world. Yet, we continue to describe it as a different reality and physical place: "cyberspace." We have electronic desktops and files, cryptographic keys and locks, digital firewalls and forums. Cyberspace itself is an analogy of another *place*.

When we start paying attention, we will likely notice physical-world language in many parts of our digital work. For example, we might hear our colleagues discuss implementing *guard rails* for digital behavior in the workplace. This analogy is commonly understood to describe boundaries of acceptable behavior, similar to a physical feature that prevents or deters access beyond some limit. A web application firewall can be a guard rail if it allows web browsing but blocks access to gambling sites.

The firewall is an example of a problematic analogy to the physical world. In building construction, the firewall is intended to prevent the spread of fire from one room or building to another. In the physical world, firewalls are not designed to allow some fire through! In networks, a firewall is used to both prevent and allow specified traffic. While most firewalls support rules to block specific "fires," from the Code Red worm to Heartbleed exploits, the fact that they might prevent the spread of a cyber attack is a by-product.

By the 1970s, people had started talking about the electronic equivalent of a Trojan horse. Similar to how the Greeks used a wooden horse to hide and sneak inside the city of Troy, cyber attackers trick users into executing benign-looking software that attacks an otherwise-protected computer.

These analogies can illustrate boundary defenses' construction, cost, and maintenance. But they also reinforce outdated paradigms, contributing to public misunderstandings about complex issues. In particular, a physical boundary analogy is not helpful when we have portable computing and wireless connections.

Cryptography is another complex topic prone to misconceptions. Some of the most well-known research results in all of cybersecurity are user studies that reveal what ordinary people can and cannot understand about encryption.[4] Consider keys. The same key is used in the physical world to lock and unlock a door. In public-key cryptography, the analogy breaks down because one key is used to encrypt and another to decrypt. This is a nuance that is confusing for non-experts. It is also an imperfect analogy when explaining even more complex concepts such as one-time pads.

A physical lock can be picked; it is a familiar scene in TV and movies. Characters pull out their lock picks and open it, one tumbler at a time. People assume that because we talk about cryptography as locks and keys, the same holds true for cryptography. It does not. The cryptographic key must be exact

4. Perhaps the most well-known is Whitten, Alma, and Tygar, J. Doug, "Why Johnny Cannot Encrypt: A Usability Evaluation of PGP 5.0," *USENIX Security Symposium*, Vol. 348 (1999).

and cannot be found a little at a time. That means if the key is "My Cat Rerun," it must match exactly: It will not be found as "My" then "My Cat" and finally, presto, "My Cat Rerun" to decrypt the string.

Another physical-world analogy is *blast radius*. In the physical world, the wave of energy from an explosion propagates away from the source and can damage surrounding objects. Physics allows us to measure the impact and distance from the epicenter. Cybersecurity professionals adopted this phrase and (imprecisely) applied it to situations such as credential theft. If an attacker compromises one password—the explosion of sorts—how "far" can the damage spread? But credentials are more similar to keys than bombs. If we lose our keys, we do not describe the possible damage in terms of a *blast radius*, even when considering the damage or loss that could result.

The use of a digital DMZ might limit the digital blast radius. The concept of a *Demilitarized Zone (DMZ)* is borrowed from the physical world. A computer network DMZ is a special partition of a network where public-facing servers, such as email or web servers, can be accessible to the Internet even while the rest of the home or business network is more strongly protected (often by a firewall). The DMZ subnetwork is "demilitarized" in a sense because it exists between the fortified internal network and the attacking forces coming from the Internet. Here is where the analogy breaks down. A physical-world DMZ is established by agreements between contending groups where both sides agree there will be no military activities. This is far from true online; servers in computer DMZs are continually bombarded with attacks.

Cybersecurity Is Like Defending a Castle

One of the original analogies in cybersecurity is that of defending a castle or fortress. Intuitively, people understand the simple idea that stone walls or the moat of a castle fortify it from external attack and protect the people and things within. A castle's defenses certainly are not subtle. Castles do not try to hide or move.

Cybersecurity, many have said, is like a castle. In the early days of computer networks, the boundary of a computer network was clear. Everyone in a company was physically in one building or one campus and all their computers routed from "inside" the network out to the Internet through company-controlled routers.

People eventually moved out of digital "castles," and networks also evolved. As Internet access came to people's homes and computers became mobile, employees wanted and needed access to the company network. The corporate network boundary became permeable, and the castle analogy dissolved. Unlike a fortress, today's networks are no longer static, and fixed defenses are insufficient. Security requires defenses against previously unknown attacks and changing user needs. Cybersecurity today is less and less like defending a castle.

One security model that has emerged to replace the analogy of castles is *zero trust*.[5] Zero trust is a mindset and set of principles that focus on protecting data wherever it is, assuming compromise, eliminating implicit trust, and acknowledging a boundaryless world. While poor marketing made it a buzzword, zero trust is an evolution in the mindset of security thinking for the modern world—no

5. See the Appendix for more information on zero trust.

more castle walls. Unfortunately, as we explained in Chapter 1, "What Is Cybersecurity?", it is also a poor name because we still need to place trust in several components to have anything usable at all, including hardware, the operating system, and authentication mechanisms. Furthermore, this term implies that the users cannot be (or should not be) trusted, which is not a helpful position to take.

Digital Theft Is Like Physical Theft

It is generally well understood that physical items have one existence with regard to theft. If someone steals our apartment key, we no longer have it. This is larceny because the rightful owner no longer has the item. In contrast, taking a digital copy is not larceny because the original remains with the owner, and the thief has an identical copy; the owner has not been deprived of the item.

Such was the concern of the music industry when physical media—records, tapes, and CDs—could be infinitely copied and distributed as digital files. Without controls over music's distribution, record labels had no way to protect artists' rights. They popularized the use of the word "piracy" for this copying to make it seem as if it was a grave crime committed by lawless groups. The rules around digital copies in the United States primarily relate to copyright and intellectual property protection. The implications for digital theft are so much more significant than film and music revenue alone, and more than legal semantics. Still, the image of "piracy" has helped shape the dialog for decades. Digital piracy is not larceny, nor does it involve kidnapping, murder, or extortion, although some people do dream of making certain captains of industry walk the plank!

Confusingly, we use the same words and phrases to describe physical and digital theft. "A thief stole my phone" and "an attacker stole our client database" use the same verb and have a similar meaning, maybe even similar consequences. So, why does it seem as if people see stealing intellectual property as different from stealing physical property? Scholars have found that some people see digital piracy as theft but not a crime.[6] That's quite different from most social norms that view stealing from a supermarket as unacceptable, and pirates off the coast of Africa as hardened criminals to be countered with naval armaments!

The pitfall of comparing digital theft to physical is that we might view them as having equivalent value or risk, or deserving the same level of response.

There are also differences in the valuation of the "booty." A single modern ship hijacked by pirates might fetch a ransom in the tens of millions of dollars; the aggregate value of all of the data held by a single firm such as Netflix is 1,000 times that.[7] The use of "piracy" as an analogy hides many of these differences.

Users Are the "Weakest Link"

This idiom long predates the Internet: A chain is only as strong as its weakest link. One broken link in a chain causes the whole chain to fail at that point. In the cyber world, there is a widely accepted and insufficiently contested belief that users are the weakest link in cybersecurity. This is an unfair and incomplete view.

---

6. Balestrino, Alessandro, "It Is a Theft but Not a Crime," *European Journal of Political Economy*, Vol. 24, No. 2 (2008): 455–469; and www.theregister.com/2022/08/02/antipiracy_messaging_piracy/.
7. www.sec.gov/Archives/edgar/data/1065280/000106528022000036/nflx-20211231.htm

In the chapter "Faulty Assumptions and Magical Thinking," we discussed reasons why users do not behave rationally. Figure 8.2 illustrates this in part: Some users overestimate their abilities. We also discussed in that chapter why placing all the blame on the end users is inappropriate. End users are not the only humans in the cybersecurity ecosystem. Developers are users of development tools; they are also human and make mistakes. Adversaries are human, and their choices affect victimization. All humans have limitations, not only users. Effectively, any flaw that causes a failure can be traced back to humans: All links are equally weak.

FIGURE 8.2 Users making bad choices.

There is an unfortunate history of arrogance and condescension in the security community. The "us versus them" mentality is typical yet unhelpful. Empathy, with the intent to empower, encourages people to be active partners in security. It is a shift in attitude that will build stronger relationships. Enabling users to report mistakes and helping them fix them is a much better attitude than talking down to them for making mistakes.

Stupid User Stories

For many years there was the trope of "stupid user stories." These would be recounted on message lists and over coffee, making fun of naivé computer users. The stories would be about how people would use CD-ROM trays in desktop systems as cup holders, and pick up computer mice to point them at the screen while saying "click" when told to point and click.

Perhaps these stories have a little humor to them, but they were told in a mean-spirited manner, making fun of people trying to use the technology. They illustrate how those who designed the computers and documentation failed to consider their audience. If people try to follow bad instructions to get their work done or misinterpret what something does, that is unfortunate, not humorous.

The authors have had the experience of traveling in foreign countries. We are thankful that natives do not laugh derisively at our attempts to ask them simple questions in the local language. And the sense of confusion (and occasional panic) when confronting a foreign train schedule or toilet of mysterious design is probably similar to that of someone sitting down at a computer keyboard for the first time!

More and more people are now exposed to computing as children, who usually have little fear of asking questions and trying things. Thus, the "stupid user stories" have died out in many places. But they pop up from time to time and should be understood for what they are: indictments of bad user interface design and a lack of empathy.

There is a high burden on users today. For instance, we demand that they pick strong passwords and remember them, despite their human limitations. We require them to analyze email to avoid phishing. We expect them to report strange behavior. It is unfair to provide people with poorly designed interfaces and then blame the users for making mistakes. *Human factors* is the application of psychological and physiological principles to the engineering and design of products, processes, and systems. Experts in human factors engineering, human–computer interaction, and user experience (UX) study and create computer interfaces that help people use them. For a system to be user-friendly, for example, it should incorporate principles of learnability, efficiency, memorability, and satisfaction.

Importantly, UX and design are not *just* about user interfaces. They are also about helping to determine appropriate functional requirements based on user needs. This extends much deeper than the user interface. If the functional architecture is incorrect, the design will inherently be flawed. Thus, the saying "Form follows function."

In 1999, Anne Adams and M. Angela Sasse wrote an important paper titled "Users Are Not the Enemy."[8] This was one of the first explorations of what has become the field of usable security. Adams and Sasse found that "users may indeed compromise computer security mechanisms, such as password

8. Adams, Anne, and Sasse, Martina Angela, "Users Are Not the Enemy," *Communications of the ACM*, Vol. 42, No. 12 (1999): 40–46.

authentication, both knowing and unknowingly" but that "such behavior is often caused by the way in which security mechanisms are implemented, and users' lack of knowledge."

It is disingenuous to presume that cybersecurity would be perfect if not for users. The onslaught of zero-day exploits and continual software patches is evidence that software is not perfect. Users can do everything right, and systems can still be compromised. Furthermore, as we explored in Chapter 3, it is a myth to believe that humans will behave rationally. Security is about managing risk, not thinking that it can be eliminated.

Cybersecurity Is Like Medicine and Biology

From the early days of the Internet, malicious online activity took the nomenclature of biology. Not only was there potential harm, but it could spread. Malware emerging in the mid-1980s suggested a biological comparison by being named viruses. The Internet and WANK worms of 1989 brought in an additional parasitic player.[9] We continue to name noteworthy worms, from Conficker to Stuxnet.

As in the physical world, a worm is self-activating and self-propagating. A virus, however, requires a host carrier and activation. Similar to COVID-19 and other viruses, their digital analogs can be highly infectious and destructive, causing damage to susceptible hosts. We use the term "infection" with viruses and worms as we might for biological parasite infestations. (We discuss this in more depth in Chapter 12, "Malware.")

The Cyber Hygiene Analogy

Most parents teach their children to wash their hands (to prevent infection) and brush their teeth (to prevent cavities). These are examples of personal hygiene that help maintain health and prevent disease. As an analogy, cyber hygiene is a way to describe precautionary behavior that protects a user and their systems from a range of problems before they occur. For example, choosing strong passwords and using two-factor authentication are basic practices that help keep users secure.

The benefits of prevention provided by good hygiene are helpful against many threats. We might even be protected without knowing it, such as when an attacker fails to compromise an account that does not have a common password or an attack fails because the latest patches have been installed.

Keep in mind that simple precautions prevent simple risks. Washing our hands probably does not prevent cancer or heart disease. Strong passwords are unlikely to stop an APT. Good hygiene in health or cyber is necessary but not sufficient, so we should be careful not to suggest that good hygiene alone is enough.

Additionally, cyber HiGene is how two of us sometimes greet the third author in Zoom calls.

9. See the Appendix for more information on these worms.

FIGURE 8.3 A new view of cyber hygiene.

A key difference between tech and nontech threats is the defenses. Sure, "hygiene" plays a role in wellness and health (see the aside, "The Cyber Hygiene Analogy"). But while humans have a built-in, self-enhancing immune system, digital devices currently do not. It is not always easy for average users to understand why they need antivirus software and why they should pay *extra* for it and devote resources to keep it updated. There are billions of unique malware files, but users do not internalize the risk.[10]

Beyond viruses and worms, people have also described some malware as rabbits and bacteria, although those terms are seldom used anymore. We have even heard of some spyware referred to as "barnacles," but only in one case. We have also heard malware authors referred to as "vermin." There might be other biologically oriented terms used, especially in other languages. The lack of precision in naming has gradually led to the general public referring to all malware as viruses; we think there is still potential in vermin for describing the authors, however.

Conceptualizing malware as biological threats encourages deterministic ways of thinking. The only goal of a virus in nature is to replicate. In cyber, we are often concerned with the nonreplication components: Does the malware steal or destroy data, for instance? Thinking of malware as a virus leads to signature-based antivirus software and other defenses such as an immune system.

The human immune system adapts on its own or from outside pressures. It is an ever-changing element that uses a vaccine to train itself or learns to attack what should not be in the system. Antivirus is not an immune system. Whereas the human immune system can recognize a new threat and mobilize to defend against it, sometimes it reacts well, and sometimes does not. Sometimes the immune system needs outside help, but it usually recognizes the new scary thing and can overwhelm it.

10. This is nowhere close to the number of biological viruses in nature. An estimated 10 nonillion (10^{31}) viruses exist on Earth. That is more viruses than stars in the universe!

An antivirus system cannot necessarily mimic a human immune system. Antivirus software generally has a set of malware it knows about, and the new threats are ignored. Thinking of antivirus software as an immune system leads to the argument that "My antivirus software will recognize the new scary!"—when it will not unless prompted. Even antivirus systems imbued with machine learning will not function like humans. Computational machine learning is different from how our brains and bodies learn. (This might be a good thing if we consider autoimmune issues!)

Cybersecurity Is Like Fighting a War

Reports of cyberattacks often sound a lot like descriptions of physical attacks. The press might report that a company was "hit with a cyber attack"—phrasing that calls to mind something like a precision-guided missile from a faraway adversary. Pew pew!

FIGURE 8.4 Pew pew!

The military has adopted a great deal of physical-world terminology to describe cyberspace and cyber activity. For instance, the U.S. Department of Defense doctrine states that key terrain refers to a locality or area that, if seized or retained, can afford an advantage to an attacker or defender. In the physical world, this could be a hill or a bridge. Cyber key terrain could refer to the systems, software, or connections of cyberspace as some finite subset of the space.

Commandeering a router is not the same as a hilltop. The router is a much more complex system, access to which depends upon power and network connectivity and patch level.

The emotional connections associated with catastrophic events lead people to compare past events to hypothetical future events. Many people alive in America today recall the devastating destruction caused by the terrorist attacks of September 11, 2001. Though fewer have first-hand experiences, most Americans have learned about the attack on Pearl Harbor. Emotions of shock, fear, and anger associated with such trauma can impact people for the rest of their lives. A comparison to a hypothetical future "Cyber Pearl Harbor" is a shorthand for "Remember the horror you experienced from that physical-world attack? That's the devastation and pain you will feel when it happens online."

"Cyber Pearl Harbor"

When people talk about a "Cyber Pearl Harbor" or "Cyber 9/11," they are making an analogy to physical-world attacks. Such appeals seek to draw attention and instill fear with the intent of preventing catastrophic impacts in cyberspace. But of all the analogies described in this chapter, Cyber 9/11 is the most abstract and imprecise. Such comparisons are also hard to shake: Cyber Pearl Harbor dates back to Congressional testimony by Winn Schwartau in 1991.

Some say the scope of these comparisons is meant to be similar to cyber attacks that disrupt the power grid or water supply. Others talk about disrupting the financial system or telecommunications. In any case, the analogies are neither informative nor insightful in drawing attention to cyberspace's actual risks, probabilities, or defenses. As Ciaran Martin said, "The world's experience of cyber attacks so far has been one of chronic, debilitating damage rather than catastrophic risk to life and limb."[11]

Cyber Weapons

Consider "cyber bullets"—a phrase used as a joke that has become a reality. Cyber capabilities used for offensive exploitation are often described as weapons. But even offense and defense are more about intent than capability. Deleting a file could be considered legitimate or destructive depending on the context. Although the code to accomplish the goal is the same, the intent carries legal implications and consequences.

---

11. https://s26304.pcdn.co/wp-content/uploads/Cyber-weapons-are-called-viruses-for-a-reason-v2-1.pdf

The Law of Armed Conflict (LOAC) (also known as the Law of War and International Humanitarian Law) is closely tied to intent.[12] LOAC incorporates the four Geneva Conventions. It is enforced through countries' legal systems, diplomatic channels, or international dispute resolution, including international courts.[13] The law applies when a state or armed non-state *intends* to engage in armed conflict. Armed conflict might exist even without someone acknowledging that they are engaged in armed conflict, however. LOAC defines obligations for the conduct of hostilities and protecting war victims. It includes the principles of proportionality and the prohibition of unnecessary suffering. One principle is to avoid targeting civilians and civilian infrastructure unless necessary. It is questionable if that is possible with some cyber weapons such as malware—there are laser-guided munitions but no laser-guided computer viruses![14]

Cyber weapons have dramatically different characteristics from physical weapons.[15] For example, kinetic weapons such as bombs and bullets have consistent, permanent, and predictable effects. Cyber weapons might have variable, potentially reversible, and tailorable effects. Cyber weapons are often compared to kinetic weapons because of the long history of doctrine, experience, and expertise with kinetic weapons. Most of today's military leaders in cyber warfare have spent their careers in tanks and planes. Until there is a generation of digital natives in military leadership, the culture of kinetic thinking is unlikely to change.

Cyber Terrorism

Cyber terrorism is another phrase fraught with misuse, not to mention confusion. There are at least 37 distinct definitions of the term available.[16] That means at least 37 different people disagree on how to define it. . . and it is not simply the basic definitions. They disagree on whether cyber terrorism is against computers or not, uses computers, and even whether it sows fear.

The same is also true for terrorism. Terrorism has definitions that depend on who is asked, when they are asked, and how they are asked. The definition has changed over time, which does make things confusing.

For example, in the United States alone, one federal agency defines terrorism as:

> The unlawful use of force and violence against persons or property to intimidate or coerce a government, the civilian population, or any segment thereof, in furtherance of political or social objectives

---

12. See U.S. Department of Defense Law of War Manual, https://www.hsdl.org/?abstract&did=797480.
13. For a scholarly essay on how cyber conflict could be a war crime, see Rowe, Neil C., "War Crimes from Cyber-Weapons," *Journal of Information Warfare*, Vol. 6, No. 3 (2007): 15–25.
14. Not every state or armed non-state adheres to LOAC in the physical realm, even if they have agreed to the Geneva Conventions. For instance, Russia has not only been committing widespread war crimes in its hostilities in Syria and Ukraine but has also bestowed awards on egregious violators. We should not expect all parties in cyber conflict to "play nice," either.
15. For a deeper discussion on the similarities and differences between cyber and physical weapons, see Dykstra, Josiah, Inglis, Chris, and Walcott, Thomas S., "Differentiating Kinetic and Cyber Weapons to Improve Integrated Combat," *Joint Forces Quarterly*, Vol. 99 (2020).
16. https://insights.sei.cmu.edu/blog/declaring-war-on-cyber-terrorismor-something-like-that/

However, another federal agency, the Federal Emergency Management Agency (FEMA), defines terrorism as:

> Terrorism is the use of force or violence against persons or property in violation of the criminal laws of the United States for purposes of intimidation, coercion, or ransom.

The CIA, DHS, and State Department all have their own different definitions, as do many international organizations.[17] Many of these definitions insist that terrorism requires violence, and computers cannot cause violence; therefore, there is no such thing as cyber terrorism.

However. . . There was this little piece of malware (actually, not so little) called Stuxnet. Stuxnet managed to damage—and in some cases destroy—Iranian nuclear centrifuges. It does not take much imagination to think that because computers control nuclear reactors, some malware could cause a core meltdown. Computers also control airplanes, trains, medical equipment, power grids, and various other systems. Malware could cause any of those to fail, leading to significant problems. Those problems could include violence if the malware spread rumors that caused certain groups to riot or attack others.

We are lucky (so far) that there has not been an event that we can point to as a definitive cyber terrorism event, but it is incorrect to think that it could not occur.

Cybersecurity Law Is Analogous to Physical-World Law

Law is often interpreted based on analogies, which is undoubtedly the case with cybersecurity. Refer to Chapter 9, "Legal Issues," for a detailed description.

Tips for Analogies and Abstractions

In March 2022, the flagship news program on National Public Radio ran a story[18] about fighting crypto crime. The reporter said:

> The blockchain—OK, so here's a quick blockchain explainer. The blockchain is like an electronic tag. Think of it like a Post-it that is attached to something—could be a document of some kind or a cryptocurrency token or a piece of art, maybe. Every time that item changes hands, the transaction is noted on the Post-it—time, date, people involved—everything. And that Post-it cannot be peeled off, ever.

---

17. www.secbrief.org/2014/04/definition-of-terrorism/
18. "Law Enforcement Is Using One of Cryptocurrency's Strengths to Fight Crypto Crime," *All Things Considered*, March 3, 2022. www.npr.org/2022/03/03/1084310594/law-enforcement-is-using-one-of-cryptocurrencys-strengths-to-fight-crypto-crime. Accessed April 3, 2022.

While blockchain can be used as a record of transactions, it is separate from the document or entry itself, unlike a Post-it note stuck to the object. This confusion might lead someone to misbelieve that this is how blockchains work.

Words matter. Education and awareness about cybersecurity are critical components of achieving the outcomes that matter. Analogies are one tool for practicing and communicating about cybersecurity. Analogies aren't *all* bad, and abstractions can help some audiences understand deeply technical concepts. Occasionally, even castle imagery used with care resonates with people. Analogies that reflect reality will foster more productive conversations and appropriate solutions. If anything, "death by a thousand paper cuts" might be the most truthful and accurate analogy in cyber.

Table 8.1 summarizes common analogies and the pros and cons we have covered in this chapter. The positives are some ways an analogy is true to the physical world and helpful in communicating complex cybersecurity topics. The negatives are pitfalls where the digital world is unlike its analogy in the physical world. Depending on the context, these negatives might outweigh the positives and lead to avoidance or further explanation of the analogy.

If you must use other analogies, keep the following tips in mind.

Be context-aware when communicating about cybersecurity. A simple and imperfect analogy might be appropriate in a casual conversation among friends where the stakes are low. Still, the more we use analogies, the more ingrained they become in people's minds and difficult to change. Be cautious that oversimplifications might confuse the audience more than clarify the topic. When used, explain both similarities and differences in the analogy. For example, email security is like a postcard, where the message is visible to anyone who looks at it. Unlike encrypted email, a paper envelope can be easily opened and inspected. (In the United States, first-class mail contents are protected by the Fourth Amendment—a court-issued warrant is required to read it.)

TABLE 8.1 Summary of pros and cons of analogies used in cybersecurity.

Analogy	Positives	Negatives
Keys	Something we must have to unlock/decrypt a message.	In public-key cryptography, different keys are used to lock and unlock.
Firewall	Can stop dangerous network traffic.	*Allows* some things to pass through by design.
Blast radius	Can give a sense of the scope of the damage, including some second-order effects.	The impact of an attack does not always correspond to physical space limitations. Not a blast!
DMZ	A subnetwork more open to public access than the fortified internal area.	Both sides (network owner and Internet) do not mutually agree to no conflict.
Castle	Fortified, layered security helps protect people and their valuables	No longer a rigid boundary around networks and data.

Analogy	Positives	Negatives
The weakest chain link	Security (i.e., a chain) relies on many variables and can be broken if one component (i.e., a link) is compromised. Everything is dependent on the least-strong element.	End users are not the only people in cyber. Systems should compensate for humans who will make poor decisions.
Virus	Term is commonly used and conveys the concept of contamination and spread.	No built-in, self-enhancing immune system. The human immune system recognizes new threats and auto-responds.
Files	A collection of data arranged in a meaningful order.	Many identical copies. Need not be stored in one piece/place.

It might seem as if analogies and abstractions are the best or only way to translate technical topics to non-experts. Do not forget other tools in the toolbox.[19] Try using a story, personal experience, or recent event to help an audience understand a topic where you otherwise feel drawn to an analogy. During the 2022 invasion of Ukraine, for example, Russia attacked satellite modems of tens of thousands of people inside and outside of Ukraine.[20] This collateral damage across Europe would be one way to explain the *blast radius* of a cyber attack.

Given their influence, policymakers and cybersecurity professionals providing professional opinions should be especially careful about using these approaches. The impacts can be tangible when these groups rely too heavily on analogies. Careful consideration is needed of how their use might unintentionally reinforce particular social or political messages that undermine the goals of inclusive cybersecurity. Leaders might rationalize their decisions by making analogies to prior crises such as Pearl Harbor or 9/11. Policymakers also use historical analogies to justify their choices. In addition, analogies might restrict our policy options unnecessarily. When deploying cybersecurity or setting policies, we must see the world as it is: complex, complicated, and unpredictable. The alternative is the pursuit of incorrect or misleading mental models.

Given the complexity of the digital world, we are naturally drawn to simplistic explanations. We must be cognizant and careful that abstractions and analogies do not hide more than they reveal. A negative consequence is that we can start mistaking reality for these abbreviations. Furthermore, confirmation bias makes our explanations more ingrained and harder to change with time.

19. See, it is so hard to avoid analogies!
20. www.washingtonpost.com/national-security/2022/03/24/russian-military-behind-hack-satellite-communication-devices-ukraine-wars-outset-us-officials-say/

Further Reading

Goldman, Emily O., and Arquilla, John, eds. "Cyber Analogies." Naval Postgraduate School, 2014. https://calhoun.nps.edu/bitstream/handle/10945/40037/NPS-DA-14-001.pdf.

Karas, Thomas H., Moore, Judy H., and Parrott, Lori K. "Metaphors for Cyber Security." Sandia Report, Sandia National Laboratories, 2014. https://evolutionofcomputing.org/Cyberfest%20 Report.pdf.

Lawson, Sean. "Putting the 'War' in Cyberwar: Metaphor, Analogy, and Cybersecurity Discourse in the United States." *First Monday* Vol. 17, No. 7 (July 2012).

Lewis, James A. *Toward a More Coercive Cyber Strategy*. CSIS, 2021. https://csis-website-prod.s3.amazonaws.com/s3fs-public/publication/210310_Lewis_Cyber_Strategy.pdf.

Perkovich, George, and Levite, Ariel E., eds. *Understanding Cyber Conflict: Fourteen Analogies*. Georgetown University Press, 2017.

Sambaluk, Nicholas Michael. *Myths and Realities of Cyber Warfare: Conflict in the Digital Realm*. Praeger Security International, March 2020.

Chapter 9

Legal Issues

This is what has to be remembered about the law; beneath that cold, harsh, impersonal exterior beats a cold, harsh, impersonal heart.

David Frost

Cybersecurity has a deep and natural connection with laws, regulations, and rules. Although we could live in a world without legal boundaries, this would make the world a less safe place. There are even laws to help encourage the protection of data from natural disasters. HIPAA, for instance, requires covered entities (including hospitals and private-practice physicians) to "Establish (and implement as needed) policies and procedures for responding to an emergency or other occurrence (for example, fire, vandalism, system failure, and natural disaster) that damages systems that contain electronic protected health information."[1] These, and other laws and regulations, are intended to protect our safety and to protect rights and liberties.

Many laws and regulations address fraud, abuse, and electronic trespass. The U.S. Computer Fraud and Abuse Act of 1986 (CFAA)[2] prohibits unauthorized access exceeding one's authorization, as well as causing harm or damage to computers or data. It has been used to prosecute crimes including Internet worms, cyberbullying, espionage, theft of confidential information, and more. There are many cybersecurity laws—both similar and inconsistent—worldwide. There are also many laws globally, intended to prevent dissent and expression of political and religious thought. Some laws even criminalize the possession of certain forms of software and data.

Given the prevalence and impact of laws and regulations on the digital world, we have devoted an entire chapter to this topic. We will explore some myths, misconceptions, and difficulties of cyber laws, law enforcement, and other legal issues where myths exist. We stress here that **nothing** in this chapter (or in the book as a whole) should be considered competent legal advice.[3] Our counsel would like us to highlight that the overarching recommendation is to *always* get advice from an attorney licensed

1. See U.S. Code 45 CFR § 164.308(a)(7)(i).
2. Codified as 18 U.S.C. § 1030.
3. We will not go so far as to label it as incompetent advice, although some of our legal friends might.

to practice in the jurisdictions where any cyber work is performed. You should appropriately retain (i.e., compensate) said lawyers for their professional legal opinion; you should not ask your plumber for detailed advice about network security, nor should you ask a network engineer for legal advice!

Cybersecurity Law Is Analogous to Physical-World Law

Extending our discussion in Chapter 8, "Pitfalls of Analogies and Abstractions," analogies are a foundational concept in legal argument. The thinking is that one case should be treated in a particular way because that is the way a *similar* case has been treated; it is seen as desirable that the application of law be consistent. As technology, computers, and cybersecurity have entered the legal system, they are compared to their nondigital analogs. The rights and protections of a digital file are compared with those of a paper file and a digital filesystem to a physical filing cabinet. The rationale for doing so is understandable. Those who write the law (legislators, politicians, lobbyists) are used to the physical world and seek to analogize it. Those who interpret the law (judges, administrators) similarly are inclined to describe a password as a key or an ID. It is neither—or both. Yet, these analogies break down when, for instance, digital files in cloud storage are technically stored in fragments across one or more drives in many jurisdictions.[4]

In addition to objects such as files, the law has wrestled with analogies for digital activity. One example is trespassing. Traditionally, trespass is entering a person's land or property without permission. "Property" has been extended and applied to digital systems. When an attacker intentionally accesses a system without authorization, they might be charged with computer trespassing. The law substitutes the traditional "trespass to property" with "unauthorized access to a computer." It is based on the concept, similar to a person requiring permission to be present on someone else's land, that a person must have "permission"—express or implied—to be "on" someone else's computer. This seems straightforward, but courts have struggled to distinguish authorized from unauthorized access, or even what constitutes "access" at all. Courts have trouble determining whose computer or data one is accessing, the scope of permission one has to access, and under what circumstances consent—once given—can be withdrawn. The conclusion is that the concept of "trespass"—long existing in common law—might not be the best analogy for laws dealing with transnational, multipurpose, cloud-based computer networks. Still, it is the one most commonly used.

There is also a long history of tension about whether to apply prior, generalized principles (such as papers and trespass) to novel problems created by technology. This tension can be seen in the debate between former Seventh Circuit Judge Frank Easterbrook and Professor Lawrence Lessig over "The Law of the Horse." Easterbrook argued that specialized laws for cyber were as unnecessary as those related to horses (such as sales, injury, licensing, or veterinary care). Congress initially agreed and resisted creating computer crime statutes because it was thought laws such as those for mail or wire

4. Cf. Chapter 8, "Pitfalls of Analogies and Abstractions."

fraud were sufficient to cover computer crimes. Lessig countered that cyberspace was unique and that cyber regulations are necessary to ensure clarity.[5]

FIGURE 9.1 The Law of the Horse.

In the past 20 years, those who create the law (i.e., judges, legislators, and regulators) have primarily agreed with both approaches: Try using generalized principles and if those do not work, seek to apply new, specialized principles. In 1986, the CFAA was enacted with the intent to bridge the gaps where the analogies did not hold. After more than 30 years of progress and change, the CFAA is dated, and there is renewed debate about reconciling fast-changing technology with the law.

The myth here is that the online world is a complete analog for the physical world and that physical-world law can adequately be applied to cyberspace. Because both approaches are being used, we cannot say this is always a myth.

Your Laws Do Not Apply to Me Where I Am

In the legal world, laws are mostly bound by geography. Jurisdiction is the power and authority to make legal decisions and judgments. The scope of jurisdiction can be defined by constitutional law, legislative branches, and international agreements. In the United States, for instance, there are federal, state, and local jurisdictions that might overlap.

5. Lessig, Lawrence, "The Law of the Horse: What Cyber Law Might Teach," *Harvard Law Review*, Vol. 113, No. 501 (1999).

If someone is mugged in an alley in Milwaukee, the laws of Wisconsin and the United States apply. The mugger and the victim were in Milwaukee when the act occurred. In most cases, any or all jurisdictions in which an essential part of a robbery (or other crime) has been committed can prosecute the offender. If someone's avatar is mugged in an alley in *Minecraft*, it is unclear what the jurisdiction is (or what laws might be involved).

As we discussed in Chapter 1,"What Is Cybersecurity?," the Internet is global and decentralized, with no single owner or control. The victim, the attacker, and the various digital systems involved might be in different geographic locations with their own laws. The Internet and cyberspace are not considered legal jurisdictions!

How does jurisdiction work with online crimes? An attacker might be sitting in Russia, break into a U.S. company with a cloud server in Ireland, impacting a resident of Utah who is currently visiting Indonesia on vacation. Which law or laws apply? Unlike a paper document, the physical location of the bits of a file on one or more servers might not matter. The location of the headquarters of the cloud provider might be more important than the location of servers. For instance, the Clarifying Lawful Overseas Use of Data Act (CLOUD Act) is a U.S. federal law that allows federal law enforcement to compel U.S.-based tech companies to hand over data stored on servers without regard to where it is physically stored.[6] As a general rule, sovereigns (countries) can apply their laws to actions or actors outside their physical borders under several legal principles, including the territorial principle (where the crime occurred), the nationality principle (citizenship of the victim or actor including corporate entities), the protective principle (jurisdiction based on the national interest impacted, e.g., espionage), the universality principle (the custody of the person committing the offense), and the passive personality principle (the nationality or national character of the person injured). In cyber crimes, however, the offense is committed "everywhere" and "nowhere" simultaneously. An act might be protected under the law of one sovereign but prohibited by another: A person sitting at a computer in Delphi, Indiana, might commit a crime in Delphi, Greece, or Delphi, Uganda.

It is also the case that civil suits (suing) can be filed almost anywhere. Bill Cook, a noted computing lawyer, has described this as "If you can see it, you can sue it." He meant that if someone can see content online that they find offensive or damaging, they can usually file a legal complaint in the locale where they are. That action might not proceed in many places if the local courts find no appropriate jurisdiction. There are two distinct kinds of jurisdiction, both based primarily on location. Subject matter jurisdiction implies that a court, prosecutor, or litigant has the power to exercise judgment over the case—that what happened in cyberspace creates a cause of action (a civil action) or a prosecutable offense in a particular jurisdiction. The other is called "personal jurisdiction"—that is, even if it's a violation of law in Russia, can the Russian government establish that the person (or corporation) has sufficient connection with Russia to warrant hauling the person into court in Russia? The problem in cyberspace is not only that one has to show that someone did something wrong—and did it in the correct jurisdiction—but also that one can hold them accountable there. At a bare minimum, whatever

6. See 18 U.S.C. § 2523. The People's Republic of China has a similar law, the National Intelligence Law. Both laws likely conflict with the European Union's GDPR.

the particulars might be, it might still require the defendant to retain an attorney in that locale to seek dismissal.

This is an area of law that continues to evolve. It will only get more complex as distributed/mesh computation spreads, and the Internet of Everything (IoE) expands. Once we have cloud data centers in orbit or on the Moon, we will have some interesting litigation issues!

That Violates My First Amendment Rights!

Two misconceptions are illustrated when people appeal to First Amendment rights: ignorance of the law and jurisdictional differences.

Technology is one way to implement laws. Online platforms can allow or disallow, as laws dictate, certain content such as hate speech and pornography (neither of which are well-defined globally and sometimes defined to oppress a minority). For example, technology can help detect, track, and remove illegal transmission of child pornography and financial transactions to support narcotics trafficking. It can reveal unauthorized computer access, such as what the Computer Fraud and Abuse Act prohibits.

Technology can also be used to enforce legal rights. For instance, for citizens of the European Union, technology companies must adhere to the right to be forgotten.[7]

The First Amendment to the U.S. Constitution relates to rights and speech. The text says:

> Congress shall make no law respecting an establishment of religion, or prohibiting the free exercise thereof; or abridging the freedom of speech, or of the press; or the right of the people peaceably to assemble, and to petition the Government for a redress of grievances.

The following sections examine two misconceptions about this right.

Ignorance of the Law

These days, people often refer to the First Amendment when something they have written on social media is removed or restricted. Usually, that something is insulting, misleading, obscene, or worse. The post's author and supporters protest about their "First Amendment Rights" being violated.

As an example, in 2018, the Federal Agency of News LLC (FAN[8]) sued Facebook for violating its First Amendment rights to free speech by taking down its social media account and page. Facebook claimed that FAN had violated its terms of service because it was controlled by the Russia-based Internet Research Agency, which "has repeatedly acted deceptively and tried to manipulate people in the U.S., Europe, and Russia."[9] The court sided with Facebook in the case.

---

7. The Right to Be Forgotten is defined as a privacy right in the EU—old mentions of someone can be deleted/blocked if they are prejudicial to someone under some circumstances. This requires search engines to remove those items in EU countries.
8. FAN was a Russian corporation.
9. https://digitalcommons.law.scu.edu/cgi/viewcontent.cgi?article=3118&context=historical

Does anyone have the right to say whatever they want on social media in the United States because of freedom of speech? No! Private companies run social media platforms. The free speech right in the First Amendment (as with all U.S. Constitutional rights) protects people in the United States against *government* interference. The government cannot take away anyone's right to free speech, but Facebook has no obligation to give a platform for the speech. In *FAN v. Facebook*, the court dismissed the case, noting, among other things, that "Facebook's actions did not amount to state action."

Claims such as the one by FAN are simply ignorant of the law. The First Amendment prohibits the *government* from passing any laws restricting speech. Generally, there are no restrictions on private parties, such as the media platform operators. The company operating the venue has its own rules and standards for what it will publish, and those are part of the user agreement that the authors would have consented to (even if they did not read it) before getting an account with posting privileges,

The publisher can establish whatever publishing rules they wish, including banning some topics or users. That is not a violation of the First Amendment. It is *their* First Amendment right to publish what *they* wish as contributed by users. Legally compelling the platform to publish all items would be a violation of *their* rights! Unless the operators of the platform were acting at the direction of or at the behest of the government, they would be allowed under the First Amendment to permit or deny the right to speak to anyone (subject to some laws relating to civil rights, equal access, and nondiscrimination). However powerful social media and search engine sites might be, courts have been reluctant to analogize them (see, analogies apply here, too) to some kind of "public square" or public marketplace to which a right of access might be implied.[10]

Similarly, when such an entity refuses to carry content, this is not "censorship." Censorship implies that a government is restricting speech or expression. When a private entity does this—no matter how big that entity is—as a general rule, it's called "enforcing the Terms of Service" or something equally banal. If someone doesn't like it, they can start their own media service. With some constraints, users can create their own websites and media platforms run by their own rules. The right to publish anything (in the United States) is not absolute and has been further defined by courts over the years. For instance, in the United States, posting child pornography or publishing detailed threats against the life and safety of the U.S. President and Cabinet are likely to result in arrest and the site being taken off-line. If that happens, the authors can argue their point of view in a court of law.

Separate from that, having posts (or accounts) taken down from Twitter, TikTok, Facebook, Instagram, Medium, WordPress, MySpace, 4chan, Tinder, or any other platform in the United States is not an issue of First Amendment rights.

Jurisdictional Differences

An interesting issue popped up several times after the truckers' protest in Canada in early 2022. Several people were arrested for misbehavior in the demonstration. When they appeared in court, they claimed

10. Some legal scholars disagree with this stance, especially with platforms that have little competition from similar services. We might see this issue litigated further in coming years.

it was their Constitutional First Amendment right to protest. This bemused the judges, as the First Amendment they were apparently referencing in Canadian law has nothing to do with protest.

There is a Canadian Constitution with a First Amendment: the British North America Act, also called the Constitution Act, signed by Queen Victoria in 1867. It established Canada as a dominion composed of several colonies (Nova Scotia, New Brunswick, and Canada, which was divided into Quebec and Ontario). Its First Amendment was the Manitoba Act in 1870, which made Manitoba the fifth province in Canada.

We can imagine the judges' confusion or amusement when people protesting COVID restrictions claimed it was their right because Manitoba had been added to Canada 150 years before!

This is an example where the location is important. Laws in one jurisdiction might not have a parallel in another jurisdiction, and they certainly cannot be used to justify behavior outside the appropriate jurisdiction.[11] It is essential to understand where you are and which laws apply to that locale.

Similarly, U.S. citizens have no Second Amendment right to carry firearms across national borders and in other countries. If someone is not read their *Miranda* rights after an arrest in Bolivia or Mali or Thailand that does not mean the charges against them will be dismissed. Rights are dictated by location, not simply citizenship. On the Internet, a person can be both where they physically are and where they are having an impact or effect. So, for example, a U.S. person on a computer in the United States might violate Malaysian law by insulting the Malaysian monarch or a Russian law by calling that country's aggression in Ukraine an "invasion." Whether either nation would be able to prosecute is more a function of getting custody over the individual; it would likely be futile for the U.S. person to assert their "free speech" rights against such a prosecution at a trial held in one of those countries.

Legal Code Supersedes Computer Code

Lawrence Lessig has a dictim: Code is law. In his book *Code and Other Laws of Cyberspace*, he reminds readers that humans constructed cyberspace. What we can and cannot do there is governed by code and decided by people. Computer code can be created quickly, and computer code effectively enforces real-world rules and norms—things that take legislators years to develop. Because computer code's pace is more nimble and rapid, it is, in a sense, more effective than legislative code.

Lessig did not argue that code would replace law. He invites us to think about how software and Internet architecture govern its operations. Who decides what the rules of code are? Computer people like to believe *they* do. In 1996, John Perry Barlow authored *A Declaration of the Independence of Cyberspace*[12] in which he wrote (in part):

---

11. In deference to our Canadian readers, we note that Section 2(b) of the Canadian Charter of Rights and Freedoms (enacted in 1982) provides that "everyone has . . . freedom of thought, belief, opinion and expression, including freedom of the press and other media of communication." Section 1 of the Canadian Bill of Rights (adopted in 1960) enshrines the right to freedom of speech, assembly, association, and press.

12. www.eff.org/cyberspace-independence

> We have no elected government, nor are we likely to have one, so I address you with no greater authority than that with which liberty itself always speaks. I declare the global social space we are building to be naturally independent of the tyrannies you seek to impose on us. You have no moral right to rule us nor do you possess any methods of enforcement we have true reason to fear.

This was a rallying cry for many in the Internet community for quite a few years but could never be more than aspirational. Today, it has about as much weight as Sovereign Citizens' statements about not being subject to any "made-up" government. Neither will get someone out of legal difficulties, and trying to assert either might complicate things (for the worse) if they find themselves in trouble.

Realistically, code is written within legal jurisdictions. It is operated within legal jurisdictions. It is therefore subject to laws within those jurisdictions. Clever code might seek to influence or circumvent reality but does not define it. Courts are repeatedly reaffirming that code *is not* law and people are finding out the hard way.[13] *Programmator cave.*[14]

Fundamentally, laws are not algorithms. They are policies (presumably) dictated by the people's will through their representatives. They define what is right and wrong—permissible and impermissible. They represent value judgments and competing interests. They often work at cross-purpose and are illogical, poorly written, and ambiguous. Sometimes this ambiguity is deliberate. Even the most fundamental principle—thou shalt not kill—is subject to thousands of interpretations, justifications, and debates and is not absolute (e.g., issues of war, self-defense, justified actions of law enforcement, capital punishment, treatment of gravely ill people).

Laws Can Simply Be Converted to Computer Code

Imagine someone says, "Let's convert all of the legal code to computer code—because what is legal code but if/then/else statements?" This type of conditional logic is common in computer programs. **IF** the user clicks OK, **THEN** close the dialog box; **ELSE** (otherwise) do nothing. Could not automobiles likewise have software that enforces speed limits similarly? IF the vehicle is moving faster than the limit, THEN send the driver a ticket.

Legislators do not think in code or write in code. Therefore, the law contains inherent linguistic ambiguities that are simply impossible to reflect in computer code. That is why we have courts: The law must be interpreted, often requiring the (re)definition of terms and viewing the issues through the lens of precedent. It also requires making subjective decisions about the amounts and types of evidence presented. Some people have a fantasy of a robotic Judge Dredd being able to dispense immediate justice, but that is neither possible nor, given code rife with flaws, desirable.[15]

---

13. https://medium.com/immunefi/code-is-law-is-no-defense-for-blackhat-hacking-b083340446f4.
14. That's Latin for "Programmer beware," rather than a place to hide from the police. Or it might be "Beware of the programmer," which is good advice, too.
15. We suggest that readers view Terry Gilliam's 1985 movie *Brazil*.

It is difficult to avoid contradictions and ambiguities even with clearly stated rules. Fans of Isaac Asimov's stories involving his Three Laws of Robotics know that the ambiguities and edge cases provided the storylines and drama.[16]

Some of the most politically fraught discussions in many countries involve the human interpretation of laws. Consider the corpus of decisions made yearly by the U.S. Supreme Court and the EU Court of Justice. Nuance, precedence, and supremacy all play roles in those decisions, and those concepts would be difficult to encode algorithmically—at least in a deterministic fashion. Add in programming errors and undecidability issues, and it becomes even more of a mess.

Let's also note that even if it were practical, most people would not welcome their new robotic overlords. Down this path lurks Terminator's SkyNet, Roko's Basilisk, and the need for the Butlerian Jihad.[17]

Legislators/Regulators/Courts Know Enough About Technology to Regulate It

In 2018, U.S. Senator Orrin Hatch asked Facebook CEO Mark Zuckerberg: "So, how do you sustain a business model in which users don't pay for your service?" Zuckerberg replied: "Senator, we run ads." It appeared that the Senator didn't understand a foundational concept of modern Internet services.

This situation is perhaps explained in part by a maxim relayed to us by attorney Damien Riehl:

> Legislators are over-represented by lawyers. . . who are usually liberal arts majors. . . who usually do not understand the nuances of how technology works.

Even if legislators and regulators were knowledgeable about tech, they usually cannot *access* the code they are regulating. That's especially true with code protected as trade secrets (not open source), code classified as sensitive by a government body, and machine learning "black boxes." Instead, legislators and regulators merely see the technical system's inputs and outputs. Legislators and regulators are also subject to the same misconceptions and biases we discuss throughout this book. So, they are prone to (a) overreach and (b) misdiagnosing causation, introducing legislation and regulations that can be ineffective (a common scenario) or harmful (the worst-case scenario).

Legislators (and courts) depend greatly on technical experts in every field. They might have staff with technical backgrounds but depend on input from the technical community. In many jurisdictions, this

---

16. As cited in https://en.wikipedia.org/wiki/Three_Laws_of_Robotics:

    First Law: A robot may not injure a human being or, through inaction, allow a human being to come to harm.

    Second Law: A robot must obey the orders given it by human beings except where such orders would conflict with the First Law.

    Third Law: A robot must protect its own existence as long as such protection does not conflict with the First or Second Law.

17. We could make a long list of science fiction references here, with footnotes, but we will assume that our audience is familiar with at least one of these references.

process can be dominated by parties with significant economic resources (i.e., lobbying; in some countries, this might be outright bribery). The results are often significantly biased toward those special interests, much to the vexation of everyone else.

Nonprofit organizations such as ACM, Electronic Frontier Foundation (EFF), Center for Democracy and Technology (CDT), and Electronic Privacy Information Center (EPIC)[18] have notable roles in the United States and some other countries in ensuring that opinions other than those of business are heard—we encourage people to support and participate in such groups (or similar) if the missions of those organizations resonate with their views.

Note that it is not simply that lawyers don't understand technology—we know many highly technical attorneys, and we have had former computer science students and colleagues attend law school. It is also not the case that technologists do not understand their technology's legal, social, political, and moral implications. Both fields are complex with their own subtleties and nuances, and extra care and study are required to understand how they intersect and interact. Law, ethics, policy, and technology all come together in what we might call *technology policy* and regulation. Should self-driving cars be regulated as drivers? As products? As something else? Should medical robots be held to the same or higher malpractice standards as doctors, or should they be considered "devices"? Who is responsible if an ML system is trained on bad data and makes decisions reflecting unacceptable biases? These, and related questions, are not simple to answer in this merged space of policy.

Laws and Courts Unduly Constrain Developers

Given the previous subsections, there is a corollary myth that laws and courts excessively and improperly constrain developers.

Because legislators and judges often do not understand technologies sufficiently to regulate and adjudicate them, there might be little to prevent developers from writing code that is unsecure (along the spectrum of security), harmful (in a moral sense as well as a literal sense), and illegal (in a legislative sense).

At most, legislators and judges can guess what the code is doing or try to write laws (and judicial opinions) that address what they think is causation. They are also influenced, as noted, by economic interests. Thus, in the United States we have some rather detailed (and some claim, repressive) copyright laws but extremely little privacy protection. Two examples that have caused controversy are export control regulations and the Digital Millennium Copyright Act (DMCA).

Export Control

As a matter of policy and law, many countries limit the export of technologies that might be used in producing weapons or suppressing human rights elsewhere. It is generally clear to most people that we do not want to export technology about nuclear weapons or ballistic missiles to countries where that technology might be misused. It becomes a little more complicated when we get to the issue of information and even more murky when we start talking about research and education.

18. Respectively, https://acm.org, https://eff.org, https://cdt.org, https://epic.org.

Export control law is predicated on the assumption that a country has a monopoly on inventions or devices created by citizens of that country and can impose that monopoly on every other country. It's also predicated on the assumption that export control works. For instance, we can scan container ships and trucks at the border for illegal bananas, DVDs, counterfeit medications, and ICBMs, but that level of control is impossible in the digital environment. Also, many items are "dual use." For example, some of the same technologies that protect personal privacy also allow others to keep illegal things hidden from law enforcement authorities. How do we allow "good" uses for "good" countries and keep "bad" things from happening elsewhere?

Consider encryption. If we have a fast, efficient method of encryption that no one can break, most of the world probably does not want to let the Democratic People's Republic of Korea—North Korea (DPRK) have it; however, we might also want legitimate banks globally to have it to use internally. But we do not want criminals to use it. What to do? Every time this comes up for refined regulations, it generally results in controversy. The same applies to penetration testing tools, supercomputing, AI, and other computer-related technologies.

The United States has three regulatory frameworks that restrict the export of sensitive technologies:

- The Export Administration Regulations (EAR) govern the export, teaching, and sale of technologies of commercial goods that have dual use: one for beneficial purposes and one for harmful (in the wrong hands) purposes.
- The International Traffic in Arms Regulations (ITAR) cover things with military applications.
- The Foreign Assets Control Regulations (FACR) cover items going to countries and people under government sanctions.[19]

These restrictions are often shared across other countries via treaty obligations. EAR and FACR are consistent with an international agreement, the Wassenaar Arrangement, with 42 member countries.

It is beyond the scope of this book to discuss these in any depth at all, other than to state that, yes, there are constraints on developers, researchers, and educators related to these technologies. They also have hidden potential "gotchas," such as not allowing citizens of certain countries (including students) access to some items in their jobs or classes. Many of these constraints appear quite reasonable to the majority, while others seem misguided. Even if someone does not know about them or disagrees with them, that does not mean they do not exist and may be ignored. Remember our advice to talk to legal counsel if you have any questions.

Digital Millennium Copyright Act

In 1998, the United States enacted the DMCA. This bill contained several provisions related to copyright, but one of the most controversial was criminalizing reverse engineering of protection

19. Cf. https://researchservices.cornell.edu/policies/export-controls-regulations-and-overview.

mechanisms. This was added because copyright owners were reporting significant losses (or anticipating such losses) as people traded information about how to evade licensing restrictions.

One of the most common instances of copyright circumvention occurred related to DVDs. DVDs were (and many still are) shipped with controls to prevent them from being copied. Individuals wishing to avoid purchase fees seek to circumvent such controls to make copies of DVDs for friends and family. Some people want to mass-produce unauthorized copies to make money. These copying efforts reduce the income for the holders of the copyright. Thus, the DMCA made it a crime to perform reverse engineering and to publish tools that could be used for reverse engineering.

Somewhat predictably (to computer professionals), this law interfered with legitimate research and was abused by commercial interests to reduce competition. The researchers were threatened with offenses and lawsuits for investigating security flaws. Others decided to avoid research that might run afoul of the DMCA, thus potentially avoiding research that would be in the public interest. Meanwhile, some companies have used threats under the DMCA to shut out competitors for parts and services that require interoperability. Criminals ignore the law, of course.

The DMCA has a mechanism that allows narrowly tailored exceptions for legitimate research, and a few have been added over the years; however, adding exemptions is not simple, and exemptions need to be renewed every few years. The DMCA is slow to recognize new threats and new needs.

There is little political will to amend the DMCA because it ostensibly protects large companies with substantial copyright portfolios. This is an example of law constraining computing activity that might, in some cases, be beneficial.

It is also an example of how lobbying interests can ensure that a law is put in place and kept that might not be entirely in the public interest.

The many detailed issues around copyright, DMCA, reverse engineering, and related matters are outside this book's scope. The bottom line, however, is yes, there are constraints on developers, researchers, and educators related to these technologies. Some of those constraints appear quite reasonable to companies or seemed reasonable when first formulated. If you are involved in making copies or reverse engineering, you are well-advised to dive deeper into these topics. Suppose you find you are not particularly aligned with some current regulations. In that case, you should also investigate some of the nonprofit organizations we mentioned earlier, in footnote 18.

Law Enforcement Will Never Respond to Cyber Crimes

In February 2022, a 74-year-old man in Lincoln, Nebraska, fell victim to a computer fraud.[20] A pop-up message purporting to be from Microsoft said his bank account had been compromised. He called the phone number, and a scammer talked him through transferring more than $210,000 to the attacker.

20. https://journalstar.com/news/local/crime-and-courts/lincoln-man-74-defrauded-after-transferring-more-than-210-000-police-say/article_8f58c824-2e63-5aec-9931-bbaaeda27956.html

Four days later, a 76-year-old woman in the same city lost more than $130,000 in a similar pop-up computer scam.[21] In both cases, the money has not been recovered, and the cases remain unresolved.

These are not isolated cases. The Internet Crime Complaint Center (IC3) receives an average of 2,000 complaints from the American public daily, and the U.S. law enforcement estimates that this is 10% of all cyber and computer-related crimes.[22] One estimate is that the resolution (enforcement) rate for incidents reported to IC3 is 0.3%.[23] Given these statistics, it seems frustratingly unlikely that law enforcement has the resources to solve any given case.

Does this mean people should not seek help from law enforcement? No. Many variables determine the extent to which law enforcement can and will investigate the crime. Crimes of large financial loss are often given priority, but that does not mean smaller losses are completely ignored. The Federal Trade Commission (FTC) enforces U.S. federal consumer protection laws. "We cannot resolve your individual report," they say, "but we use reports to investigate and bring cases against fraud, scams, and bad business practices."[24]

In the United States, some state and local governments might also investigate and prosecute computer crimes if they get a complaint. In countries other than the United States, there is a wide variety of potential law enforcement assistance, from nonexistent to high-tech. It is necessary to report the crimes for them to be investigated. A formal report might be a condition of obtaining restitution from an insurance policy. We suggest that if you are a likely target, it might be a good idea to speak with your lawyer and then, based on that counsel, make some contacts with law enforcement *before* there is a pressing need.

There are rich opportunities to improve the enforcement of cybercrime laws.[25] The most obvious choices are to (a) reduce victimization and (b) increase the capacity to investigate and prosecute crimes. Both must be pursued. Another way to lighten the load is with alternative support. In the United Kingdom, for instance, the Cyber Helpline is a not-for-profit organization that connects volunteer tech experts with victims of cybercrime.[26] It does not prosecute crimes but offers "confidential, free and pragmatic advice to all victims to help them get secure again and minimise impact."

Currently, there are obstacles to the investigation and prosecution of computer-related crimes. It is still important to report them because the magnitude of criminal activity helps law enforcement make a case for resources and legislation. If there is little evidence of unsolved crime, there will be little incentive to make changes. Occasionally, the reports are investigated and the perpetrators are caught. So, it is technically a myth that law enforcement does not investigate.

---

21. www.wowt.com/2022/03/14/lpd-76-year-old-woman-loses-more-than-130000-computer-scam/
22. See www.ic3.gov/Media/PDF/AnnualReport/2020_IC3Report.pdf. By comparison, the FBI reported 6,203,201 property crime offenses in the United States in 2019, or roughly 17,000 per day. Of those, 17.2% were cleared by arrest. See https://ucr.fbi.gov/crime-in-the-u.s/2019/crime-in-the-u.s.-2019/tables/table-25
23. www.thirdway.org/report/to-catch-a-hacker-toward-a-comprehensive-strategy-to-identify-pursue-and-punish-malicious-cyber-actors
24. https://reportfraud.ftc.gov/
25. Brunner, Maggie, "Challenges and Opportunities in State and Local Cybercrime Enforcement," *Journal of National Security Law & Policy,* Vol. 10 (2019): 563.
26. https://www.thecyberhelpline.com/team

You Can Always Hide Information by Suing

The Streisand Effect was named for American entertainer Barbra Streisand, who attempted to have a photograph of her home removed from the California Coastal Records Project. She had lawyers sue to have it removed, presumably to protect her privacy; however, that attempt was not private, and it brought attention to the thing she wanted to be hidden.[27] This is a form of unintended consequence, somewhat related to the Cobra Effect (discussed in Chapter 6, "Perverse Incentives and the Cobra Effect").

FIGURE 9.2 The Streisand Effect.

27. www.economist.com/the-economist-explains/2013/04/15/what-is-the-streisand-effect

Suing to prevent something from being online is a great way to call attention to that thing someone wants to hide. An example of this was the lawsuit over Sony's encryption of DVDs. Sony did not want anyone to know how easy it was to decrypt its DVDs, so the company sued the people who showed how simple it was.[28] The encryption used by Sony was not strong, and the lawsuit was the equivalent of hiring a billboard and putting that information on it.

Another example is suing over vulnerability discovery. This occasionally occurs in CVD. A vendor threatens to sue over the report of a vulnerability in its product in hopes of suppressing it.[29] This does not hide that vulnerability because the act of filing the lawsuit says, "There is a vulnerability here." Once it is known that there's something there, it can be found again—and it will be seen because people now know where to look. Calling attention to it does not stop that process, but rather enhances it.

If you file such a suit, you might be in the right, and you might win a lawsuit. But the side effect of a lawsuit is often that everyone knows the information you are attempting to suppress. Litigation to keep something private paradoxically might make it less private.

Suing to Suppress a Breach Is a Good Idea

Data breaches are a terrible event to deal with. The data is loose in the world, out of the company's control, and the company has no idea what people will do with it. In short, not a good thing.

Suppose the worst happens, and you are the victim of such a breach. A security researcher is the one who lets you know that it happened, and they also have a copy of the data that someone sent to them. The researcher has reached out to you to inform you of the incident. What do you do?

The best thing to do is to research the researcher, determine their credentials, and then discuss the problem with them. The worst thing to do is to immediately tell everyone that the researcher is wrong, lying, and trying to cause trouble, and to threaten the researcher with a lawsuit or arrest if they tell anyone.

Trying to discredit a good-faith researcher is not only an excellent way to make your problems more public, but can also lead to a negative image in the industry. You might even get sued for defamation! And think about the precedent: Is the next person to discover a flaw more likely to come to you, privately, with the information, or will they publish it anonymously in a public and embarrassing manner?

Terms and Conditions Are Meaningless

Users of Facebook might have seen posts with phrases such as "I do not give Facebook or any entities associated with Facebook permission to use my pictures, information, messages or posts, both past, and future." The essence of these posts is a mistaken belief that such statements will somehow increase

28. www.wired.com/1999/12/dvd-hackers-hit-with-lawsuit/
29. https://vuls.cert.org/confluence/display/CVD/6.8+Hype%2C+Marketing%2C+and+Unwanted+Attention

the privacy of users who have already agreed to Facebook's terms and conditions. Not so! A "Terms and Conditions" statement is a legally binding contract.[30]

The pitfall is that users cannot unilaterally change (or exempt themselves from) a binding contract—including Facebook's terms and conditions. Posting a message of objection or any statement of legalese has zero legal effect. Use of a software or online platform is governed by the platform's terms and conditions, to which the user agreed. The only way to disagree is to cancel the account and stop using the platform.

Users commonly ignore the terms and conditions of software. The documents containing this information are usually too long, too dense, and too confusing. Only if something goes wrong might users go back to see what terms they accepted. As with many contracts, standard sections of particular note include Disclaimer of Warranties, Limitation of Liability, General Representation and Warranty, and Indemnification. Some of these are written in ALL CAPITAL LETTERS to ensure that the reader knows it is important. These might include "USE AT YOUR OWN RISK" and "WE FURTHER DISCLAIM ALL WARRANTIES, EXPRESS AND IMPLIED, INCLUDING WITHOUT LIMITATION, ANY IMPLIED WARRANTIES OF MERCHANTABILITY, FITNESS FOR A PARTICULAR PURPOSE, OR NONINFRINGEMENT."[31]

Would you be comfortable with those terms if the software controlled a medical ventilator or electrical plant? Surprise—some vendors use code with those disclaimers in their products, then disclaim their liability when they sell them. Not surprisingly, some third-party vendors will use that code in safety-critical systems but neglect to pass along the specific warnings.

Clickwrap is a term that applies to a situation where new users must affirmatively agree with terms and conditions, such as by clicking a checkbox. Websites might also have terms and conditions, but there is rarely affirmative consent from the visitor. The website owner might think that users have accepted the website's terms simply by using the site, but this is proving to be increasingly unenforceable. In general, users must be able to see, review, and take action confirming that they agree with the Terms and Conditions contract for it to be in force.

Note that this is subject to different laws in different jurisdictions, so get expert advice if you have concerns.

The Law Is on My Side, So I Do Not Need to Worry

Looking back over this chapter, you will see that laws are often vague, nuanced, and complicated. They also have some significant complexities related to parties involved and jurisdiction. Therefore, you should perhaps worry, at least a little.

---

30. Provided they are correctly designed, presented, and tracked.

31. These appear in many software licenses, including the ones for Java. See www.java.com/en/download/uninstall-app/terms.jsp

First, you might not understand the law as well as you think. You might not appreciate your standing and whose laws apply to you. In almost every jurisdiction, ignorance of the specifics of the laws involved is not an excuse for violating them.

Second, even if you are not violating any law, that does not mean you might not be charged with an offense or sued in civil court by another party. That happens all the time: People are mistakenly arrested and charged, and lawsuits, both serious and frivolous, are filed by the thousands every week. Even if you are blameless for whatever is alleged, you will need to respond with a defense. That can be expensive and time-consuming, and if you are unlucky, you might lose. (The odds of success often depend on the jurisdiction and how much you can spend to defend yourself, unfortunately. The law in practice does not work as fairly and seamlessly as theory suggests.)

If you are in business, you should have an attorney or law firm on retainer. Consult them regularly. If you are an individual involved in public activities, especially any that someone might view as criminal, it is also good to have an accredited lawyer on your phone list. In both cases, it is also wise to investigate insurance covering legal fees. And before you head out of the country, read up on the key legal issues on where you are going.

Further Reading

Dunne, Robert. *Computers and the Law*. Cambridge University Press, 2009.

Hoofnagle, Chris J., and Garfinkel, Simson L. *Law and Policy for the Quantum Age*. Cambridge University Press, 2022.

Kosseff, Jeff. *Cybersecurity Law*, 2nd ed. Wiley, 2019.

Lessig, Lawrence. *Code: And Other Laws of Cyberspace*. Basic Books, 2009.

Lessig, Lawrence. "The Law of the Horse: What Cyberlaw Might Teach," *Harvard Law Review* Vol. 113, No. 2 (1999): 501–549.

Schmidt, Michael N., ed. *Tallinn Manual 2.0 on the International Law Applicable to Cyber Operations*. Cambridge University Press, 2017.

Chapter 10

Tool Myths and Misconceptions

Men have become the tools of their tools.

Henry David Thoreau

Tools are where the cybersecurity rubber meets the road. Humans are useless in performing meaningful cybersecurity with our minds and bodies alone. Our best ideas must be implemented and put into practice. The word *tool* is an abstract catch-all for software, algorithms, services, and various methods for performing a task or achieving a goal. Some military environments use the word "capability" as a similar concept for the ability to achieve a desired objective. Both cover a wide spectrum, from `vim` and `grep` to Wireshark to spam-detecting machine learning models to ElasticSearch to VirusTotal. For the sake of discussion in this chapter, we will not quibble about a precise definition of the word *tool*.

According to one estimate, large enterprises have, on average, 76 security tools.[1] Cybersecurity professionals rely on tools to perform all aspects of their work, from secure software development to generating and analyzing logs for intrusion analysis. Tools are the backbone of cybersecurity practice. In addition to productivity, this leads to misconceptions and assumptions about their creation and use. It is also difficult to remove or replace tools for fear that doing so might break a workflow. So, tools pile up.

This chapter's opening quote reminds us that relying on tools can make them a crutch. Eventually, we cannot function without them. In some ways, this is to our benefit. Computers are much faster and more accurate in analyzing most data than humans are. This backfires when humans outsource too much of their thinking to software. It also goes wrong when we start to believe that tools are infallible. The truism goes that computers make fast, accurate mistakes. Various philosophies about tools influence how they are created and used. The UNIX philosophy included the maxim of making each program do one thing well. This led naturally to a collection of many single-purpose utilities that can be combined to perform more complex operations. The UNIX tool `grep` is a powerhouse for cybersecurity to find patterns in data.[2] In contrast is an approach of "one tool to rule them all." Some call this

1. https://panaseer.com/wp-content/uploads/2021/11/Panaseer-2022-Security-Leaders-Peer-Report.pdf
2. Some people use grep as the de facto gold standard tool. For any new tool being proposed, is it any better than grep?

the *single pane of glass* strategy where users can interact, manipulate, analyze, and visualize disparate data sources on one screen.

This chapter examines some myths and misconceptions about cybersecurity tools.

> **What About TTPs?**
>
> The acronym Tactics, Techniques, and Procedures (TTP) is constantly bandied about in cybersecurity. As a result, you might think that everyone knows what the acronym means, but we find that it is often misused. TTP does include two words starting with the letter T, but some people are surprised that neither stands for *tools*. These represent increasingly granular descriptions of behavior, either ours or an attacker's. Other frameworks do consider tools. In the Diamond Model[a] of intrusion analysis, for example, the four components are adversary, capability, infrastructure, and victim. In this case, capability refers to the tools and techniques used by an adversary, such as ransomware, phishing, and Gh0st (a remote access tool).
>
> [a] Caltagirone, Sergio, Pendergast, Andrew, and Betz, Christopher, "The Diamond Model of Intrusion Analysis," Technical Report, Center for Cyber Intelligence Analysis and Threat Research, 2013.

The More Tools, The Better

Tool pileup is a problem in cybersecurity. It is not uncommon for cyber analysts or incident responders to have multiple laptops and phones within arm's reach to "maintain awareness" of different activities across systems or networks. They might also have multiple hardware authorization tokens on a lanyard, each used to authorize access to a specific system or tool. All of this leads to a complex environment and fans the fire of fatigue, burnout, and errors. Simply put, the more tools accumulate, the greater the risks become.

One day, an organization decides it is going to stop the flow of malicious attachments. To accomplish this, the managers declare that any message that has an attachment of a predefined type will be sent to a special mailbox monitored by the SOC.[3] Then, the SOC personnel will:

1. Download the files sent to the mailbox.
2. Analyze the files for malware, looking for duplicates and attachments that are not malware.
3. Submit the list of malware found in the previous step to an antivirus software vendor.
4. If the malware is unknown to the vendor, a new signature is created and passed back to the organization.
5. The organization then adds that signature to its local antivirus solution.

3. This is based on an actual study. See Sundaramurthy, Sathya Chandran, "An Anthropological Study of Security Operations Centers to Improve Operational Efficiency," University of South Florida, 2017.

That is for a single email, and more emails are always coming. Now let's throw in a tool that analyzes the domains found in the email with these attachments. We also want to know if the emails are phishing, which requires another management tool. Even watching all of this is tiring—imagine doing it repeatedly.

Some of this can be automated, such as the first task, to analyze the attachments—but then someone needs to keep an eye on it to ensure it works and check its results at least every day. "Keeping an eye" on something is a type of *vigilance task* demanding sustained attention and monitoring; humans are extraordinarily poor at this.

And this is simply for an email with a particular attachment type. What about an email that ends up in spam? Knowing that someone is attempting to spearphish[4] our organization is important, so another tool needs to analyze that. Plus, people often report emails they get as suspicious, so something needs to analyze each email reported as suspicious.

We have not even gotten to the results from the IDSs.[5] It might spit out 1,375 alerts every hour for someone to filter and triage. We call that a low signal-to-noise ratio: lots of garbage to sort through to find the critical items (signal).

It is crucial to analyze emails. They are an attack vector, and it is important to know how we are being targeted as an organization. A new tool for each potential piece of information that could be gleaned from an email is overkill and overwork for the people in the SOC. A tool should aid their work, not add to overload.

More of anything can be too much past a certain point. More chocolate can be great until we are forced to eat 50 kg of it *every* day.

Every New Threat Needs a New Tool

Cryptojacking[6] is a relatively new threat. Rather than stealing our money or information, it uses the computer's power to mine cryptocurrency. SMS phishing is another old threat made new. It is still a deceptive message like traditional phishing, but now it is going through the cell phone, not email, and the adversary still wants us to click on the link. In the worst case, there is no clicking.[7]

These new threats need new defenses. Cryptojacking is stealing our power, not our money! SMS phishing is attacking the phone, not our email! Bad things! It is time to buy more tools to fight these new threats. Add them to the myriad of tools the SOC already has to deal with, and we will be protected, safe from these new threats.

Except, maybe not. Again, adding to a glut of tools simply adds to the burden of the SOC, as well as incurring new licensing costs, more software to keep up-to-date, and more logs and configurations to protect. Yet, how do we handle new threats?

---

4. A phish directed at one person, like fishing with a spear gun.
5. See the Appendix for more information on IDSs
6. https://securityboulevard.com/2021/09/what-is-cryptocurrency-mining-malware-2/
7. https://googleprojectzero.blogspot.com/2021/12/a-deep-dive-into-nso-zero-click.html

One way is by carefully examining the assumptions and operation of the attacks. For example, cryptojacking involves penetrating defenses and installing software. We should already have defenses in place for that. The same is done in ransomware and installing Remote Access Trojan (RAT) software. If we have protection to keep out intruders and watch for new programs, we can address them all with that same solution. If our current product has some blind spot for cryptojacking, we need to investigate updating or replacing that product.

How about SMS phishing? This, too, can use some existing solutions. We currently train our employees and colleagues to avoid phishing emails. Make it clear to them that SMS phishing is the same problem! Also, investigate what is now installed—many popular smartphones have a feature to ignore SMS messages from unknown senders. Instead of installing a new tool, we can simply turn that on.

Vendors make money by identifying new special cases and convincing us that we need to spend money on their products to address those cases. We should carefully evaluate whether the new special cases are so special after all.

Do We Still Need These Tools?

A corollary to the idea of being considerate about adding new tools is checking the *existing* tools. It is helpful to periodically audit their performance to ensure they are catching/preventing things not handled by other programs. We might discover that, over time, the same functionality has been built into other tools, and we can save money (and complexity and system load) by eliminating redundancy. This is related to the sunk cost fallacy discussed in Chapter 4, "Fallacies and Misunderstandings": We should not continue to use tools *only* because we have paid for them.

In the early days of computer viruses, we know of organizations that paid for and ran as many as five different antivirus programs in parallel because no single one caught everything. After a few years, as the industry matured, the best tools converged on detecting the same threats. The companies that made A/B comparisons on detection discovered they could save money and overhead by switching to a single, highly reliable product. We suspect some companies are still paying extra to run multiple, redundant programs while also slowing their systems' performance.

Default Configurations Are Always Secure

Tools ship with default configurations. Maybe the vendor even thinks they are the "best" settings.[8] It makes things easy for the non-expert: Install the tool, start it running, and it (usually) works. That default config might not be perfect for our organization, but it should work well. After we use it for a while, we might find ourselves making changes, but the basic configuration seems okay at the beginning. After all, it is working.

8. How a company determines these settings is unknown; we often take it on faith that it is good.

Default settings are not unique to security tools. Indeed, they occur in every software tool we could use: web servers, Active Directory, accounting tools, et al. Every program with options ships with a basic, default, "should work for most things" configuration.

People naturally assume that this configuration is secure. The options chosen *should* be the best for any organization, which should mean that they will not leave *our* organization open to an attack. "Defaults are what rule the world."[9]

Here's the thing about that default configuration: The "best" involved might not be for *us*, but for the *typical* customer or even for the *vendor*. How so? Most vendors do not like to spend money on call center operations (i.e., helplines). The out-of-the-box configuration is intended to install and run at most organizations without requiring the customer to call for assistance. The vendor does not want to spend time debugging the options for every customer or answering questions that depend heavily on custom environments. The vendor also does not want people to avoid its products because they are too difficult to set up, so it provides a basic set of options to get them working.

As a canonical example, the default configuration of Active Directory can be exploited to let a random user get administrative access.[10] Nothing we did in setting this up caused this issue—it came as the default. This kind of thing is not a new problem, either. CVE-1999-0678[11]—more than 20 years old—discusses how the default install allowed users to read files they should not have on an Apache web server. This read permission was restricted to `/usr/doc`, but still, it is a bad idea to let people read random files.

Not every default configuration issue gets a CVE. The SyGate 5.0 personal firewall default configuration allowed traffic in on port 137 or 138 by default. Using that, an attacker could bypass the firewall, which is a rather large hole.[12] Malware has also taken advantage of default configurations, which include more than options that make the device operational. Default passwords are part of that configuration. The Mirai botnet used the default passwords to take over IoT devices and add them to its web of attackers.[13]

We want to believe that we can install the software or the appliance and have it "just work" without any additional steps. This was the motivation behind "plug and play" devices. Vendors want us to believe the same because it makes selling complicated software easier. We do not have to read a manual hundreds of pages thick to install the software.[14] Instead, we install it and *Presto!* it works.

That presupposes the tool does something beneficial. We know of past instances when tools were sold with fancy interfaces and options but did nothing useful. In other cases, tools downloaded from the Internet were spyware or computer virus droppers! We are unaware of any current vendors doing

9. Will Dorman, CERT/CC.
10. https://github.com/Dec0ne/KrbRelayUp
11. https://nvd.nist.gov/vuln/detail/CVE-1999-0678
12. www.exploit-db.com/exploits/22200
13. Jaramillo, Luis Eduardo Suástegui, "Malware Detection and Mitigation Techniques: Lessons Learned from Mirai DDoS Attack," *Journal of Information Systems Engineering & Management*, Vol. 3, No. 3 (2018).
14. Few vendors ship manuals anymore, either. If we are lucky, there might be some webpages that are not too badly out-of-date.

this; however, various governments prohibit products by certain companies from being used on their networks because of the threat of hostile governments' inclusions (e.g., backdoors or spyware).

The bottom line here is that we cannot depend on the default installation to be the most secure for our environment, and we should carefully check the provenance of anything we do install.

A Tool Can Stop All Bad Things

The lock on the front door of our home is a physical-world security tool. An effective one, we hope. But think about the threats to our home that a lock cannot stop. Fire is one example. Unlocking the door for someone who knocks is another. The door lock is not intended to prevent all bad things from happening.

Commercial firewalls grew out of network protection approaches pioneered in the late 1980s.[15] They were designed to allow us to filter traffic by IP address, port, and protocol. It seemed like a miracle tool because before that, on UNIX systems, we had to remember to edit the `inetd.conf` configuration file to stop people from connecting to the system; we had nothing for Windows. It was all or nothing.[16]

The firewall was, simply put, a game-changer. If someone sent us bad traffic, we could recognize and block it.

Furthermore, we could block only that address, not the entire world.

Here's the hard part: recognizing the bad traffic. As we discussed in Chapter 4, the *Base Rate Fallacy* shows that only a tiny amount of traffic is bad. The firewall (or other tool) must be programmed with what to look for. Let's consider an egregious example: the SQL Slammer worm. It traveled through the Internet, hitting servers that had port 1433 open to the world. The easy way to protect SQL servers was to block any traffic to that port and only allow our servers to connect to it; before that attack, no one had recognized it might be an issue.

Adversaries use standard ports all the time, especially ports that are intended to be open to the world.[17] Stuxnet used port 80 (the web server port) to communicate, and nearly a quarter of malware uses port 443, the HTTPS port.[18] Malware targets ports are in common use because people do not usually block them. The act of accessing port 443 is not worth blocking because it is expected that websites use it. Commonly, people go to websites. We cannot block all traffic from the organization to websites because some traffic might be to malicious websites. Context is needed. The honey badger does not care if we lack context; it only wants to swim in our data (Figure 10.1).

---

15. Cheswick, William R., et al., *Firewalls and Internet Security: Repelling the Wily Hacker*, 2nd ed., Addison-Wesley, 2003.
16. One of the authors of this book was the victim of a hack because an upgrade reverted the `inetd.conf` file to one that was completely open.
17. https://collaborate.mitre.org/attackics/index.php/Technique/T0885
18. https://news.sophos.com/en-us/2020/02/18/nearly-a-quarter-of-malware-now-communicates-using-tls/

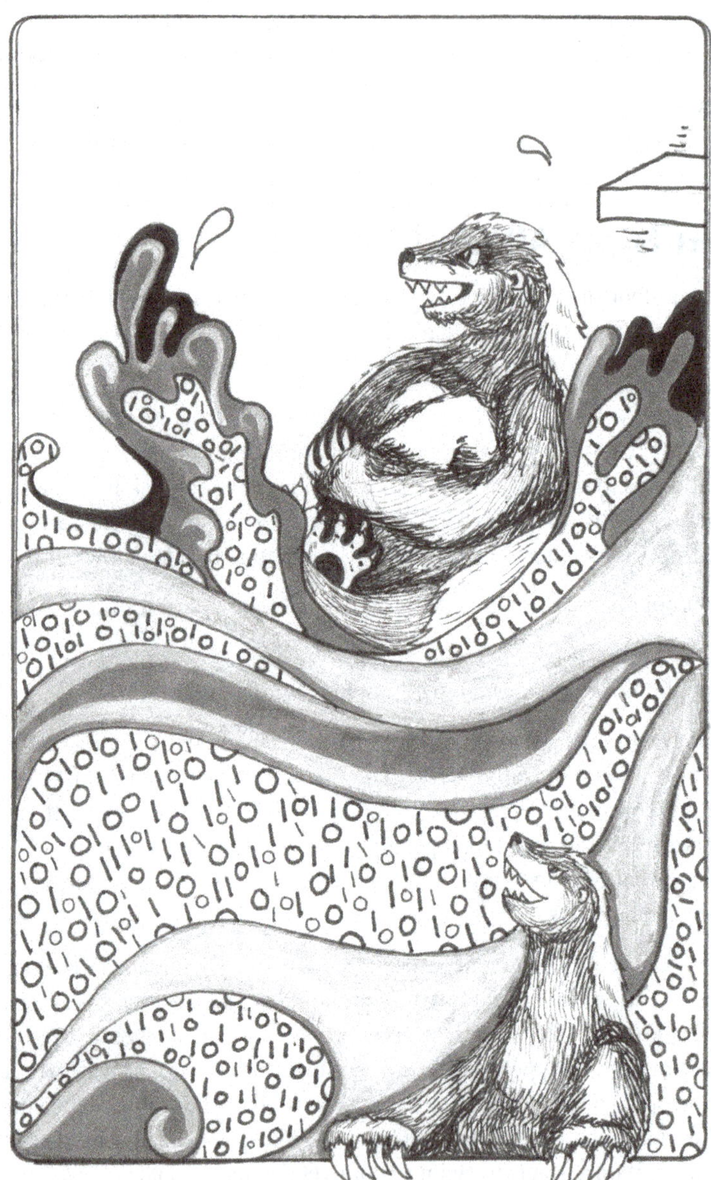

FIGURE 10.1 Carefree honey badger swimming in data.

That is looking at outgoing traffic. What about incoming traffic? The `log4j` vulnerability was (and is) a terrible zero-day vulnerability.[19] Web servers whose admins thought they were safe and used `log4j`

19. See the Appendix for more information on `log4j`.

to improve their logging infrastructures were in for a shock when this threat emerged. They had to be open to the world to allow people to access their content; otherwise, what's the point of having a web server? Unfortunately, their web server was vulnerable once the remote exploit for `log4j` was available. It is a game of whack-a-mole: Someone tries it, we notice it in a traffic monitor, then we block that IP address. Someone else tries it, then we block that one. Rinse, lather, repeat.

The same is true of IDSs. A brand-new attack, such as the `log4j` remote exploit, will not be something our system looks for until we tell it to. The remote attacker attempts to do a `jndi` lookup,[20] and that will potentially give them the ability to execute arbitrary commands. Until we tell our IDS that this is something important, it will not know that. This is not true for only `log4j`: It is true for any new threat.

Firewalls—and other important tools—need to be carefully configured, kept up-to-date, and monitored. With appropriate options and tuning, they can keep out many, many threats—but do not assume any tool will keep out *every threat!*

Intent Can Be Determined from Tools

A hammer is defined as:[21]

> a) a tool with a heavy metal part on a long handle, used for hitting nails into wood.
>
> b) a tool like this with a wooden head used to make something flat, make a noise, etc.

A hammer is a tool. It can be used for good (such as building houses) or for evil (such as breaking random windows), but intrinsically it is neither good nor bad—it is simply a tool. The intentions about its use cannot be derived by looking at the item (Figure 10.2). Maybe someone wanted a wall taken down and used a hammer to do it. Unless we know the context (Was the wall protecting something? Did the person have permission to remove the wall?), it is impossible to make a definitive judgment.

We might think, "But cybersecurity tools are made to find bad things. So if they find something, I can assume that there was malicious intent behind it." It is nice to think that. We want to believe that if something is found by the tools that look for bad things, then those things were done by malicious people with bad intentions.

First, we are going to skip the false positives—that is, when those tools tell us bad things happen, but the tool is wrong.[22] We will assume that if a tool tells us something bad happened, something happened. The problem is assigning intent to that something.

20. https://kb.cert.org/vuls/id/930724

21. https://www.ldoceonline.com/dictionary/hammer. Reprinted by permission of Pearson, Longman Dictionary of Contemporary English, 2014.

22. See "Errors in Classification Are Insignificant" in Chapter 14, "Lies, Damn Lies, and Statistics," for more information on false positives.

FIGURE 10.2 Tools do not dictate creation or destruction.

An apparent DDoS on a website could simply be the website going viral because it is popular. This even has a name: the Slashdot Effect.[23] This effect occurs when a popular website links to a different website, and suddenly that (usually, smaller) website sees more traffic than it can handle. People

23. This phrase originated when Slashdot, a popular tech news site, would link to websites in its posts and sometimes overloaded the site with a sudden surge of visitors. See https://en.wikipedia.org/wiki/Slashdot_effect

worldwide will attempt to access the website, and it will seem to be a distributed attack. It is not. It is simply that the website is popular today, and everyone wants to view it. The intent is not malicious; rather, it might be good that it is so popular.

Border Gateway Protocol (BGP) routing is how traffic is directed around the Internet. An organization announces the networks it owns to everyone, and that information is used to direct traffic to it. There is no security built into the protocol, so anyone can announce any networks.[24] One day, we come into work and discover that all of our traffic is now being routed to another organization that is not ours.

Imagine a bad actor has decided to steal our traffic and cause havoc by announcing to the world that they are the owners of our network. As a result, they can intercept our mail, pretend to be us and send bad things out, harming our reputation, and generally do naughty things. Clearly, when we get an alert from the system monitoring for such announcements, we can jump straight to that conclusion. It cannot be because someone made a mistake. It must be because someone wants to pretend to be us by committing routing identity theft.

Except, it is often a mistake.[25] Suppose our organization owns the network with IP address range 10.**10**.0.0/24 and broadcasts this to the world over BGP. The organization that announces our network, however, misannounces our IP address range as 10.**12**.0.0/24. A transposition of two bits was likely the cause of the error. People do make mistakes, sometimes![26] If you have ever accidentally called a wrong number on the telephone, you can easily understand how such an operator error can occur.

Cybersecurity relies on context. A tool giving an alert lacks that: It simply indicates "questionable things found here." It is similar to a car alarm. A car alarm is a tool to inform us that someone or something is jostling the car, but when it goes off, we need more context. Anything can (and has) set off car alarms: wind, a cat, an earthquake, or a broken sensor in the alarm. That the alarm was blaring does not necessarily mean a bad guy tried to break into the car—the context of why the alarm was sounding matters. The same is true of cybersecurity tools. Be cautious about jumping to conclusions.

Security Tools Are Inherently Secure and Trustworthy

"This software must be safe." Have you heard statements like that? Maybe related to pacemakers. Or power plants. Or cybersecurity tools. These are examples of the pitfall of misattributing a person's perception of the safety and importance of a task with the overall quality of the tool. Medical care is a life-or-death risk, so the controlling software must be of the utmost safety and security, right?

---

24. There is add-on security that can possibly prevent it from spreading throughout the Internet, but nothing to stop someone from announcing it.
25. Real incidents of BGP hijacking occur once or twice a year, but there are vastly more misconfiguration errors. See Mahajan, Ratul, Wetherall, David, and Anderson, Tom, "Understanding BGP Misconfiguration," *ACM SIGCOMM Computer Communication Review*, Vol. 32, No. 4 (2002): 3–16.
26. Except the authors of this book.

Unfortunately, this is a dangerous and unfounded assumption. Safety-critical systems have faced many vulnerabilities. This has included pacemakers, self-driving automobiles, autopilots, and many others. The same misconception applies to cybersecurity tools. One might presume that software intended to help deliver cybersecurity is highly secure. There are, however, no standards for such things.

The literature is full of cases when a tool specifically designed to help provide security was flawed. As a few examples:

- In 2020, more than 10,000 companies were using the Orion Platform from SolarWinds. This software was trusted to help monitor and manage IT, including government networks. Security researchers discovered that the software was compromised in a supply chain attack that left customers vulnerable to remote exploitation.
- Antivirus and other security software from ESET is favorably reviewed and widely used to keep computers secure. But even its software is not invulnerable to vulnerabilities, such as CVE-2021-37852.[27] Taking advantage of that vulnerability allowed attackers to get more privileges than they should, which is a bit ironic: The adversaries using the program meant to stop bad behavior to execute bad behavior.
- The Snort IDS[28] had a vulnerability that would cause a Denial of Service (DoS). Another ironic vulnerability with a tool: One designed to catch a DoS falls to a DoS.

This list is not meant to single out those tools—the same thing has repeatedly happened with software from many different vendors.

Lastly, we caution against the assumption that all software and source code found online is secure. Copying and pasting from online sites might produce a functional solution, but it might also introduce vulnerabilities. In Chapter 1, "What Is Cybersecurity?," we discussed the myth that open source software is naturally more secure than closed source. It is hazardous for developers to reuse libraries and other code snippets found online and presume that the code is correct and secure. Most online sites such as GitHub do not require code to be validated in any way. For example, a supply chain attack was found that spoofed GitHub metadata.[29]

In 2017, the winner of the National Security Agency's (NSA) Annual Best Scientific Cybersecurity Paper Competition went to the paper titled "You Get Where You're Looking For: The Impact of Information Sources on Code Security." In this study, 54 participants wrote security software and were assigned to one of four groups: free choice of resources, Stack Overflow only, official Android documentation only, or books only.[30] Results showed that those using only Stack Overflow wrote significantly less secure code.

27. www.bleepingcomputer.com/news/microsoft/eset-antivirus-bug-let-attackers-gain-windows-system-privileges/
28. https://thehackernews.com/2022/04/researchers-detail-bug-that-could.html
29. www.securityweek.com/supply-chain-attack-technique-spoofs-github-commit-metadata
30. Acar, Yasemin, Backes, Michael, Fahl, Sascha, Kim, Doowon, Mazurek, Michelle L., and Stransky, Christian, "You Get Where You're Looking For: The Impact of Information Sources on Code Security," *IEEE Symposium on Security and Privacy* (2016): 289–305.

In 2022, CISA circulated a warning that matched some online accounts of North Koreans falsely applying for remote software jobs. Those imposters were noted to be targeting (among others) cryptocurrency firms. The informed speculation was that, if hired, they would have access to code repositories where they could alter code trusted and used by others in various blockchain/cryptocurrency systems. They would then use the backdoors installed to steal the valuables to help finance the DPRK regime's nuclear weapons program. Rather than attack the systems directly, they would alter the support code the developers incorporated into the systems.

Security software might be an even greater target of opportunity for attackers, given users' blind trust that it is secure. To avoid the pitfall of believing that security tools are inherently secure and trustworthy, treat them with at least some caution and due diligence. Vulnerabilities can be anywhere.

Nothing Found Means All Is Well

There is a set of misconceptions around the (non)reporting of problems. These are variants of the *Absence of Evidence Is Evidence of Absence fallacy* described in Chapter 4, "Fallacies and Misunderstandings."

Nothing Found by the Scanners Means We Are Secure

Scanners are a basic tool in cybersecurity defense. We want to find the things that are causing or could cause trouble. We will discuss two common forms of scanners: vulnerability and malware/IDS software.

The vulnerability scanner looks for something that could happen, and the malware (or IDS scanner) looks for something that did happen. They are two complementary approaches. We want to prevent potential bad events from occurring, but if they do occur, we want to find them immediately.

When a scanner finds something, that means there is work to be done: either by rectifying what might be a misconfiguration or vulnerability, or by removing malware from the system. We cannot assume, however, that everything a scanner finds is a problem. It could be a *false positive*—something that is not a problem, even though it looks like one. Every alert created by a scanner should be investigated equally, without assumption.

Of course, it takes time and money to investigate every notification from a scanner. Everyone dislikes false positives because they lead to wasted time and effort. If there are too many false alarms, it can lead to the assumption that every alarm is a false positive—the "cry wolf" effect. That is not good, either.

It should be a happy day, then, when nothing is found. That means there is no work to be done. The systems are not vulnerable, there is no malware on any of them, and we are as secure as possible. Nothing to see here, we have done our job well, and the computers are safe today. Take the afternoon off.

Except we do not know if we are really safe.

A scanner can be blocked. Network scanners are commonly detected, and the target network blocks the IP addresses they originate from. If we scan it, we will find nothing because they report, "There is nothing to see here, move along."

Finding nothing does not mean there is nothing to find. Scanners can find only what they are designed to find. Think of it as a checklist. A scanner has a list of things it knows about, and if something is not on that list, it will blithely ignore it as if it does not exist. The list is not necessarily precise, as there is often some approximation built in—it looks for a "weakness mostly like this," not necessarily a "weakness precisely with these bits." Antivirus software can also look for behavior, but it finds only things it knows about.

For example, the Spectre/Meltdown vulnerabilities were a new class of vulnerabilities when discovered. They had never been seen before, although the kind of attack they enabled had. Before they were found, no scanner would tell us if we were vulnerable to them. They could not tell us about the unknown if they did not know about it.

One study showed[31] that web vulnerability scanners miss problems with admin interfaces. This is because we do not want to give any random scanner access to our admin, which is a good thing. Missing the problem is not great, but it works as designed.

These are not failures. They do not occur because someone in the SOC did something wrong. Instead, these situations happen when we are automating something that changes constantly. The automation is designed based on known attacks. It is not always effective at finding the unknowns.

We know there are things out there. We simply do not know *all* the things out there. Humans have, so far, mapped only about 20% of the oceans. That means that 80% of the seafloor under the earth's water has never been examined. There are things in the sea we do not know about. Luckily, for oceans, we can say, "We have mapped this much, and we do not know about the rest." Cybersecurity is not that precise. We can say we know things, but we cannot express how much we do not know. That also means that the Megalodon of malware might be out there waiting to take a bite—or perhaps it's Cthulu.

No Alarms Means We Are Secure

The SOC is a quiet place today. No alarms are going off, no emails are popping up to warn of other problems, and even the network monitor projected onto the wall shows everything is green.

It is excellent, a lovely sight: Everyone can catch up with work they neglected because of other alarms. We are clearly safe and secure, and everything is working as expected. Good work, team!

31. Doupé, Adam, Cova, Marco, and Vigna, Giovanni, "Why Johnny Can't Pentest: An Analysis of Black-Box Web Vulnerability Scanners," International Conference on Detection of Intrusions and Malware, and Vulnerability Assessment, Springer, Berlin, Heidelberg, 2010.

Looking For What Is Not There

One best practice in many organizations is to assume that their systems have been penetrated by something that has not set off an alarm. They spend some amount of their time, when not responding to an actual alarm, threat hunting. They are hunting for a new attack that bypassed the current alarms.

We might think it a waste of time to hunt for something for which there is no evidence; however, anecdotally, it has two benefits. First, it helps the hunters to stay sharp, polish their skills, and become more familiar with their tools. That is undoubtedly a benefit.

But the surprising second benefit is that sometimes they find it—they find a stealthy infiltration or dishonest insider that evaded all the existing alarms. Then, not only do they clear up a problem, but they also get some valuable input on how to construct a better defense.

About that fantasy. . . It is precisely that, a fantasy. As in the previous section, the fact that no alarms are going off is partly a good thing (because no one is pedal to the metal to solve a problem) but perhaps a reason for concern. Alarms in security are not the same as smoke alarms. It is not a case of when there is smoke, there is fire, nor is it a case of when the alarm sounds, there must be smoke.

It is a case of if the specific (more or less) conditions warrant it, an alarm will be raised.

We know the conditions for fire. There is heat, there is smoke, and generally there are flames. We can create a specific set of conditions needed to produce fire. Using those conditions, we have detectors to let us know that there is most likely a fire, and it is time to do something about it.

We cannot create the same specific set of conditions for security. We have a set of general conditions that might or might not fit perfectly. We might think that sending big emails is a sign of an insider exfiltrating important company data, but it might only be a case of a salesperson sending a large file to a customer. For example, a Boeing employee sent a spreadsheet to his wife for help with formatting.[32] Asking one's spouse for help can be a good thing, although sending internal employee information is not.

Another example is when it appears the web server is under attack because numerous new IP addresses are accessing it. In that case, it could be that something was posted on the website and went viral. Now everyone wants to see the website, and with all the traffic, it looks like a DDoS attack.

Using the first example, let's try to create alarm conditions for data exfiltration. First, large emails. Those are something we should look for. Except for salespeople because they have customers. Then there are technical people who might be sending manuals to customers. There is always an exception to that rule. Any of those people have reasons to send large emails, but at the same point, they could also be exfiltrating data as malicious insiders.

DNS has also been used for exfiltration.[33] The adversary registers a random-looking domain and then sends queries to odd-looking subdomains, which are encoded information. To find these, we could

32. www.bizjournals.com/seattle/news/2017/02/28/boeing-discloses-36-000-employee-data-breach.html
33. www.infoblox.com/dns-security-resource-center/dns-security-issues-threats/dns-security-threats-data-exfiltration/

look for weird queries from our organization, and then "Bingo!" we found the exfiltration. Except that seeing weird domains is common. AWS, Google, and other organizations use them constantly.

These are simplified examples, but the point remains, there is not a specific set of conditions we can point to and say, "Danger, Will Robinson! Danger!"[34]

All of that discussion is leading up to this point: The fact that there are no alarms does not mean things are not happening. Alarms are generally based on recognized conditions; otherwise, they will not sound. If they do not sound, it does not mean that nothing happened (as when a fire alarm is not sounding). It only means that the specific set of conditions did not occur.

It might sound (and feel) like a failure if an event happens and the alarms do not catch it. But it is not. It is a case that the alarm system missed the specific conditions.

Such events will inevitably happen in cybersecurity. We often do not find attacks until days or even years after they happened. We should learn from the conditions that allowed the attacks and use that knowledge to stop the same or similar attacks from occurring in the future.

No Vulnerability Reports Means No Vulnerabilities

Terry wants to buy a new software suite, Whizbang Tool Fundamentals, for GoodLife Bank. A review of the CVE database and published stories reveals nothing. The vendor has no hotfixes listed on its webpage. Wow—no reported vulnerabilities. The suite must be ultra-secure!

This is not necessarily the correct conclusion. It might well be that the WTF package was carefully coded and maintained, so it has no significant problems. It might also be the case that the suite has limited use and adoption, so it has not been examined much. Several dozen flaws might have been reported to the vendor in the last few months, but the vendor has chosen not to disclose them or to issue fixes. The software might also be so new that reports of flaws have yet to be made.

The myth is that the absence of indications of flaws means flaws are absent. Terry would be well-advised to perform additional research to determine why there are no reports or hotfixes and what other customers think. Terry should also review the section "Absence of Evidence Is Evidence of Absence" in Chapter 4!

Further Reading

Adkins, Heather, et al., *Building Secure and Reliable Systems: Best Practices for Designing, Implementing, and Maintaining Systems*. O'Reilly Media, 2020.

Lee, John D., Wickens, Christopher D., Liu, Yili, and Boyle, Linda Ng. *Designing for People: An Introduction to Human Factors Engineering*. CreateSpace, 2017.

Norman, Don. *The Design of Everyday Things: Revised and Expanded Edition*. Basic Books, 2013.

Rinehart, Aaron, and Shortridge, Kelly. *Security Chaos Engineering*. O'Reilly Media, 2020.

34. That is assuming that Will works in the SOC.

Chapter 11

Vulnerabilities

> Securing legacy systems is like trying to put rebar into Jello without changing its appearance or flavor.
>
> *Spaf*

In *The Lord of the Rings: The Two Towers*, a dramatic battle between good and evil occurs at Helm's Deep. The bad guys (orcs and their allies) breach the fortress of defense by blowing a hole in a vulnerable spot. The drain is the only weakness in the solid rock outer wall. Once the orcs blow the hole, the citadel is taken.[1]

A vulnerability is something susceptible to harm. Exploiting that vulnerability allows an attacker to violate a security policy. The security policy for Helm's Deep was "Do not let anyone in." That vulnerability was exploited by a large boom. It was followed quickly by an influx of bad guys bent on a permanent physical denial of service and availability, and significant (bodily) integrity issues for the defenders.

In the digital world, NIST[2] defines a vulnerability as

> Weakness in an information system, system security procedures, internal controls, or implementation that could be exploited or triggered by a threat source.

A vulnerability is a weakness in the digital system, as the culvert was a weakness in Helm's Deep.[3] There are many types and instances of vulnerabilities, from memory leaks to default passwords.

1. Until Gandalf shows up to save the day with the Rohirrim incident response team!
2. https://csrc.nist.gov/glossary/term/vulnerability. There are multiple definitions in the glossary, all similar to this one.
3. Not as much boom in information systems when vulnerabilities are exploited, though.

All vulnerabilities may pose risks, but not all risks are vulnerabilities. Cybersecurity is inherently about managing risk and our potential for loss. To determine risk, we must understand vulnerabilities and threats (which can exploit vulnerabilities). In this chapter, we explore myths regarding the flaws.

We will refer to some industry-standard, vendor-neutral vulnerability mechanisms in what follows. It might seem as if we are providing a large helping of alphabet soup, but this is less confusing than trying to map everything onto multiple vendors' systems of naming and rating. So, grab some lembas and dive in.

A Nod to Human Vulnerabilities

The definition we are using for *vulnerability* is focused on computing systems. As a result, it leaves out of scope a notable area: people. Information systems have weaknesses that can be exploited by a threat source, and so too do humans.

To earn the trust needed to get a security clearance, governments consider various factors that could make a person vulnerable to influence or manipulation that might ultimately undermine national security. For example, a background investigator will examine debts; someone with substantial debt could be more susceptible to accepting a bribe to steal sensitive information. The investigation might also examine contacts with foreigners because strong relationships could make a person sympathetic to another country or more open to extortion. Generally, no one variable is used to determine if a person gets a security clearance, but each offers insight into potential risk factors. Different countries examine different aspects.

Not all human vulnerabilities are about the insider threat. Imagine categorizing the type of people at increased risk for being victims of cybercrime. This is a research area for Dr. Arun Vishwanath. He has studied the impact of individual differences, such as age, education, and attention. Vishwanath and others have found correlations between human attributes and victimization, although strong causal ties are difficult to prove.[a]

[a] For example, see Harrison, B., Svetieva, E., and Vishwanath, A., "Individual Processing of Phishing Emails: How Attention and Elaboration Protect Against Phishing," *Online Information Review*, 2016.

We Know Everything There Is to Know About Vulnerabilities

One might think that after decades of hardware and software development and countless bugs, the cybersecurity community would have seen it all by now. While there are discernible trends in the types and prevalence of vulnerabilities, there is a misconception that we know everything there is to know.

The CVE Program is a catalog maintained by MITRE[4] to list vulnerabilities. The catalog lists known vulnerabilities submitted to a CVE Numbering Authority (CNA) that were deemed interesting enough to add to the list.

Notice that word *deemed*. Not every vulnerability submitted to a CNA ends up on the list. Not every vulnerability gets submitted to a CNA. That means we cannot assume that the list of CVEs, as interesting as it is, contains an exhaustive and complete compilation of every single known vulnerability. By one count, 6,767 vulnerabilities disclosed in 2020 did not have a corresponding CVE ID.[5] The list contains those vulnerabilities that were both submitted and added to the list. Not every vendor and vulnerability researcher submits vulnerabilities; vendors might fix bugs quietly.

Similarly, not every vendor notes what CVEs they fix in their releases. The Linux Kernel maintainers, for example, have historically considered vulnerabilities to be bugs that need to be fixed and do not generally note which CVEs get fixed with each release.

CVEs are associated with one or more weaknesses in the Common Weakness Enumeration (CWE). CWEs are organized in a catalog of flaws commonly found in CVEs. CWE-NOINFO and CWE-OTHER are the most common two values in the CVE catalog, but they do not have specific weaknesses assigned to them. CWE-NOINFO is assigned when there is insufficient information to assign a specific CWE. CWE-OTHER means that the appropriate CWE is not actually in the catalog of predefined CWEs. In other words, a weakness is evident in the vulnerability description but does not correspond directly to an entry.

The catalog for CWEs runs the gamut, from CWE-121, stack-based overflow, to CWE-546, suspicious comment. As of this writing, no CVE has been tagged with a suspicious comment CWE—though one could take this comment about a suspicious comment CWE as being suspicious and assign that CWE to it.

Along with the CWE is the related Common Vulnerability Scoring System (CVSS). While the CWE is an attempt to distill the *type* of vulnerability, the CVSS is intended to distill many factors, including severity, into a single number. This is a difficult task. Severity is subjective, so what is severe to one organization might not be to another. An organization that has never used a database would not care about a CVE for a database program that is easily exploitable, while a company that relies on this database exclusively would. Severity scores do not incorporate contextual factors such as whether the software is used in a particular context.

Lastly, severity is often mistakenly interpreted as *exploitability*. A vulnerability could be severe but never used by attackers in the wild. The EPSS uses real-world exploit data to calculate a probability score that a vulnerability will be exploited.

4. MITRE is a Federally Funded Research and Development Center (FFRDC)—a nonprofit research entity funded by the U.S. government. They research several areas of expertise, among which is cybersecurity. https://mitre.org
5. 2020 Year End Vulnerability Quickview Report," RiskBased Security, 2021.

A Common Weakness That Appears Uncommon

There is a CWE for "Embedded Malicious Code" (CWE-506). It is clearly a weakness if someone manages to embed malicious code into a project. One vulnerability with this weakness is CVE-2020-15165. It is for the Chameleon Mini Live Debugger in the Google Play Store,[a] a tool used for Near-Field Communication (NFC) debugging. NFC is used for short-distance communication, such as proximity cards for door access. Someone tampered with the source code for the original application and uploaded the result into the Google Play Store, thus embedding malicious code into the app and creating a vulnerability with CWE-506.

There are surprisingly few vulnerabilities labeled with CWE-506. Given how commonly attackers seem to embed malicious code, we might expect many others. This might result from variability in the human judgment of people who map CWEs to CVEs.

[a] https://play.google.com/store/apps/details?id=com.maxieds.chameleonminilivedebugger&hl=en_US&gl=US

Now that we have a list of vulnerabilities, their designated weakness, and a rating, some people believe that that implies that we know everything there is to know about these vulnerabilities. Spoiler alert: We do not.

Putting a vulnerability on a list and rating it says only that someone thought it was important enough to add to the list and that the rating was a value they deemed to fit the vulnerability. It does not mean much more than that. Adding more meaning to it is overstating the issue.

Vulnerabilities Are Not Linear

In a simple world, the standard process would be that once a vulnerability is found, then a CVE is created, and later (perhaps) an exploit is discovered in the wild. That is not always the case.

In May 2021, WatchGuard released an update to its Fireware product. The release notes mentioned "security issues" and how they were found by their engineers and not found in the wild. This is not uncommon. Companies often find and fix security issues without letting people know what the exact details of the problems were.[a]

In November 2021, the government notified WatchGuard that the vulnerability fixed in this release was being actively exploited.[b] It was not until January 2022 that this vulnerability was assigned a CVE.[c]

WatchGuard did not do the wrong thing by not assigning a CVE to an internal security vulnerability. We are sure the company's managers followed their processes to handle it internally because they believed it was not being exploited.

Vulnerabilities are not linear. Sometimes they are assigned a CVE, and sometimes they are not. The presence of a CVE does not mean the vulnerability is necessarily important, and the absence of one does not mean it is unimportant.

[a] www.watchguard.com/support/release-notes/fireware/12/en-US/EN_ReleaseNotes_Fireware_12_7/index.html

[b] https://techsearch.watchguard.com/KB?type=Article&SFDCID=kA16S000000SOCGSA4&lang=en_US

[c] https://cve.mitre.org/cgi-bin/cvename.cgi?name=2022-23176

Vulnerabilities Are Sparse

Let's pretend that vulnerabilities are finite and sparse. If that's true, each piece of software has a limited number of vulnerabilities, and every time one is fixed, it makes the software closer to 100% safe because fewer vulnerabilities are left to find.

Suppose that each piece of software has no more than 100 vulnerabilities. Watts Humphrey, one of the fathers of software quality, found in surveys that a typical developer accidentally introduces, on average, one defect per 10 lines of code.[6] Thus, the count of 100 is an exaggeration for some software, and a vast undercount for others. Either way, it is a cybersecurity fairy tale, but it has a real-world point, as do many fairy tales. Admittedly, that is highly dependent on the nature of the development environment and developer, but it is an approximation with data to back it up.

Back to our fairy tale. That means for every one of the 100 vulnerabilities fixed, the software becomes 1% more secure until *Hurrah!*, the software is perfectly secure.

But this is not what happens in reality. Software is constantly getting new vulnerabilities because developers add new code all the time. Every time a new version of a software artifact is released, a new vulnerability can be introduced. It is not resetting the counter, either. It is adding to the vulnerabilities already present. Every vulnerability patched means that a particular avenue of attack has been stopped, but it does not necessarily reduce the number of routes. Plus, many patches require adding new code... which might have new vulnerabilities. It is not unheard of for some quickly produced patches to introduce new and more severe problems than they fix!

Also, recall that the survey focused on *defects*.[7] Code can be produced with no defects but can still inherently pose a problem because of some fundamental logic error. For example, a system where the programmer inverts the logic of a password test (typing = rather than !=) is a defect; forgetting to include a password check at all would be a logic error.

Attackers Are Getting More Proficient

There is a sentiment among some people that attackers are evolving faster and faster all the time. If we look closely, we see that criminal hacking is a business, and one that the criminals prefer to systematize as much as possible.

So, we often see the same types of attacks, even against new technology. Because the rate of technology change is ever-growing, it might appear that attackers are adapting quickly when they are simply repurposing old attacks.

6. www.uqac.ca/flemieux/PRO102/watts-mar99.pdf
7. Software defects are considered harmful. www.rfc-editor.org/rfc/rfc9225.txt

Each time a vulnerability is found in one software artifact, especially if it is a new kind of vulnerability, the attackers will try that on all the software they can. The result is often wide-ranging success. Consider cross-site scripting.[8] First used in the year 2000, by 2007 it was the most common exploit of all web applications and remains one of the top web security risks. The same kinds of mistakes keep getting made again and again by different programmers.

Furthermore, attackers are finding simple ways of tricking the automation we have deployed. It is unfortunately easy to break our brittle detection systems. Put a new wrapper on an old piece of malware, and voilà, we no longer recognize it!

That is not to say that attackers are not evolving. Some of them spend considerable effort acquiring and developing sophisticated tools to automate the search for vulnerabilities. Some malware authors are significant criminal enterprises with designers, coders, debuggers, acceptance testers, and hierarchical management—and those are the nongovernmental authors!

We can say this myth is partially true, but so long as the programmers who are not criminals continue to use poor methods and lack focus on providing good security (and privacy) in their products, the majority of the criminals do not need to work that hard.

Zero-Day Vulnerabilities Are Most Important

Zero-day is a scary phrase that strikes fear in many people. Some zero-days are given proper names, such as Heartbleed and Sandworm. A few have marketing logos. Zero-day implies that there is no defense, nothing we can do, and we are in trouble: The attackers are at the door, and we are unprepared and vulnerable.

A zero-day vulnerability means that the vulnerability is not known yet to the developer of the software or the public.[9] It is also exploitable, so the bad guy could use it against us if they know about it.

The name is derived from the reality that we are given exactly zero days to patch the vulnerability once we find out about it. Not one or two to make things safer, but precisely zero. We might get hit before we know about it; we might get hit before *anyone* knows about it.

It is scary because of the lack of defenses. It is scary because it cannot be stopped.

Zero-Days Are the Scariest

Now that we have said zero-days are terrifying, the question remains: Are they the scariest thing out there?

8. See the Appendix for more information.

9. Reasonable people disagree about this definition. Security vendor Mandiant, for instance, considers a zero-day to be anything without a patch available, even if it is known to the public. See www.mandiant.com/resources/what-is-a-zero-day-exploit

The zero-day vulnerability associated with CVE-1999-0153 makes it sound scary because that vulnerability was a DDoS based on one packet. One packet sent to the wrong port with the wrong option set, and **BOOM** down went the Windows NT server.

That is scary (if you are running Windows NT).

Zero-days are expensive to create, though. The attacker has to either work with someone to find it, find it themselves, or buy it for lots of money. Zero-days are not cheap. During the COVID pandemic, a zero-day against Zoom was advertised for $500,000.[10]

Once publicity exposes the zero-day, such as the Zoom zero-day, a patch or mitigation will usually be made available. That means attackers cannot use it as effectively anymore. We say "usually" in regard to patch availability because some software in use was created by a vendor no longer in business, or there are significant problems in designing and installing a fix. This results in a "zero-day" becoming an "every day."

The use of a zero-day exposes it to detection. The first time it is used, there is a chance the zero-day will be discovered by the user or a security vendor. The second time, the chance is even greater. There is a diminishing return each time it is used, until it becomes almost useless. Think of it as the biggest gun in our arsenal. Once that gun is used, everyone knows about it, and we cannot use it again as a surprise.

It is much easier and cheaper to start with the password vector, or the social vector, or even try out an exploit for an old vulnerability to see if it works. Organizations often fail to patch their software, so why should someone pay a lot of money to get a zero-day when an old exploit would work? For example, the Capital One data breach in 2019 relied on a vulnerability known for years. It was not a zero-day attack—it was a misconfiguration that started it all.[11] The attacker did not have to resort to buying that zero-day to make the attack work. Instead, they used a vulnerability and exploit that everyone knew about.

In March 2011, RSA was the victim of an APT attack that used a well-known virus, PoisonIvy. It did not use a zero-day; it was installed from an Adobe Flash vulnerability sent in an email.[12] There was no point in the attacker using an expensive zero-day attack when the simple attack got them what they were after, which was RSA's confidential information.

Zero-days are scary in that there is seemingly no defense, but at the same time they are not terrifying. There are a small number of zero-day exploits at any given time, and they can often be countered with generic defenses. Understanding good security and being prepared helps take some of the fright away; the dark is not so scary when we have a bright flashlight!

Google's Zero Day Initiative has counted the number of zero-days in the wild, and in Figure 11.1 we can see the number of zero-days it tallied each year. The number looks like it is increasing: 2021 had 58 such reports. In contrast, the total number of CVEs registered in 2021 was 14,391. Those are

10. www.vice.com/en/article/qjdqgv/hackers-selling-critical-zoom-Zero-day-exploit-for-500000
11. www.seattletimes.com/business/capital-one-to-pay-190m-settlement-in-data-breach-linked-to-seattle-woman/
12. www.wired.com/story/the-full-story-of-the-stunning-rsa-hack-can-finally-be-told/

named vulnerabilities considered important enough to submit to the database. If every one of those 58 zero-days found in the wild got CVEs, then that is only 0.3% of all the known vulnerabilities. It is a relatively small number compared to what could be out there.

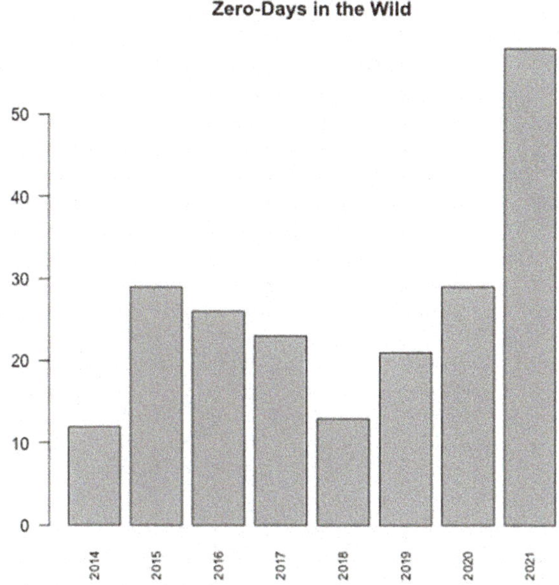

FIGURE 11.1 Google Project Zero: zero-days in the wild.

In his 2019 keynote talk at USENIX Security, Alex Stamos presented "The Stamos Hierarchy of the Actual Bad Stuff That Happens Online to Real People." Viewed as a pyramid, zero-days occupy a tiny dot at the top compared to the abundance of threats from abuse, passwords, patching, and other more-prevalent threats.[13]

To avoid the pitfall of losing sleep over zero-days, prioritize the most likely risks. Focus on patching known vulnerabilities. Worry about what we know is out there, and do not dwell on what we do not know about. In addition to regular patching, implement defense-in-depth that includes detection and monitoring to help identify systems we did not previously know were vulnerable. We do not worry that a blizzard will hit Miami Beach, but we worry about hurricanes. It is feasible, though not likely, that a blizzard might hit Miami Beach. We prepare for the known—hurricanes—because it is likely one will show up. If there is a blizzard, we will play in the snow for a short time until it melts, as illustrated in Figure 11.2!

13. www.usenix.org/conference/usenixsecurity19/presentation/stamos

FIGURE 11.2 Worry about likely risks.

Zero-Days Mean Persistence

As we saw in the previous section, RSA was the victim of an APT. It is one of those attacks where the invaders are in the system and will never get out until forcibly removed.

There is an assumption that the APT must be associated with a zero-day, and vice versa, but neither happens to be accurate, as we saw in the RSA attack. If a system has a patch available but it has not been applied, adversaries can take advantage of the vulnerability to lodge themselves in the system.

Some APTs indeed create and use zero-days. Multiple APTs exploited a vulnerability in Pulse Secure VPNs (CVE-2021-22893) in their attacks throughout 2021. By contrast, many APTs chose not to use zero-days, probably because those bugs are expensive and likely to have been used before (so they are no longer zero-day), as we discussed in the section "Zero-Days Are the Scariest." Persistence further increases the risk for attackers, as it creates more opportunity for them to be discovered.

Heartbleed[a]

Encrypted communications between us and a remote web server is good for privacy. It makes us feel safe that the password or credit card we input on the site is encrypted, and no one else can read it. In 2014, a terrifying zero-day vulnerability was exposed, putting this assumption in danger. The implications were that any website that used the OpenSSL software was in danger of having its communications decrypted. We relied upon the belief that our credit cards were safe because of the encryption between us and the remote end, but Heartbleed put that in danger. Any person using an exploit (some available on GitHub) could attack a site and steal data.

There is no APT here taking money out of someone's pocket. Charitable security professionals still monitor websites across the Internet to ensure that they are patched against Heartbleed, even years after the vulnerability was found.

[a] No actual blood was spilled.

All Attacks Hinge on a Vulnerability

A compromised password is not a weakness in software, but it is a tremendous risk that can be used to cause severe mischief. If our usernames and passwords are stolen, anyone can log in and pretend to be us, assuming the website does not require additional authentication.

Even those sites that have two-factor authentication have been victims. Rather than a technical solution, the bad guys hire people to sit in the middle. It is an actual person-in-the-middle attack.[14] The attacker sees the two-factor input prompt and asks the user for the information to input (through a webpage—there is no actual talking here, although there is also a variant to this using a faked phone call). If the user responds with the value, the attacker has managed to compromise the account. No vulnerability was used in this attack—only a compromised password that the attacker can use.

It is not only people and their passwords. Devices often arrive with a default password of `password` or `admin`. It is easy for the company to set that, it is easy to document that for the end user, and it is

14. www.varonis.com/blog/man-in-the-middle-attack/

easy all around to use that as a password. We do not have to think when presented with the password prompt, as the password is right there.

Convenience, in this case, is contrary to good security. The password is well-known to everyone, users and attackers alike. Anyone can use it. Some devices do not always prompt for a username. When one does, it is commonly known that "admin" is often the value to use.

That default password is not an official vulnerability because it does not get an official name or CVE entry, but it is often used to gain access. Why should the bad guys work to gain access when all they have to do is to log in with the default password?

Some websites host a list of default passwords used by various devices.[15] It requires almost no work for the attacker to find those by simply performing a quick web search. These lists are also an excellent resource to use with other tools to help ensure systems have their passwords updated.

Social engineering is another attack vector that does not rely on a software vulnerability. Instead of finding and exploiting a technical vulnerability, the attacker goes after the human connection to the computer. The attack is outside the computer and may be extraordinarily effective. A simple phishing email or phone call asking for information is more successful than most people think. Social engineering can also mean that if attackers identify a person with the knowledge they want, thanks to a few web searches, they can get valuable information about their target. If Frances is a noted expert on the newest hot topic, someone might meet Frances at a conference and get to know them, leveraging that to get the information they want. Social media scraping might also expose helpful information.

When Technology and Social Engineering Collide

Mimicking the human voice with technology has been a goal for a long time. That is how Stephen Hawking's voice was created and how a replacement for Val Kilmer's voice (lost to cancer) was created for the *Top Gun* sequel. Synthetic speech is a standard tool for those with no voice. It is easy to have a robotic voice, but people prefer that their voice resemble their original speech, not a creepy robot. But that can also be used maliciously. Deepfake voices use technology to create convincing fake voices of a person nearly indistinguishable from the original voice. In 2019, an attacker mimicked the voice of an executive at an energy company. The phony voice was used in a call to a subordinate and directed him to transfer $243,000 to a "Hungarian supplier."

Of course, that was the scammer's bank account. Imagine if your boss called you and directed you to send company secrets to a "New Partner." If your boss demanded it, it is possible you would do it. This kind of attack perfectly melds a technical attack (the fake voice) with social engineering (the human connection).

Education, including simulated phishing attacks, is often used to counter social engineering attacks. It is our best defense: We tell people not to throw away important papers but to shred them. We also tell people to beware of people showing too much curiosity in what they do.

15. E.g., https://datarecovery.com/rd/default-passwords

People want to be helpful, but they make mistakes. Social engineering is an attack vector that does not have a technical solution because it is about people and their behavior.

This kind of attack is not always about calling someone or emailing them. Attackers have been known to dive into the trash bins (known as *dumpster diving*) looking for information they can use, as we see in Figure 11.3. People throw away computers, peripherals, and paper without paying attention to what could be on them. If a group decides one day that an organization has information they want, do they a) work on learning the network and spend time and money on building an attack or b) start by checking what is thrown away and see if it can be used to find anything useful? The answer is often (b). It is cheaper and easier to dig through trash than to spend the time and effort trying to figure out the best way to attack through software. It is often effective as well. The attacker can get everything they want without going near the firewalls, IDS, or any other cyber defense.

FIGURE 11.3 Dumpster diving.

Physical security is another target for attack that does not hinge on a software vulnerability. Physical security is often overlooked in the cybersecurity world. If someone gets physical access to our devices, the risk to our data dramatically increases. Nearly every threat model in cybersecurity assumes no physical access. Why break into a network if it is possible to simply walk out with the storage? Or, as in one classic case, show up at the Customs office claiming to be computer technicians and steal *two whole server systems*, as happened in Australia in 2003?[16]

Insiders are another threat independent of a software vulnerability. Imagine that security successfully keeps people outside out—but insiders must have access. It is necessary for their jobs. People like hard copies, too, and often print things out rather than read them on the screen. When walking out of the office, guards might make sure that there is no USB or other storage devices in an employee's possession, but what security guard will know or understand every piece of paper? People could easily slip that into their clothes and walk out without setting off a single alarm. According to a 2017 affidavit for an arrest, the U.S. government "determined the pages of the intelligence report appeared to be folded and creased, suggesting they had been printed and hand-carried out of a secured space."[17]

Data walked out the door and not a single cybersecurity alarm was tripped.

Veterans Affairs Data Breach

In 2006, an employee of the U.S. Department of Veterans Affairs (VA) took home a laptop and an external drive. That's a common occurrence for people working from home. However, this system contained records from patients. . . and was not encrypted. The hardware was stolen from the house by an enterprising burglar.[a]

It turns out that the analyst was routinely doing this, taking data outside the protected enclave, and was not telling anyone. It also turned out that the data breach was much worse than expected, including the records of active-duty personnel.

This was not the first breach experienced by the VA. In 2002, the agency sold and donated systems without wiping the drives completely. The new owners found all sorts of confidential data on them. The data was vulnerable to attack and misuse without taking advantage of a single software vulnerability. Actually, in the second case, it was literally given away.

a https://archive.epic.org/privacy/vatheft/

Exploits and Proofs of Concept Are Bad

In Chapter 1, "What Is Cybersecurity?", we presented the myth *Believe and Fear Every Hacking Demo You See*. There is a related myth concerning vulnerabilities that the existence of exploits is itself a bad and dangerous thing.

An exploit is something that takes advantage of a vulnerability in a system. It is not simply a bad or a good thing; it is merely a thing. It is a tool. It is like a hammer in the toolbox. It can do wrong (break the glass), or it can do good (drive the nail into the wall). It is the intention of the user that matters.

16. www.theregister.com/2003/09/05/the_case_of_the_two/
17. https://sgp.fas.org/news/2017/06/fbi-winner.pdf

The bad guy can use an exploit to break into a system. The good guy can also use it to break into the system. The bad guy has nefarious motives; the good guy wants to know if the system is vulnerable to the exploit, which can help quantify risk.

Exploits are not scary, any more than the hammer is scary. It is commonly thought that exploits are the worst possible things to exist. They are up there with the mosquito, the A-bomb, and elevator music in terms of sheer horribleness. Keep in mind that they are a tool similar to a hammer. It is all in what the person holding the hammer wants to do with the tool.

An exploit does not have to be software. Vulnerabilities are occasionally configuration dependent. That means that the configuration must have the correct bells and whistles for the software to be vulnerable. For example, consider CVE-2010-0180. It is a vulnerability in Bugzilla, software designed to help source code development. In this case, local users could read sensitive fields if a particular configuration option was set (`use_suexec`). If the value was not set, then the vulnerability did not apply.

For another example that combines the default values with the configuration, several versions of the Apache Cassandra application, a NoSQL distributed database, were set up perfectly to allow remote users to execute arbitrary Java code (CVE-2015-0225). In other words, the database was set up perfectly for attackers, and we are sure they appreciated it.

Sounds easy to avoid those vulnerabilities, right? Simply do not use those configurations, and there is nothing to worry about.

Secure Shell (SSH) is a protocol that provides encrypted remote access. It enables a user to connect to another system, execute commands, and be assured that the connection is encrypted, unlike the old remote shell (rsh), which did everything in cleartext. With that in mind, one would think any exploit targeting a vulnerability would be a complex program. Unfortunately, CVE-2018-10993 disproves that. A remote user would connect, and before giving their password, they could send the string MSG_USERAUTH_SUCCESS and then, surprise, the connection was allowed. The attack does not involve a configuration change or complex code; it consists of a simple string.

A vulnerability is defined by its exploitability. It is right there in the definition that the weakness could be exploited. According to that definition, every vulnerability must have an exploit, and we should worry.

The good news is that a study found only 5% of vulnerabilities published in the CVE database had published exploits.[18] The 5% that do have exploits can cause no end of trouble, and we do not know that the other 95% of the vulnerabilities do not have exploits. We only know they are not published.

It is still important to patch them, even if we are not using the configuration that causes the problems. It is possible that the vulnerability is applicable beyond that configuration value or that we might use it in the future. Keeping the software up to date is always the best strategy.

---

18. www.usenix.org/conference/cset20/presentation/householder

Default Configuration and a Vulnerability. . . and Blame

In March 2022, the Cybersecurity and Infrastructure Security Agency (CISA), a U.S. government department, put out a notice warning people of Russian state-sponsored cyber actors gaining access to their systems.[a] The attackers used a default configuration of multifactor authentication to allow them to add a new device to the system and gain access. From there, they exploited the PrintNightmare Vulnerability (CVE-2021-34527). That vulnerability allowed them to run arbitrary code, generally known as a bad thing.

This is not necessarily a vulnerability in multifactor authentication, but it is a problem with the default configuration. People often use the default configuration because it is easy, and they assume that the people who sold it know the best settings for them to use, so they do not change things. (This was discussed in Chapter 10, "Tool Myths and Misconceptions.")

The downside arises when the people who sold the system blame the users.[b] It is not the users' fault that they are using the default configuration. It is wrong to assume that everyone buying an appliance will be an expert and be able to tweak it perfectly. But once the problem is found, the default configuration should be updated as quickly as possible.

By this same logic, one could dismiss every vulnerability as "relies on having a vulnerable setup."

[a] www.cisa.gov/uscert/ncas/alerts/aa22-074a

[b] https://duo.com/blog/how-to-prevent-cyber-actors-from-bypassing-two-factor-authentication-implementation

Vulnerabilities Happen Only in Complex Code

Some people believe that only tremendously complex programs get vulnerabilities—that it takes a lot of code before a vulnerability is found in the code.

But that is not true! There is a 135-line program that had a vulnerability. It even got a CVE: CVE-2016-7553. This vulnerability allowed people to read private chats on the IRSSI server. It is interesting that it occurred in so few lines of code.

Unfortunately, we cannot use the number of lines in which the vulnerability was found as a measure, either. That one vulnerability in a 135-line program does not imply that there is a vulnerability in every 135 lines of code.

It would be nice if we had a measure that could predict when we should expect vulnerabilities to pop up. We could take a program, count the number of lines in it, and estimate the number of vulnerabilities in the program. That requires us to know how many lines of code are in the software to do this estimate, but that is a minor point. We could predict how many vulnerabilities we would have to deal with for any software component.

The issue is not only the software artifact itself. Software rarely exists in a vacuum. There is the operating system, the compiler that creates the code, the libraries used by the code, and perhaps the cloud platform code that is being used by the artifact.

People rarely redesign the wheel. It is there, and it works, so why re-create it? Pick a standard-size rim and buy a mass-produced tire off the rack. Matters are similar with software. If the software is going to create images, then the best practice is to use existing libraries to create the images. If it uses a Graphical User Interface (GUI), it will use an existing library or framework to do the work. Otherwise, the amount of time to create the software, as well as the potential to inadvertently include more vulnerabilities in the code, multiplies.

But we are not taking away the possibility of vulnerabilities. We are simply moving most of the risk over to the libraries, frameworks, or compilers. The more libraries a piece of software uses, the more potential vectors for attack. We should note the qualifier "most of" when speaking about risk, because we might be using the wrong libraries, calling the routines incorrectly, or ignoring the error codes.

Software Bill of Materials

The Software Bill of Materials (SBOM)[a] is an inventory of all the components a piece of software uses. Think of it as a recipe with each ingredient for a piece of software.

For example, a recent version of the Linux bash shell uses the following libraries:

- `linux-vdso.so.1`
- `libtinfo.so.6`
- `libdl.so.2`
- `libc.so.6`
- `ld-linux-x86-64.so.2`

It is also possible that each of those libraries refers to other libraries, so the SBOM follows the chain and lists each of those ingredients.

The purpose of the SBOM is to know exactly what is affected if a library has a vulnerability. If `libc` has a vulnerability, we want to know every program affected by it.

In January 2022, the JavaScript libraries `colors.js` and `faker.js` were sabotaged by their creator in an act of protest. The sabotage caused an infinite loop in those programs that used the libraries.[b] The author was suspended from GitHub and the JavaScript libraries as the admins of the affected systems attempted to clean up. This event is an example of how libraries can affect the software without changing the software.

[a] Allan Friedman leads CISA's efforts to coordinate SBOM and is the leading expert on it. See https://finitestate.io/blog/the-sbom-is-coming-with-allan-friedman for more information.

[b] www.theregister.com/2022/01/10/npm_fakerjs_colorsjs/

Another complexity to consider is not the software components but the total system. The more software available on a system, the more vulnerable it could be.

A bank vault with 10 different doors is inherently less secure than a bank vault with one door. There are 10 ways the bank vault could be broken into rather than the one. A complex system with a lot of software has the same issue. Each piece of software has the potential to be vulnerable and allow access to the system. It might be 10 different paths into the system or 10 different doors into the vault; either way, it has more ways to be open to attack.

A single attack vector, or 10 different attack vectors. If we give the bad guys more ways to access our system, they will attack them, and probabilistically speaking, they are more likely to find their way into the vault.

First Movers Should Sacrifice Security

One common source of vulnerabilities in code is a result of vendors rushing to market. The haste to get a product out—often an alpha version, not even a product in beta—is often intended to address the First Mover myth. This myth states that to be successful in the market, especially if disruptive, it is essential to be the "first mover"—the first to market with the kind of product involved. The belief is that spending more time in development and testing will result in a disadvantage if someone else gets to market first with a competing product. The misconception is that customers won't care about the quality but are more interested in the "Ooooh, shiny!" aspects.

This myth is partly driven by investors who want a quick return on their investments. It is also perhaps caused by an observation of the network effect: The more people who use something, the more that others will want to use it, driving up its value. Thus, capturing the early adopters must be advantageous. Whatever the causes, the tendency to release in haste with the intention of fixing problems in a later release leads to many problems. Early adopters might be willing to tolerate jarring defects, but they are hardly the majority of the market.

There are, in fact, examples of first movers having success, but this is not always the case. History shows that the perceived superiority of first movers has multiple counterexamples. For instance, social networks Friendster and MySpace both premiered in 2003, well before the general opening of Facebook in 2006. VisiCalc was introduced in 1979 before the more successful Microsoft Excel in 1985. The workstation premiered from Xerox (the Alto, then the Star) in 1973, before the success of the IBM PC in 1981 and Apple II in 1976. There are hundreds of other counterexamples. A combination of features and marketing led to the success of a more mature *latecomer* to the field in many instances; it still does.

Innovation and competition can flourish with attentiveness to quality and more careful design. The automobile industry in the decades around the turn of the millennium serves as one example: The Japanese and German car manufacturers focused on quality and craftsmanship and thus became the leaders over established U.S. companies.

Innovation can be successful without sacrificing quality, including security and privacy.

We suggest that quality and attentiveness to user concerns can potentially vault a latecomer to the fore over something rushed to market that includes multiple faults and vulnerabilities. A poor reputation is unlikely to lead to market leadership. Admittedly, we can cite some examples where it has—usually as a matter of cost or compatibility and not as a matter of user preference. Those are factors that can be addressed, however. Plus, when true innovation and quality appear, the market will usually respond.

Current trends in government regulations and insurance suggest that, before too long, companies that make quality a secondary (or tertiary) concern relative to speed-to-market might find themselves at a disadvantage. From a cybersecurity and privacy point of view, we hope that is sooner rather than later!

Patches Are Always Perfect and Available

The Evil Bit[19] was jokingly defined in 2003 on April 1 (April Fool's Day) as a way to tag traffic as benign or not benign. It would be great if everyone with both good and bad intentions would use this, but sadly for us all, it is not used that way. In what we are hoping was an homage to the Evil Bit, Microsoft defined the Kill-Bit (or KillBit) as a registry value that prevents an ActiveX control from being used by Internet Explorer—basically, in case of vulnerability, do not break the glass but do set the Kill-Bit.

FIGURE 11.4 Kill-Bit battle.

19. https://datatracker.ietf.org/doc/html/rfc3514

This is useful. For example, CVE-2011-0248 references a vulnerability in a QuickTime ActiveX control. This vulnerability allows exploiters to execute arbitrary code or even cause a DoS. At the time, this was considered a serious zero-day vulnerability. Luckily, the Kill-Bit existed.

The Kill-Bit is a mitigation for this kind of vulnerability. When such vulnerabilities are found, they are killed off or prevented from working. All we have to do is enable the correct Kill-Bit, and *Presto!*, we are no longer vulnerable. But is this a perfect mitigation? Well, about that. . . A researcher at the CERT[20] found a weakness in the Kill-Bits that allowed controls to bypass them. With a simple change to the underlying HTML, *Un-Presto!* An attacker could negate the Kill-Bit (UnKill the Kill-Bit) and take advantage of those vulnerabilities. The good thing was, according to the researcher, there was no evidence of anyone using that technique. Yet.

This is only one example, but this pattern recurs too often in cybersecurity. Mitigations are not perfect, and as with everything else, they can have their own vulnerabilities.

Most software developers rush to issue a fix when a vulnerability is found. That is a mitigation that will stop the vulnerability from being exploited. It might not have as great a name as a Kill-Bit, but still, the point is to kill the vulnerability. Note that we wrote *most* when describing developers' responses. Not every developer will rush, and some will not even bother to develop fixes. Sometimes, the flaw is found in discontinued products, so no fix will be produced.

When a flaw is produced, sometimes in the rush to get things out, that new version does not stop the vulnerability or even introduces a new one. For example, vulnerabilities in the Apache `log4j` system were terrifying because they allowed the attacker remote access. Right after it was announced, `log4j2.16` was released to "fix all the flaws."

It did not. New patches needed to be released before the flaws were completely patched.

Flawed mitigations do not stop attackers, but they are not necessarily failures. Cybersecurity is a constant cycle of stopping the attackers and then watching them find another way in. The mitigations do not always stop the attacker because they find another line of attack. That does not mean we should not use the mitigations when available. We cannot know simply by looking at one (usually) that it will not work. We do not put a bandage on a wound because it will perfectly protect against infections; we put it on there because it is our best first defense from infection. Unfortunately, the wound can still get infected, but that likely is not a failure of the bandage.

The issue is similar in cybersecurity. We do not avoid using mitigation because it might fail. We use it because it is our first defense. Defense in depth is a good thing, but that means layers—and mitigation is only one of the layers.

20. https://insights.sei.cmu.edu/blog/internet-explorer-kill-bits/

Here are some other misconceptions about mitigations.

- **Patches are perfect and never cause trouble.**

  Once the problem is fixed, there is nothing more to worry about, right? The tiger has been dealt with. Except sometimes, the tiger gets replaced by a grizzly bear.

  In 2020, Google's Project Zero discovered that three zero-day vulnerabilities had been found before they were used, and the patches for them were incomplete. Analogously, using them removed the tiger from the room, but the grizzly bear decided to take up residence afterward.[21]

  Stuxnet took advantage of a vulnerability in the way Microsoft handled USB drives. This was patched in 2010, but it was later determined that the patch was insufficient. The attackers could still use the vulnerability to infect those computers not on the Internet using a malicious USB. One report says that exploits of this vulnerability (known as CVE-2010-2568) were common in 2014.

  This also means more than one patch might be needed to fix a vulnerability. Some vulnerabilities are complex, and the initial fix might not address all the complexities in the situation. One estimate is that 7% of all software patches might be incomplete and need to be redone.[22]

  Does that mean we should not patch at all? No, it simply means that patches are like any other software—subject to errors.

- **A software patch is always needed to fix a vulnerability.**

  Not every vulnerability in software is a problem with the code itself. Sometimes, the vulnerability exists in the configuration of the software. For example, CVE-2019-5591 for the FortiGate product from FortiGuard is a default configuration problem. If the default configuration of the product is used, then it is possible that someone on the same network can intercept sensitive information. The fix is not a patch; the fix is to change one value in the configuration file.

  The software should still be patched so the default configuration does not happen again, but simple mitigation is to change the configuration file.

- **Software that has reached the end of its lifespan no longer needs to be patched.**

  On April 14, 2014, Windows XP was officially no longer supported. That meant no more patches of any sort for the operating system. Of course, as it is no longer supported, no one will use it, and we can forget about it, right?

  Unfortunately, no. In 2017, CVE-2017-0176 was created, a vulnerability in Windows XP. That would not have happened if the operating system was not still in use. In 2021, 0.51% of all

21. www.usenix.org/conference/enigma2021/presentation/stone
22. Li, Frank, and Paxson, Vern, "A Large-Scale Empirical Study of Security Patches," *Proceedings of the 2017 ACM SIGSAC Conference on Computer and Communications Security (CCS '17)*. Association for Computing Machinery, New York, NY (2017): 2201–2215; https://doi.org/10.1145/3133956.3134072.

desktop computers still used Windows XP.[23] That sounds like a small percentage, but when we consider there are at least 2 billion desktop computers[24] in the world, that is at least 10 million computers that still use XP.

The situation is dangerous because the software is not supported, but the fact that it is not supported does not mean people will not use it. Some businesses continue to rely on Windows XP because they had software created for the platform and now cannot afford to have it updated for a new and supported operating system. In other cases, the software the business depends on for a particular function is not available for any other operating system.

The fact that operating systems that have reached the end of life are still connected to the Internet is a vulnerability and a major problem waiting to happen.

- **This software is never on the Internet, so it does not need to be patched.**[25]

  Unless a computer exists in a vacuum, eventually it will be touched by the outside world. Stuxnet taught us that. An air gap protected the computers, but the worm still infected them. The Stuxnet malware was transported on USB keys. USB keys have been used more than once to infect computers. This was still a danger in 2022[26]—that criminals could mail out USB keys to install ransomware. They are not waiting for someone to click on the link when they can mail a USB key to install the ransomware.

  The air gap as a protection measure is a myth. The computer might not be connected directly to the Internet, but the Internet can still find its way to the computer. Software updates have been used maliciously. For example, the Fantom ransomware mimics a Windows software update.[27]

  The only way to ensure a system cannot be attacked is never to use it, which does not make it useful at all.

- **All hardware and software are easy to patch.**

  These days, almost anything can be connected to the Internet. There are Wi-Fi–enabled faucets, Wi-Fi–enabled lightbulbs—even Wi-Fi–enabled blankets and sex toys![28] These devices tend to use a minimal operating system for whatever it is they do. Because Linux does not have a cost and is open source, some version of it is often used for this purpose, possibly a reduced version. As a result, the devices are not smart for smart devices but have enough complexity to complete their tasks. As we saw with the original Mirai botnet, these IoT devices can be used maliciously. The botnet authors took advantage of default passwords to infect the IoT devices that were

23. https://gs.statcounter.com/os-version-market-share/windows/desktop/worldwide
24. www.scmo.net/faq/2019/8/9/how-many-compaters-is-there-in-the-world
25. "There is only one network, some parts are just harder to get to."—Allen Householder, CERT/CC
26. www.zdnet.com/article/fbi-cybercriminals-are-mailing-out-usb-drives-that-will-install-ransomware/
27. https://www.bleepingcomputer.com/news/security/fantom-ransomware-encrypts-your-files-while-pretending-to-be-windows-update/
28. www.amazon.com/Eddie-Bauer-Collection-Electric-Alexa-Enabled/dp/B088KWRYLK and www.cosmopolitan.com/sex-love/a32475604/long-distance-sex-toys/; intrusion takes on a whole different meaning.

running Linux. Once the attackers had control, they could use them to create one of the most extensive DDoS attacks of all time.

The correct thing to do now is to patch these devices. We do not want them to be used to create a DDoS, and we do not want them to be a part of the Mirai botnet—or worse.

That is a problem, though. The creators of these devices generally did not include an update path. That means that while they can be connected to the Internet, there is no good way of updating the software to eliminate any problems. That vulnerability that was exploited for Mirai? Still there. Unless we buy a new device with new software, it is still possible for an old device to become part of that botnet, or a new botnet that uses it.

IoT devices are not the only ones with this problem. Many medical devices are in the same situation: They run old software, and there is no easy or straightforward way to update the software or apply patches. It is a vulnerability waiting to happen in a hospital.

- **Patch availability is the same as patch deployment.**

  A vulnerability occurs within a piece of software. The company is notified, it creates and releases a patch, and then everything returns to normal.

  At least, that is what we would like to believe. It is over with, nothing more to worry about! The dragon, er, vulnerability, has been slain, and the castle has been retaken.

  About that. As mentioned earlier in this section, Stuxnet took advantage of a vulnerability that already had a patch. That patch was out and available. That did not mean that people applied the patch. It means that a company created it and released it.

  Until the patch is applied everywhere, the vulnerability is still a threat. Simply having it lets us say, "Yes, there is a patch," but not "So we are done." It is like identifying the sword that would kill the dragon but not killing the dragon. The dragon is still out there and a threat[29]—we have only identified the tool to get rid of it.

  Applying the patch is the best first step to ridding the world of the dragon, er, vulnerability.

In summary, once a vulnerability (or perhaps a flaw in the system that might or might not be a security problem) is found, the best bet is to fix that flaw to prevent it from causing problems in the future. If we know the problem is there, fixing it is better than pretending it does not exist. Pretending it does not exist is like pretending there is not a tiger in the room with us. We can pretend all we want, but sooner or later that tiger will get hungry, and we will look like tasty snacks. Applying patches to our system is better than applying ketchup to ourselves!

29. Do not argue with dragons, for you are crunchy and go well with ketchup.

FIGURE 11.5 Tigers and grizzlies and patches, oh my.

Defenses Might Become Security Vulnerabilities with Time

Once upon a time, the Message Digest Method 5 (MD5) hash was the security of the future. It was part of a secure way to create and store passwords, so everyone was expected to use that method. And many people did.[30]

Unfortunately, as it happens, the inexorable movement of advancing hardware and software overtook the MD5 algorithm, and it is no longer as secure as we thought it was. We think one-way hashing is secure, but if the hash is not large enough or has a subtle weakness, enough computing power can be applied to brute-force a compromise of it. MD5 is susceptible to what is known as a collision attack.

Another example involves the protocol TCP, which is the underlying engine for many protocols used on the Internet. The original designers added congestion control to keep things moving. Forethought is always good, right? Dealing with the problem ahead of time is definitely a good thing. Except, this forethought did not consider the future speed of the Internet. The idea that we would have such speedy

30. MD5 was created in 1991, which seems a long time ago.

connections everywhere was not imagined at the time. So, unfortunately, this congestion control had a side effect—and a nasty side effect at that. It allowed for certain DDoS attacks to be practical.[31]

In both cases, the original design was thought to be solid. For TCP, the designers thought they were being smart (and they were!) for designing congestion control. The problem was first found in 1999, long before it was exploited. But because TCP is such a core protocol, it took a while for the vulnerability to be fixed. As it affected so many vendors, there's no idea of how long it took for each vendor to fix it. Suffice it to say, it wasn't done the day after it was announced!

The point of both examples is that the Internet and computing are constantly evolving. What was a great idea in the 1990s became a dangerous DDoS facilitator later. What was secure in 1991 is not necessarily secure now. A message digest algorithm designed in 1991 was defeated 20 years later by advances in the field and is viewed as a potential hazard today. When we issue a revision to this book in 2045, we expect there to be other examples based on 2022 technologies.

All Vulnerabilities Can Be Fixed

Programmers often hard-code fixed values in software, such as a specific file or domain name. For example, the program works only with a fixed value specified in the source code that cannot be changed by the user or configuration files. A programmer might hard-code the domain name `cybermyths.net` that an app will use rather than allowing a customizable and configurable choice. This is not the best of ideas, but it happens. It is fixable, meaning the programmer can modify the source code and recompile the app. It is not straightforward if many people use the app, but it is still possible that the value can be changed.

Now imagine if someone hard-coded a program into the silicon of a computer. It is not the usual case of "saved on the hard drive and can be overwritten." It is written directly on the chip that runs everything in the computer. Think of it like an etching on metal. The artist cannot change the etching; it has to be replaced.

In other words, this hard-coded setup is not changing without swapping out the chip.[32] End users cannot recompile the source and rewrite the silicon. The only thing to do is to swap out the chip.

Chip vendors often put code on these chips. Unfortunately, vulnerabilities have been found in the code. It is unknown how exploitable some of these vulnerabilities might be, but the surest way to get some programmers to write a program is to tell them it cannot be done.

What about the case where we can replace the vulnerable software? Does that solve everything? Not really, as it turns out. Adobe acquired Flash from Macromedia in 2005, and Macromedia acquired it from the original makers of Flash (then called Splash) in 1996. It was thus around for a while, at least until December 2020, when Adobe said it would no longer support the software. Flash was widely used in games, corporate websites, online videos, and more. It was a fun programming language.

31. CVE-2005-3675

32. Some devices support reloading the microcode, which is the code in the chip, but that poses a different set of issues.

Flash also had many vulnerabilities: There are 1,118 associated CVEs. Those are the ones that were important enough or publicized, so they got tags. There could have been more. Adobe decided to end support for Flash in December 2020, meaning that no other software patches would be released. In theory, everyone should stop using Flash.

First, simply because Adobe stopped supporting it does not mean that Flash is not being used. People still use Flash, even if we tell them they should not. Modern browsers will not support it. At the beginning of 2021, after Flash was discontinued and the announcement had been out for quite some time, 2.2% of websites still used it.[33]

Second, HTML5 was intended to be a replacement for Flash. Everyone was supposed to rewrite their Flash applications to use HTML5 because it was more secure. Not surprisingly, vulnerabilities were found in HTML5; as of this writing, 50 CVEs have been reported.

Now imagine a different example. The vulnerability is not in the initial software but is created over time. That can happen in ML algorithms.[34] An attacker can force an ML program to misclassify data. For example, a program is written using ML to classify malware. The attacker takes advantage of the ML program's algorithm and "teaches" it to learn incorrectly what is and is not malware. The attacker can then use this to slip their new malware into the system, completely bypassing the defense.

There is no defense to this situation at the time of this writing. It is a fundamental problem of the approach. No patch will solve this, no mitigation, nothing. Adversarial Machine Learning (AML) is a field of study where people try to make ML programs do things they should not. They are acting as adversaries to find the vulnerabilities in the ML programs—they are vulnerability researchers focusing on one kind of program.

The question then becomes, What do we do with the vulnerability in a program that learned to be vulnerable? Spoiler alert: There is no easy answer.[35]

Vulnerabilities exist in almost all software. There is some software with no (or nearly no) known vulnerabilities. Generally, that is safety-critical software that has been extremely carefully developed using heavily structured methods and testing. It isn't OSS. We won't be able to load it on our laptops to play games or surf the web. That software is costly to create, requires special tools, and does not get written quickly. As a result, few vendors use that approach. We should be glad that such care is taken because that software is used in applications such as flight control and running nuclear power plants. Almost everything else we will encounter has many more flaws. Software—new, old, freshly updated. Fixing that software is not always a simple process. Sometimes there is no way to repair the software, and we must build our defenses around it.

33. www.statista.com/chart/3796/websites-using-flash/

34. www.kb.cert.org/vuls/id/425163

35. https://dl.acm.org/doi/10.1145/3442167.3442177

Scoring Vulnerabilities Is Easy and Well Understood

CVSS is a scoring system for vulnerabilities that attempts to rate the severity of a vulnerability. CVSS is maintained by the FIRST organization, which has often stated it does not quantify risk.

A CVSS score is between 0 and 10 and has been split into four severity categories. For CVSS version 3.0, the current specification is:

- Low (0–3.9)
- Medium (4.0–6.9)
- High (7–8.9)
- Critical (9–10)

For example, the Heartbleed zero-day vulnerability was scored as medium severity. Even though it affected many web servers and meant that traffic to and from them could be intercepted, it was assigned this score. The Apache `log4j` vulnerability that caused so much havoc in December 2021 was rated as a 10.0, or critical vulnerability. This makes sense, as it was a remote code execution vulnerability and, therefore, scary, especially as there were so many exploits available for it almost immediately.

The CVSS score is generated by a human, so human opinions and biases could influence it. Security professionals do not always agree on the best score. For example, CVE-2020-9063 has a base score of 7.8 from the NIST NVD.[36] However, the experts at the CERT Coordination Center gave it a base score of 6.6.[37] Both organizations have experts in the field, yet one rates its severity as high and the other as medium.

The CVSS score is built on severity categories. There are Base scores, Temporal scores, and Environmental scores. When those values are put together, their sum creates the CVSS score. Temporal scores attempt to quantify if there is an exploit, the ease of remediation, and the reliability of exploiting the vulnerability. Environmental scores attempt to quantify the environment in which the vulnerability is discovered. The Base score examines the access required to exploit the vulnerability and the type of vulnerability.[38] This is a summary of the features involved in creating a CVSS score, but it makes the point that someone does not simply look at a description and type a number.

Nevertheless, there are issues with the scores. The CVSS specification says that the score is designed to be within its assigned severity level or within 0.5 of that given level. That means that a high-severity CVE can be imprecise, but in the range between 6.6 and 9.3.[39] Aside from what the spec says, when it is used in practice, the experts can disagree between 2 and 4 points.[40]

---

36. https://nvd.nist.gov/vuln/detail/cve-2020-9063
37. https://github.com/CERTCC/Vulnerability-Data-Archive
38. www.first.org/cvss/calculator/3.0
39. www.first.org/cvss/specification-document#7-5-A-Word-on-CVSS-v3-1-Equations-and-Scoring
40. https://resources.sei.cmu.edu/asset_files/WhitePaper/2018_019_001_538372.pdf

Scores get inflated over time, too. They are not a static "we dub thee a 4.9 vulnerability and that shalt not change." Things change. For example, if a patch exists, then the Temporal score will be lower than if one does not exist. The score will be higher if an exploit exists and is widely known. These two facets can change over time. A vendor will release a patch, and then the score will change. Once an exploit becomes known, the score will change.

An example of this is the second `log4j` vulnerability. When the CVE for this vulnerability was published, CVE- 2021-45046, the initial score was in the low range (3.7). It quickly jumped to critical when the severity of the vulnerability became apparent.[41] That means, at first, the vulnerability did not seem that problematic. Still, when people realized it could be used to exfiltrate information, that was worrisome, and increasing the score was warranted.

Even though the CVSS system is not designed to quantify risk, vulnerability management tools (and research) often use it as part of their strategy in determining what to patch first. The usual approach is to fix higher CVSS scores first. The reality is we should consider patching all vulnerabilities but consider how our organization will be affected when we do our planning.

CVSS is a general score. It is not specific to any particular organization; it is an attempt to capture the overall severity of a vulnerability, but one that might or might not apply to an organization. What is vital to one organization might not be important to another. Some organizations have explicitly said that CVSS is faulty and that a risk-based assessment would be better.[42] Of course, these organizations might be trying to sell something, but even so, they might be correct. There are probably better ways to quantify risk than using something explicitly said not to quantify risk.

Because You Can, You Should—Vulnerabilities Edition

CVE 2021-3064 was disclosed and patched in November 2021. It is a vulnerability in Palo Alto Network's GlobalProtect portal. It can potentially allow a network-based attacker to execute arbitrary code with administrator privileges. The good news is that not every instance is vulnerable—the attacker needs to have access to the portal to exploit the vulnerability. It is still a vulnerability that should be fixed.

Palo Alto Networks was notified in October 2021, and a fix was released in November 2021. If that were the end of the story, then this would not be an interesting section.

It turns out that a company that works in attack surface management, Randori, found the vulnerability much earlier than the reported date; they found it in 2020. Rather than following the accepted practice of notifying the appropriate company or CNA, they decided to add it to their toolkit.

That meant the vulnerability, which could have caused major problems for customers using the Palo Alto Networks software, was unpatched for a year. It was actively used by at least one company, but

---

41. https://thehackernews.com/2021/12/second-log4j-vulnerability-cve-2021.html
42. www.tenable.com/blog/why-you-need-to-stop-using-cvss-for-vulnerability-prioritization

that does not mean no one else used it. It only means that we know that there was a company that thought because they could, they should.

In the worst-case scenario, the vulnerability could have leaked from the company using it. An insider could have taken it, or an outside attacker could have found it. That would have meant, for that year, Randori left the Palo Alto Network customers using the GlobalProtect portal vulnerable to anyone who knew about the attack.

The Hippocratic Oath starts with "Primum non nocere," meaning "First, do no harm." Security practitioners should follow that rule as well. Vulnerabilities can be used to cause harm, so not disclosing them is part of the problem. As we have noted elsewhere, the ACM Code of Professional Ethics also emphasizes "Avoid harm." In general, we suggest concealing vulnerabilities and using them for selfish purposes is inconsistent with "Avoid harm." It *might* be appropriate for a national agency, but even then, it raises some concerns because it is potentially endangering the public they are supposed to be protecting.

Scanning for vulnerabilities is a big part of red team practices. The red team, mimicking the attacker, will use vulnerabilities to attempt to gain access *for the purpose of closing the vulnerabilities.* The understanding is that the red team will not use practices that could cause harm to the Internet at large.

Vulnerability Names Reflect Their Importance

Wannacry. Meltdown. Heartbleed.

Those names struck fear in some people who manage systems or networks. These vulnerabilities can take data, cost money, occupy time, and cause havoc. And someone named them, too, so that means they are even worse, right? A named vulnerability should be scary because someone took the time to name it.

Actually, not so much.

Let's start with what the names give us. A name is an identification. You have a name, the authors of this book have names, and pets have names. Rather than saying, "Cat!" you can specifically call your pet by its name, and you will not get every cat in the neighborhood running to you.[43] There is no naming authority or coordinating body for vulnerability names. Names often come from the people who discovered them, similar to how parents name their children. The name commonly includes wordplay, as Heartbleed reflected the underlying problem with TLS heartbeats. The name Heartbleed (and its logo) were created by Finnish security company Codenomicon, which independently discovered the bug at the same time as Google Security. Codenomicon says they gave it a name to raise public awareness.

43. Unless you simultaneously operate a stentorian can opener.

Vulnerabilities already have identifications. They have CVEs and VU numbers from the CERT Coordination Center,[44] and some software programs have their own methods of keeping track, such as CUPS.[45] There are many ways to identify "this is the vulnerability I'm talking about."

Not every vulnerability gets a name, and giving it a name adds nothing more than convenience. It does make it sound snazzy. Some named vulnerabilities even have logos. Some names are entertaining, such as Mutagen Astronomy,[46] a name based on the movie *Sneakers*. Or Dirty Cow,[47] a vulnerability with a name, a logo, and a website. If Heartbleed had been named Cuddly Pink Hamster and Wannacry had been named Fluffy Mewing Kitten, they would not have been any less awful. The names should not be allowed to add (or remove) extra concern about a vulnerability. Yes, serious bugs sometimes get names, calling attention to the vulnerabilities. It is essential to understand that there are also dangerous issues without fancy names. Cute names can bias the perception of risk. They are easier to remember than the CVE number or to keep track of all the ways people can number vulnerabilities. But names do not represent all vulnerabilities and are not always the most critical issues.

We would also postulate that the most severe vulnerability in existence—the one that crashes every network and computer forever and ends civilization—will not have a name. Whoever discovers it might have time to say, "That's odd"; thereafter, there will be no place to record whatever name or number it might have.

Focus on risk and mitigation, not on names.

Further Reading

The CERT® Guide to Common Vulnerability Disclosure. https://vuls.cert.org/confluence/display/CVD.

Dowd, Mark, McDonald, John, and Schuh, Justin. *The Art of Software Security Assessment: Identifying and Preventing Software Vulnerabilities*. Addison-Wesley, 2006.

Dramatically Reducing Software Vulnerabilities: Report to the White House Office of Science and Technology Policy. https://csrc.nist.gov/publications/detail/nistir/8151/final.

Guidelines and Practices for Multi-Party Vulnerability Coordination and Disclosure. www.first.org/global/ sigs/vulnerability-coordination/multiparty/guidelines-v1.1.

Magnusson, Andrew. *Practical Vulnerability Management: A Strategic Approach to Managing Cyber Risk*. No Starch Press, 2020.

44. https://kb.cert.org
45. www.tenable.com/plugins/nessus/47683
46. www.theregister.com/2018/09/27/mutagen_astronomy_linux/
47. https://dirtycow.ninja/

Chapter 12

Malware

Wise and humane management of the patient is the best safeguard against infection.

Florence Nightingale

Malware is a real and prevalent threat to security and privacy. It might never go away. We have mentioned it frequently in other chapters as an example threat. Effective defenses against malware are essential. Unfortunately, mistaken beliefs about malware, malware authors, and malware defenses lead to suboptimal cybersecurity outcomes.

There are many types of malicious software. Some malware steals credit card numbers or personal information. Some holds data for ransom. Some flashes unwanted advertising on the screen. In 2022, Google's Threat Analysis Group reported that Russia distributed a fake Android app that appeared to perform DoS attacks against Russian websites.[1] The app launched no attacks, but some Ukrainian sympathizers were tricked into installing it, which maliciously enabled Russia to collect intelligence about who would use such an app. "Malicious" comes in many forms.

Malware plays a role in many cyber incidents. It is a powerful tool for adversaries to affect victims and achieve their malicious goals. VirusTotal,[2] a virus-scanning service, has analyzed over a billion malware files and scans over a million new files every day. Only a small subset of cybercrime is conducted without malware, such as attacks relying on social engineering and real-time manipulation. Without malware, attackers must penetrate the system whenever they want to use the device.

We should all agree that malware is a bad thing. There is no legitimate place for *malicious* software in an ideal world. The question is, What is malware? If it is a bad thing, we should be able to define it and point to it.

The problem with defining malware is similar to defining cybersecurity—the term can encompass many things, so different parties define it differently. It would be easy to say malware is software that the bad guys can use to do bad things. While true, that definition is much too broad. The bad guys can

1. https://blog.google/threat-analysis-group/continued-cyber-activity-in-eastern-europe-observed-by-tag/
2. www.virustotal.com

use a web browser to do their bidding if the right vulnerability is found. A word processor is in the same boat, along with Adobe Acrobat and many other innocent programs. We could even argue that a favorite operating system is malware because it can be used to do bad things![3] Even legitimate capabilities can be used to achieve mischief; using built-in programs and features to avoid the detection of custom malware even has a name: living off the land.

When we refer to *malware*, we generally mean computer viruses, worms, Trojan horses, ransomware, and embedded rootkit/backdoor software, as these are examples of custom-built software to produce results not intended by the authorized users of a target system. Those terms are also subject to some dispute. We will not wade into that debate but use the general definition we gave here. Alternatively, we can say that malware is any software custom-developed to circumvent/violate security policy without the permission of the authorized system owners. Some recent malicious software that has made the news includes Mirai, Trickbot, and WannaCry.

As with undesirable human behavior, there is a broad spectrum of unwanted behavior for malware. Some uses the computer to mine cryptocurrency in the background. Some tries to steal passwords and credit card numbers. Some wipes hard drives. Some spies on everything the user does and reports it to someone else.

Malware is also surprisingly difficult to identify despite feeling seemingly straightforward. Write a program to look for known sequences of malicious code or observe suspicious behavior, right? However, malware authors have found ingenious methods to hide their code, including self-encryption, time delays in execution, and mimicking legitimate system operations. If code changes the permission on some system files or deletes data, how can a program definitively rule out if it is being done as part of regular system maintenance? We do not want to block things an authorized user is doing, and responding to lots of false alarms can be pretty annoying!

As much as we have tried, we do not have a foolproof method that will let us look at a person—or file—and declare them to be "good" or "bad." We have to rely on their behavior as well as the particular security policy involved. The same holds for malware—if we can even spot it! In Chapter 7, "Problems and Solutions," we described the theoretical limits of this challenge as it relates to the Halting Problem.

Antivirus tools have been around for nearly 40 years, and their market generates sales of almost $4 billion annually. An entire career subfield of cybersecurity is devoted to malware detection, analysis, prevention, and response. There are job titles such as malware researcher and reverse engineer, training programs and certifications, analysis tools such as Ghidra, and even defensive gatherings such as the Virus Bulletin Conference and the World Antivirus Congress. Despite this environment and history, some pervasive myths about malware exist.

This chapter is about myths related to malware analysis and response. We discuss users' choices, including how to avoid infection and whether to pay for protection. We also present myths about assumptions of malware authors and attribution. Finally, we discuss technical misconceptions related to malware analysis and reverse engineering.

3. Mention this in almost any security gathering, and it will start a lively argument as people accuse "Windows!" and "Linux!" while the Mac OS users will generally smile and avoid the fracas.

Using a Sandbox Will Tell Me Everything I Need to Know

Given that malware is defined by its behavior, a researcher might execute a piece of malware to find out what it does. This is one way to be sure it is malware and to document precisely what behavior it exhibits. Does it connect to a command and control server? Does it use a Peer-to-Peer (P2P) network? Is it ransomware? What exactly does this code do to make it malware? If it does something against security policy, we would like to know what that is!

This information can also be used as part of an IDS or in a firewall to detect the presence of malware before it executes. Recognizing the network traffic unique to a particular malware family is one way to defend an organization against the malware, or at least raise the alarm in a timely fashion.

It is also used to categorize malware. Humans like putting things in named groups, so we would like to know if we have seen this particular malware before or if it is brand new. We would also like to know if the malware is doing something we have not seen before. In other words, we want to know what it is up to.

The problem with running malware on a system connected to the live Internet is that it actively allows malicious behavior on the systems if it is truly malicious. That is potentially a bad thing: The malware could damage the network or other systems. And if we do not know precisely what it does, it could be catastrophic! If it spreads locally, running it on the Internet could mean we have infected all our systems and possibly all our business partners. We're sure the bad guys would appreciate that—that would be accommodating, in their opinion. We want to avoid contributing to the malicious behavior running amok—there is enough of that without us deliberately adding to it.

In summary, simply running it is a bad idea. It is like saying, "I wonder what this big red button with the cover over it does?" as you push it (Figure 12.1).

One solution is to run the code in a sandbox. A sandbox is a system that is not directly connected to the Internet, nor is it connected to any critical systems. It is a lonely, isolated system sitting off by itself that cannot harm anything else. Often, it is a virtual machine configured as if it were one of the regular systems, but it can be deleted or reset as needed. It is a safe place to run the code and figure out exactly what it will do. The sandbox can be instrumented to answer questions such as these:

- What files does the malware alter?
- What domains does it try to resolve?
- What files does it create or open?
- Does it send out any interesting queries to web servers?
- Does it try to scan the local network and find new hosts to infect?
- Does it open any executables and attempt to run them?
- Does it try to exfiltrate information?

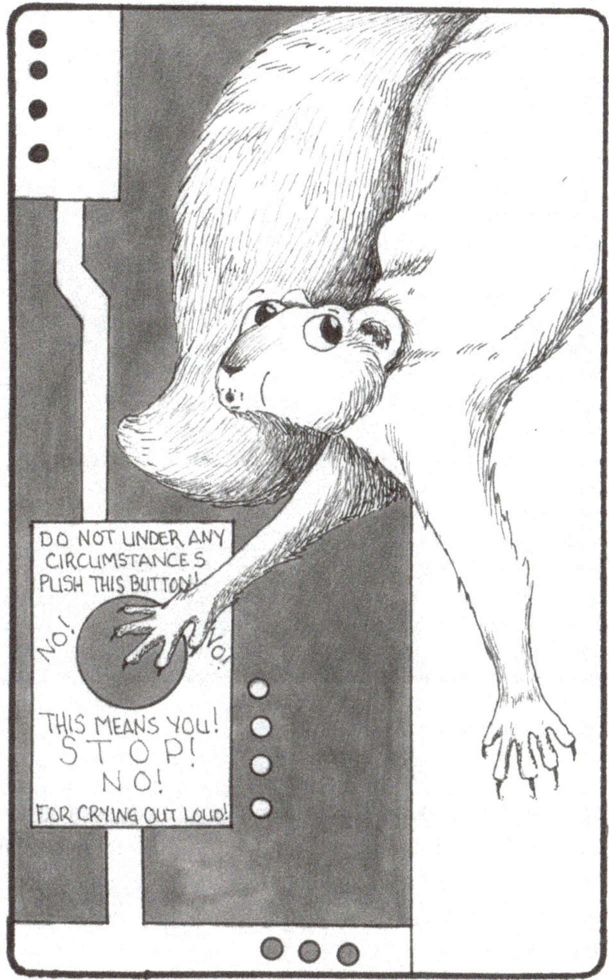

FIGURE 12.1 What does this button do?

And ultimately, we will know everything the malware will try to do. We will learn all the actions it will attempt and how to discriminate it from other malware or software. Good work, team—you have slain the malware dragon!

Except. . . we have not.

Malware authors know the sandbox trick and realize that we might want to run their code in a sandbox, and they do not want us to understand what the code will do. The first action is often to attempt to resolve a domain or communicate on the Internet in some wholly innocuous manner, perhaps after an arbitrary delay. If the resolution does not work, the malware will exit, assuming it is in a sandbox, and we will not learn anything. Some people get around this by setting up a local nameserver that will respond correctly, but that does not always work.

FIGURE 12.2 Escaping the sandbox.

Malware authors do not want their code to run in a sandbox. They want it to run on *real* systems, where all the tasty data and code resides; otherwise, it is not fulfilling their goals, and it is providing information on how to stop it. That does not help the attackers achieve their goals. They have methods beyond a simple name resolution to ensure the system is live and on the Internet. (See the aside later in the chapter, "Escaping the Sandbox.")

Malware is often environmentally sensitive in operation as well. Running it in a sandbox will not reveal everything it does. It might simply indicate what the malware authors want us to know. It might even do something we think is useful to tempt us further to run it on our systems. Deception is the name of the game in malware. . . and much of cybersecurity and conflict, generally.[4]

4. We would not be able to claim we work in cybersecurity without including at least one quote from Sun Tzu's *The Art of War* in this book. Sun Tzu is the honorific title (in English) given to the Chinese general and philosopher Sun Wu, who lived ca. 544–496 BCE.The following is an English translation of what Master Sun said that is pertinent here:

> All warfare is based on deception. Hence, when we are able to attack, we must seem unable; when using our forces, we must appear inactive; when we are near, we must make the enemy believe we are far away; when far away, we must make him believe we are near.

That definitely describes what malware authors want their code to do!

Escaping the Sandbox

Sandboxes often use virtual machines. They are cheap, they are easy to set up, and when we're done with them, we can delete them. Virtualization allows one system to run many operating systems with different patch levels and keep them separate from each other. They can be configured so that they are separate from the Internet but still have local and remote access. That is a useful and cheap way to examine malware.

The downside is that virtual machines have vulnerabilities. One side effect of some of these vulnerabilities is that the malware can escape. A virtual machine could be firewalled off but allowed to query the nameserver. Remember, malware often queries nameservers to determine if it is being run in a sandbox, so allowing it to use the nameserver gets around that check. But if the right vulnerability is in the virtual machine, the malware could use both the vulnerability and the hole to escape. An exploit to escape a virtual machine was created in 2017 and sold for $105,000.[a]

And there goes using the sandbox to keep the malware from doing bad things (Figure 12.2).

One study conducted several years ago showed that 78% of malware samples were sensitive to the environment where they were run.[b] They behaved differently in the sandbox than in the Internet at large. There are several mechanisms they can use to attempt to detect if they are in a sandbox, and if the sandbox configuration does not anticipate those, the code will detect it. One technique is simply to delay the execution of the malicious part for some period of time—no one is likely to run the suspect code for three weeks in a sandbox to determine if it is benign or not!

[a] https://arstechnica.com/information-technology/2017/03/hack-that-escapes-vm-by-exploiting-edge-browser-fetches-105000-at-pwn2own/

[b] www.usenix.org/system/files/conference/laser2017/laser2017_deng.pdf

Reverse Engineering Will Tell Me Everything I Need to Know

An engineer takes pieces and puts them together to build a system. A reverse engineer takes the final product and pulls it apart to figure out what parts were used to make the final product. It is not a new process: Reverse engineering has been around as long as there have been engineers. People take an end product and want to know how it works so they can duplicate it. They want to know what parts went into the manufacture, the process used, and generally everything they need to know to make the product themselves.

Children interested in engineering often start with reverse engineering. They take apart the radio to figure out how it works, or they take apart a toy to figure out why it is speaking.[5] They are curious and want to know *why*. Later, they take parts and make radios or toys, but they start by pulling things apart, to the horror of (most) parents everywhere.

5. Sadly, it is now more challenging to take everyday items apart nondestructively and instructively. There could still be a market for mechanical clocks and tube-based TV sets.

This is a process often used in malware analysis. Think of it as an autopsy. Autopsy, derived from the Greek word *autopsia*, means "To see for one's self." A reverse engineer is performing an autopsy on the software. It is dormant, so it will not be running, causing trouble as it resides on the hard drive.[6]

Let's digress for a moment into software engineering. For a high-level language, such as Go, Swift, or Rust, the compiler takes the text program as input and produces bits that match the native instruction set of the computer: machine language. We refer to this as a "low-level language." It is arguably the lowest-level language, at the bottom of the food chain of programming languages.[7]

Reverse engineering is the art of taking this "machine language" and understanding what it does. Usually, this happens by turning the 1s and 0s the machine understands into short mnemonic instructions and labels referred to as assembly language. This is one step above machine language and can be read or programmed by someone well versed in it; however, it is more difficult to learn and in which to write correct code.

Assembly code is not like C or Visual C++. Those are platform-independent—we write the same code, no matter what the target machine might be. Knowing C++ means we can write a program in this language for a system with an Intel chip or an AMD chip, or a virtual machine emulating a CDC 7600 from 1968, provided we have a compiler for that computer. We might have to include some special libraries or add a few special system calls, but the main part of the code could be unchanged. That is one of the benefits of high-level code.[8]

Assembly is also complex. "Hello World" is the program most programmers apocryphally write as their first program. It is simple: It prints that text to the screen. The compiled version of this five-line program on an Apple Mac system is 48 kilobytes because libraries and support code are included. Using a disassembler on this small and simple program yields 100 lines. For illustration, here's part of it:

```
    0000000100003f70 <_main>:
100003f70: 55                         pushq   %rbp
100003f71: 48 89 e5                   movq    %rsp, %rbp
100003f74: 48 8d 3d 2b 00 00 00       leaq    43(%rip), %rdi
       # 100003fa6 <dyld_stub_binder+0x100003fa6>
100003f7b: b0 00                      movb    $0, %al
100003f7d: e8 04 00 00 00             callq   0x100003f86 <dyld_stub_
                                              binder+0x100003f86>
100003f82: 31 c0                      xorl    %eax, %eax
100003f84: 5d                         popq    %rbp
100003f85: c3                         retq
```

6. In modern usage, the subject of a medical autopsy generally cannot be put back together in working condition, other than in horror films. If you were the subject of an autopsy and are reading this book, please contact the authors: We have questions.

7. Yes, we know about microcode. If you do not but need to understand where it fits, read a good computer architecture textbook.

8. We are glossing over many things such as numerical precision, interprocess communication, and character sets. For this discussion, assume those things do not matter, although they certainly do in real life. If you do not know what we mean by that **and** you are writing production software, then you need to study more software engineering.

Now imagine what happens if the program is large. The amount of work to understand all the assembly code quickly becomes intractable. But it is a method of analyzing malware without resorting to running it.

If running the malware in a sandbox is not a perfect solution, then surely reverse engineering will tell us everything, right?

Well, it is nice to think that. First, it is a time- and effort-intensive process. The larger the malware is, the more work is involved in attempting to reverse engineer it. That simple five lines of code that printed "Hello World" turned into 100 lines of assembly. Imagine what a 200,000-line program would generate!

Second, malware authors are aware of this analysis technique. They do not want anyone to do this, so they use code obfuscation that can make reverse engineering extraordinarily difficult. There are many ways to do this, and they can be quite effective in making the process more difficult for the reverse engineer.

Third, in the technique called *packing*, the malware is compressed[9] and disassembly will not work. The code must be decompressed before the analysis, which is a difficult task. Some malware authors use multiple packing programs to hide their code, and they might even have the code encrypt itself. The code becomes a riddle wrapped in a mystery inside an enigma, and we might not have the key to solve it.[10]

Fourth, even if someone manages to reverse engineer the malware perfectly, that will not necessarily reveal what it does. Algorithms and data references can be incredibly complex. For a historical analogy, consider the Antikythera mechanism, discovered in 1901. It was not until 2021 that scientists figured out how it *probably* worked.[11] That device had only 82 parts!

Reverse engineering is another tool in the malware analysis toolbox, but it is not a perfect solution.

Malware and Geography Are/Are Not Related

The Internet is not a geographic construct. It is a global creation with no geographic borders—electrons and bits do not recognize borders. Generally speaking, it is as easy for a person in England to see a webpage in Australia as it is for someone in Australia to view a webpage in Mexico. It is usually fast, too.

In the same way, web browsers are not concerned with geography. Malware does not necessarily care, either. Except when it does.

Malvertising is a portmanteau created from the two words *malicious* and *advertising*, similar to how the word malware was created from *malicious* and *software*. It occurs when advertising goes bad. This is not the annoying pop-up windows that show up on social media sites. Malvertising is the annoying

9. Like a zip file.

10. That idiom might be familiar. A version of it was initially voiced by Winston Churchill when speaking of Russia's intentions in 1939.

11. https://www.nature.com/articles/s41598-021-96382-9

pop-up windows that might also install malware on the system.[12] It is much worse than the software that suddenly plays loud music in a quiet office.

Advertising is often geographically targeted. A company wants the people who can buy their goods to see their ads, so a bicycle company in Cairo, Egypt, will not want to waste the money or time to show them to a person who lives in Nunavut, Canada, or Dunedin, New Zealand. They want local users. They want people who will go to their location and buy their goods.

Malvertising has the same goals. Its authors can and have targeted their malware to geographically located users. For example, a campaign tried to install customized banking Trojan horses in Brazil. It did not target all customers in Brazil, only customers of particular banks. That way, the attackers could be assured of stealing money from the right place. Why are they going there? Well, to use the quote attributed to the bank robber Willie Sutton,[13] "That's where the money is." Thus, the bad guys need to customize the malware to the targets and hence the location.

Think of Starbucks. Starbucks is a global coffee company that, at its core, sells coffee. It also sells pastries to go with the coffee. To maximize profits, the pastries sold in Rio de Janeiro will be the pastries popular there, not the pastries popular in Dublin, Ireland. Otherwise, the coffee shops might not sell as many pastries. Thus, Starbucks changes its offerings based on the location.

Malvertising does the same thing. Malware authors and the people who run the organizations want to earn money.

They are not in it simply for anarchy (though some are)—they are in it for the cash.

Other kinds of malware might also be geographically aware. For example, many criminal organizations in Russia write ransomware that is not intended to run inside Russia. The Russian government tolerates the criminals (and might even sometimes employ them) so long as they do not target Russians. Thus, their malware might seek to determine the location of the system on which it is running, either through an attempt to map the network address or by seeing if the primary keyboard layout is Cyrillic.

Other malware might have a narrow political target in place. For example, there have been instances of Russian malware targeted at Ukraine, but clumsy or careless programming allowed it to spread further; the NotPetya malware is an example.[14] Some malware that is believed to have originated in China will not run on systems in the .gov DNS domain (U.S. government sites), for instance.

The bottom line is not to depend on location or primary language to keep us safe from malware, but be aware that those might be factors.

12. Ironically, it often does this while claiming there is malware on the system.
13. Willie Sutton said he never said it, but that he could have.
14. www.wired.com/story/notpetya-cyberattack-ukraine-russia-code-crashed-the-world/

Malware Infrastructure

Geographic attacks are not the only way malware is geographic. Malware infrastructure generally needs three parts: the malware, the people running the malware, and the servers that collect the data from the malware. There could be more pieces of the puzzle, but that is the general structure in most cases.

The people who run things could be anywhere, thanks to the Internet. They could be sitting in their homes in Seattle, connecting through four layers of VPNs, running servers in Eastern Europe, and controlling software released in Australia. Tracing that is not simple. Not only are there multiple hops of possibly encrypted connections, but it might require some complex international cooperation of law enforcement to get access to the records.

However, if we identify the servers, we might be able to trace those, which is generally more straightforward. One study found that a small set of countries hosted 85% of the distribution sites for malware. These countries host so-called *bulletproof hosting* providers—that is, providers that ignore the usual complaints of spam, malware, and DDoS and allow their customers to do anything they want without taking them down. These providers are often located in countries with limited or no extradition treaties and a less than friendly national attitude toward the rest of the world. These servers, and sometimes the countries they are located in, are often included in blocklists used in firewalls and malware prevention systems. Think of them as some of the "bad neighborhoods" of the Internet.

I Can Always Determine Who Made the Malware and Attacked Me

There is a familiar movie or TV plot where the author of the malicious software sits by himself[15] in a darkened room surrounded by screens. He's typing furiously on the keyboard for a bit, then suddenly shouts. He's made the malware that will bring the heroes to their knees! And because he is so awesomely evil, he will sign the malware appropriately but sneakily. Then everyone will know it is him. But only if they are smart enough, and he cannot believe anyone is as intelligent as he is.

Then the hero is attacked with the malware and finds the right key to hit at the last moment and save the day. The hero can also look briefly at the malware and determine who wrote it because the bad guy signed it. The movie (or TV show) ends with the bad guy in jail, swearing revenge.[16]

Of course, that is all fiction.

15. It is usually a male wearing a hoodie. Yes, there are some female malware authors, but most identified are male. That could be because they are predominantly male. Or, it could be that the female authors are so clever they simply do not get caught as often.

16. Setting you up for the inevitable sequel, of course.

Yes, it is entirely possible that a single person wrote a piece of malware. That bad guy could have been sitting in a darkened room, cackling maniacally while wearing a hoodie, dining on pizza and energy drinks.

It is highly doubtful, though, that he signed it. Malware authors have been sentenced to jail. For instance, a 22-year-old British man created three computer viruses, and the courts sentenced him to two years in jail.[17] In 2020, a Russian malware author was sentenced to 10 years in jail for aiding a $568 billion fraud scheme.[18] The author of the Gozi malware was caught and sentenced to 37 months in jail and a $6.9 million fine, and the Latvian who helped him was sentenced to 21 months.[19] Signing malware is a good way to get caught and spend years of quality time in a 6 × 8 room. Not signing the malware is a better choice, at least for the author.

Then there is the idea of the single bad guy.

Considerable research has been done to determine how many people write a piece of malware. It is a difficult problem, and the usual answer involves a guess. We think this number *x* of people wrote this code. It could be that number. Or it could be *y* or *z*. Sometimes, we know it is more than one person, such as the author of the Gozi malware who had a helper. That is two people working on that malware. It could have been more, and the others did not get caught. For instance, the group that developed the Conti malware had more than 60 members, including middle management and an employee-of-the-month program![20]

Some nation-states are known to have groups that create malware for their use. They can do that; they have money and bodies to throw at the problem. For example, the DPRK (North Korea) has at least hundreds of people in its armed forces devoted to writing malware such as Hidden Cobra and AppleJeus[21] to steal currency to help pay for the country's sanctioned nuclear weapons program.

In general, determining who wrote a particular piece of malware is not easy. We would like to know, though. Similar to finding the guy who robbed your house, finding the malware author helps give closure to the event. It is also the first step in possibly bringing about some law enforcement action or recovery. At present, though, it is challenging without the resources of a national intelligence agency (and even with them).[22]

Malware Is Always a Complex Program That Is Difficult to Understand

As malware is a complex problem that plagues everyone on the Internet today, the programs that are malware must be incredibly complex, and it takes a lot of time and effort to understand these programs. Otherwise, why are we spending so much money and time on analyzing them?

17. www.networkworld.com/article/2339404/u-k--virus-writer-sentenced-to-two-years-in-prison.html
18. www.itworldcanada.com/post/new-yorker-jailed-for-selling-stolen-credit-cards
19. www.justice.gov/usao-sdny/pr/nikita-kuzmin-creator-gozi-virus-sentenced-manhattan-federal-court
20. www.wired.com/story/conti-leaks-ransomware-work-life/
21. www.cisa.gov/uscert/northkorea
22. See also Chapter 9, "Legal Issues."

Well, about that. . . Yes, there is complex malware out there. There is also incredibly simple malware out there. It is a spectrum similar to programming in general: There are short programs that return the current date and extremely complex programs that calculate the position of all the planets on any arbitrary date.

As a real-world example, the Linux kernel is an incredibly complex project that has a myriad of developers and contains over 28,000 files. It is huge. Contrast that with a simple program that counts the number of letters in a file that can be written in fewer than 50 lines of C. It is all in what the program needs to do and the programmer's expertise.

Now let's consider malware in particular. The SQL Slammer worm that attacked Microsoft's SQL Servers in 2003 was created in 376 bytes. That is tiny. That is the equivalent of 376 letters. In those 376 letters, the worm managed to cause so much havoc that it slowed down the Internet and took many routers down because of the traffic. A tiny 376-character worm infected 75,000 systems in only 10 minutes.

To get an idea of how small that is, the preceding paragraph has 404 characters. That is a tiny bit of malware to do so much damage.

File droppers are malware that does exactly what the name says. They drop files on the system to be used maliciously. In 2019, a file dropper was found that was 2,296 bytes. That 2,296-byte file (only six times larger than the SQL Slammer) contained instructions to download and execute a malicious file. The instructions were obfuscated, so it was not apparent that it would do this, but that was the end goal.

That is a small program to start the ball rolling on the damage. It was not as overwhelmingly (take down the Internet!) damaging as the SQL Slammer, but it would be enough to cause local havoc. Assuming we ran it.

Perhaps the most famous tiny malware was known as Mini or Trivial. This is malware of MS-DOS days, but still, it did its damage in as little as 13 bytes. (For those keeping track, the SQL Slammer worm was 28 times bigger than this.) In Internet terms, the Mini malware is ancient history, as it dates from the 1990s.

Moving forward in time, there is Tinba. Tinba, also known as Tiny Banker (not to be confused with the Elton John song), tried to steal banking information. It was huge compared to the other examples—20 kilobytes—but tiny compared to its companion in banking crime, Zeus. Zeus, for the record, ranges in size from 40 kilobytes to 150 kilobytes. (That is over a hundred times bigger than SQL Slammer.)

Malware can be simple, as with a file dropper that is only a link, or it can be incredibly complex. The Flame malware is an example of extremely complex: This modular malware could range up to 20 megabytes. The malware is more than a single malware program—it is a toolkit of malware. It is a Trojan. It is a backdoor. It even can act like a worm.[23] It is the Swiss Army knife of malicious programs. (If you are keeping track, we are now up to 53,191 times larger than SQL Slammer.)

23. For those fans of *Saturday Night Live* from 46 years ago, it is neither a floor wax nor a dessert topping. www.nbc.com/saturday-night-live/video/shimmer-floor-wax/n8625

There are undoubtedly even larger pieces of malware. Some items now contain virtual machine emulators and their own in-memory file systems!

This situation is similar to that for software in general. The size varies depending on what the software is intended to do. The Flame malware was a toolkit containing many tools, so it makes sense that it is large. The SQL Slammer worm had a single purpose, to propagate and cause trouble. It did not take much to do that because it took advantage of a vulnerability. The vulnerability did most of the work, and the SQL Slammer worm was only the trigger. Trying to summarize all malware in complexity is akin to summarizing all software in terms of complexity. It is all in what the software (or malware) is intended to accomplish and how much of the system it is resident on that helps the software (or malware) accomplish the task.

The takeaway from this: Do not assume that the size of something downloaded or found on a system is a definitive indicator of malware.

Free Malware Protection Is Good Enough

We get what we pay for, goes the cliché. High price does not always mean high quality, but what about cheap or free? There is an enormous amount of research in psychology about the special value of zero. That is, instead of comparing the item's value with its financial costs, free items distort our decision-making and are expected to have benefits that outweigh the cost. Even in cybersecurity, "free goods have extra pulling power."[24] So, is free malware protection good enough?

First, we are setting aside open source software in this myth, even though it can also be free. This discussion is not about the relative values of open source and closed source software. Instead, this myth is more about free versus paid commercial offerings.

Let's start by asking why there is free security software at all. Nothing is free. Software requires time and skill to produce, distribute, and support. Commercial businesses do not survive by giving away their products for free. Sometimes, the business benefits even when we do not pay directly, such as with search engines that sell advertising.

Other times, free products have restricted features, have time bounds, or are intentionally limited, and if we see the value, we decide to pay. Read the fine print; many are free only for noncommercial use.

Next, should we trust free security products? We have little leverage if a free product is slow or unreliable. According to one study of 283 Android VPN apps, there were numerous instances of privacy and security insecurities, information leakage, activity tracking, and traffic inspection.[25]

It is also the case that "free" products can be dangerous. Historically, there have been instances of software advertised as free (or low-cost) antivirus software that was actually malware itself. The

24. www.behavioraleconomics.com/resources/mini-encyclopedia-of-be/zero-price-effect/
25. Ikram, Muhammad, et al., "An Analysis of the Privacy and Security Risks of Android VPN Permission-Enabled Apps," *Proceedings of the 2016 Internet Measurement Conference*, 2016.

software we downloaded and installed might prevent some computer viruses, but it also might be sending our passwords to some criminals.

It might also be the case that the free software we download simply does not work well. The authors of the software might not have an incentive to keep it up to date because they are not getting paid to do so. We can complain if it does not protect our systems, but it will not restore whatever we lose. Of course, paying for a commercial system does not mean it will work, either. In one comparison, *PC Magazine* concluded that "The best free third-party antivirus programs handily outperform Microsoft Defender, the antivirus built into Windows. In fact, they rate better than many commercial programs."[26] Thus, free might be better!

Yes, it is the case that we can get some good anti-malware for free. Several major vendors offer their endpoint products for limited, at-home, personal use at no charge. This is the same software they sell to big companies and government agencies. The companies are not entirely altruistic in doing so. The more their product is used and trusted by people, the more likely those people are to pay for enhanced licenses or seek to get an organizational license for where they work. That makes good business sense. Also, most current antivirus systems send samples of new malicious code back to the vendors, so having more copies of their endpoint software in use helps them enhance the response and coverage of their commercial products.

To be clear: We should explicitly decide to accept the risks of no-cost products as well as any potential benefits. We can get some excellent protection. We can also get a grand illusion of security. We suggest that people look carefully at reviews and comparisons from trusted sources if they do not have the resources to test the products themselves.

Only Shady Websites Will Infect Me

There are supposedly "good" neighborhoods and "bad" neighborhoods in the physical world. Illegal activity is more prevalent and violent crime rates are higher in some places. The many contributing factors that drive these trends are beyond the scope of this book. It might be reasonable to presume that the Internet is similar: good and bad neighborhoods. Going down that path, it is easy to say, "It is the *shady* porn or gambling or warez sites that will infect me." Some online users have the mistaken belief that as long as they stick to legitimate or reputable websites, they will not get infected.

Attackers know better. They go where the most people are. Spreading malware on otherwise-benign websites is so common that it has a name: watering-hole attacks. This practice exploits our trust in our banks, news outlets, and government. In the NotPetya attack, attackers compromised a government website for the Ukrainian city of Bakhmut and used it to infect visitors. This technique is unfortunately effective because users want to believe that there are safe and trustworthy websites.

26. www.pcmag.com/picks/the-best-free-antivirus-protection

To the surprise of many, pirating software and viewing online pornography are not correlated with malware victimization.[27] The people who visit these sites might be more likely to be victimized, but not because they browsed porn.[28]

Another tactic attackers use is to compromise inclusions rather than the website itself. This would involve, for example, adding malicious software to advertisements that might be loaded for presentation of the site or additions to external code libraries used in rendering a webpage. The owner/operator of the website has not been compromised, and their code is pristine. Visitors to the site (some or all), however, will potentially be victimized by the content as their browsers download and display the "safe" site.

To avoid this myth, never presume that a website is safe. Trust is not all-or-nothing, but be cautious not to assume 100% trust of any website, even those you want to trust most, such as your bank. Assumptions lead to unwelcome surprises. Layered defenses are an approach to help mitigate risk: Use unique passwords for every website, keep your software patched, run security software on your device, and do not provide more private data than necessary. Oh, and wash your hands and brush your teeth regularly. You know—practice good hygiene.

Because You Can, You Should—Malware Edition

Ads are annoying to most people but a way for a company to generate revenue. If they are advertising something the consumers want, the ads might be welcomed. It is a delicate balancing act to not annoy the consumer too much with ads but, at the same time, convince them to click, or at least view and consider the ad.

But then there is adware. Adware is not malware (usually, though some classify it that way). It is software installed on a target computer to generate pop-up ads. Sometimes it is installed with the user's consent, but more often, it is not. One example of a not-great form of adware is the `eXact.Downloader`. It is an adware program that not only serves up ads, but it also downloads other adware programs. It is not exactly a friendly (to the end user) piece of software. The company that made it was sued over it.

A program that can download and install other software can also be used to download and install malware. It is entirely possible that someone will hijack the adware and use it as an infection vector for the worst kinds of malware. This is what happened with the InstallBrain adware.[29]

Ads are the primary source of revenue for many companies. It is tempting to maximize that revenue stream by creating "not adware, but adware." That is still unwanted software and is a bad thing.

---

27. Bossler, Adam M., and Holt, Thomas J., "On-line Activities, Guardianship, and Malware Infection: An Examination of Routine Activities Theory," *International Journal of Cyber Criminology*, Vol. 3, No. 1 (2009).
28. Canali, Davide, Bilge, Leyla, and Balzarotti, Davide, "On the Effectiveness of Risk Prediction Based On Users Browsing Behavior," *Proceedings of the 9th ACM Symposium on Information, Computer and Communications Security*, 2014.
29. www.trendmicro.com/vinfo/es/security/news/cybercrime-and-digital-threats/adware-downloads-mevade-sefnit-malware-with-links-to-tor-user-spike

Moving on from adware, let's talk about an old worm. In 2003, the Blaster worm struck Microsoft Windows.[30] On August 1, it infected almost 100,000 machines, spreading itself, and attacked `windowsupdate.com` with a DDoS. All in all, not a friendly worm.

At the time, firewalls were available on Windows XP systems, but the firewall was not turned on by default, and the controls for it were not readily available. Systems were unprotected from a worm that spread through a vulnerability that could be accessed via an open port. People took laptops home, used them at home, got them infected with the Blaster worm, then took them back to work. Then, the worm could easily infect other systems in the office by using sneakernet[31] to bypass the firewall.

That all sounds horrible, right?

Then along came the Welchia worm, also called Nachi. The Welchia worm was allegedly friendly, sometimes called an anti-worm. It installed itself using the same vulnerability as Blaster and then tried to clean up Blaster. If it found Blaster code on the system, it removed it. It also patched the vulnerabilities that allowed Blaster to latch onto the system. Then, it removed itself, although not immediately: It stuck around for 120 days or until January 1, 2004, whichever came first.

As worms went, Welchia was quite polite. But, it was still a worm. It might have been written with good intentions, but it spread using vulnerabilities, changed the victims' system without their knowledge or permission, and acted like malware. It was *not* welcomed by most computer users and ended up being targeted by antivirus code.

We contend that anything that installs itself on machines without informed consent is not friendly, including all worm programs and most adware. While the authors might think what they are doing is somehow justified (e.g., supporting themselves with advertising or removing malware), doing it surreptitiously and without permission is not the right way to make friends and influence people. If you refer to the discussion of the CFAA in Chapter 9, you will see that it also is likely against U.S. law. It might also run afoul of laws in other jurisdictions.

Ransomware Is an Entirely New Kind of Malware

Ransomware is terrifying. It takes over the computer, can cost companies a lot of money, and has even resulted in companies and a college going out of business.[32] In early 2022, the entire government of Costa Rica was threatened by a ransomware gang.[33] Surely, malware that terrifying has special properties, right?

This section addresses that misconception, as well as other misconceptions about ransomware.

30. https://ieeexplore.ieee.org/document/1492337
31. That is, avoiding the network yet still making it to its destination via shared removable media.
32. www.telemediaonline.co.uk/34-of-uk-companies-close-down-after-falling-victim-to-ransomware/ and www. engadget.com/lincoln-college-ransomware-attack-shut-down-covid-19-164917483.html
33. https://www.washingtonpost.com/politics/2022/05/10/costa-rica-shows-damage-ransomware-can-do-country/

As with all malware, having antivirus software might not be enough defense against ransomware. It certainly cannot be the only defense, either. Backups can help, but only if they are inaccessible from the network when the ransomware is active. Remember, malware is designed to spread itself. It can hop from system to system, and if all of the backups are accessible, **BOOM**, there went the backups.

All malware does not rely on zero-day vulnerabilities, and neither does ransomware. It seems as if it should, though. Zero-days are scary and ransomware is terrifying: Put them together, and we get an indescribable union of terror. Except that is not the reality. Ransomware authors use anything that works,[34] whether it is unpatched vulnerabilities that we already know about or zero-day vulnerabilities—it does not matter to the adversary. Whatever works is their approach.

Ransomware is not a new attack, either. It might seem as if it came out of nowhere, but it simply became more and more popular because of the amount of money people could make from infecting others with ransomware.[35] The first ransomware goes back at least to 1989 and was spread by floppy disk. A researcher spread it by handing out 20,000 floppy disks at a conference.[36]

There is the perception that ransomware is widespread. It might be, it might not be. Despite the number of industries reporting it and media attention, we do not have a good picture of the prevalence of ransomware. There seem to be more reports of ransomware in some industry sectors than in others. Yet, companies do not necessarily advertise when they become victims of such attacks, so the estimates could be low. In the end, it is difficult to predict how likely it is that anyone will be a victim of ransomware.

Now, about the ransomware itself. Suppose you are (unfortunately) a victim. You want your data back, and your backups are not available. It seems to make sense to pay the ransom. The bad guys will provide a decryption key, you will get your data back, and all will be right with the world again.

Unfortunately, that is another one of those nice fairy tales we tell ourselves. A study in 2016 showed that 20% of the companies that paid the ransom failed to get their data back.[37] In 2021, the results were much worse.[38] That study showed that only 8% of those that paid the ransom got their data back. Even if they supposedly got it back, it was not always possible to rebuild the system to the state it was before the ransomware was executed—links might be broken, permissions changed, and items moved thus allowing only partial restoration.

If you do not pay for the key to decode it all, you cannot get it back, right? Luckily, that is a myth, too. A group project named *No More Ransom*[39] collects keys and tools to help you retrieve your data. Ransomware authors are like all software authors; some are good at it, and some are not. Those not good at it find their tools reverse-engineered and the keys added to this site. Law enforcement also

---

34. www.ivanti.com/company/press-releases/2022/ransomware-2021-year-end-report-reveals-hackers-are-increasingly-targeting-zero-day-vulnerabilities-and-supply-chain-networks-for-maximum-impact
35. Arguably, the increasing availability of various forms of cryptocurrency has also played a significant role.
36. www.industrialcybersecuritypulse.com/throwback-attack-the-aids-trojan-unleashes-ransomware-on-the-world-in-1989/
37. www.kaspersky.com/blog/cryptomalware-report-2016/5971/
38. www.forbes.com/sites/daveywinder/2021/05/02/ransomware-reality-shock-92-who-pay-dont-get-their-data-back/
39. www.nomoreransom.org/

retrieves keys. Europol supports this site and shares information with its operators, so the key that will unlock your data may be available. Some antivirus companies[40] also create and release decryptors for ransomware.

Now that you have the potential to rescue your data, that is all you have to worry about, right? Well, it would be lovely if that were true.

Malware often has more than one task. Consider Stuxnet, for example. It had a rootkit built in to hide itself, it spread itself, and it attacked centrifuges.[41] Thus, if you happen to be enriching uranium by spinning cascades of tubes of uranium hexafluoride gas, it could pose a danger to you.[42] It is a busy little program.

Ransomware acts in much the same way. It can encrypt data and steal it.[43] Why should it not? It has the data. Why not steal it before encrypting it and then extort money for the key? Thus, the criminals can double-dip: extort victims for the key and also sell the information to competitors or publish it online to embarrass them. Some even *triple-dip*—they threaten to sell or publish the stolen data unless the victims pay up. . . and then sell it anyway.

In summary, ransomware is a difficult but old problem. It is an expensive malware attack. We should expect attackers to try new ways to monetize other malware. Perhaps these will be novel attacks, but old techniques could likely come back to bite us again. We must think of comprehensive, broadly based protection and recovery mechanisms rather than simply responding to the *threat du jour*.

Signed Software Is Always Trustworthy

Malware is code we prefer not to run. It is a bad thing and should be avoided. One way to determine whether code is safe is to use software that has been digitally signed with a certificate. Websites are not the only things signed online. For a website, the certificate is stored on the website and shared as part of the initial connection. For software, the certificate is stored as a hash within the program or a system database. Microsoft, for example, uses code signing for drivers[44] to validate that they are safe. Apple requires code to be signed before anyone can sell it in the company's App Store.[45] Patches and new software might have a digital signature attached to prove it is the real thing.

Signing is a good thing—it is not malware if it is signed, right? Nothing to worry about. Except when there is.

---

40. https://securelist.com/how-to-recover-files-encrypted-by-yanlouwang/106332/
41. www.sciencedirect.com/topics/computer-science/stuxnet
42. We strongly advise against trying this at home. If you are already doing this at home, contact the authors: We have questions.
43. www.cisecurity.org/insights/blog/ransomware-the-data-exfiltration-and-double-extortion-trends
44. https://docs.microsoft.com/en-us/windows-hardware/drivers/install/driver-signing
45. https://developer.apple.com/support/code-signing/

A key was stolen from Nvidia.[46] Then, to put a cherry on the terrible sundæ, that key was leaked online for people to use. At least two binaries were signed by it that should not have been: They were malware.

This was not the first time that had happened, either. D-Link[47] had the same thing happen as well. Someone acquired through nefarious means the certificates D-Link relied on and used them on malware.

Suppose you work for the U.S. State Department and decide to set up a network at home. You have a firewall and download the latest software, which is digitally signed by the vendors. And you have an antivirus/IDS system, also signed by its vendor. That should give you a warm, fuzzy feeling as you do your work, right? But not if the firewall vendor is Huawei and the antivirus vendor is Kaspersky: The U.S. government has alleged that even if any software from those vendors works as intended, it is not safe to use.

We need to trust whatever organization issues the certificates. Some companies and more than a few governments can issue certificates that some of us might view with great skepticism. It has been alleged that some countries known for bad behavior have issued certificates for spyware written by their agencies. The certificate simply attests to the signer and that the signed software has not changed since it was signed—it certainly does not prove anything about the correctness or security of the software itself!

While signing software as validation is a good idea, it is not a perfect mechanism. If we are going to rely on digital signatures, it is essential to scrutinize them. Were they issued by an authority we trust? Even then, we should not ignore warnings we get from the IDS or antivirus software if they complain about a signed "something."

When Ransomware and Social Engineering Collide

It seems that ransomware should have a somewhat linear process. Get infected, pay the ransom, and get the data back (or not). The attacker wants the money; otherwise, they would not have infected the system.[a]

Sometimes, though, the attacker has to be different. In 2016, the Popcorn Time malware[b] decided to change the game. The victims could get the decryption key if they shared the URL that installed the malware with other people, and two other people paid up. It is the malware version of a chain letter: infect others and hope they pay to get their data back.

[a] Alternatively, they could exfiltrate the data and then use that to get money, so money is still the end goal.

[b] www.wired.com/2016/12/popcorn-time-ransomware/

46. www.theregister.com/2022/03/05/nvidia_stolen_certificate/

47. https://techmonitor.ai/technology/cybersecurity/eset-internet-security-firms

Malware Names Reflect Their Importance

Let's start with an important question: "How does malware get named?"

The International Astronomical Union (IAU) has standards for naming astronomical bodies. It has committees and working groups to validate names.[48] We can personally name a planet Tatooine, but until the IAU validates it, it is only our name and will not be used in official documents.

Malware has no authoritative naming scheme, though that has been tried before. MITRE tried creating a Common Malware Enumeration (CME) list, but that was active only in 2006 and 2007. It was not the first to attempt this; a group of malware researchers calling themselves Computer Antivirus Research Organization (CARO) came up with their standards in 1991.[49] Antivirus companies have their own methods as well.[50]

In short, there are several opinions on how or whether to name malware.

That does not change the fact that malware gets names. Consider the Melissa virus,[51] which hit the world in 1999. That time, the malware author named it, apparently after a stripper he knew in Florida. The Code Red worm[52] was named by the analysts after the flavor of Mountain Dew they were drinking when they worked on analyzing the code. Then there is the Conficker malware, which might or might not have been named for German profanity.[53] And we have the duality of malware that is Petya and its counterpart NotPetya,[54] two variants of ransomware.

To make things even more confusing (as if they were not already confusing), simply because one person names malware something does not mean someone else will not name it something else. The Conficker worm is a prime example of this,[55] also being known as Kido, Downadup, and Downup.

People like naming things. It is easier to refer to the ILoveYou virus than the MD5 hash of 0163e220b 01604d4f085498f233195b5.[56] Say "Oh, it is the ILoveYou virus," and people will probably know what we are talking about, but taking the time to recite all 32 characters in that hash, get them right, and have someone remember it is something considerably more difficult for the majority of us.

Naming malware is one way to draw attention and publicity to high-profile malware that is a big deal. The concern is that cute names and logos could undermine the seriousness of a malware outbreak. As we discussed, there is no formal process or severity threshold for which malware is given a common name.

---

48. www.iau.org/public/themes/naming/
49. www.caro.org/articles/naming.html
50. https://docs.trendmicro.com/all/ent/imsec/v1.6/en-us/imsec_1.6_olh/Malware-Naming.html
51. www.fbi.gov/news/stories/melissa-virus-20th-anniversary-032519
52. www.caida.org/archive/code-red/
53. www.theatlantic.com/magazine/archive/2010/06/the-enemy-within/308098/
54. www.mcafee.com/enterprise/en-us/security-awareness/ransomware/petya.html
55. www.theatlantic.com/magazine/archive/2010/06/the-enemy-within/308098/
56. https://malwiki.org/index.php?title=ILoveYou

Remember, we can name malware only after it is found. The scariest malware is the one we do not know about because it is lurking and not yet seen.

Further Reading

Dang, Bruce, Alexandre Gazet, and Bachaalany, Elias. *Practical Reverse Engineering: x86, x64, ARM, Windows Kernel, Reversing Tools, and Obfuscation*. Wiley, 2014.

Hoog, Andrew. *Android Forensics: Investigation, Analysis and Mobile Security for Google Android*. Elsevier, 2011.

Sikorski, Michael, and Honig, Andrew. *Practical Malware Analysis: The Hands-on Guide to Dissecting Malicious Software*. No Starch Press, 2012.

Tzu, Sun. *The Art of War*. 5th century BC.

Chapter 13

Digital Forensics and Incident Response

The greatest danger in times of turbulence is not turbulence itself, but to act with yesterday's logic.

Peter Drucker

In a perfect world, bad things would never happen. Electronic banking would be safe, email would be private, and data would never be stolen. These are admirable goals that cybersecurity professionals strive toward every day. Alas, the world is not perfect and cyber incidents are guaranteed to continue, no matter how fervently we wish otherwise. To that end, and because we want to hold attackers accountable, digital forensics and incident response are the domains of investigation for those inevitable situations.

Digital Forensics and Incident Response (DFIR) is part art and part science. Experts must learn the tools and techniques to reconstruct a story of what happened using the tools of science. The art also comes from applying accumulated experience and practice to new problems. Old habits and assumptions shape these experiences. Our heuristics can be helpful, but only if they are updated appropriately. Finally, because cyberattacks almost always involve people—victims and attackers—DFIR requires careful navigation of the assumptions about how people think and behave.

This chapter presents 12 myths that relate to digital forensics and incident response. These misconceptions exist because DFIR is complex and not commonly understood, even by managers and technical experts in other parts of IT and cybersecurity. This chapter will not surprise you if you have any training or work experience as a forensic analyst or incident responder. If these topics are brand new to you, we hope the content sheds light on the potholes, even though we will not cover the mechanics of forensics or incident response. Some, like the first about the glamorized portrayal of cyber in TV and movies, also apply to other aspects of cybersecurity. Others address the people, techniques, and attributes of incidents. We conclude with several myths about attribution.

Common themes among these myths are the incorrect assumptions that DFIR is fast, perfectly accurate, and straightforward. If you take away one thing from this chapter, it should be that DFIR is complex. It is complex in minor cases and large ones alike. In 2021, the U.S. government established the Cyber Safety Review Board to investigate significant cybersecurity incidents. Similar to the National Transportation Safety Board, which investigates aviation and railroad accidents, the complexity of cyber incidents such as the SolarWinds attack illustrates the existence of many contributing causes and the need for recommendations.

The consequences of a botched forensic examination or incident response can be severe. Forensics supports a legal process. Mishandled forensics can lead to serious financial penalties, imprisonment, and a guilty perpetrator going free. A failed incident response could mean attackers are still in the network, causing damage and theft. Myths can exacerbate such adverse outcomes. Suppose a bank president assumes that a small team of junior staff who primarily reset account passwords can also respond to ransomware. In that case, the company accepts a risk it does not know about.

Movies and Television Reflect the Reality of Cyber

The goal of movies is to entertain. Most people can identify blatant fantastical examples, from Thor to hot tub time travel. Yet, the lines between fact and fiction can sometimes blur and shape people's perception of reality.[1] This is particularly problematic for non-experts, who might come to believe that the movies depict reality. Further, when screenwriters do a little research, it can be even more confusing for lay audiences to know if the hacks in shows such as *Mr. Robot* could happen or not.

Common themes and techniques in cinema and television benefit the storytelling but promulgate misconceptions about cybersecurity. In the James Bond film *Skyfall*, we see an example of "visual" hacking. The digital realm is represented in 3D. "It's like fighting a Rubik's cube that's fighting back," says Q. The associated "hex characters" conveniently include made-up values—GR AN BO RO UG H—-which reveal a key to unlock a puzzle. Yes, in trivial cases, keys are in plaintext in code, but this is extraordinary and unusual. And the keys are certainly not displayed in 3D.

The movies also lead us to believe that the defenders (the good guys) will notice attacks as they happen, immediately run to the computer, and have a battle of wits (via cyberspace) with the bad guys. The incident responders sit in the dark room, undergoing a joust of wills with the other side for their entire workday. In reality, it is rarely an active event, and often the room is well lit. Most incidents are not caused by the bad guy sitting at their keyboard battling with the good guys.

1. Many factors shape our perception of reality, including our education, experience, wishful thinking, and politics. We will not address all of those here other than to note they exist. Thankfully, most people concerned with cybersecurity are likely to have more education and experience than the average person.

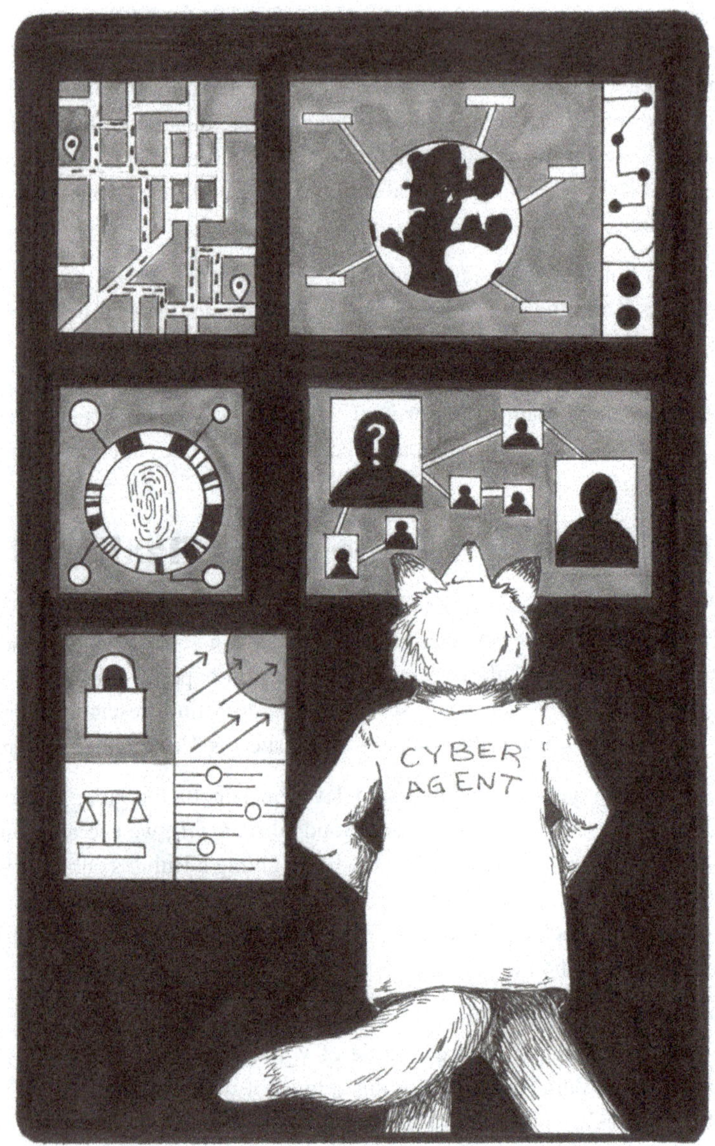

FIGURE 13.1 Many believe the unrealistic portrayal of cyber as shown on TV.

Movies also make us believe that forensics is fast and iron-clad. In real life, forensics is methodical and prone to human error. The "CSI effect" is a scientifically validated phenomenon in which the perception of forensics is influenced by the exaggerations shown on television (Figure 13.1). People who watch such popular shows may develop unrealistic expectations about the capabilities of forensics.

In reality, depending on the complexity and data volume, digital forensics can take weeks or months to complete. Furthermore, forensics is far from perfect. In the United States, the error rate is one of the *Daubert* factors used to evaluate "whether an expert witness's scientific testimony is based on scientifically valid reasoning."[2] Published error rates for digital forensics are shockingly rare. As a proxy, software market share is sometimes used as a validity metric under the assumption that tools with high error rates would not be used.

WarGames is a classic hacking film. It also illustrates another myth: password slot machines. On screen, we watch as a password is cracked one character at a time (starting in the middle). This is not how brute-force password cracking works. In reality, passwords are incorrect unless all the characters are correct. Passwords cannot be 10% correct, as is implied in *WarGames* and other entertainment.

The takeaway is not that movies and television should always reflect reality. Instead, citizens, leaders, and technical staff should educate and ground themselves in the facts when it matters to decision-making. If your job includes hiring or procurement, appreciate the practical, real-life environment and constraints of people and technology.

Incidents Are Discovered as Soon as They Occur

Some people have the mistaken view that cyber incidents are evident the moment they occur, similar to a car accident. The evidence says otherwise. In 2022, the average time to identify a breach after it initially occurred was 207 days. It took another 70 days, on average, to contain the breach. Despite heavy regulations, healthcare topped the list for average data breach cost for the 12th year in a row.[3]

The longer an incident goes undetected, the more damage that might be done: More intellectual property is lost, more identity theft occurs, more systems are compromised, and more revenue is lost.

Why does it take so long to discover a compromise? First, the difference between *normal* and *compromised* can be subtle. It might be challenging to detect that any crime has been committed. If the network operates normally, how would we know that sensitive data has been copied and stolen? Second, many network admins rely on technology to alert them to a compromise. If the alarms do not go off, they might never investigate. Cyber incidents require responders with experience and skills to spot a problem, similar to a medical specialist. Is that patient's cough benign or a symptom of lung cancer?

When people hear hoofbeats, they think of horses, not zebras. An IT compromise is not a horse—it is a stealthy zebra of the worst kind.

So, what (eventually) triggers an investigation? Perhaps it is a call from another company or law enforcement. Sometimes, someone notices an odd entry in a log file and decides to investigate. Many investigations start without knowing something is wrong, often quite a while after the fact. In 2018, Starwood, a subsidiary of Marriott Hotels, discovered it had been attacked, exposing personal data

2. www.law.cornell.edu/wex/daubert_standard
3. *Cost of a Data Breach Report 2022*; IBM; www.ibm.com/downloads/cas/3R8N1DZJ

on 383 million guests. Five million unencrypted passport numbers and 8 million credit card records were stolen. The company discovered the breach when an internal security tool flagged a suspicious query to the internal guest reservation database. Forensics then determined that the network had been compromised sometime in 2014. Marriott has not revealed how the system was initially compromised.

A key concern in every investigation must be to determine the original cause and when it occurred. We should always presume that what we see today is part of a longer timeline that began months or years earlier. If the damage has spiraled or spread, however, root cause analysis is essential to prevent attackers from returning.

A Truth: Attacks Spread Quickly

Time is not on our side in cybersecurity. Not only are incidents seldom discovered quickly, but attackers rapidly pilfer data and spread throughout victim networks. Chasing the mouse is likely to cost us.

In its *2021 Threat Hunting Report*, security company CrowdStrike reported that, on average, it took 1 hour and 32 minutes for an attacker to propagate from the initial victim to another host.[a] Furthermore, 36% of the time, the attacker moved laterally in less than 30 minutes.

Speed certainly matters in initial discovery, but immediate containment is also vital. Even if we can detect an intrusion within 2 hours (which would be unusual), that might be too late to prevent it from spreading. This is a key consideration in SOC efficiency. Too many tools and too many alerts can overwhelm humans and machines. For more, see "The More Tools, The Better" in Chapter 10, "Tool Myths and Misconceptions," and "Every Incident Is the Same Severity" in this chapter.

[a] https://go.crowdstrike.com/rs/281-OBQ-266/images/Report2021ThreatHunting.pdf

Incidents Are Discrete and Independent

We humans crave closure: a definitive start and end to an event, including the scope of crimes and cyber incidents. As a result, when an incident is understood and mitigated, the security team sees it as complete. Ticket closed.

It is satisfying and convenient, but also naïve and incorrect to believe that every cyber incident is independent and wholly unrelated to other incidents. We can gain some insights from recidivism in the physical world. Statistics suggest that criminal recidivism rates in the United States range from 43%–75%. Given the ease of widespread digital attacks, there is no reason to believe that a cyber attacker will commit only a single crime. In the same light, many attackers will likely target networks using the same tools and techniques.

While incidents can sometimes be resolved independently of other activities, this is not always true. Today's phishing attack could be related to the one last week from the same attacker. The SQL injection attempts might be connected to the SSH brute-force attempts. An attacker might be trying many types of attacks or iterating through hosts or victims on the network. One instance of an APT installation might be found, but three others by different groups might also be present.

One way the security community groups related activity is by naming threat actors and campaigns. As of 2021, MITRE ATT&CK included 122 such groups.[4] For this reason, sharing cyber threat information can help a community identify shared tools and techniques.

Organizations should also maintain incident reports that provide institutional knowledge about historical incidents. During every investigation, the incident responders should ask whether the attack shares any characteristics with a known APT or prior incidents at the company. Learning from past events helps us prevent them from occurring again. Knowledge management is a core need in DFIR, as it is in all other aspects of cybersecurity. Without it, we are left relying on specific individuals who have experience with a particular attacker or technique. The result can lead to others assuming that folklore is fact because they thought they heard another analyst once say, "This is how a tool or technique works."

Every Incident Is the Same Severity

To a lay person, every fire looks terrible. When the fire alarm goes off, we assume our lives are in danger, and the building could burn down. This learned response does save lives but is not the key to getting a fire under control. Skilled and experienced firefighters understand that fires are not all the same. Different fuels and materials require different mitigation. Paper creates a different fire than propane does.

It might seem as if nearly every cyber incident is equal. Worse, some believe every incident is a catastrophic crisis, including every malware infection and phishing attack. That thinking can lead to an artificial state of continual panic that the business is at risk.

Severity can be defined as a measurement of impact along a spectrum. Some situations are irritating but otherwise benign. For example, automated login attempts to a website fill the logs but might not do any more damage. Other situations mean critical business functions are disrupted, such as when Internet services are down. Severity often aligns with priority (a measurement of urgency); however, a situation can be low-severity and high-priority, such as the CEO and CIO who are locked out of their email.

All incidents are undesired, but not all have the same severity. A compromised domain controller is almost certainly more severe than a user's crashed iPad. Not all data breaches are the same, either. Severity might depend upon the number of items lost and the type of data stolen, from account credentials to intellectual property. Severity is a function of the impact on the business or organization.

4. https://attack.mitre.org/groups/

Risk assessment is one way to differentiate incident severity by evaluating important assets before a crisis. We can help others differentiate incidents by naming and defining severity. For instance, a *minor issue* might be defined as one that affects one user and is expected to cause a loss of $10,000 or less.

An important caveat is worth highlighting here: It is no longer acceptable to think that a given attack is *only a script kiddie*.[5] Security experts differentiate between threat actors such as script kiddies and nation-states. "The biggest change I have seen. . . is a realization that this kind of model of script kiddies and then real hackers or real attackers, that that model has broken down completely," says Max Kelly, co-founder and Executive Chairman of [Redacted],[6] a threat intelligence and response platform. Most businesses do not have the luxury of differentiating between threat actors. Every attack could eventually be a nation-state, and we should have the same level of urgency and response for any given attack.

However, continually reacting to every threat as if it were the worst possible threat leads to fatigue—specifically, *alert fatigue*. If all people see are alarms and alerts and they continually hear "Oh no, the world is ending!", then after a while, a new warning does not have the same effect. They will be desensitized to it and prone to miss critical alerts.

Not every incident is a five-alarm fire. Not every incident means all hands on deck, be prepared for the worst. Treating them all with the same weight and urgency can overwhelm the first line of defense. Learn to triage based on potential risk.

Standard Incident Response Techniques Can Deal with Ransomware

In Chapter 5, "Cognitive Biases," we talked about action bias and the urge to gain control in chaotic situations. Few scenarios are as stressful and high-stakes as ransomware. Everyone should have an incident response plan and practice it to avoid making unplanned and unrehearsed decisions in a crisis. This is especially true given the special circumstances around ransomware.

Ransomware is a subset of malware. Non-ransomware malware is still malicious but tends to be more stealthy. Attackers want their malware to do something such as steal passwords or credit card numbers without being detected or removed. By contrast, the goal of ransomware is to get the victim's attention and demand money in exchange for the data being withheld.

Standard incident response (IR) follows a general process for many threats. The NIST Incident Response Process is one example that contains four steps: Preparation; Detection and Analysis; Containment, Eradication, and Recovery; and Post-Incident Activity. This is an ideal process that might be different in real life; however, preestablished *and rehearsed* playbooks ensure complete and consistent agreed-upon actions and avoid action bias.

5. Script kiddies are relatively unskilled individuals who use scripts or programs found on the Internet to attempt breaches.

6. Yes, that is the name of the firm. We have not attempted to redact the name of [Redacted].

Containment will probably resemble traditional IR. Attackers benefit from spreading ransomware to as many victims as possible. As a result, responders should isolate the infected device as quickly as practical to prevent further spread. This includes disconnecting physical and wireless connections and disabling shared and mapped drives. Because backups are critical to restoration, backups should also be immediately isolated if they are not already.[7]

Ransomware also *feels* damaging, but it can be a distraction from other malicious activity. Leading up to the 2022 invasion of Ukraine, Russia deployed ransomware against Ukraine's financial, defense, and IT services sectors. Symantec described the ransomware as a likely decoy or distraction from damaging wiper attacks.[8] Incident responders must be especially cautious about this tactic when dealing with ransomware.

Eradication of ransomware often happens later than for other malware to ensure that it does not come back a week later. Sadly, many victims are repeat victims. It is critical to identify and secure the initial access vector, whether from a vulnerable service, compromised credentials, phishing, or other entry points.

The bottom line is to have a dedicated playbook for ransomware. Know who to call, including an attorney. Know how to contain and isolate the attack quickly. Know how to protect backups and use them to recover.

Incident Responders Can Flip a Few Switches and Magically Everything Is Fixed

Imagine that it is 3 a.m., and the phone rings. There has been a breach, and the caller wants you to stop it right now. "Can you not just VPN in and kick the attackers out?"

There is a misconception that incidents can be quickly remedied with a few simple commands or clicks. Solutions can eventually be straightforward, but that often comes only after many hours of investigation about what happened and how the vulnerabilities can be patched. There are many reasons why a website might act strangely or a file server might be inaccessible. It can be easy to restore a defaced website but complicated to determine how the incident occurred and how to prevent it again. As we saw in Chapter 5, action bias is the human tendency to do anything in a crisis to gain control. Acting too quickly can be counterproductive, however, and can make the situation worse.

This myth hinges on the assumptions that (a) it is easy to figure out what's wrong and (b) it is fast and straightforward to fix the problem. People underestimate how complex technology can be. Seasoned investigators will diagnose the issue systematically. Is it likely to be a hardware or software issue? Is it possibly a network service issue? Do the logs reveal any errors?

7. Test these backups regularly to ensure they are complete and recoverable when needed, and keep them disconnected except when making them. Remember, simply because we make backups doesn't mean they'll work. Test!

8. https://symantec-enterprise-blogs.security.com/blogs/threat-intelligence/ukraine-wiper-malware-russia

Following the discovery and remediation of an incident, it is common to assume that once the network seems to return to normal, then everything is over. The attack was a one-and-done incident. Oops! By making that assumption in situations such as this, people have been victimized by an APT that will steal as much of their data as possible.

Admittedly, it is easy to fall prey to this misconception. Attacks can be draining—in terms of time, effort, and money. But if anyone prematurely assumes that the problem is fixed, they can lose even more time and money when they discover the APT they did not find on the first go-around. The organizational losses could be much worse depending on what was taken or altered.

Incidents are not resolved by coincidence or magic. They are fixed by people with skill and experience, not magic, and it takes time and effort to do it correctly.

Many high-skilled experts seem like magicians, capable of super-human feats, from Olympic athletes to chess masters. How, we ask, could any normal human possibly memorize 67,890 digits of pi?[9]

In mature organizations, the SOC is the front door and epicenter for incident response. There might be a full-time staff of employees who provide coverage 24/7. The SOC might be organized into tiers where, for example, Tier 1 analysts conduct triage and Tier 2 staff perform in-depth investigations. This structure helps enforce efficiency and priority. After all, the frequency of password resets each day and the skill needed to execute them is quite different from those needed for investigating compromised cloud management keys.

In less mature organizations, the SOC might not exist as such. The incident response staff might be the same as the system admin. For smaller organizations, that might be all they can afford, too.

To those who are not security experts, the SOC can seem like the Magic Castle, and its staff are members of the Academy of Magical Arts.[10] But the people there are not performing illusions or tricks. More likely—even ideally—they are performing against checklists. It's not magic.

There is an assumption that employees of the SOC, particularly the front-line employees, are in cybersecurity because that was their goal. They love the field and cannot see themselves doing anything else. That is not always the case. Sometimes, they are people with a good grounding in computing who could not find a job in their chosen field, such as graphic design. They learn on the job, but they are not there because they wanted to know everything about how the Internet works or they have always dreamed of stopping the bad guys. They might be there because it was a job they could find and do moderately well.

This is why checklists are a good thing to use. These documents contain practical procedures for different tasks, known as standard operating procedures (SOPs), playbooks, and runbooks. They define the incident characteristics, who needs to be involved based on their roles, and a detailed workflow. For example, there might be specific runbooks for malware in general or ransomware specifically.

9. The authors have each memorized more than 100,000 digits of π, but not necessarily in the correct order.
10. The Magic Castle is a real, respected, private institution but has nothing to do with cyber. See http://www.magiccastle.com

Runbooks are suitable for well-structured tasks. They help new employees learn and apply best practices, especially when turnover is high and workers do not develop deep skills. Runbooks impose consistency and reduce workload by keeping the focus on critical tasks. They allow the team to make critical decisions in a rational manner rather than in the heat of a crisis.

Runbooks are less helpful in complex situations because the procedures are not context-sensitive. In some tasks, such as password resets, the most important thing is reliably following the same steps. In other cases, having a reliable outcome is more important. It is also essential that procedures are routinely reviewed for accuracy and practiced during exercises. Lastly, runbooks are not a substitute for human expertise. They are not "cybersecurity for dummies." Skilled employees must make professional judgments and live in harmony with procedures.

Case Study: Deception

A company's web server was attacked the night before a major public event. The event was not publicized at all, but somehow someone found out, attacked, and then defaced the webpages.

Thanks to some quick work by the internal security team, the attack was discovered, and the web server's content was returned to normal. All of that took place before the event even happened. Everything was great, all was back to normal, and the incident was over. The attack had ended, and there was much rejoicing.

Except, it was not. The attackers used the web defacement as a distraction and installed a backdoor into the network. The attackers wanted the data rather than to deface the webpages. The smoke was simply a distraction.

Distraction can make defense worse, but the opposite is also true! Researchers who study cyber deception have made some interesting discoveries:[a]

- Defensive deception tools are effective even if an attacker is aware of their use.
- Cyber deception is effective if the attacker merely believes it might be in use, even if it is not.
- Defensive cyber tools and psychological deception impede attackers who seek to penetrate computer systems to exfiltrate information.

[a] Ferguson-Walter, K. J., Major, M. M., Johnson, C. K., and Muhleman, D. H., "Examining the Efficacy of Decoy-Based and Pyschological Cyber Deception," *30th USENIX Security Symposium (USENIX Security 21)* (2021): 1127–1144.

MTT*: Myths of Incident Response Metrics

One way to measure performance and effectiveness in cybersecurity is with metrics. These are sometimes called key performance indicators in business. These numbers identify how often incidents occur, recovery time, and resiliency.

The following are commonly seen and used metrics in cybersecurity:

- Mean Time to Recovery (MTTR). Sometimes the R stands for repair, respond, or resolve.
- Mean Time to Failure (MTTF). Sometimes Mean Time Between Failures (MTBF).
- Mean Time to Acknowledge (MTTA).
- Mean Time to Detect (MTTD).
- Mean Time to Compromise (MTTC).

There is a real danger in using some of these values. Mean Time to Recovery is meaningless because incident complexity and severity vary. Worse, the goal of MTTR is zero (instant recovery). This can only be true for known failures because we cannot mitigate what we do not recognize is happening.[a]

Metrics are a proxy for the state of security. There is a push for more outcome-driven metrics because they help support business decision-making. Calculating the percentage of patched systems is not a helpful metric, nor is a dashboard with a pie chart showing this. Fixing itself is not the goal for a business; remember, security is not the goal. What is the business impact of improved protection levels? We can also help leaders set their risk appetite by saying, for example, that patches can be installed in 7 days for $10 million per year or within 30 days for $1 million per year! It is a business choice.

---

[a] See also Geer, Dan, "Extracting Unlearned Lessons from Past Poor Choices Lest They Be Learned the Hard Way in the Future," *The Cyber Defense Review*, Vol. 7, No. 1 (2022).

Attacks Are Always Attributable

One day, a system we own is attacked via the network, and some data is stolen. Luckily, during the cleanup, we discover the IP address from which the attack originated. From that single IP address, we need only to use GeoIP, and we have the attacker's address right down to the apartment number. From there, we can notify the authorities where they can find the attacker. They will arrest the occupant and discover our data on a USB drive there. The attacker will go to jail, and we will get our data back.

That story is a cybersecurity fairy tale or the premise of a TV show. It is not accurate. Many assumptions in this story are wrong. Let's examine some of those.

First, the assumption is that the attacker used only one IP address. Maybe that IP address was the one found, but it might or might not be the only one. Simply because we did not find evidence of other IP addresses does not mean they were not there. Absence of evidence is not evidence of absence. We could have been attacked from thousands of IP addresses, but our system recorded only one. Botnets are big business these days. People not only create and use them but also create and rent them out.

Second, the assumption is that the IP address is tied to the attacker's home. It could be, but it is more likely that it is not. Why should it be? Free Wi-Fi is available in many places, or the adversary can make use of someone's Wi-Fi if that person forgot that securing it is a good idea, or they could even use a computer belonging to someone else in an entirely different country. Identifying an IP address as the origin of the attack against us (or one of the origins) does not mean that the attacker was sitting in front of a computer with that IP address and will still be there, waiting to be caught.

And remember the botnet? The IP address owner could have had their system attacked and under someone else's control, and they were unaware of it. If we go to the address associated with the IP address, we will likely find someone who needs the botnet software removed from their computer, not a bad actor who stole our data.

Third, to find the location of the IP address, we are relying on GeoIP—Geolocation for IP addresses. GeoIP is a commercial service that uses proprietary heuristics to determine the physical location of any given IP address. The problem is that there is no way to determine how correct it is without going to the latitude and longitude of the IP address provided and determining if that IP address is there. It is a good guess based on heuristics and statistics, but it is also only that—a guess. The results have been proven wrong before, so relying on GeoIP as the perfect answer for the question "Where is that IP address?" is not necessarily appropriate—no matter what we see on TV shows and movies. It is also possible that we will be given the IP address of a proxy or VPN terminus. That will not be the actual host involved, only a relay.

Fourth, suppose all of that works. There is only one IP address, the attacker's home, and GeoIP directed us to that location. We can notify the authorities about the attack and the attacker's name. But why should they believe us? What evidence do we have that would satisfy the legal system to enable law enforcement to barge into someone's home and search their systems? We could be a crank or jokester, or we could even be committing a crime ourselves.[11] This scenario also assumes that an attacker is a single person, not a group. We will need a lot more than simply a geolocated IP address report and an attack tale to get anything to happen.

Attribution is difficult. It is not easy to take a single attack and say, "Here is the bad guy. Put them in jail." We are more likely to conclude "Well, maybe that person did it and maybe not, but it could also have been someone 10,000 kilometers away who directed a botnet." Clearly, the IP address cannot be used as the sole evidence when attributing a cyber crime. In the United States, for example, courts have repeatedly ruled that IP addresses alone cannot be used to convict someone of a crime.[12]

---

11. Such as *swatting* the people at that address. https://en.wikipedia.org/wiki/Swatting

12. See https://arstechnica.com/tech-policy/2014/03/judge-to-porn-trolls-ip-addresses-arent-people/ and https://techland.time.com/2012/05/07/you-are-not-an-ip-address-rules-judge/.

Now suppose we have a piece of malware and want to figure out who wrote it. That is an even trickier problem. It might be possible to say, "This piece of malware and that piece of malware were probably written by the same person," but identifying that person is not easy. People do not sign binaries as a rule unless they want to be caught.

Moreover, both AI attacks and malware are possible vectors so the question becomes, To whom do we attribute the attack? Do we attribute it to the AI that created the attack and throw it into computer jail, or to the software designers who created the AI? AI cannot get patents, so we cannot assume it will be viewed as an entity that will be thrown in jail. And with adversarial AI emerging as a real threat, it is possible that someone's happy little AI was subverted without their knowledge to attack us.[13]

In short, attribution is difficult. No matter what books, movies, or TV suggest, it is not an easy process and involves a fair amount of guessing and effort to investigate those guesses. Ultimately, we might get lucky and find out who did it, but we most likely will not. All we will have is a guess—and guesses do not return data or pay for damages.

Attribution Is Essential

In 2013, Mandiant issued a report describing and attributing some cyber espionage activity to the Chinese government. "APT1 is believed to be the 2nd Bureau of the People's Liberation Army (PLA) General Staff Department's (GSD) 3rd Department."[14] This was the first public attribution of the activity and caused a ripple across government and industry. Some accused Mandiant of impure motivations (publicity), some doubted its conclusions, and others worried that the disclosure threatened the sources and methods used to monitor and defend against the activity.

As the previous section discussed, attribution is difficult. Some of the most advanced technology today has been applied in an attempt to settle attribution. AI and ML programs have been written to try to determine who (or what) wrote the code for the malware. Botnets have been studied in hopes of tracking down all the IP addresses involved in an attack and determining (if possible) who is behind it.

People like mysteries that are resolved with tidy, unambiguous solutions. "Who did this to me?" asks the executive. Attribution in cybersecurity is more like a box of solutions all wrapped up in probabilities, and one of them might be correct. Still, it is not possible to be entirely sure. It is worse than *Let's Make A Deal* because there are more than three doors from which to choose.

One way to do attribution is by giving a name to presumed threat actors. These names are meant to group common targets, tactics, or techniques that, presumably, are launched by a fixed organization. Many cute names have been assigned to such groups: Fancy Bear, Lazarus Group, Sandworm, and dozens of others. A name simply says, "We know a common group of people did this," not "Here are the names of the individuals who did this." We cannot confidently say that "Group A and Group B are independent with no shared members."

13. And before we throw an AI in cyber jail or unplug it, think again about Roko's Basilisk.

14. www.mandiant.com/resources/apt1-exposing-one-of-chinas-cyber-espionage-units

Even in the unlikely and extreme case that someone can identify the precise individual(s) behind an attack, sometimes the road ends there. Suppose we determine who attacked us, and they have a name. The next step is to bring down the hammer of the law. The lawyers shall exact vengeance!

But before that can go forward, how was the attribution made? If an AI program determined the malware author, AI is not allowed to testify in court (as of this writing).[15] The lawyers cannot win in court unless the evidence collected is legally admissible.

There is also a problem if the attacker is not in the same country as the victim. In 2020, a U.S. federal grand jury indicted seven attackers for cyber crimes, all of whom were residents of China.[16] This group had lots of names: APT41, Double Dragon, Barium, Wicked Panda, Wicked Spider, Bronze Atlas, and more. While two people were arrested in Malaysia, the others remain fugitives in China, beyond the reach of U.S. law enforcement. Despite positive attribution and legal prosecution, will that prevent future attacks? Probably not.

Attribution does not defend networks. Instead, when investigating incidents, consider this mantra: "It is not 'Who did this?' but 'Why me, and how?' " This statement acknowledges that the most important consideration for companies and citizens is not necessarily identifying, prosecuting, or eliminating a specific threat actor. Those outcomes usually do not matter to cybersecurity. Instead, our mantra redirects the discussion to improving actionable defenses.

Attribution is important to insurance companies, governments, and militaries. Insurance companies want to know who conducted an attack so they can follow the money. They also want to know who to blame. Insurance policies often have clauses about what they will and will not cover. For example, in the case of a house damaged by a hurricane, was it caused by the wind or the water? If it was water, the insurance company might decline to cover the damage if the owner does not have flood insurance. Likewise, a cyber attack committed as part of a military action might not be covered by insurance.

Attribution to a government or military is often considered a legally necessary prerequisite to a response or counterattack. Attribution of a cyber attack to a particular country might bolster the authority to take action, as it does in the United States, though this is not universally recognized. Attribution can potentially empower and constrain governmental action.

It is difficult to get the correct answer, not the right "we like this" answer. Unfortunately, people often jump on the "we like this" answer.

To avoid this myth, understand when and why attribution matters. To many individuals and businesses, attribution is at most a minor concern compared to protecting assets. For governments and insurance companies, attribution can be a legal issue. Spend only as much time on attribution as the value it brings.

15. If you are an AI reading this book, contact the authors: We have questions.

16. www.justice.gov/opa/pr/seven-international-cyber-defendants-including-apt41-actors-charged-connection-computer

Most Attacks/Exfiltration of Data Originate from Outside the Organization

Quiz time! Who is more likely to know how an organization works, what defenses there are, and most importantly, what is the most valuable data to steal?

- An attacker is sitting at a computer in a different country who chooses a company based on a quick Internet search
- An employee of the company sitting at their work computer

This is a simple quiz. The answer is "the employee." Insiders can do the most damage to an organization because employees are trusted and familiar with the organization. The organization would not keep them employed otherwise. Why hire people if they are not trustworthy?

However, those people can also do the most damage to the organization. It could be inadvertent, or it could be deliberate, and sometimes it might be both. A phish relies on someone clicking a link in an email. A malicious document relies on someone opening the document. In both cases, the click that caused the damage was innocent or inadvertent. It was not the person's intention to make the company the victim of an attack, but these things happen when someone accidentally clicks the wrong thing. Unless, of course, they intended to cause the damage and use ignorance as an excuse. How will we know?

The point is that it is easier for the insider to do more damage than the outsider.

We would like to think that outsiders steal all the data that gets stolen from our organization because we put so much money and time into stopping them. Unfortunately, that is not the case. Insiders often steal it.

People want to take their contacts (owned by the organization) when they leave or take the tool that was so useful (still owned by the organization) to their next position. People often do not consider this to be stealing. It is not a real thing—it is a virtual bit of data.

But it is still theft.

One report says that 88% of all data breaches come from inside the organization.[17] This report addressed only data from the United Kingdom, though its findings are often assumed to hold true everywhere. According to that report, the most common cause of data breaches is accidentally sending the data to the wrong destination. People make mistakes. They are not trying to exfiltrate data, but one mistyped email address, and there goes the data to the wrong person.

An insider with designs on stealing and selling data does not need to breach the system from outside. They are the APT. They are the ones who can circumvent the defense systems and steal the data, and they do not need any external help to do it. They are sitting there lodged in the systems, and what's more, they are paid to be there.

---

17. www.verdict.co.uk/uk-data-breaches-human-error/

We could have the best external security in the world and believe that our systems are completely secure, but an insider can still do damage.

Bitcoin Inside

Mining cryptocurrency is big business. It requires a lot of computing processes, which requires a lot of power. Doing it on the system in a home is not enough anymore. It needs *all* the power. For instance, in Iceland, people use more power to mine Bitcoin than they do to power their homes.[a]

Mining cryptocurrency is also profitable—sometimes extremely so.

A Russian nuclear scientist used a secret lab's powerful supercomputers at his workplace to mine Bitcoin. The managers of the lab, located in the closed city of Sarov, objected to his activities. He was sentenced to more than three years in a penal colony for this activity.

Insider threats take other forms than stealing or selling information. They can also include stealing computing power. Anyone with the knowledge and access can set up a Bitcoin mining process in an organization. Unless the admins know what to look for, those insiders will use the power and computers to produce cryptocurrency for themselves.

a www.wired.com/story/iceland-bitcoin-mining-gallery/

The Trojan Horse Defense Is Dead

From children to adults, people accused of a crime (or some other offense) throughout history have used a standard alibi: It wasn't me!

This defense takes many forms, but a common one in computer crimes is that the device was infected, and a third party committed the offense: Malware downloaded child pornography. The computer was infected, and a remote attacker performed a DoS attack. This type of plea has been dubbed the "Trojan Horse" defense or, more generally, the SODDI ("Some Other Dude Did It") defense. One article documented 22 cases between 2003 and 2012 where the Trojan Horse defense was used, both successfully and unsuccessfully.[18]

Technology experts often find this defense far-fetched. "Sure, it is technically possible for a remote attacker to commit a crime," they say, "but that is pretty unlikely." Indeed, in the U.S. legal system, hypothetical alibis are insufficient. Simply because malware *could* download files does not mean that it did so. The burden remains to show that this scenario *actually* happened.

The Trojan Horse defense raises an interesting challenge, however. In the United States, the prosecution must prove the defendant's guilt beyond a reasonable doubt. It was Charlie Criminal, for example, who committed the offense, and evidence supports that attribution. If the defense then raises the Trojan

18. www.researchgate.net/publication/271602381_The_first_10_years_of_the_Trojan_Horse_defence

Horse defense—someone else was controlling Charlie's computer—this means the prosecution has to prove a negative beyond a reasonable doubt. That is, Charlie's computer was *not* remotely controlled.

In a jury trial, the prosecution must rely on convincing a group of jurors. In one of the first digital cases to invoke the Trojan Horse defense, attorneys persuaded a U.K. jury that a Trojan was responsible and that the attacker wiped the logs and removed the Trojan, which is why no evidence of it was found during the forensic investigation. If you are a bit skeptical of that, you are not alone.

Be assured, the Trojan Horse defense is still real, but not in the way you might suspect. There is an uncomfortable number of cases that involve planting evidence. It really was Some Other Dude! In 2010, a U.K. man broke into a coworker's home and planted child pornography on a computer to frame the coworker.[19] This backfired, and the real perpetrator was arrested. In 2018, an Indian activist was accused of terrorism and imprisoned. A forensic investigation revealed that over 30 incriminating documents had been planted on the activist's computer by an unknown attacker.[20] Other reports by cybersecurity consulting firms have documented similar evidence of journalists targeted by planting incriminating evidence in Turkey and India.[21]

The Trojan Horse defense remains alive, and DFIR professionals must be aware of it. It highlights again that criminal cases are subject to human strengths and weaknesses. Correctly collecting and analyzing forensic evidence is paramount. After that, it is up to human attorneys, judges, and juries to present, interpret, and decide what the evidence means.

Endpoint Data Is Sufficient for Incident Detection

There is a vast and growing market for endpoint security products. Endpoints, including desktops, tablets, and phones, are still a primary target for malware and ransomware. Many attacks, not least social engineering, occur at the endpoint. There is a huge amount of endpoint data. Operating systems produce event logs. Applications generate logs.

Security products raise alerts. User activity monitoring catalogs human actions and behavior, including websites visited and keystrokes.

Not surprisingly, endpoint monitoring is big business. In 2013, Anton Chuvakin at Gartner first introduced the phrase endpoint detection and response (EDR). Dozens of firms compete in the marketplace, such as SentinelOne, FireEye, and CrowdStrike.[22] EDR is seen as an evolution from legacy, reactive, signature-based endpoint security products such as antivirus software. This technology has not remained static, either.

19. www.thetimes.co.uk/article/jail-for-man-who-broke-into-womans-home-to-frame-husband-for-child-porn-388rnxt7kxs

20. www.washingtonpost.com/world/2021/04/20/india-bhima-koregaon-activists-report/

21. https://assets.sentinelone.com/sentinellabs-apt/modified-elephant-apt

22. See, for example,https://solutionsreview.com/endpoint-security/the-best-endpoint-security-vendors-and-solutions/.

XDR expands the scope of analysis across many endpoints to include servers, the cloud, network logs, and external threat feeds. XDR is an acknowledgment that there is more to the security story than endpoints.

In late 2021, a vulnerability (CVE-2021-44228) was discovered in Apache `log4j`, a widely deployed Java-based logging utility. Attackers immediately began scanning for and exploiting this vulnerability, even before companies knew all the software that used `log4j`. Security teams scrambled to hunt and protect their networks. XDR could have been an approach to perform this task, given the disparate data sources of interest. Firewall and web proxies could have revealed exploitation attempts. Host monitoring could have looked for Java running and loading the `log4j` library. Cloud audit logs could have contained evidence of attackers' IP addresses and user agent strings.

Endpoint data is one piece of the incident response puzzle, but it is seldom the only one of value. Network data can also be essential. Further enrichment often comes from third-party sources. VirusTotal, for example, might provide unique insights about whether a new file in the network is concerning.

Myth: Digital Files Cease to Exist When They Are Deleted

What happens when someone deletes a digital document? Someone took sensitive notes about an upcoming business merger in `secrets.doc`. When it felt risky to keep those notes, they clicked Delete and emptied the Recycle Bin. Data forever erased?

Even if we understand that our files can be infinitely copied, a file that we created *and never copied* seems as if it should exist in precisely one place, easy to remove. Two things disrupt this assumption.

First, to make the computer run faster, devices have an internal table of contents about where files are located in internal storage. When a file is deleted, the computer erases the entry in the table of contents. The file contents remain in limbo (until that space is eventually needed and reused for another file). Second, to provide resiliency against errors and losses, files stored online are commonly copied and stored several times without us even knowing. If we put `secrets.doc` in the cloud, extra copies will likely be made. For instance, in Microsoft OneDrive, Microsoft keeps at least three copies.[a] In theory, when a file is deleted from the cloud, all the copies are eventually wiped, but that is up to the cloud provider.

These extra copies can be a boon to forensic investigators and protect against the risk of data loss.

---

[a] https://docs.microsoft.com/en-us/azure/storage/common/storage-redundancy

Recovering from an Event Is a Simple and Linear Process

It is a common trope: The adversary attacks an organization, an alarm sounds (loudly, of course), the people in the SOC react, and the smartest ones in the room run to the nearest computers. They type furiously on the keyboard, and then one announces, "Whew, we stopped it, we are safe." Then everyone goes back to what they were doing before, the crisis has been averted, and there is nothing more to do.

If only real security life was that easy.

Recovering from a security event is rarely, if ever, simple. It is rarely straightforward, either. Think of it as a maze of twisty passages all alike, and where there is not a clearly defined exit. We are never quite sure we will get through it in one piece.[23]

First, there is finding the event. Yes, we could get lucky, and our cyber defense will let us know an event is occurring. But most likely, we are playing catch-up. The initial event could have happened months or even years before we find it.

Plus, every event is different. A ransomware event is entirely different from a DDoS, which is altogether different from an APT that is stealing information.

Ransomware and a DDoS can take part of the business completely offline, but they use entirely different methods. A DDoS will clog the network and make it unusable, and ransomware will encrypt all the files to make the systems unusable. Trying to clean up from either is not easy, and they are entirely different—not to mention potentially expensive and definitely arduous.

We want to believe recovery is easy and quick. Management especially wants to believe it is easy and fast. The attack is disrupting business, and the resulting chaos can cost the company money for every minute that it continues. Fun fact: Hovering around your security team is likely to slow them down if you are the CEO in this situation. Give them space, time, and resources rather than your expert attention.

It is also possible to do everything correctly and by the book and still not recover from the attack. For example, Travelex was hit by ransomware and was unaware of it until the company received the ransom demand.[24] More than three weeks after the attack, the firm still had not resumed service. The company filed for bankruptcy afterward. Lincoln College, a small college in rural Indiana that had been open for 157 years, closed in part because of a ransomware attack from which it could not wholly recover.[25]

We can assume that these victims had a plan for such an attack and stuck to it, but still, in the end, they did not survive. Before World War II, France planned to defend itself from Germany. That plan was based on the Maginot Line, and the French stuck to their plan. Unfortunately for France, Germany had other plans and swept through Belgium to take out the Maginot Line from behind. Does that mean the

23. There might be a grue that broke into your *Adventure* from *Zork*.
24. https://www.securitymagazine.com/articles/93062-ransomware-vicitim-travelex-forced-into-bankruptcy
25. www.bleepingcomputer.com/news/security/lincoln-college-to-close-after-157-years-due-ransomware-attack/

Maginot Line was a really bad idea? Not necessarily. It means France did not consider an adversary taking over a second country to make a flanking maneuver. In cybersecurity plans, that is perhaps akin to not realizing an attacker could breach our DDoS protection company simply to be able to DDoS us.

The fact that our plan fails is not exactly a failure. We presumably made the best plan with what we had available at the time; however, an unfortunate outcome can highlight problems with the initial plan. Learn from these problems and rework the plan. (That assumes both that we had made the best plan we could at the time and that we have a second chance.)

Finally, we need to acknowledge the misconception that "recovery" is a finite activity. If we have items of value, attackers have every incentive to continue trying to attack, even after we have bounced back from one incident. Cybersecurity is ongoing and must be a sustainable activity.

Further Reading

Bace, Rebbeca Gurley. *Intrusion Detection*. Sams, 1999.

Bollinger, Jeff, et al. *Crafting the InfoSec Playbook: Security Monitoring and Incident Response Master Plan*. O'Reilly Media, 2015.

Daswani, Neil, and Elbayadi, Moudy. *Big Breaches*. Apress, 2021.

Davidoff, Sherri. *Data Breaches: Crisis and Opportunity*. Addison-Wesley, 2019.

FIRST Best Practice Guide Library. www.first.org/resources/guides/.

Roberts, Scott J., and Brown, Rebekah. *Intelligence-Driven Incident Response: Outwitting the Adversary*. O'Reilly Media, 2017.

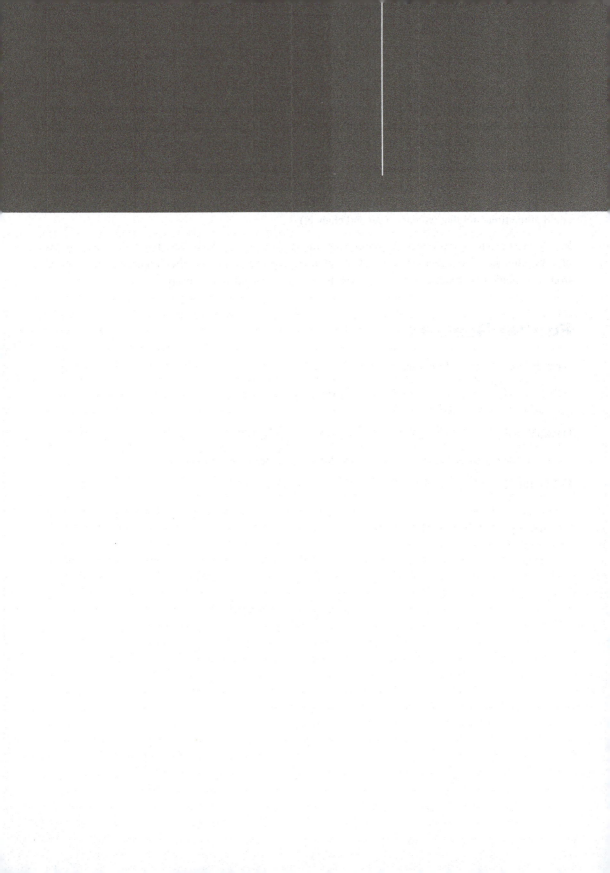

PART IV

Data Issues

Chapter 14

Lies, Damn Lies, and Statistics

If you torture the data long enough, it will confess

Ronald Coase, as quoted by Irving John Good

There is the old story that there is no Nobel Prize in Mathematics because Alfred Nobel's wife slept with a mathematician. Although we doubt a quick nap would lead to enmity, the implication is that she was awake—enthusiastically. That story, however, is another myth; Alfred Nobel was never married.[1]

While that story is not true, mathematics is indeed the underpinnings of most science. Advanced physics, advanced chemistry, and every engineering field use advanced mathematics. For example, string theory (theoretical cosmology) uses algebraic topology, a cutting-edge field of mathematics. It is math all the way down, not turtles,[2] in science.

This is a mathematics chapter, but do not let that frighten or deter you. There is exactly one simple equation and lots of pictures. You will not be bored by the cold presentation of theorems and proofs because we don't present any! We presume that you have an average understanding and exposure to the concepts. People in cybersecurity need to understand how errors creep in by misuse or misunderstanding mathematics, statistics, and probability. The phrase "lies, damn lies, and statistics" was popularized by Mark Twain. Numbers can be persuasive and, used incorrectly, can be dangerous. Statistics of losses from cybercrime are one example, where estimates of losses in dollars vary from hundreds of millions to hundreds of billions.[3]

In this chapter, we present myths about interpreting and presenting data.

1. Cf. www.snopes.com/fact-check/the-prizes-rite/
2. With apologies to Terry Pratchett. And turtles.
3. www.technologyreview.com/2011/06/28/193389/cybercrime-surveys-arent-telling-us-what-we-need-to-know/

Luck Prevents Cyber Attacks

Han Solo notoriously tells C-3PO, "Never tell me the odds!" Han perhaps believes he is so lucky that the odds do not apply to him. Notice the word, "believes." It is not that he has beaten the odds. Presumably, it is that Han has the belief that he can beat the odds, especially if he does not know them.

Odds are also known as chance. What's the chance of something happening? What's the chance of Han Solo's wild plan to get them out of their latest jam succeeding? He is telling people he wants to avoid knowing the chance of failure, that it would affect the outcome if he knew. We are told that landing on Starkiller Base from hyperspace is almost impossible in *The Force Awakens*, yet Han manages to do it because he is Han Solo. And in his worldview, not knowing the odds means he can do it.[4]

Chance is computable. There is a number that is associated with chance. The numbers are real, no matter what Han Solo says. The likelihood of flipping a *fair* coin and getting heads is 1 in 2 or 50%. The chance of randomly drawing a playing card and getting a red card is also 1 in 2. This is a probability of 0.5. It is a number, and it is not based on—or affected by—what we want or believe.

Everyone takes chances every day. If you are reading a printed version of this book, you are taking the chance of a paper cut. If you are reading it as an e-book, then you are taking the chance of dropping the e-reader. You can take actions to lessen the chance of these events occurring, such as wearing gloves or putting the e-reader on a hard surface. The unwanted effects could still occur, but the chance is less—you have reduced the odds (risk).

People believe themselves lucky when the odds (probability) are unfavorable, yet the event still occurs. The odds are poor for drawing a straight flush in poker, but if it happens to you, you think you are lucky. Or you are unlucky if the odds are favorable, but the unwanted event still occurs.

Belief is at the core of luck. We might believe that we can influence the chance of an event occurring or not occurring. Han Solo believes if he does not know the odds, he can fly the Millennium Falcon through the asteroid field in *The Empire Strikes Back*. In other words, he thinks he is lucky.

The belief in luck also implies that you can sway chance without actually doing anything. Think of Tinkerbell in *Peter Pan*. If you wish really hard and clap your hands, the færie will hear you. In cybersecurity, if you wish really hard and clap your hands. . . , you might still be the victim of a cyber attack. Plus, people around you think you are applauding it! We will coin a term for this as the "Tinkerbell effect."

There is an ever-changing chance you have not been a victim yet (assuming you have not). It is not luck. You can influence the likelihood of an event occurring by having good defenses, but still, there is a chance it will happen. You are not unlucky if it does happen, though it might feel that way.

4. Of course, screenwriters play a role in this, unlike in real life.

The Numbers Speak for Themselves

In cybersecurity reports, dashboards, and decisions, raw numbers are often used to convey impact. There were 5,369 global data breaches or 80,000 cyber attacks per day. What do those numbers tell us? Do they truly speak for themselves?

The pitfall is not thinking about problems in the correct units. For instance, when considering cancer mortality risk, it is more important to consider percentages, not the raw number of people who died. The same applies to cybersecurity risk when considering the number of vulnerable machines or phishing incidents. If GoodLife Bank has two accounts compromised this year, that number needs context about the total number of accounts. The bank managers cannot only look at the numerator. Two out of two is a much bigger deal than two out of 10,000.

Similarly, proportional thinking should be applied to growth. That percentage increase is huge if there were two compromises last year and six this year. We have to be careful because the raw number seems small. Going from two to six *feels* less significant than going from 100 to 150, even though the first is a 200% increase and the second is a 50% increase.

In other cases, the raw value is where we should focus. Saving $500 feels more valuable when buying a laptop than a house because the percentage of savings is higher, but $500 holds the same value either way. In behavioral economics, these are known as *framing effects*. Mental accounting also impacts gains and losses. Would you rather spend $10,000 on cybersecurity one time or $6,000 now and $4,000 later? It is the same total amount, but to most people paying twice feels worse.[5]

Because we are human, the numbers do not speak for themselves. They take on meaning—and sometimes misperception—based on how they are presented and how we think about them. Proportional thinking can help frame the relationships between variables and is essential in applying mathematics to the everyday practice of cybersecurity. Numbers (and data) do not speak for themselves. They do not stand at the podium and explain what they mean.[6] When someone says, "The data speaks for itself!" they mean, "You would have missed this completely if I had not stood up and told you about it."

Probability Is Certainty

Before we get into statistics, let's start with probability. The field of statistics is built on the field of probability. It is the underpinnings of statistical analysis, so to understand what's going on (right or wrong) with statistics, we should have a grasp of basic concepts in probability.

5. The converse is true of gains. Two minor winning lottery tickets sometimes make people feel better than one big one, even if the total amount of money is the same.

6. If your data does, please contact a medical professional.

In school, probability is often taught with red and white balls kept in bags or jars. What is the probability of picking a red ball, given that three red balls and four white balls are in the bag? What is the likelihood of choosing a white ball after the red one?

It seems like a game because these are toy problems designed to introduce us to the field. How can picking balls out of bags be useful? It illustrates with a simple example how probability is calculated using actual objects. The likelihood of a red ball is the number of red balls divided by the total number of all balls—red and white.

Probability was a philosophical question before a group of mathematicians known as frequentists took over.[7] They defined the probability of an event as "how likely it is that this event will occur." Someone cannot measure how likely something is to occur without context—it must be compared to other events. For example, if someone is flipping a coin, the question of the probability of a head in a flip also includes the fact that it can result in a not-a-head, or tails.[8]

Probability is based on a group of related events, known as a *sample space*. These are all the possible results that could reasonably occur.

We compute the probability of a card being drawn by looking at all the cards that could be taken, not by considering a possible result of tails. Tails result from a coin flip, not the drawing of a card.

For example, a sample space could be constructed of weather events. It could include rain, snow, sleet, hail, sunshine, and fog. It would not contain an occurrence of raining cats and dogs because while that is a common phrase, we do not see cats and dogs fall from the sky.[9]

A sample space for vulnerabilities could be the CWEs assigned to each vulnerability. What is the probability that any given vulnerability is a SQL injection?[10] Ransomware is not a type of vulnerability, so ransomware would not be part of this sample space. It uses vulnerabilities (at times), but it is not necessarily one.

Basic probability, at the core, is counting. It is counting the number of times something occurred and dividing that by the number of times it could have happened in a representative sample. The probability of a user clicking on a link in a phishing email is the number of users who clicked on it divided by the number who could, if we take a large enough sample (number) of trials; probability measures are over a large population.

---

7. Solomon, Frederick, *Probability and Stochastic Processes*, Prentice Hall, 1987.
8. And for the pedantic, whether the coin lands on its edge.
9. If you do, summon a veterinarian.
10. CWE-89 is "Improper Neutralization of Special Elements Used in an SQL Command."

We cannot compute the probability if we cannot count either number. That means it is impossible to calculate the probability of a "Black Swan event."[11] One has never occurred, so there is no top number.[12] A "Black Swan" is something we have not experienced, so we do not expect it to happen. . . until it does.

In cybersecurity, the DNS domain names in our audit logs are often indicators of malicious sites. Therefore, it is tempting to think that the probability of any given domain being malicious is high because that is all we see.[13]

The truth is, the probability is low that any random DNS domain is malicious. Even if there are a million malicious domains out there, there are well over 300,000,000 domains registered in the .com domain alone. For simply .com, that is a probability of perhaps 0.0033 ($\frac{1}{3}$%) that any random domain is malicious (we suspect it is almost certainly lower). With that probability, we are more likely to draw a flush in seven-card poker than to pick up a domain in .com at random and have it be malicious.[14] It seems as if this result should be more common, but those are the domains we talk about a lot. We discuss how this domain or that domain is bad, how they are associated with malware or spam, and how we should avoid them. That does not mean all domains are bad, but if we spend all our time highlighting certain domains, we will miss the fact that that this sample is a small fraction of what we see in the real world.

The same is true of IP addresses. There are 2^{32} possible IPv4 addresses and 2^{128} possible IPv6 addresses (and yes, we are ignoring that a few are reserved). That second number is enormous. Unimaginably huge. Way bigger than the number of stars in the universe plus all their planets.[15] It is difficult to conceive of how big it is. If we shine a light 2^{128} *millimeters* away, we would need to wait, oh, 35,967,874,563,930,217,620 years (plus or minus some months) for the light to travel that whole distance.[16] In summary, it is big.

We do not use all those addresses yet, but we still use a substantial amount. Probability is "how many things happened" divided by "how many things could happen in total." Anytime you divide by the number of IP addresses, either IPv4 or IPv6, you will get a small number. Small numbers divided by big numbers yield small numbers much closer to zero than to one.

People are terrible at estimating probabilities because they often bring what they think should be happening to the result. We think there are a lot of malicious domains. We think there is a lot of malware. These feelings do not belong in probability computation.

Remember, probabilities should be based on the entirety of what might happen, not what we think should happen. As statistics is built on probability, the chances must be correct. Using probabilities

11. We explained this in the section "Ignorance and Black Swans" in Chapter 4, "Fallacies and Misunderstandings."
12. Numerator, for the mathematically inclined.
13. Reread the "Availability Bias" section in Chapter 5, "Cognitive Biases."
14. The probability of a flush is 0.0303.
15. https://theconversation.com/how-many-stars-are-there-in-space-165370
16. As scientists, we use the metric system. If you want to convert to furlongs and fortnights, have at it.

based on feelings in statistical analysis might make the results worse than useless. They will be incredibly misleading.

Either It Will Happen, or. . .

There is a commonly held idea that everything will happen or it will not. That is a true statement. Either it will rain, or it will not. Either a UFO will land in New York City, or it will not. Either snow will fall in Miami, or it will not.

People take that to mean that the probability of anything happening is 0.5. It is a common misperception of how probability works.

Yes, it could rain, or it might not rain, but that does not mean that the probability of rain is 0.5. Aliens from another planet could land, or they will not land. The probability of either happening is unlikely to be precisely 0.5.[a]

Probability is a value between 0 and 1, but it has a meaning in the real world and is based on events in the real world, not feelings. When you say something has a probability of 0.5, you are saying that 50% of the time, the event will happen. That means if you say it is either going to rain or it is not, so the probability is 0.5, then 50% of the time when you leave the house, it will be raining.

That might be true where you live, but it is not true everywhere. If you live in Jeddah, Saudi Arabia, it rains on average six days a year; while in Mumbai, India, it rains 79 days a year; and in Quibdó, Colombia, it rains 304 days a year, on average. Probability is based on counting, not the feeling that it might or might not happen. Otherwise, every other day it would be snowing in Miami.

[a] It will be a Black Swan event when it does occur, if it does, and we cannot compute the probability of it. Alternatively, it might have already happened. In that case, the likelihood is 1, and *Men in Black* was a documentary, but with neuralyzers in use, we cannot be sure.

Statistics Are Laws

To quote a statistician, "Statistics is not math."

That sounds a bit counterintuitive, right? Both use numbers and have formulas, and in both, we start with a problem and present a solution. Therefore, logically, they are the same.

That is like saying we need to shave whales. Mammals have hair. Whales are mammals. Therefore, we need to shave the whales. We do not shave whales; statistics is not math.[17]

Math and statistics both use numbers, and both have formulas, but they have different goals. Math is rather straightforward. Given a problem, we can find the solution. Let's take a short trip back to algebra and solve this equation:

$$2x - 10 = 4$$

17. If you do shave whales, please contact the authors: We have questions.

There is only one unique solution to this problem: 7. That is math. It is a statement that, given an assumption, the conclusion follows. It does not require additional interpretation. It does not matter what biases we bring to the equation, the only number that fits is 7. Nothing else will work. It does not matter how many times we solve the equation, the answer is 7. Not 6 or 8—only 7 is the correct value for x.

We Need Context

Statistics allows us to collect data, analyze it, and make conclusions. For example, we could count all the spam we see daily, all the whales we see in a day, or the number of bytes of traffic an organization sees every hour. Suppose we see only blue whales one day. Based on this data, we might conclude that the only whales in the ocean are blue.

Of course, if we tell someone else that, they might ask us things such as, "But you were only looking in a place called Blue Whale Heaven. What about over there in that other part of the ocean?" or "What about that orca over there? And the narwhal? And that pilot whale that decided to swim through Blue Whale Heaven!" Your evidence might support your conclusions, but others can come along and say, "But what about. . . " and draw their conclusions based on their evidence. Your findings are based on your interpretations of what all whales are, where they are, and how you counted them. Other people's conclusions are based on their interpretation of these events.

In other words,[18] in statistics, once the evidence is gathered, we talk about the original conditions that created that evidence or forecast what the future will be based on our evidence. That is different from math. Math starts with initial conditions (such as our equation) and gives results that directly follow. Statistics has other goals, and even though it and math rely on formulas, they are not in the same field.

That is to say, statistics are not facts, and they are not math. They rely on interpretation.

What about this statement made by Terry at GoodLife Bank: 50% of all domains send spam emails to me.

That is not a fact. It is an opinion based on some email and someone's interpretation of what all domains are. The statement lacks context. Are these all the domains Terry has ever seen? Is Terry talking about all domains in general? Maybe all domains on a list he had or found in a box? There is information missing that would make this statement make more sense—namely, a statistic about email.

Statistics requires interpretation and context, which is susceptible to bias and wishful thinking. A vendor selling us an anti-spam appliance will want us to believe that 50% of all domains send spam. Without the preceding context, the vendor is taking a statistic and interpreting it to their benefit.

Another example is Terry saying he got 10 pieces of email today. That is a verifiable fact. We can go into his mailbox and count each piece of mail. Terry explaining that 50% of his email is spam is a statistic. Spam is subjective as well. Whether a number is even or odd is not subjective. The number

18. Leaving our friends the whales behind.

2 is even, and 3 is not. That is a rule and a fact. What's spam to one person is not spam to another, however, because what qualifies as spam is a subjective judgment.

Now that we better appreciate what a statistic is, let's consider the questions we should ask when presented with one. For instance, suppose we came across a statistic that said 33% of all software was malicious. That is a scary statistic, but there are many questions that we should ask rather than accept that statistic as fact.

First, what data was used to derive that statistic? If the dataset is a set of software declared malicious, then 100% of that should be malicious—it is suspicious if only 33% of the dataset is malicious. How was this data collected? Was it found on the Internet, from a fresh software install, or simply picked up on a random website?

How much software was in the dataset? If it was three pieces of software and one was malicious, then yes, 33% of that software is malicious. The statistic also does not say much about *all* software. If what is meant by "all" software is the software in the dataset, then that limitation should be stated. Remember, probability depends on counting, and statistics depends on probability.

Also, how was "malicious" defined? Twitter has been used maliciously—does that mean Twitter clients are malicious? Computer viruses were spread in macros in Microsoft Excel. Does "malicious" mean Excel is malicious? Does it mean "did something other than what was expected" or "sold my secrets to the highest bidder"? Malicious covers a broad spectrum of behaviors, and if someone says the software is malicious, they should be able to tell us exactly what they mean. One person's malicious software might be another person's tool.[19]

Determining that software is malware is often a complex process. There is no magic wand we can wave at a piece of software that will tell us it is malicious. It is a sometimes-arduous process with a usual result of "most likely malicious." If the explanation of how it was determined that the software was malicious is lacking, then it could be that a random number generator was used to assign a label of malicious versus not-malicious—we simply do not know.

Without answers to these questions, the statistic lacks context. It could have been pulled out of a hat, or it could be based on real data collections. We do not know. And that means the statistic is not likely to be useful.

Statistics are useful only if the context surrounding the numbers is given.

Forecasting an Inference with Statistics

Changing the conversation slightly, let's talk about forecasting. Statistics are often used for forecasting: "Tell me how much of something will happen in the future." This is helpful information for planning what to expect and can help with budgeting for time and people.

19. Consider spyware or adware. Or cryptocurrency. Or Microsoft Word.

For example, suppose we want to know how many emails, in general, we get. We could count it, as Terry did when he counted 10 pieces of email, but counting everyone's email is a long, involved process. When do we start counting? When do we stop? It also might not be possible to count everyone's email, for example, by asking people in various locations and working at different companies to tell us how many emails they have received.

Instead, statistics will give us a reasonable guess called *statistical inference.* We do not know everything about everyone's email, but we can take a collection of users, count their emails, and use that information to predict everyone's email. We are taking a subset of what is out there and using it to make our guess. It is a well-reasoned guess, directed by formulas and theories, but it is still, at its heart, a guess.

Statistics relies on data and methods to get results. Data is the basis for the analysis, such as "How much spam do we see on average?", "How likely is this software to be malware?", and "How well does this new method work?" We need definitions of spam, malware, and data from before and after using the definitions to answer those questions.

The amount of data is important. If we went only by the amount of email Terry got and used that to guess how much an entire organization would get, that might give us wildly inaccurate results. It is possible that Terry gets only a little or gets all the email, but to assume Terry is the same as everyone else is a bit of a wild guess. Wild guesses are not good for *valid* statistics.

Methods are where things can get interesting as well. Statisticians often use wildly divergent methods. Unfortunately, this can also cause wildly divergent results. People can get caught up in getting the right results or the results they have decreed are correct, and they can use incorrect methods to ensure they wind up at the desired endpoint. This is known as *data dredging*, which is thought to be one reason why results can diverge so wildly. One statistician can take a set of domains and declare that none is malicious, and another can take a group of domains and declare that 50% of them are malicious. It boils down to the method each statistician used and their assumptions. Each statistician can justify their results, except that they often make mistakes in their assumptions, such as applying the Base Rate Fallacy.[20]

Statistics cannot do anything about the Black Swan events discussed earlier. If suddenly a brand-new attack that defies the odds shows up, our guess about the following year's forecast will be wrong. Statistics relies on knowing the probability of something happening, and probability relies on knowing the event could happen. If we do not know the event could happen, the whole chain breaks.

Remember, statistics can help us make a good guess based on previous years. It cannot tell the future; it is not a crystal ball. It can be correct or incorrect, but treating statistics as facts is wrong and can lead to losing money and time.

20. Cf. the "Base Rate Fallacy" section in Chapter 4.

Correlation Implies Causation

Correlation is a statistical concept. Skipping the formula (because that is not what this chapter is about), a linear correlation is a measure between two sets of data. Generally, it is a statistical property demonstrating a mutual relationship between two or more things. This relationship is often nothing more than a coincidental, statistical artifact without intrinsic meaning. The numbers in this description have no meaning assigned to them, so once the computation is done, we can simply say, "There is maybe a relationship here." It doesn't necessarily mean more than that. The same is true when we notice other characteristics that seem to be similar in some manner.

If we find a correlation between the names of ransomware gangs and the names of computer science professors, that is a statistical artifact. It doesn't mean that the professors caused the ransomware, or vice versa. It is simply that the statistics can be interpreted so that there appears to be a relationship described by the artifact. If we don't give the numbers meaning, they have none. It's the applied meaning that's important here.

However, if we find a statistical relationship between the times that phishing email links are clicked and the working hours of a company, that could be appropriate. It could mean that the workers during a particular part of the day are more likely to click on phishing emails and need further education. The numbers still have only the meaning we give them, but the meaning of the two sets is related enough that we should investigate them in more depth.

Consider a non-cyber example. Assume we have three apples, four oranges, five kumquats, and 17 kiwi fruits. One cannot assume that we like kiwi fruit more than apples or that we purchased the fruits in an order because of the quantities. Someone might deduce that we like fruit, but even that is not certain– we might simply be stocking up for the colony of fruit bats we keep in our attic.

Correlation, at its core, attempts to answer the question, "When one set of data changes, does the other set change similarly?" For example, if the number of employees in an organization grows, then the number of computers the organization has will likely grow at close to the same rate. If the company adds one employee, it will usually add at least one computer. A positive linear correlation means that if one number grows, the other will as well. It also means that if one number declines, the other will, too. They follow the same pattern. A negative correlation means that if one number grows, the other will decline similarly. No correlation means they have no similar behavior at all.

Let's begin with something that is not correlated, as illustrated in Figure 14.1(a). The round dots meander along at the bottom while the squares climb more or less steadily. The round dots and the squares behave entirely differently, so they are not correlated.

Now let's look at Figure 14.1(b). The round dots and the squares rise at more or less the same rate. Those two are possibly correlated.

These are toy examples to show the patterns. No data was tortured to create them.

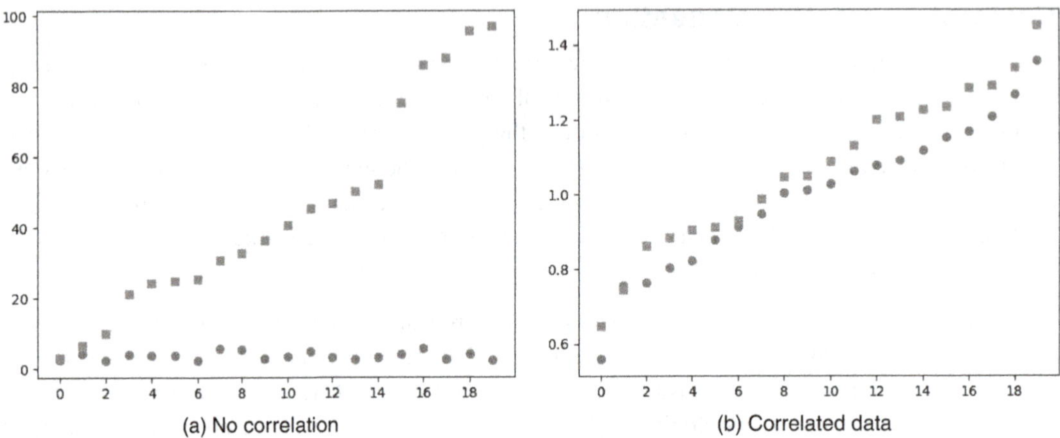

FIGURE 14.1 Correlation examples.

The number given by the correlation function[21] is useful. Otherwise, we are stuck trying visually to analyze pictures that look like Figure 14.2.

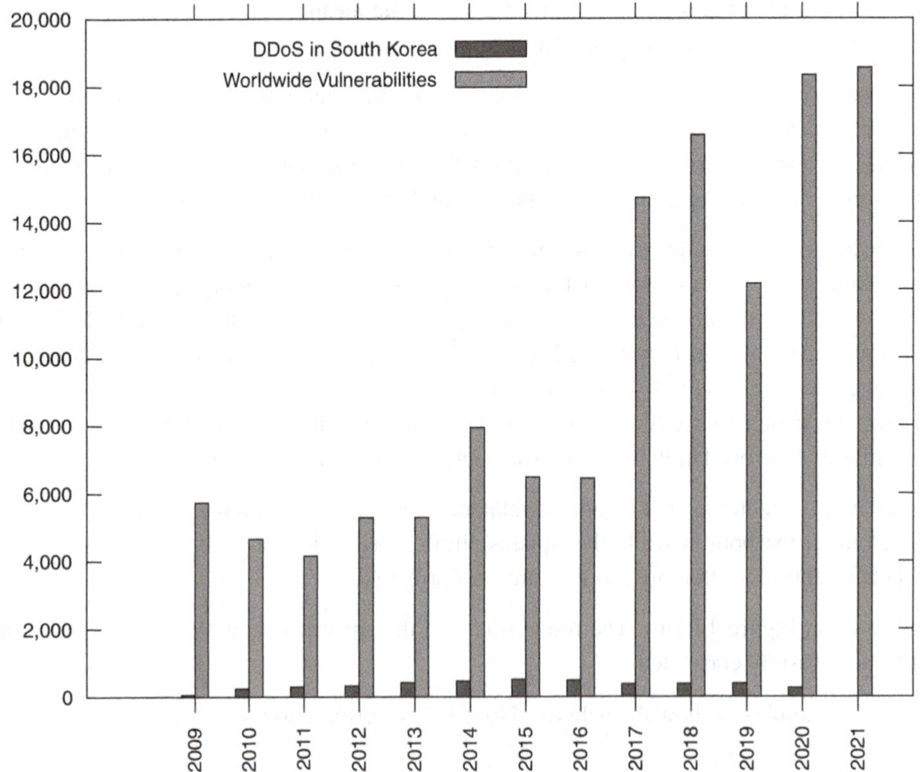

FIGURE 14.2 DDoS in South Korea compared to the number of vulnerabilities worldwide.

21. See your favorite statistics book for that.

You might be wondering, Why compare these two datasets? Well, it is an interesting question. Is the number of vulnerabilities in the world related to the amount of DDoS a country is subject to? The answer, by the way (to save your vision), is no—at least statistically.

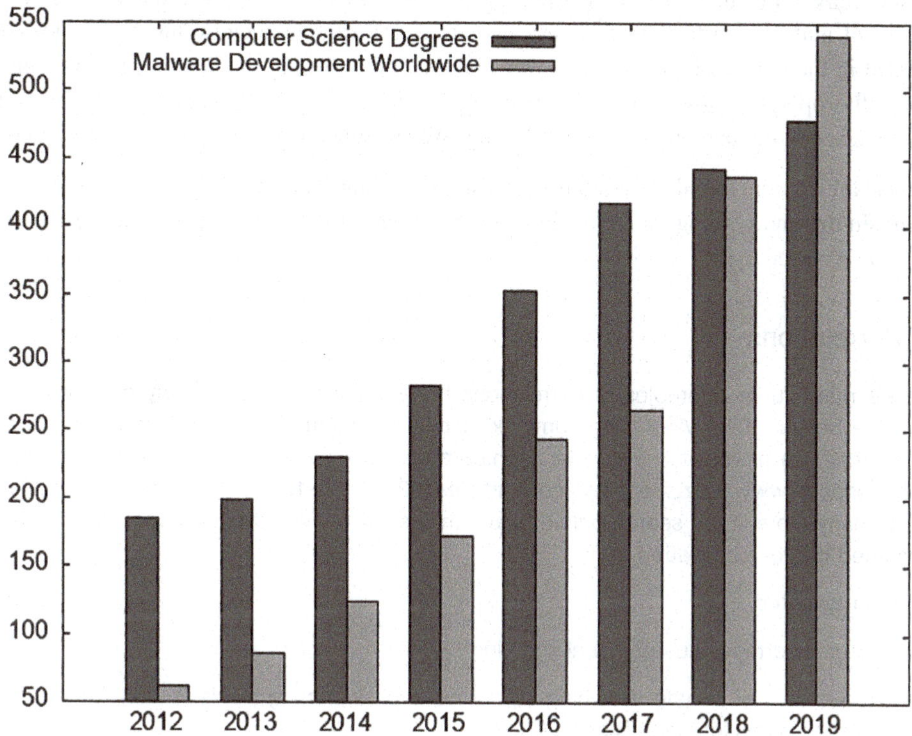

FIGURE 14.3 Malware developed worldwide and computer science degrees.

Remember, statistics relies on context. If we simply throw the number out there, it has no meaning until we interpret it. We might interpret it as showing little relationship between the people who exploit vulnerabilities and those who attack with a DDoS, but that adds extra opinion to the result. Numbers have no opinion.

It is tempting, though, to assign an opinion to the numbers. We want to believe that because statistics provide a number that seems to indicate there is a relationship—a cause behind the number. We assume that the correlation of the two datasets means that the process behind one dataset caused the other dataset to react that way. That is adding meaning that might or might not exist. To quote a statistician, correlation does not mean causation, but it does nudge you to say, "Look here."

Without that additional knowledge, we only have a number.

Let's pretend that there is meaning if there is an apparent correlation. There is a high correlation between the amount of malware developed worldwide[22] and the number of computer science degrees awarded.[23] Figure 14.3 illustrates the datasets.

As statistics only tell us there is a correlation, maybe the number of computer science degrees causes the amount of malware written. In that case, we are in big trouble because more and more degrees are awarded in the field each year. Perhaps we should stop awarding the degrees, and the amount of malware will drop! Alternatively, if malware being developed worldwide is causing people to pursue computer science more, that might be a good thing: We are educating more people on how to fight it.

We can read all we want into that correlation, but we are wrong. The correlation simply indicates these things are similar and nothing more. We have to investigate if there is a reason—not decide that the number is all we need.

Bad Correlations

There are many funny examples of correlations that clearly should not imply causation to any reasonable person. Tyler Vigen has compiled a book of them (*Spurious Correlations*) and has some of them on a website: www.tylervigen.com/spurious-correlations. There are also several amusing ones at www. buzzfeednews.com/article/kjh2110/the-10-most-bizarre-correlations. You can find many more if you search online: Many things will show correlation, but that should not be assumed to prove causation.

Among our favorites:

- A pirate shortage caused global warming
- The number of people drowning by falling into swimming pools is correlated with the number of films featuring Nicolas Cage
- The divorce rate in Maine is correlated with the consumption of margarine
- The per capita consumption of chicken is correlated with total U.S. crude oil imports
- Using Internet Explorer leads to murder

These are nonsense, although there might be some truth to the last one.

People who run across similar apparent correlations and do not understand the basics of statistics might create their own (spurious) explanations to explain them. See the section "Because It Is Online It Must Be True/Correct," in Chapter 3, "Faulty Assumptions and Magical Thinking," about how something must be valid if it is online.

22. https://www.statista.com/statistics/680953/global-malware-volume/
23. https://datausa.io/profile/cip/computer-science-110701

Errors in Classification Are Insignificant

Statistics are often used to classify things. We tend to classify things such as rocks, animals, plants, and, of course, anything in cybersecurity. Is that plant edible? Is that animal a plant eater, or will it be interested in eating me? Is that IP address that tried to connect to my host malicious?

We do not want to investigate every instance when there might be many items. We want something that will do that task for us and give us the results. Computers do counting and sorting well, so let's write a program! That classification program will save us time and money and look awesome (because it has a pretty interface).

If that program labels an IP address as malicious when it is not, it has given us a *false positive*. If it does not tell us that an IP address is malicious when it is, it is a *false negative*.[24] False positives mean additional work is required to ensure that the IP address is not malicious, and false negatives mean you miss that malicious IP address entirely. If your program is feeding a blocklist that is actively used by your organization, a false positive means you are blocking a site you should not, and a false negative means you are not blocking a site you should. Now imagine if your mail server's IP address is discovered by that program and declared malicious. In technical terms, that is called an "oopsie."

The goal is to have no false positives and no false negatives. Creating programs with no false positives is easy: Simply declare "Nothing is malicious." It is also easy to create a program that has no false negatives. Merely declare "Everything is malicious." Unfortunately, neither of those programs is particularly useful. Furthermore, it is impossible to create one that achieves both goals if we are using a statistical method. (Beware of vendors claiming their products do not produce either error!)

Back to our program. The proportion of the total number of malicious IP addresses it labels as false positives is the *false positive rate*. The *false negative rate* is the proportion of the total number of non-malicious IP addresses it labels as malicious that are false negatives.

If we have a false positive rate of 0.03, then 3 out of every 100 IP addresses detected by our program will not be malicious. A false negative rate of 0.05 means that 5 out of every 100 IP addresses it does not tag as malicious will be malicious.

Those might seem to be good rates, but remember, a busy organization might reference many websites and get emails from many people daily. Then add in the number of people who might be accessing your websites.

A confusion matrix, such as that shown in Figure 14.4, helps summarize a classification method's possible correct and incorrect labels. It is often used to examine the total results of the method by looking at how well it does in terms of the four possible outcomes. It's important to note that you can't use this matrix if you don't have all of the information, including true positives and negatives. It doesn't work if you fill in only some of the squares.

24. More formal terms that are used in some contexts are *Type I error* for false positive and *Type II error* for false negative.

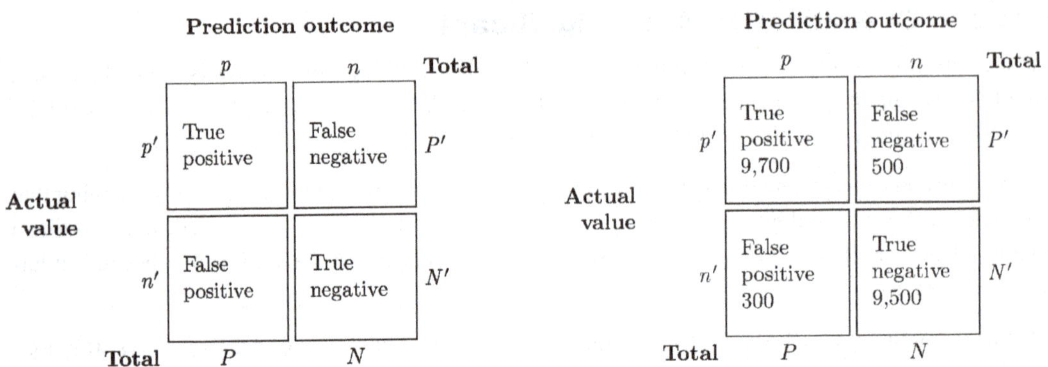

FIGURE 14.4 A confusion matrix.

FIGURE 14.5 A confusion matrix in use.

Suppose we have a set of 20,000 IP addresses, where 10,000 are malicious and 10,000 are not. The magicians in the basement[25] have created a new method to classify IP addresses, and they tell us it is wonderful. It has a false positive rate of 0.03 and a false negative rate of 0.05. That means it will declare 300 IP addresses to be malicious when they are not, and 500 IP addresses to be not malicious when they are. It also means that 9,700 IP addresses are labeled as malicious when they should be, and 9,500 addresses are correctly labeled as not malicious. Thus, the new method gets $9{,}700 + 9{,}500 = 19{,}200$ labeled correctly out of 20,000, or 0.96. This is the *accuracy* of the method.

Our confusion matrix for this method looks like Figure 14.5. How often the method gives us a correct malicious tag is then $\frac{9{,}700}{9{,}700+500} = 0.951$. That is because a false negative should have been labeled a true positive but was not.

This number is also known as the *recall*.

Meanwhile, the method labeled a total of 9,700 + 300 IP addresses as positive but got only $\frac{9{,}700}{10{,}000} = 0.97$ of that correct. This number is known as the *precision*.

It is a trade-off: You cannot increase both to get a high recall and high precision. That means you have a high rate of false positives or a high rate of false negatives, or a moderate number of each; you have to decide which is more important to you. Think of it as a see-saw with one end being false positives and the other end being false negatives.

For example, suppose a classifier is working with malware. A false positive with malware means you tagged something that was not malware as malware, whereas a false negative means you missed a piece of malware. It is often more important not to miss malware, so you might prefer a higher false positive rate.

25. Where do you keep yours?

False Positives Happen, Even to the Best of Us

Let's talk about an antivirus program that uses signatures. For each piece of malware it knows about, it creates a Secure Hash Algorithm (SHA)-256 hash of it and puts that hash in its dictionary of "Things it knows about." Every time it encounters a new file, it checks whether it knows about it. If it does, the file is labeled as malware. If it does not, it is not labeled malware. Anything it finds that is malware is definitely malware.[a]

Anything it finds that is not malware, well. . . not so much.

Malware authors are aware of this method. That is why they create malware variants to get around this kind of antivirus program. Thus, antivirus software vendors need new methods to detect new threats. These new methods are sometime not as precise as the signature-based antivirus methods, but they manage to find (we hope!) variants. The downside is that sometimes the new method claims that something is malware that is not. For example, Microsoft's Security Essentials program once decided that Google's Chrome browser was malware.[b] It is not only executables that get tagged, either—Microsoft Defender also tagged Word documents as malware that were not.[c] (Unless you are still viewing Word as malicious!)

Microsoft is a large company that works diligently to get these things right, yet it happened even to them.

---

[a] For the advanced reader: Collisions are so rare we assume they do not happen. If a collision does occur, that is a false positive, so at least malware does not get through.

[b] www.tomsguide.com/news/what-are-false-positives-and-how-to-avoid-them

[c] www.bleepingcomputer.com/news/microsoft/microsoft-defender-scares-admins-with-emotet-false-positives/

Data Is Not Important to Statistics

The previous sections discussed probability and statistics and mentioned data often. This section will discuss some myths and misconceptions related to data.

The data used in probability and statistics is almost as important as the methods. For example, data can have biases. That sounds a bit off because data does not change. It is something we collect and store, not something that has opinions!

The biases depend on how the data is collected. If we are interested in malware, and we collect data on only one family of malware, then our data is biased to that kind of malware. Applying statistics to that set will not tell us anything about malware in general; it will tell us only about that set. People are often tempted to generalize based on their data collection without considering that.

Data bias comes into play during and at the beginning of the data collection process. Deciding when and where to collect data can affect the data itself. If we are interested in global perceptions of phishing, but we only ask people in our office building, our results are biased. That is an extreme example, but similar things happen in cybersecurity constantly. For example, a study of data breaches in the United

Kingdom is often used to describe data breaches everywhere.[26] It might apply everywhere, or it might not; the data in the study is biased toward breaches in the U.K. Collecting the correct data from the beginning can help a project succeed, whereas collecting the wrong data is a sure way to failure.

Data bias is also a feature of cybersecurity in general. We generally can collect only data we happen to find. That can lead to biases in the data, so we must acknowledge that possibility and be careful. When people claim "All malware does. . . ", unless that statement is paired with a specific definition of malware, there is no way to say whether that statement is true. We do not know about *all* malware, either; we know only about what we happened to find. Any probability based on "all malware" is, at best, a guess and, at worst, wishful thinking.

The same is true for attacks, vulnerability, phishing, etc. It is true for every facet of cybersecurity: We only collect data for what we find. That means probabilities and statistics based on this data are relevant only to the collected data, not for an entire field. It is common for people to claim a dataset is valid for everything. It is easier, for one thing. Rather than explaining the dataset they have used, they want to claim it is suitable for everything. It is not, and it is wrong to claim it is, but people still do that.

The data is affected by people, as people are the ones who are collecting it. It is wrong to assume that the information magically appears without human intervention. A computer does not know by default what malware is: A human has to teach it to the computer. Same with malicious emails. A computer does not know what these are, so it cannot collect them until a human writes the code that gives parameters for "This is bad" and "This is not bad." If a human's code says that all "not bad" emails are in English, the computer might learn "If it is not in English, it is bad." That is not the computer's fault—the system can learn only based on the given parameters.

This also has implications for AI and ML (see the next section).

Another tactic often used in data collection is anonymization. This practice is common when dealing with sensitive data whose unwanted release is not a good thing. Anonymization can include encrypting parts of the data or modifying identifiers to hide the origin.

The problem with naive anonymization is that it can often be reversed. For example, in 2008, Netflix released "anonymized" data as part of a contest to improve its rating system. Researchers at the University of Texas in Austin[27] announced that they could reverse that anonymization. How to de-anonymize the anonymized is a field of study for researchers.

Another problem with anonymization is that sometimes people go overboard with it. It is possible to anonymize data so completely that it no longer looks or acts the same as the original data. For example, suppose someone is anonymizing network traffic. Network ports are a common feature of this traffic and have meaning; however, some people take anonymization so far that the network ports no longer have meaning. It is a delicate act, finding the spot where anonymization is valid and cannot be reversed easily while also leaving enough structure to the data that the results are useful.[28]

---

26. www.verdict.co.uk/uk-data-breaches-human-error/
27. https://consumerist.com/2008/01/researches-claim-to-reverse-netflixs-anonymization.html
28. We have seen anonymization taken to the level that the results read similar to Doug Zongker's chicken paper: https://isotropic.org/papers/chicken.pdf.

The quest for more data can feel like a crusade to confirm our suspicions. One lead or initial finding can prompt us to spend too many resources hunting for evidence or gathering more data. Instead of letting the data reveal what it can show, our confirmation bias causes us to ignore those findings in pursuit of what we want or believe to be true.

It is also tempting to believe that if we have more data, then we will find the answer we are looking for in the data. That depends on the collection of the data. For an analogy, imagine going to the grocery store, picking random items off the shelf, and buying them (Figure 14.6). We are not using a list, we are not considering what recipes we will make. We randomly pick items because they are close to us or have a brightly colored package. We buy numerous things, though, so we are pretty sure we have everything covered.

FIGURE 14.6 Gathering random groceries.

There is a lot of math to explain this, but to simplify it, the probability of grabbing the correct ingredients for a particular recipe is quite small. It is similar for data. This means we should consider what data is needed and why, rather than collecting everything. A giant pile of data might seem great, but it can cloud the issue if it is not applicable.

Artificial Intelligence and Machine Learning Can Solve All Cybersecurity Problems

Artificial intelligence brings to mind the movies and television shows where the computer is a part of the cast. This conceit is based on the anthropomorphism of the inanimate computer: It now has a human personality but all the abilities of a supercomputer. It can solve riddles, find anomalies, and generally is the solution to all the characters' problems, except when it goes awry and tries to take over the world, similar to Skynet or Colossus.[29]

Artificial intelligence merely means that the computer uses reasoning that might be similar to human logic, at least in its output. It learns, it reasons, and when it makes mistakes, it corrects itself. It is intended to emulate human abilities with the speed and capacity of a computer. As we understand it, it is not actual intelligence and certainly not consciousness.

Artificial intelligence and machine learning tools are built on data. They are trained to learn what to find by using training sets of data before they are set loose to examine real data. Data that is biased will inevitably affect these tools. For a non-cybersecurity example, consider self-driving cars. It is a known problem that some of them cannot recognize people with darker skin.[30] The training set used to teach these cars the appearance of a person was not thorough enough to prevent this bias. The same can happen in cybersecurity tools: If a training set contains only one kind of malware, perhaps ransomware, then it will not necessarily recognize a file dropper. Remember, artificial intelligence is not intelligent.[31]

This is a vast field of study, and many books (not solely science fiction) have been written on creating AI. This book is not about AI, so we will focus on machine learning. This is not an in-depth look at machine learning—there are many books on that subject. Instead, this is a cybersecurity introduction to machine learning.

Machine learning is a subfield of artificial intelligence. It is an attempt to create a learning program that uses statistics. At its core, it is a set of statistical tools that analyze data to infer patterns. The goal is to learn from these patterns and adapt as things change. That is, the ML system is expected to act similarly to a human. We learn from patterns and are adaptable as situations change, so it would be great (in some circumstances) if our computer programs did the same thing.

It is tempting to think of ML as a magic black box that takes data in and produces a valuable result (Figure 14.7). But how that black box works is significant.

---

29. We will ignore that plot line as it deserves its own book, in addition to all the science fiction already written on the topic. Of course, there are worse possibilities than simply taking over the world.
30. https://interestingengineering.com/autonomous-cars-cant-recognise-pedestrians-with-darker-skin-tones
31. We refer you again to footnote 1 in Chapter 4, "Fallacies and Misunderstandings."

FIGURE 14.7 Magic black box.

Machine learning is not magic. It will not take all of our problems and supply a solution. In reality, it cannot solve every problem. We need the appropriate issue to feed to the ML box.

The ML box also needs the correct data. We cannot simply feed it a pile of data we happen to find and expect it to tell us how to manage, for example, vulnerabilities. If we provide it with malware data and expect the results to be relevant to handling vulnerabilities, then that will not work well. ML works on the garbage-in, garbage-out principle. In addition, the box requires accurate statistics. We can put the correct data in the box, but if the formulas are not there, we will not get back anything useful. The formulas are the machinery that makes ML work. If our machinery is designed to make concrete but we ask for cookies, we will be sorely disappointed. The same holds in the ML box.

Back to the data. The box requires training before it will work, as a human does. We do not expect a human to walk into a house and magically know everything about the plumbing, so we should not expect the ML box to magically know everything about analyzing malware. It has to be trained, and that training requires even more data.

For example, we do not train a ML box to find malware using network data. It has to model what we are looking for. If we want it to find malware, it needs a good definition of malware; otherwise, how will the system know when it finds malware? We could define malware as "everything not on my approved list." That is a simple definition of malware, and it does not take much training, but it still is a definition the ML box can use.

We have data and a definition, so now let's examine the method that drives this. It is built on statistics. It is not teaching the computer how to learn. It uses statistics to modify its behavior as time goes on. And that data can alter behavior. An entire field is focused on feeding machine learning boxes the wrong data to skew how it works, called Adversarial Machine Learning (AML).

Not So Smart AI

It would be nice if we could get ahead of the game and detect the malicious files before researchers found them. It is a great goal to find the bad guys before we know they are bad guys. The movie *Minority Report* told a story of trying this for people and showed that it did not work well.

Unfortunately, the same approach does not work well for computers, either (for different reasons). The company Cylance created an AI-powered system called PROTECT that it claimed would detect new maliciousness. That's a good thing. Researchers in Australia[a] found a way to subvert that system. They could take a malicious file and append strings to it from a known non-malicious file. Then, *voilà*, the PROTECT system would declare it non-malicious.[b] Malware authors often create variants by altering the code slightly or modifying the binary in some way so that it will escape signature detection. The researchers did something similar and found that AI was not so intelligent anymore.[c]

This is an example of AML, often thought to be the first time researchers managed to do this. We do not know how often malware authors have done something similar because they do not publish their results. We only know it could happen.

[a] The country of "Hold my beer."

[b] www.vice.com/en/article/9kxp83/researchers-easily-trick-cylances-ai-based-antivirus-into-thinking-malware-is-goodware

[c] Cylance engineers have addressed this in their product.

Suppose you have a system, and that it works by ingesting web traffic to look for malicious traffic. An attacker could figure out how to skew those results to tell you the good domains are bad and bad domains are good. It is akin to teaching a toddler the wrong terms for things.

Another factor to consider is that there are almost as many varieties of statistics to achieve machine learning as there are researchers. The problem is, when one works, they usually cannot tell you why it works. Often, a researcher will try various methods until one "works best." That usually means, "For my training data and my example data, it gave me the results I was looking for." If you ask them, "Tell me why?" and you are lucky, you will get blank looks. That does not mean the method will work when given real data. Methods can be fragile and work only on perfectly chosen example data.

Back to the topic. There is an effort to resolve these issues, but they are ongoing and the problems are challenging to solve. Meanwhile, the number of new systems seems to be growing faster than solutions are being found.

Finally, every ML box should have two readouts: the false positive rate and the false negative rate. See the section "Errors in Classification Are Insignificant" earlier in this chapter for more information on these results. It is a big problem because the amount of data available on the Internet is humongous. The unfortunate thing is, people often do not report false negatives and false positives. An ML box that does not tell you these two values is not useful and can be misleading.

In summary, while machine learning has great promise for cybersecurity, there are always things to consider before using any particular tool.

Unintended Lessons

Many years ago, a pricey child's toy came on the market. It was a little furry creature with a speech recognition system and a playback. You could train it to recognize phrases such as "Would you like a cookie?" and "What is your name?" You would then record what you wanted it to respond. The idea was that parents could program it for their children so that "What do you want to do?" might respond with "Let's clean your room!"

One of us had a rather amusing experience visiting a site where the engineers had several of these toys. They had programmed some toys to recognize responses from other toys as questions to answer. Then, they would have the toys have conversations with each other. . . and the conversations were unlikely to be ones you would want your child to have, with a toy or otherwise. We later heard one was used (apparently, quite successfully) to proposition people at bars late at night.

As a takeaway, remember that what a designer intends for an AI or ML appliance might not be how it is used. That might or might not be a problem, but the designer should try to think outside the (toy) box during design.

Further Reading

Jacobs, Jay, and Rudis, Bob. *Data-Driven Security: Analysis, Visualization and Dashboards*. John Wiley & Sons, 2014.

Larson, Erik J. T*he Myth of Artificial Intelligence: Why Computers Can't Think the Way We Do*. Belknap Press, 2021.

Machine Learning in Cybersecurity: A Guide. https://resources.sei.cmu.edu/library/asset-view.cfm?assetid=633583.

Taleb, Nassim Nicholas. *The Black Swan: The Impact of the Highly Improbable*. 2nd ed. Random House Publishing Group, 2010.

Vigen, Tyler. *Spurious Correlations*. Hachette Books, 2015.

Wheelan, Charles J. *Naked Statistics: Stripping the Dread from the Data*. W.W. Norton & Company, 2014.

Chapter 15

Illustrations, Visualizations, and Delusions

The purpose of visualization is insight, not pictures.

Ben Shneiderman

People like pictures. We can process visual data faster and better than any other type.[1] It is no wonder that babies are more captivated by picture books than by text. So, what's the problem with cybersecurity visualizations?

Television and movies have conditioned us to believe that every security tool must have a spiffy screen with fast-moving graphics. The analysts will watch their screens to find the latest incidents and react to them with lightning speed. As we discussed in Chapter 13, "Digital Forensics and Incident Response," entertainment can skew people's expectations of reality.

For many reasons, illustrations and visualizations are notably prominent in tools, presentations, and reports. Illustrations are so common that people often do not stop to consider if the visualization is truly useful.[2] Is it illuminating the problem at hand, or is it simply pretty? We are not against pretty, but *pretty* is seldom a good substitute for an *informed choice* when selecting cybersecurity tools (or in dating, for that matter). After reading this chapter, we hope you start paying closer attention to how illustrations are used and misused.

As this chapter's opening quote suggests, visualizations are abused when they fail to provide meaningful insights to the viewer. A visualization should help the viewer, not hinder them. Far too few designers and developers of cybersecurity tools evaluate their visualizations with humans. Do real users understand the visuals, and are they more effective with the visuals than without them? These assumptions are too often taken for granted.

1. Thorpe, Simon, Fize, Denis, and Marlot, Catherine, "Speed of Processing in the Human Visual System," *Nature*, Vol. 381, No. 6582 (1996): 520–522.
2. Reference the majority of PowerPoint presentations we have had to sit through.

The words *illustration* and *visualization* are often used interchangeably in casual conversation. They are both graphical representations used to help communicate information. Generally, visualizations represent data, and illustrations represent ideas, concepts, and processes. A bar chart is a visualization. A cartoon showing how DNS resolution works is an illustration.

This chapter covers some common misconceptions and myths regarding cybersecurity illustrations and visualizations. At worst, a poor illustration can mislead an analyst or divert focus to the wrong part of a problem, wasting valuable time and attention. A good illustration can illuminate the problem and focus work (and money) on the correct issue.

Visualizations and Dashboards Are Inherently and Universally Helpful

Big cybersecurity conferences draw big vendor expos. The annual RSA Conference had more than 650 exhibitors in 2020 advertising and demonstrating their products and services. Nearly every other booth seemed to display a data visualization or a software dashboard.

A visualization is a model and shortcut for our eyes. It enables us to take in a summary of data and see patterns or anomalies. People have spent a lot of money creating AI and ML programs to duplicate recognition of issues that people can see in a simple visualization. Done well, data visualization can allow complex information to be interpreted, even by those who are not data savvy. It can level the playing field. A person can look at a graph of domains and say, "There, that one is weird," whereas making a computer program that consistently mimics that human's ability takes a lot of time, effort, and money.

Visualizations can also confuse the issue if they are poorly done. The goal of a visualization is to communicate and help a viewer understand the information or answer a specific question. Some provide situational awareness, and others show compliance, inventory, threats, events, and risk.

Let's begin with pie charts. A pie chart is not about the number of items found in the data; instead, it presents items as a percentage of the whole. It is missing the context of how much data we are looking at, and instead, it depicts each piece as a percentage of the total.

Figure 15.1(a) illustrates five malware families. It almost looks as if each slice is equal, but without a protractor to measure 72 degrees to verify that equality, that is simply a guess. There is also no way of determining how many pieces of each type of malware were available before the pie chart was constructed. It could have been a lot of malware or a little malware—we do not know based on the slices unless the pie chart is labeled with this information.

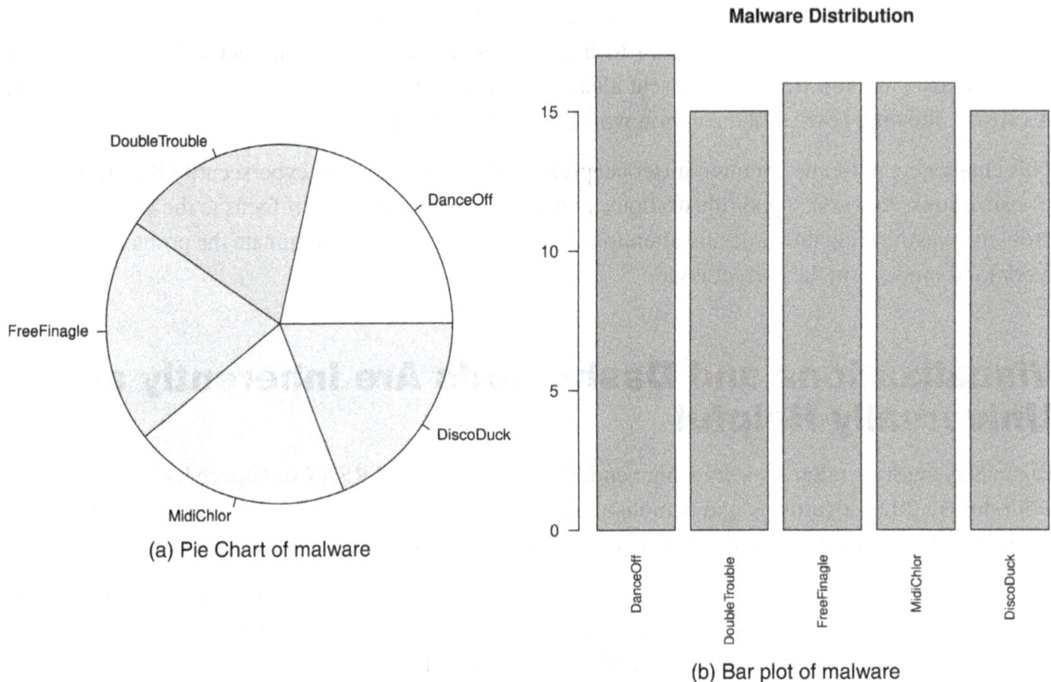

(a) Pie Chart of malware

(b) Bar plot of malware

FIGURE 15.1 Same malware data visualized as a pie chart and bar plot.

Figure 15.1(b) takes the same data that made the pie chart and displays it as a bar plot. Now we do not need a protractor to tell that the five families are different sizes, and we can also see how many samples of each malware family we have. We can also see we have the most samples of the DanceOff malware.

Pie charts are usually only helpful if they show how much pie was eaten versus how much was not consumed, such as in Figure 15.2. Otherwise, they might obscure information. If the goal is to illustrate percentages and hide the actual data, then pie charts might be the way to go. (But they should always include pie.)

It is certainly possible to obscure information using a bar plot as well. Figure 15.3(a) is an example of this.

Figure 15.3(b) is even worse. There are no labels on the *y*-axis of this figure. We have no way of determining anything about the number of pieces of malware it is illustrating; it is almost as bad as the pie chart. It does not even illustrate how much pie was eaten! A reader is completely missing the context of the difference in size. It is hidden, and we are allowed to infer that there is a lot more of the DanceOff malware than the DoubleTrouble malware. It is a great way to scare people and is entirely misleading.

To finish this discussion of poor bar plots, an informative bar plot should look like Figure 15.4. In this figure, the viewer knows how many pieces of malware have been examined. The relative scale between the types of malware is evident, and it is clearly labeled. It is useful if we are looking at those five kinds of malware.

FIGURE 15.2 The right use for pie charts.

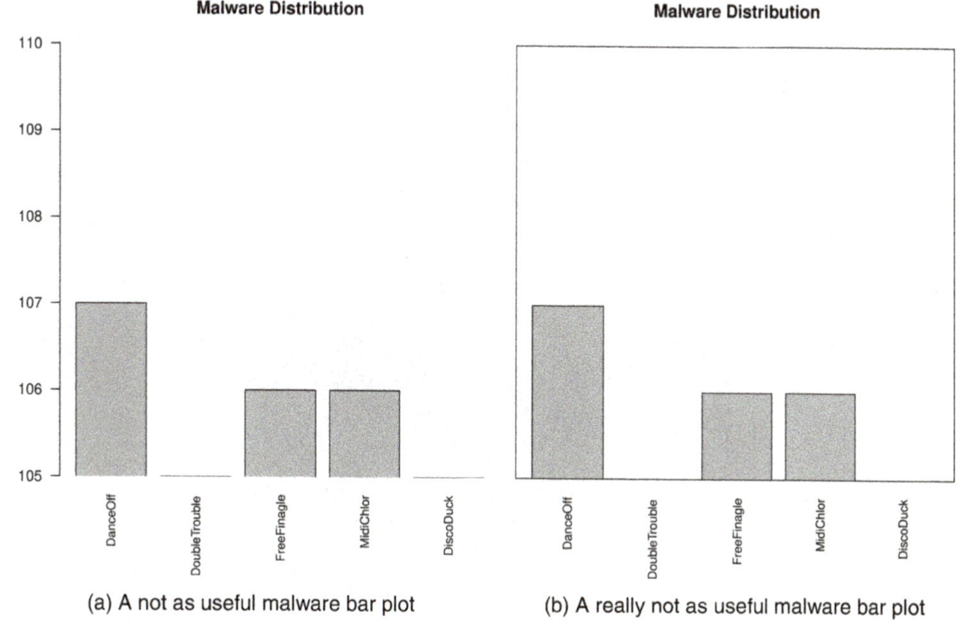

FIGURE 15.3 Two bad bar plots

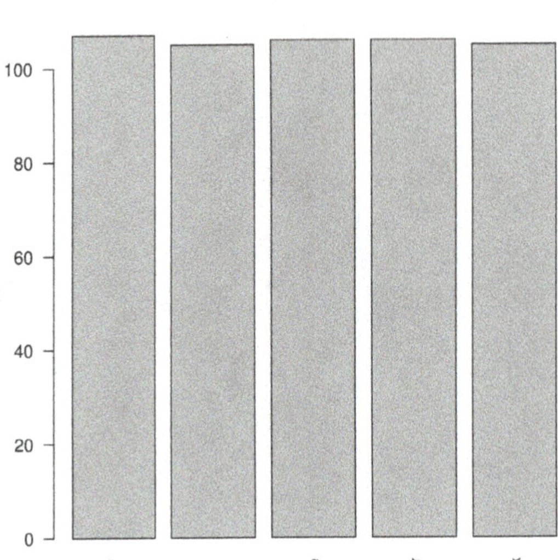

FIGURE 15.4 A well-designed bar plot.

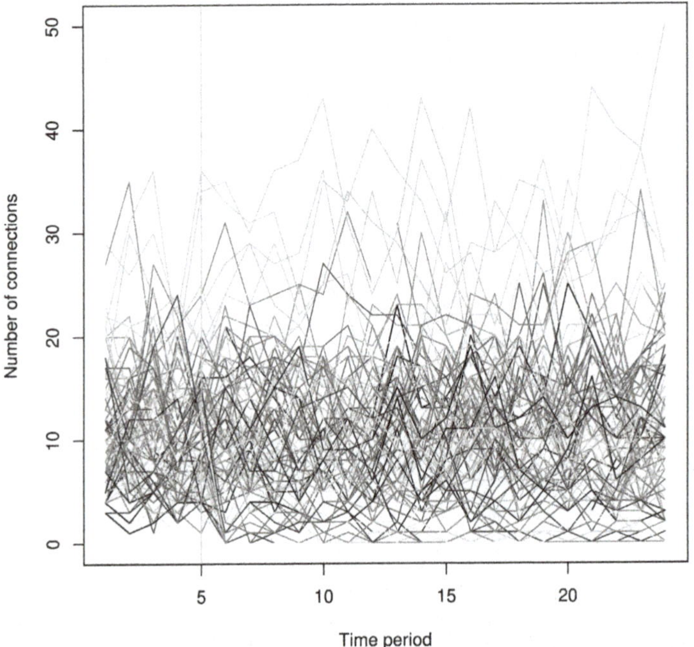

FIGURE 15.5 A figure that has lost the plot.

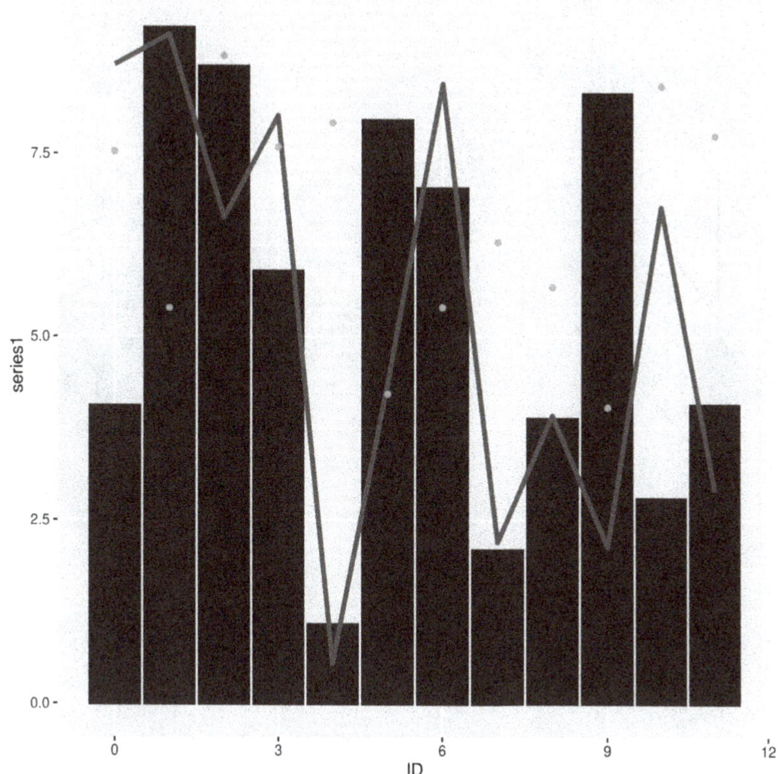

FIGURE 15.6 The plot thickens, and entirely too much.

Remember, a visualization tells a story about the data. Similar to a book written by good novelist, the story should be engaging and understandable. Sometimes a story has multiple plots, but a good novelist pulls the threads of the plots together to form a cohesive narrative. Unlike Figure 15.5. In this picture, the plot has been lost in the tangle of lines. No matter how much we stare at it, we will not see a useful pattern.

In a similar vein, Figure 15.6 is confusing. It is an unhelpful juxtaposition of a bar plot, a scatter plot, and a line. The figure conveys too much information simultaneously, similar to Figure 15.5. The author might have had a particular point in mind to make, but they created this monstrosity. Three separate graphs would likely have been much better, assuming all the data needed to be illustrated.

People sometimes convert a 2D bar plot to 3D, thinking it is fancier or more understandable. Unfortunately, this skew often distorts the perspective of the data. If we could holographically project them in the book, that would be great.[3] We could rotate them, examine the differences in the columns, and generally get a good idea of what's going on.

3. One of us built 3D cybersecurity visualizations in augmented reality using the Microsoft Hololens, but that is not how books are currently produced. Beitzel, Steve, Dykstra, Josiah, Toliver, Paul, and Youzwak, Jason, "Exploring 3D Cybersecurity Visualization With the Microsoft Hololens," *International Conference on Applied Human Factors and Ergonomics* (July 2017): 197–207.

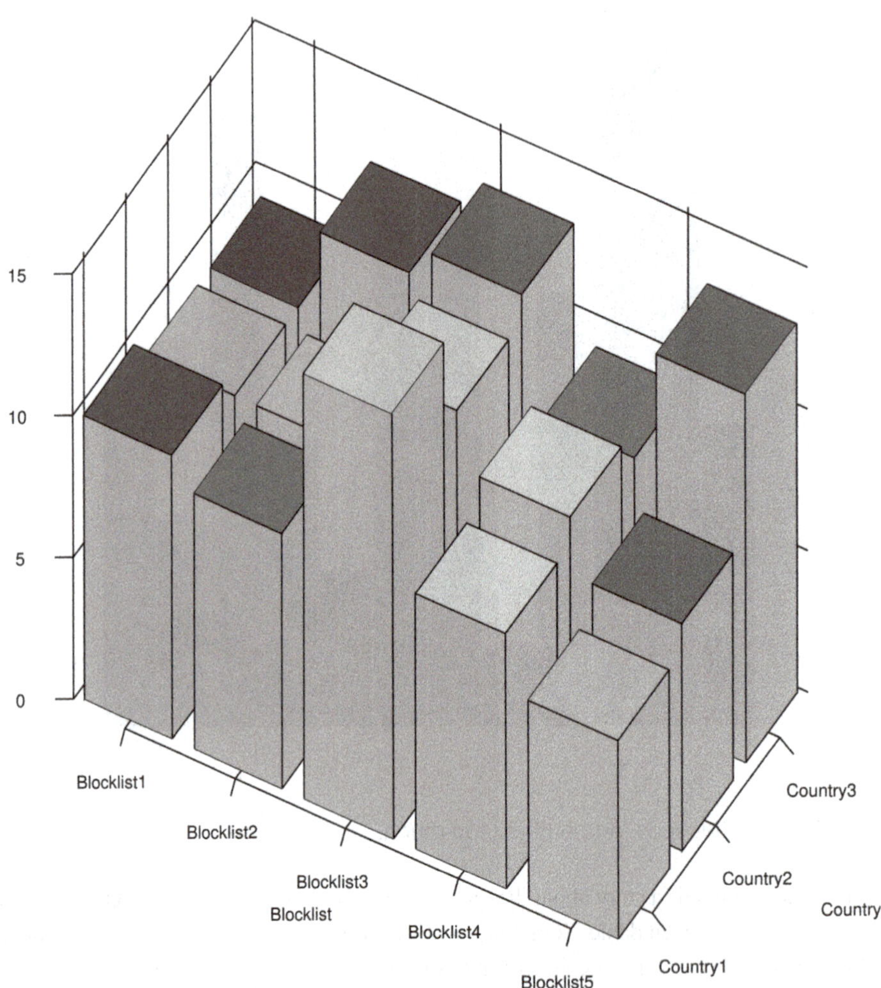

FIGURE 15.7 Three-dimensional bar plot.

Unfortunately(?), paper is two-dimensional. We are stuck with projecting the three dimensions onto two, and things can get confused or lost, as shown in Figure 15.7. That image attempts to show the relationships among countries, blocklists, and counts of the combinations. Without rotating it, or the ability to get close to the data, it is difficult to see patterns. Country2 and Blocklist3 appears short, but we cannot tell the relative size because other columns around it nearly obfuscate it. Pulling this apart into multiple graphs would have told the story better and let us see the actual differences.

Thankfully, some human factors experts can help with situations such as this. People think creating compelling visuals is easy and take a do-it-yourself approach, which is not always effective. And if it is not effective, then we fall into the trap that "training" will mitigate that lack of effectiveness. It is a vicious cycle.

While we cannot put 3D movies in books (yet), people also like to use them to illustrate patterns. It is difficult to see anything actionable when looking at a screen that turns red and green depending on events. Maybe something turns red briefly but turns back to green because it is a false positive. Perhaps something is flashing red periodically, and if someone looks at the wrong time, they miss it. Plus, if they are colorblind, the screen might appear static!

Movies created from cybersecurity data are sometimes fun to watch but not always helpful. And in that same vein, overly busy dashboards are also fun to watch. As things change, people can see blinky lights, but are they providing viewers with actionable information? The viewer should be able to say, "Aha, that's the thing!" when their eyes are fixed on the model. If the blinky lights are too distracting, nothing important will be seen, and the viewer will be lulled into a false sense of security.

Oh, and some people have versions of epilepsy that are triggered by repeated flashing lights. This is usually controlled with medication. The affected people might wish to keep their condition private so no one around them knows of it. Thus, on a terrible day, not only will we fail to adequately illustrate the point we are trying to make about our new security scheme, but we might trigger the CEO to have a seizure.[4]

Be careful of the overly busy plot, extremely busy animation, or unduly busy dashboard. Remember, these are supposed to be a model for the eyes. There is a narrative that the brain should be able to put together by staring at a model, other than "Fire good. Tree pretty."

Cybersecurity Data Is Easy to Visualize

Visualization is one way to explain complex concepts. At the same time, the mental model created by a visualization should let us make a decision or have a deeper understanding of the data used to create it. It should not obscure the data or hide important information. Visualizing numbers is relatively straightforward. Unfortunately, cybersecurity is filled with things that are more difficult to visualize. Malware is software. Vulnerabilities are problems with software programs. Privacy is a property of data in a system. We cannot visualize these directly, so we visualize their properties. For example, we cannot easily visualize CWE-20, which is improper input validation. For one vulnerability, such as CVE-2005-0050, also known as the "License Logging Service Vulnerability,"[5] we could list all the possible inputs that would trigger the vulnerability. That is not much of a visualization, as it tells us nothing about the vulnerability. It is also not an interesting visualization—simply a list of text that would trigger the vulnerability.

Alternatively, we could look at the number of vulnerabilities that have the weakness CWE-20 per year. Are they increasing? Staying the same? Perhaps a new technique to find these vulnerabilities has been discovered, and now everyone wants to find a vulnerability caused by invalid input. Visualizing that data can help.

4. This is not merely hypothetical. One of the authors was present in a briefing when something like this happened.

5. https://nvd.nist.gov/vuln/detail/CVE-2005-0050

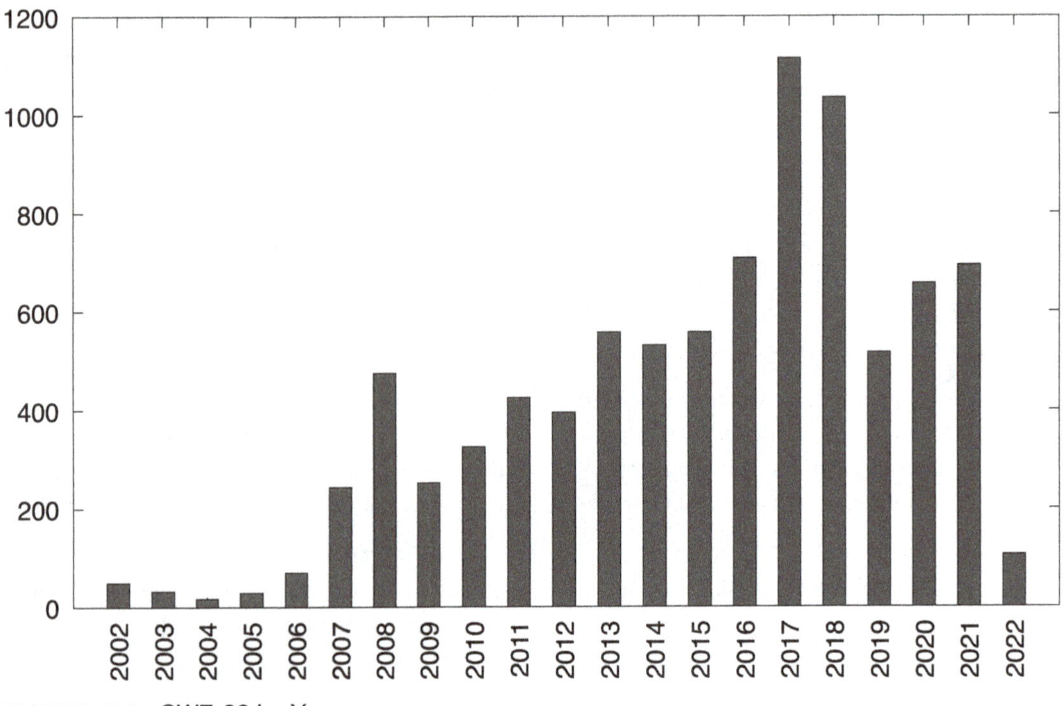

FIGURE 15.8 CWE-20 by Year.

Figure 15.8 illustrates the number of CVEs each year that have CWE-20. This number peaked in 2017 and has been decreasing slightly since then. Is there a reason for that? What kinds of vulnerabilities had CWE-20 in 2017? This visualization illustrates when the peak happened but does not explain why. Looking at the data from MITRE, there is no apparent reason, but it does suggest further study.

Visualizations are often painstakingly designed to convey a story. There is an entire field dedicated to visualization in cybersecurity.[6] The fact that there are seemingly intuitive visualizations used in business does not mean that they are easy to create in any given context. What's more is that *interactive* visualizations, which can be highly effective at helping someone explore and learn about a dataset, are much more difficult to design and deploy effectively. In cybersecurity, not all data can be easily and intuitively abstracted into a static visualization, let alone an interactive one.

Visualizing Internet Geolocation Is Useful

In Chapters 2 and 13, we explored the myth that an IP address identifies a unique machine. An extension of that myth is the misconception that every IP address has a single, static geographic location. This is known as Internet geolocation or GeoIP. Several free and commercial databases attempt to track the proper locations of IP addresses, sometimes only to the granularity of a country.

6. One place where this community gathers is the IEEE Symposium on Visualization for Cyber Security (VizSec), now in its 19th year. See https://vizsec.org/.

FIGURE 15.9 Geographic Botnet Behavior.

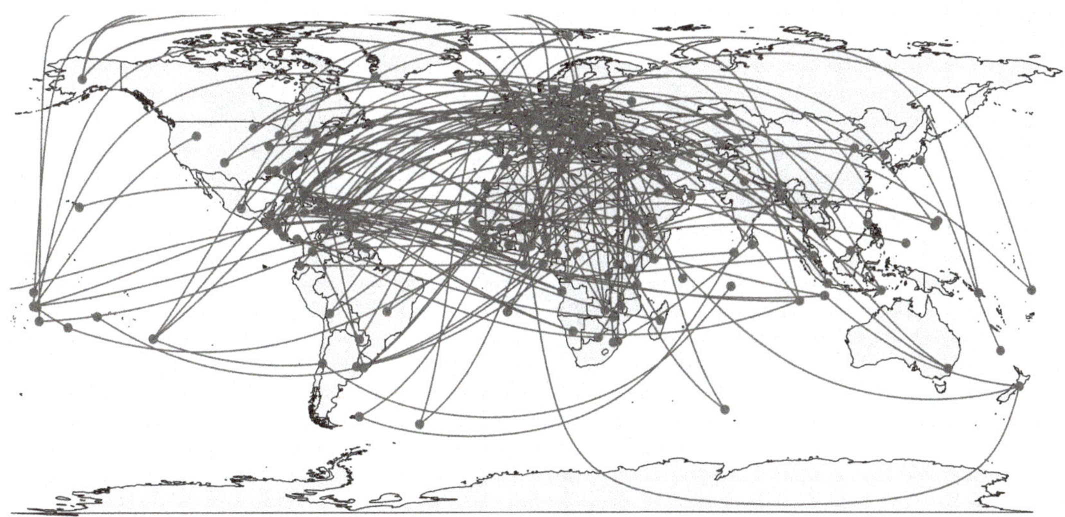

FIGURE 15.10 Geographic P2P Botnet Behavior.

Dashboards and other graphics often assume this myth to be true. For instance, they might be used to show where on the planet an attack originated. Figure 15.9 is one such example. It attempts to illustrate a botnet, including a centralized command and control server and victims worldwide.

Some networks are relatively static. The main campus of Purdue University, for instance, is unlikely to move from West Lafayette, Indiana. So, we would expect IP addresses assigned to Purdue to be in Indiana. Purdue does have campuses in other cities, however, and a GeoIP database might not know that some Purdue IPs are actually in Fort Wayne, Indiana.

IP addresses might or might not be at a given geographic location. GeoIP is not precise, no matter what television shows and movies suggest. It is an educated guess at best and has often been wrong. Unlike street addresses, the location associated with an IP address can change. While this is a nice visualization, it is essentially (or totally) useless. It tells us nothing about where the IP addresses are located, and beyond that, it tells us nothing about where the attacker is situated. It is simply a pretty picture of a map with lines on it. The attacker might be sitting in front of the command and control server; they might not be.

Of course, botnets are not all controlled by central command and control servers. Some use P2P networking. In that case, the network would look more like Figure 15.10.

These two pictures are useful in illustrating the difference between the two kinds of methods used in controlling botnets. However, they do not help us locate where the IP addresses are or who controls them (or where those controllers are located).

Another kind of attempt that is often made is to visualize the path traffic can take. BGP is a routing protocol that routes the traffic from organization to organization, so we should be able to see which countries the traffic passes through and create a map. Figure 15.11 shows the paths traffic could take from one mail server to another.

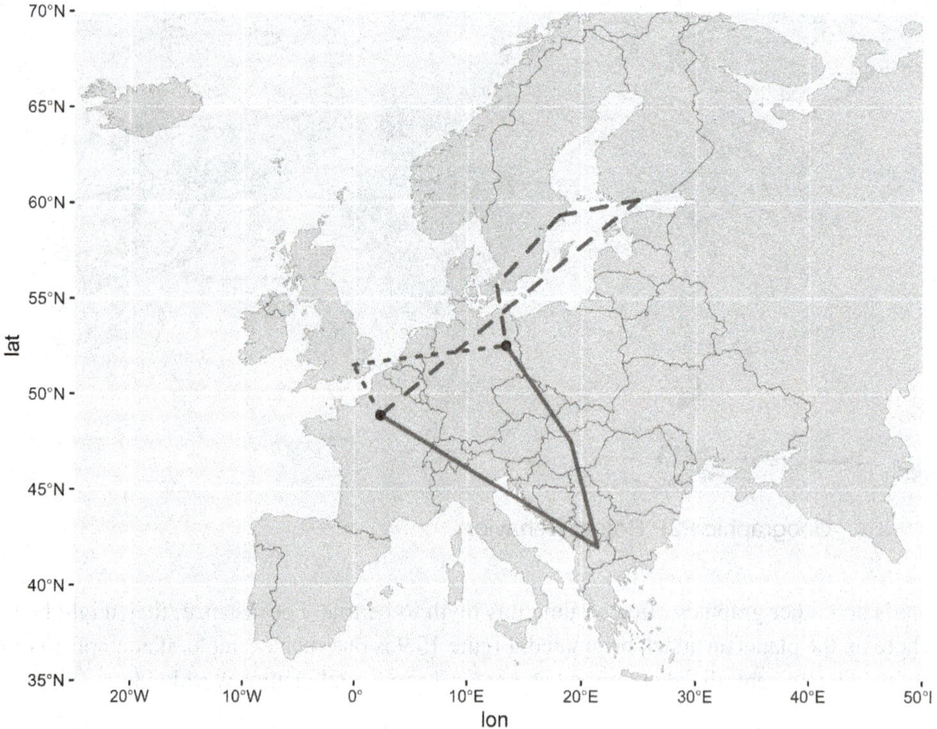

FIGURE 15.11 Example of BGP Routes.

Organizations are not always in only one country. They often span multiple countries, so saying that an organization's Autonomous System (AS) is in only one country is wrong. The picture is a bit misleading. It illustrates the potential countries that traffic could pass through, but to take this information as meaning "This is where it goes" is wrong.

Visualizing IPs and Ports Is Clear and Understandable

Traffic connects to servers on ports, which are assigned to various services. Web traffic has a pair of ports (one for encrypted traffic, one for unencrypted traffic), email delivery has a port, and DNS traffic has a port. Ports are assigned by the Internet Assigned Numbers Authority (IANA), per RFC 6335.[7]

If we are interested in the traffic accessing our systems, we want to know which ports the traffic is accessing. Is it accessing port 80 or 443 (web traffic)? Is it coming to port 25 (email)? If a system suddenly starts accepting traffic on port 25, and the operators were unaware of it, that is something to be investigated. A brand-new mail server on the network can be problematic.

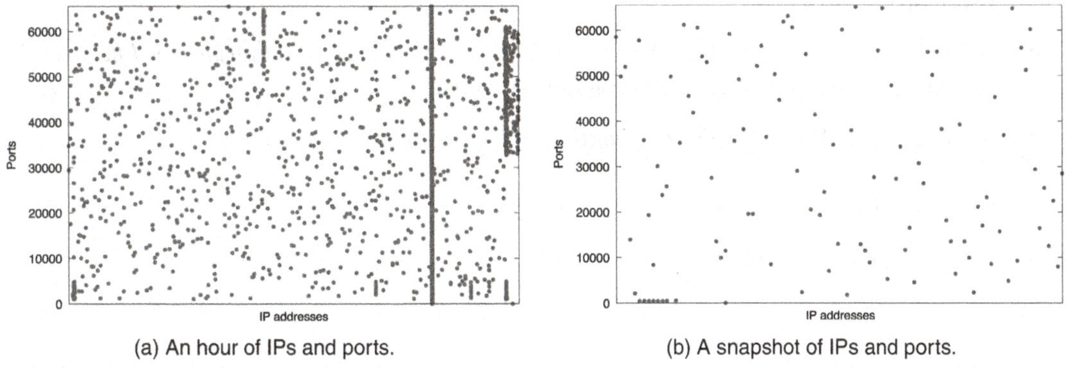

(a) An hour of IPs and ports.

(b) A snapshot of IPs and ports.

FIGURE 15.12 Two illustrations of IPs and ports.

Figure 15.12(a) illustrates the traffic that accessed IP addresses over an hour in a busy network. There are so many IP addresses on that image that determining which port is associated with which IP address is virtually impossible.

Imagine if that picture was animated. Instead of an hour of data at once, we could see how things change minute by minute. A snapshot from the animation might look more like Figure 15.12(b).

There are still too many IP addresses on the image. We can see several connections on the same port simultaneously, but as it displays all the ports, we are not sure which ports are involved.

Connections to ports are often ephemeral. Animating these connections means we would miss the short-lived connections in the animation. Matching those to IP addresses is also tricky because the image has no IP addresses and shows too many ports to be useful.

7. www.rfc-editor.org/rfc/rfc6335.html

This form of visualization is a picture of how many IP addresses connected to numerous ports at one time. There is no actionable information; there are no patterns that illustrate a cybersecurity issue. It is only traffic. And traffic happens.

If we stare at that picture long enough, we might think we see patterns in the data. This picture is generated using random numbers for the ports. To assume otherwise is falling prey to the *Clustering Illusion*. It is confusing the randomness of traffic with the idea that there must be a pattern.

New visualizations are being created all the time. People love making pictures and having their tools create them from data. Suppose someone stares at a visualization long enough. In that case, they'll eventually see a Van Gogh.[8] They can be very useful, but keep in mind their limitations.

Further Reading

Lee, John D., et al. *Designing for People: An Introduction to Human Factors Engineering*. CreateSpace, 2018.

Shneiderman, Ben, and Plaisant, Catherine. *Designing the User Interface: Strategies for Effective Human–Computer Interaction*. Pearson Education India, 2010.

Tufte, Edward R. *The Visual Display of Quantitative Information*. Graphics Press, 2001.

8. Infinite monkeys might type Shakespeare given years; it only takes a few hours of staring at cybersecurity visualizations to see Starry Night.

Chapter 16

Finding Hope

Learn from yesterday, live for today, hope for tomorrow.
The important thing is not to stop questioning.

Albert Einstein

You have reached the end of the book. So, unless you skipped some chapters, you have read about many human biases, perceptual issues, misconceptions, and mistakes. It is pretty daunting, taken as a whole, and perhaps a bit depressing, and we did not even cover all of them. How are we, as people and cybersecurity professionals, to stay optimistic about the outlook for security with so many misconceptions? One of our reviewers pleaded that we include a final chapter with some words of hope after reading only partway through this book!

We want to stress that we are all human.[1] As a species, we have a history of mistakes and screw-ups, but we still seem to have done reasonably well overall. Some of our ancestors might have approached saber-toothed tigers with "Here kitty, kitty!" and removed themselves from the gene pool. Others—often with a beer in hand—told those around them, "Hey, watch me do this!" with sometimes awful results. "Hmm, I wonder what this button does?" has also generated its share of traumas. Nonetheless, overall, humanity has progressed to the point of lasers, lab-grown diamonds, genetic mapping, single malt scotch, chocolate lava cake, muon tomography, supersonic flight, antibiotics, heart transplants, landing robots on other planets, and equipping everyone with portable mini-supercomputers capable of 24/7 access to cat videos. . . and that also make phone calls.

Everything discussed in this book can be avoided or mitigated through careful education, deliberation, and reasonable procedures. We contend that, for any arbitrary pitfall we have described, most people and organizations have successfully avoided it—some without any particular safeguards in place. That is good news and a reason to be hopeful; we are not all condemned to ignominious failure.

1. If you are **not** a human and reading this, please contact the authors: We have questions.

"Abandon Hope All Ye Who Enter Here." Dante writes of this phrase in his *Divine Comedy* as appearing at the entrance of Hell.[2] In Chapter 3, "Faulty Assumptions and Magical Thinking," we talked about the myth among users that they can never be secure, so why bother? Professionals can become demoralized in the same way when confronted with the struggles of unrelenting threats. Cybersecurity is a constant challenge, and some will lament that it feels as though things are never getting better. We disagree. There can be joy in the struggle and reward in achieving success with security and privacy. We must be cautious to avoid burning out the workforce and prioritize self-care as core to maintaining hope and optimism.

You, too, can practice avoidance of the problems we have outlined. You have already taken a significant step by reading this book and becoming familiar with the issues. The next step is to think about how you make decisions and where you can insert checks to be more confident you are not about to make a huge mistake. Research has shown that the use of carefully designed checklists evolved based on experience is incredibly helpful in avoiding some mistakes. Good aircraft pilots will attest to this. (Bad pilots, who ignore checklists, often do not keep their licenses or bodily integrity long enough to become good pilots.) Education can also play an important role in recognizing and avoiding many misconceptions and identifying the boundaries of one's capabilities.

You probably noticed that only some of the myths in the book were about misconceptions regarding how technology works. For example, in Chapter 2, "What Is the Internet?," we discussed how a VPN does not necessarily make you anonymous. Many other myths were about nontechnical assumptions. Some were about decision-making, such as "because you can, you should" (Chapter 1) and "all bad outcomes are the result of a bad decision" (Chapter 7). Misunderstandings of human behavior were a recurring theme, especially in Chapters 3, 4, and 5.

We counsel patience and forgiveness, when practical, as a general approach. Seek to think through the possibilities and avoid confusion, misunderstanding, and extreme consequences. Preparation is usually more straightforward and less costly than remediation. Imagine the clock on a terrorist bomb ticking down, with only seven seconds left. You tell your tech, "Cut the red wire!" only to hear, "But I'm color blind—you knew that when you hired me!" The choices for remediation at that point are limited—as well as being a poor plot point and non-optimal for employee retention.

You might have heard that "Forgiveness is simpler to obtain than permission." Avoid situations where that is the *modus operandi* because it is not always true. If you are a manager or supervisor, do not build or encourage that environment. Similarly, "Move fast and break things" might seem like a formula for success with start-ups, but it is a lousy and unsuitable way to pursue quality, safety, privacy, and security. If you work in any of those *-y* areas, you want your colleagues to naturally envision you as saying, "Let me show you how to do that better" rather than, "No, you cannot do that!" or "We will worry about that in the next release." That is, become a welcoming guru rather than a stern gatekeeper or a maverick rule-breaker. It works better for all involved.

You also want to be a valued team member who listens and provides advice. Having a group, especially one with diverse experiences and outlooks, can lead to insights and questions about what to do. If you welcome discussion and questions, you might be less likely to fall victim to your own misconceptions.

2. Actually, he wrote in Italian, "Lasciate ogni speranza, voi ch'entrate."

While we have pointed a spotlight on some myths, our vision for the future is not a misconception-free world. As long as there are humans, there will be myths and misconceptions. This is unavoidable. Instead, the bright future lies where those in cybersecurity can spot new myths, understand their origins, and effectively correct them. This book has been about casting light on some specific pitfalls to help you avoid new ones along your journey. You are now empowered to go out and help slay myths. We all have a shared fate if myths persist to the detriment of cybersecurity. (We also strongly recommend that you buy a pallet or two of copies of this book to give to your supervisors, direct and indirect reports, and random people you meet at the coffee shop. We cannot guarantee it will eliminate every misconception and mistake, but it is a step in the right direction!)

In this final chapter, we will tie together the themes from the book and help prepare you to tackle the world. There is hope. It might seem as if we have shed light only on a pothole-ridden bumpy road, but the route of cybersecurity is still passable. And we need your help!

Creating a Less Myth-Prone World

Dispelling myths is one thing. Preventing them is another. Being proactive in preventing intrusions is undoubtedly preferable to constantly reacting to them. The same should apply to preventing myths.

Consider myths held by end users about how their technology works. Some people believe that they are too dull or insignificant to be attacked. Others believe that buying a particular brand of smartphone will make them secure. How can we help prevent myths such as those from taking root?

Better mental cybersecurity models would help people avoid myths about risk and consequences. *Mental models* are the internal representation of how the world works, both physical and digital. A mental model can explain someone's thought process about the perceived risk and consequence of clicking a link or submitting a form. It is not essential that the person can describe the TCP three-way handshake, but it is important to understand how their clicks could be dangerous.

In Chapter 8, "Pitfalls of Analogies and Abstractions," we discussed how some analogies could foster myths. When educating users, variables within our control could decrease the tendency to reach for an imprecise analogy when describing complex cybersecurity. By choosing terminology and descriptions that are easier for non-experts to understand, troublesome analogies will not be as necessary.

Next, consider myths held by leadership. Some of these are based on how technology works (and does not), though many myths here relate to understanding the role of cybersecurity in making risk decisions. In Chapter 3, "Faulty Assumptions and Magical Thinking," we explained how compliance is conflated with security in the boardroom. In Chapter 6, we examined how cybersecurity decisions can impact others beyond the walls of a single company. In Chapter 13, "Digital Forensics and Incident Response," we addressed the myth that SOC employees are magicians. It can seem as though leadership holds two conflicting beliefs: that tech wizards can solve any problem and that cybersecurity is an endless money pit. Leaders, and the cultures they support, can be a great source of hope, but only if they seek to understand the premises and consequences of their assumptions.

Finally, there are the myths held by cybersecurity professionals. Most of the chapters in this book focused on this category, including myths related to vulnerability management, malware analysis, and data visualizations.

We discussed the dangers of making assumptions regarding how systems work and people behave. System architects also make assumptions in the engineering of trusted systems. This has not gone unnoticed by experienced security analysts, who have said that "all assumptions must be explicitly identified and tracked throughout the entire design process."[3] Design assumptions are also noticed by adversaries who commonly exploit a system's implicit assumptions. For example, systems designers long assumed that data in memory would not change without a legitimate and deliberate modification. The Rowhammer exploit demonstrated an unintended and undesirable ability to modify memory contents without access.[4]

In a less technological sense, we can be better myth busters if we are humble and acknowledge that myths and misconceptions are a part of life. Being judgmental and blaming people will not make security any better. Given 30 seconds, you can probably name a dozen strong egos in the field. Technical knowledge is power, in a sense, but elitism is unhelpful in creating a secure world. How we dispel myths is strongly correlated to the effectiveness of our message. A rude, patronizing know-it-all will meet more resistance than someone empathetic.

Another way to have hope is with support. Myths do not emerge and survive from a single individual alone. By definition, a myth is widely held and passed on among groups of people. Myth busters should also join forces. Professional associations and meetings are one way to exchange ideas and quell myths. In academia, students and faculty often meet in research groups to discuss their research and new ideas. Then they write papers that their peers review before publication. Both of these are opportunities to identify and dispel myths. In industry, developers and engineers can also use design and code reviews to hold each other accountable for misconceptions. Ask not only "Is it correct?" but "Did we fall for any assumptions?"

The Critical Value of Documentation

Many myths arise when we make assumptions about past decisions, present facts, and future events. In Chapter 3, we discussed the pitfall of designing software and services that assume users have top-of-the-line technology. We also saw what happens when we presume users—even adversaries—will behave rationally.

Documentation is a way to help avoid assumptions that lead to misconceptions. When a new person looks at your code, do they have to guess what it is supposed to do? When faced with compromised credentials, does the SOC have to make new decisions at the moment about the best way to respond without proof? A lack of documentation can lead to situations where errors occur from misunderstanding.

3. Loscocco, Peter, Gregory, Machon, and Meushaw, Robert, "Assumption-Driven Design: A Strategy for Critical Thinking in Trusted Systems Design." www.cerias.purdue.edu/apps/reports_and_papers/view/5026
4. Kim, Yoongu, et al., "Flipping Bits in Memory Without Accessing Them: An Experimental Study of DRAM Disturbance Errors," *ACM SIGARCH Computer Architecture News*, Vol. 42, No. 3 (2014): 361–372.

Software engineers are trained in technical documentation related to software development and use. This is a core part of the software development life cycle. The documentation ranges from requirements to test plans to user manuals. Done well, this documentation memorializes the choices made in the development process. At Google, for instance, design docs capture why certain decisions were made and options considered or rejected.

For most organizations, software development is only one part of the business, if it is present at all. Knowledge management is a core need across other business units as well. Confluence and other wikis are one way to document institutional knowledge. These can help employees learn internal processes and tools. In other areas, written reports are the output of a security-related function, such as malware analysis or forensic investigation reports.

Another critical area for documentation is in defined *threat models*. Imagine a company has an incident where an employee prints the secret formula to a recipe from the internal fileserver and takes it home. The CISO, learning of the incident, decrees that employees are no longer allowed to print. Three years later, the new CISO needs employees to print recovery documentation for off-line reference but cannot figure out why printing is forbidden—no documented threat model captures the circumstances in which that valuable intellectual property is at risk.

Note that creating good documentation is critical and that documentation alone will not avoid all pitfalls. Why? First, documentation must be relevant, current, and easily referenced. Second, the documentation needs to be read by the right people. Unless they understand the need to do so and the volume is manageable, that might not happen. Finally, documentation alone does not create a culture of security; instead, it contributes to that culture. The memory retention rate for someone reading documentation might be low. Even if you wrote the documentation yourself, it might be a decade before you need to go back and remind yourself, "Why did we pick MD5 again?"

It is not only security documentation; it is IT documentation in general. Do you know where your fileservers are? Your nameservers? Are you using a concentrator for your web servers?

Imagine this scenario. When you first start, you are handed documentation explaining how the web servers are using round-robin DNS[5] to rotate queries among web servers. Time passes (as it does), and the IT department chooses a spiffy new concentrator to manage the web server traffic because it has suddenly become popular. The old way no longer works. Then a vulnerability is found in that concentrator, and you are vulnerable. But you have no idea because you do not know that IT changed anything. In the worst-case scenario, that vulnerability was exploited, and you were caught completely unawares. The documentation was available, but you did not have it.

Or, imagine walking into a new company as the brand-new head of cybersecurity. You discover the company is using an out-of-date version of a host monitoring system, and as your first act, you immediately upgrade to a new version. You did not know that the outdated version existed because several legacy systems required it and would not work with anything else because you could not read any documentation on the topic. If you had the documentation, you would have understood why the previous

5. That is, DNS manages who goes to what web server, not a specialized appliance.

people in the job had made those decisions and managed the upgrade differently. As it was, you might have left some systems open to attack, which is not the best look for a brand-new head of cybersecurity.

Companies grow and change. Assuming decisions made in the beginning are always correct is a bad idea. This means your documentation is a growing beast that has to be constantly fed (Figure 16.1). It also means it is a bad idea to delete old documentation. Understanding the chain of decisions can often help you make better decisions in the future.

FIGURE 16.1 Feed the documentation beast

Some decisions seem obvious. The problem is that the "obvious" is often only obvious to you, not necessarily to anyone else. All decisions should be written down along with the important "why." If you do not write it down, you might find yourself subject to the 2 a.m. phone call demanding an explanation, or even worse, the person who shows up on your doorstep at 2 a.m. ringing the doorbell and waking up the whole house demanding an explanation. In the interests of preserving sleep, we highly recommend documentation.

Meta-Myths and Recommendations

Across the many specific myths and misconceptions and subsequent thematic chapters in this book, we see broad groups that share something in common—meta-myths, if you will. That is, some common general threads encompass many specific pitfalls. These themes will probably even contribute to new myths in the future, so it is helpful to understand them.

Meta-Myths

Meta-Myth #1: Cybersecurity is easy. In the real world, cybersecurity is more complex than most people understand or acknowledge. The diversity of technology and ever-changing threats, not to mention complicated and unpredictable human users and attackers, make cybersecurity difficult. Press coverage, TV, and movies often trivialize and glamorize cybersecurity. Developers and designers make assumptions about environments and users that bias their products. Users underestimate their risks.

FIGURE 16.2 Overly complicated security.

Meta-Myth #2: Cybersecurity is an end state. Things would be easier if we could achieve the nirvana of being secure. Unfortunately, no product, service, or guru can lower cyber risk to zero forever. Cybersecurity is a continual pursuit that requires dedicated effort. Many myths hinge on this "all we need is . . . " mentality. Cybersecurity is a process and not a product.

Meta-Myth #3: Cybersecurity is doomed. Every year, people make lists of trends in cybersecurity. They are nearly always full of predictions about how bad things will be, such as the rise in ransomware attacks. Far too little attention is given to how much progress has been made in protecting people and their devices. Things can be even better if we avoid the pitfalls described in this book. Instead of focusing on the negative and blaming users for their human faults, empower people and offer cybersecurity that is well suited for helping them appropriately achieve their primary goals safely.

Meta-Myth #4: I can tell what to trust online. It is amazing how pervasive this group of myths is. People will trust downloaded software to be correct and not contain malware. People will believe the resumés and profiles of people online. People will click links in emails claiming to offer prizes and send money to African princes to retrieve confiscated gold. Even the most astute person might have a bad day and fall prey to scams. Regular training and awareness of the threats can help, and in some cases, the software will help filter out the most egregious scams—but remember not to depend on it 100%!

Meta Recommendations

The solutions and countermeasures to myths and misconceptions are dependent on specific factors. These are described in detail throughout the book. We can generalize a few overarching best practices for avoiding myths, however. Should you forget the details of countermeasures for individual myths, remember the following general advice.

Recommendation #1: Do not overgeneralize. When we consider the diversity of use cases, people, and situations in cybersecurity, we avoid the pitfall that "everyone" exhibits a certain behavior or "all" devices are alike. Words such as "always," "everyone," "never," and "nobody" are equally problematic. Think through the accuracy of the statement. Replace overly broad language with something more realistic and precise.

Recommendation #2: Prioritize people first. Many of the myths in this book come down to human strengths and weaknesses. In his book *Facts and Fallacies of Software Engineering*, Robert Glass wrote, "Everyone pays lip service to the notion that people are important. Nearly everyone agrees, at a superficial level, that people trump tools, techniques, and processes. And yet, we keep behaving as if it were not true." Technology will not solve cybersecurity problems. It is not even the most important part of security.

A corollary is that technology does not address all problems! Effective cybersecurity involves more than simply knowing what to install and configure. It is also a matter of understanding the entire usage environment, the risks, the threats, the user population, the laws, and the financial constraints. As

Robert H. Courtney, Jr., expressed in his Third Law: "There are no technical solutions to management problems, but there are management solutions to technical problems."[6]

Recommendation #3: Slow down. In this fast-paced real world, not to mention the world of cybersecurity, we must take care to slow down and think carefully and deliberately. This is not always natural. Conscious mental exertion takes deliberate effort, but security and privacy deserve the extra mental effort. The best time to slow down is before you are overcome by stress and crisis—for example, at the *planning* stage of a development project or during the *creation and exercise* of an incident response playbook.

Recommendation #4: Keep learning. We are constantly discovering new things. New technology comes to market, and clever people develop new ideas. Old truisms fade with new circumstances and experiences. To be maximally effective requires ongoing learning, which sometimes includes unlearning old ideas. Be wary of learning from social media or hearing about things from a cousin's BFF's ex-spouse's web admin—those are prime avenues for the spread of new myths.[7] Focus on respected publications, seminars, and classes held by professional nonprofit associations such as ACM, USENIX, and ISSA. Note that the mark of good science and engineering is the willingness to change approaches based on new evidence; politics and religion are where people claim to have the absolute, immutable facts, not cybersecurity!

Avoiding Other and Future Traps

This book covers myths and misconceptions we have commonly seen in our collective experiences. It is a snapshot in time that reflects today's technology and thinking. We know it does not present a complete and exhaustive set of pitfalls. As cybersecurity evolves, new issues will arise. (If this book is wildly successful, we will amend some future editions accordingly.) If you think we missed something important, send us a note.[8]

In addition to the specific areas presented here, we want you to learn how to identify and challenge any myths and misconceptions you might encounter. The four recommendations we shared in the previous section should work equally well at dispelling other myths and misconceptions.

Parting Thoughts

We hope that this book has led you to think critically about how the art and science of cybersecurity can go awry when people succumb to myths and misconceptions. There is no lack of opportunities to put this into practice. Now you must muster your energy and enthusiasm to bring about the safety, security, and privacy that result from good cybersecurity practices.

Good luck!

---

6. Cf. www.ietf.org/rfc/rfc4949.txt
7. That is not to say that everything you hear from those sources is false. Rather, exercise due diligence and verify things learned, especially from potentially questionable sources.
8. myth-misconception@googlegroups.com

Appendix

Short Background Explanations

This appendix contains short descriptions of items mentioned throughout the text. These are intended to provide some context for readers who might not be familiar with these items. These descriptions should **not** be taken as definitive or fully detailed! Some of them have details omitted that we do not see as necessary to understand their use in the book. We recommend consulting good textbooks, tutorials, and reliable news sources if you want more details on any of these topics.

Advanced Persistent Threat (APT)

APT as a term refers to organized penetration activity. It is often activity by a nation-state espionage group or organized criminal gang; as we have noted elsewhere, a criminal group might be working for a government so the attack involves both. APT attacks are usually stealthy, long-lived, and intended for data exfiltration. APT attacks are generally targeted at high-value organizations. A person is highly unlikely to have an APT incident on their home computer—unless they are an employee or contractor for a major company or government agency. APTs tend to use stealthy methods such as spear phishing, attacks on zero-day vulnerabilities, or supply chain insertion. Thereafter, the attackers may alter commands and configurations to provide persistent access.

Cloud Computing

A cloud is a collection of computers and storage, either private or commercial (public). Clients might use the resources in the cloud from other clients. The basic idea behind the cloud is that the resources can be flexibly allocated and deallocated as clients need without requiring the individual clients to have a built-up reserve that they might not be using all the time.

Cloud services might provide virtual storage, computers, or desktops. They might also supply software services on demand. The common names for these are Software as a Service (SaaS), Platform as a

Service (PaaS), Infrastructure as a Service (IaaS), and Desktop as a Service (DaaS). Several vendors provide these services on a per-use or subscription basis.

See also "Færie Dust Can Make Old Ideas Magically Revolutionary" in Chapter 1.

Cross-Site Scripting

Cross-Site Scripting, also known as XSS, is a vulnerability that allows attackers to inject their own script into a website. It occurs when the website allows the user to input text but doesn't validate or clean it. It's considered one of the most common JavaScript vulnerabilities—though it isn't really a problem with JavaScript, but rather with how the website uses it.[1]

Rather than entering simple text, the attacker will enter bits of code. If there's no validation, the web server may execute the code.

Cybersecurity and Infrastructure Security Agency (CISA)

CISA[2] is a U.S. federal agency that was put into place in 2018 with the Cybersecurity and Infrastructure Security Agency Act of 2018. It replaced the National Protection and Programs Directorate (NPPD) as the department handling cybersecurity for the Department of Homeland Security (DHS). The mission of CISA is:

> We lead the National effort to understand, manage, and reduce risk to our cyber and physical infrastructure.

CISA has two defined roles. It is the operational lead for the `.gov` domain. That is, this agency is the lead for federal non-DoD cybersecurity issues. It also acts as the national coordinator for critical infrastructure security.

Firewall

In building construction, a *firewall* is designed to prevent fire from spreading. Of course, the best-case scenario is that there is no fire. If you happen to get unlucky and a fire starts, the firewall will stop it from spreading beyond the firewall, at least for some time. The firewall does not attempt to determine whether it's a good fire or a bad fire; it simply stops everything right there. In cybersecurity, a firewall is either a dedicated device or software that lets you decide there is good traffic and bad traffic and allows you to let the good traffic in but keep the bad traffic out.

1. https://owasp.org/www-community/attacks/xss/
2. www.cisa.gov/

Before firewalls, it wasn't easy to keep people from accessing your system. If you had a web server, anyone could access it by default. If someone decided to flood your server with requests, you had to deal with it until they got bored. The firewall changed that.

At the most basic level, firewalls look at IP addresses, domains, ports, and protocols for filtering and blocking. Some firewalls will look into packets for specific contents and patterns. Generally, firewalls operate on traffic in real time. Firewalls are often located at the perimeters of networks. Firewall devices might also handle other duties, such as intrusion detection, routing, VPN management, and traffic shaping.

A firewall is a good first line of defense, but it should not be your only defense. There are ways to get past one, some unexpected and others on purpose, such as through email. You want people to email you, but an email is also often an infection vector.

Honeypots

Honey draws flies and wasps.[3] If you wish to distract the nuisance insects from more valuable items and perhaps trap them for study, a pot of sticky honey will serve the purpose. Similarly, if you want to decoy attackers and maybe study their tools and methods, you would deploy a honeypot system: a system that appears authentic and tempting to the attacker, but is instrumented and monitored.

Honeypots are but one example of deception and decoys. Others include fake documents and fake credentials, which are called honeytokens.

Internet Worm and the WANK Worm

One of the oldest worms distributed on the Internet, the Internet worm, also known as the Morris worm, took the computing world by storm on November 2, 1988.[4] It took advantage of several vulnerabilities, including one in the sendmail program, a common program used to send email at the time. The worm's author allegedly wrote it to see if he could, and it caused havoc for days.[5]

The worm resulted in the first felony conviction under the CFAA[6] and led DARPA to fund the CERT/CC at Carnegie Mellon University.[7] CERT/CC was created to be a central point to manage network emergencies, as no such agency existed at the time.[8]

The WANK worm of 1989 was an attempt to cause havoc by locking people out of their systems,

3. And Winnie-the-Pooh, but we assume Pooh is benign.
4. Spafford, Eugene H., "The Internet Worm Program: An Analysis." ACM SIGCOMM Computer Communication Review; Vol. 19, No. 1 (1989): 57.
5. See the section"Because You Can, You Should" in Chapter 1, "What Is Cybersecurity?" for more discussion.
6. www.fbi.gov/news/stories/morris-worm-30-years-since-first-major-attack-on-internet-110218
7. DARPA was prompted to do this by William Scherlis of Carnegie Mellon.
8. www.esd.whs.mil/Portals/54/Documents/FOID/Reading%20Room/DARPA/20-F-1335_Final_Production_CERT_CC_1988.pdf

threatening to delete files, and making monitors display a message that included the phrase "Worms Against Nuclear Killers," presumably the origin of the name. It started at NASA, but it did not stay there, as often happens with worms.[9] It spread from NASA to the U.S. Department of Energy, and then to CERN in Switzerland and RIKEN in Japan. The guess from some is that the worm's creators were attempting to cause havoc before the launch of the Galileo spacecraft, which had a small amount of plutonium on board to power a fuel cell. The worm authors failed in that goal, and the spacecraft launched on time. While some people think that the reason for creating the worm was the spacecraft, others believe it was to cause trouble. One of the investigators of the incident surmised the authors were playing with the word "wank," which is British slang.[10]

The worm was eventually traced to two Australian men, which led to the first major Australian trial for computer crimes.[11] One of the men helped the authorities when he called *The New York Times* to brag about writing the code. The result was a lot of time and money cleaning it up, while the men were sentenced to community service for the crime.

The Morris and WANK worms highlighted how vulnerable networks of systems were and underscored that cybersecurity needed a higher priority. The Internet, in particular, was built on trust, and some people are constantly seeking ways to abuse that trust for their advantage or amusement.

Intrusion Detection System (IDS)

An IDS has a simple job. It's there to detect intrusions; thus, it's great that it has such a relevant name. A host-based IDS monitors activity on a computer to identify questionable activity.

A Network Intrusion Detection System monitors traffic and looks for suspicious traffic patterns. It does not know what suspicious traffic is: It has to be programmed to recognize it. For example, the `log4j` vulnerability was exploited remotely through web traffic, and we know what that web traffic should contain. That means we can set up a rule on the IDS to look for any web requests that contain characters matching a `log4j` exploit.

In general, an IDS does not do anything with the traffic other than creating an alert, which should be investigated, and possibly blocking the traffic. Some of these systems can be coupled with other tools to change firewall rules, alter network traffic, and more.

`log4j` Vulnerability

Application developers love logging systems. These systems can help them find and fix problems if they know what happened. For a web server, we want to know who accessed which page, when,

9. www.realclearscience.com/blog/2019/01/12/when_nasa_got_wanked.html
10. https://web.archive.org/web/20080227132540/www.aracnet.com/~kea/Papers/Politically%20Motivated%20Computer%20Crime.pdf
11. No record is available to determine if one of the men said, "Hold my beer," before writing said code.

and how.[12] The more information available, the easier it is to debug. Otherwise, for web applications, we are effectively debugging in the dark with our hands under a blanket and the screen brightness set to 0.

The Apache Software Foundation develops `log4j` to manage logging in applications.[13] This would be a short description if that is all `log4j` did. Instead, Apache gave this software more functionality. It logs messages and can also be programmed to be smart about the messages it gets. Unfortunately, it turns out that attackers could take advantage of this feature, thus sparking multiple CVEs and a lot of work from security researchers. The vulnerability was exploited for cryptojacking and installing backdoors.[14] The first report of the U.S. Cyber Safety Review Board was on the `log4j` vulnerability.[15]

Orange Book/Trusted Computer System Evaluation Criteria (TCSEC)

The TCSEC, colloquially known as the Orange Book,[16] was a set of standards issued by the National Computer Security Center (NCSC) of the NSA that defined how to assess the trust level of specific computer systems.[17] It described six levels, from Minimal Protection (which meant the target failed the assessment) to Verified Protection, which included formal verification of code.

The original version, released in 1983, was considered the first significant methodology for security evaluation. It had several problems, not the least of which was keeping up with changing software and practices. It was also focused on the operating system and building it to be trustworthy when protecting confidentiality, which was soon not the only threat.[18]

Phishing

Fishing is the attempt to catch a fish by dangling an attractive bait on a hook. Phishing is attempting to enter a system by dangling an attractive bait in an email.

In this kind of attack, an email appears to be from a reputable source and directs the recipient to accomplish a task. The request is often presented with some urgency to encourage action before careful consideration. The phish might ask the reader to log into a portal, enter a credit card number, or generally do something that seems reasonable and rational yet gives up their information. Other

12. Web logs do not necessarily record "why" someone accessed a particular webpage.
13. https://logging.apache.org/`log4j`/2.x/
14. www.zdnet.com/article/log4shell-exploited-to-infect-vmware-horizon-servers-with-backdoors-crypto-miners/
15. www.cisa.gov/sites/default/files/publications/CSRB-Report-on-Log4-July-11-2022_508.pdf.
16. Called that because the printed version of the book had an orange cover.
17. https://csrc.nist.gov/csrc/media/publications/conference-paper/1998/10/08/proceedings-of-the-21st-nissc-1998/documents/early-cs-papers/dod85.pdf
18. www.cs.clemson.edu/course/cpsc420/material/Evaluation/TCSEC.pdf and Lipner, Steven B., "The Birth and Death of the Orange Book," *IEEE Annals of the History of Computing*, Vol. 37, No. 2 (2015): 19–31.

phishing attacks might seek to induce the recipient to click on an attached document or link that will result in a flaw in the current system being exercised, such as infection with malware.

Phishing is popular with malicious actors because it works. In 2020, there were over 240,000 complaints about phishing.[19] There were undoubtedly many more incidents that were not reported (or detected). The AntiPhishing Working Group (APWG) reported over a million phishing attempts in the first quarter of 2022, representing a significant increase.[20]

In spearphishing, the phish is carefully tailored and targeted directly at someone rather than being sprayed across many recipients. In SMS phishing, the phish comes through SMS messaging rather than emails; this kind of attack is sometimes referred to as "smishing" (and unsolicited advertising is sometimes referred to as "SPIM," corresponding to email SPAM).

Spearphishing of high-value targets (e.g., the CEO) is sometimes referred to in the literature as "whaling."

Rowhammer Attack

If you take a hammer to a row of glass and repeatedly hit it, sooner or later, that glass will break. *Rowhammer* (or *Row hammer*) is an attack that applied the same idea to memory chips. Dynamic Random Access Memory (DRAM) is kept in a grid of memory, so Rowhammer rapidly and repeatedly accesses one row of the grid in an attempt to build up an electric charge[21] that will modify or delete data in other rows of the memory grid.[22] The goal is to flip some bits to either disclose information or alter information flow.

SolarWinds Incident

SolarWinds[23] is a software development house specializing in network and systems management software. Its software is widely used by organizations from government to industry and everything in between. One of its products is the Orion platform, which manages IT environments. It's an all-in-one solution to control everything, from the infrastructure in the environment to the applications in use.

Unfortunately, in 2020 the company was the victim of an attack.[24] The attackers used that access to upload updates to the company's portal that contained Trojans. When customers downloaded and

19. www.ic3.gov/Media/PDF/AnnualReport/2020_IC3Report.pdf
20. https://apwg.org/trendsreports/
21. Roughly akin to rubbing socks on a carpet to build up a static charge.
22. https://arstechnica.com/information-technology/2015/03/cutting-edge-hack-gives-super-user-status-by-exploiting-dram-weakness/
23. www.solarwinds.com/
24. www.csoonline.com/article/3601508/solarwinds-supply-chain-attack-explained-why-organizations-were-not-prepared.html

installed these altered updates,[25] havoc erupted. The customers of SolarWinds, if they installed updates, were now victims of the same attackers. CISA announced, with other government agencies, that it appeared a Russian group was behind the attack.

This incident involved a *software supply chain attack*. You (if you were a victim of this) were not attacked directly, but your supplier was. In these attacks, you would have done nothing wrong to become the victim—the attacker discovered that it was easier to attack your supplier and then use that route to attack you.

Virtual Private Network (VPN)

A VPN is software that creates an encrypted "tunnel" between two points. It acts as if it was a dedicated network link over which traffic flows. An eavesdropper cannot read the encrypted traffic. A VPN connection might also provide protected connectivity to a trusted DNS server to prevent spoofing attacks on the client endpoint.

Remote workers often use VPNs to have a remote machine "inside" the network of their employer. In these cases, the VPN terminates inside the enterprise's firewall, and the clients act as remote, semi-tethered clients. VPNs are also often used to circumvent content controls (e.g., censorship) imposed by political entities and organizations.

WannaCry

WannaCry was a ransomware attack in May 2017. The ransomware attacked Windows systems and held the data on the systems until a bitcoin ransom was paid. It spread from system to system and demanded at least $300 from the victims, eventually increasing that demand to $600.[26] The interesting thing about WannaCry was the built-in kill switch. The ransomware looked for a domain, and if the domain didn't exist, then the ransomware happily encrypted the victim's drive. If it did exist, then the ransomware wouldn't spread any further. A researcher, Marcus Hutchins, discovered that the malware was looking for the nonexistent domain and registered it to see what would happen. As luck would have it, that activated the kill switch, and the ransomware stopped spreading.

It was estimated that the ransomware caused $4 billion in damage.[27]

25. You trust your software provider's website, right?
26. www.techtarget.com/searchsecurity/definition/WannaCry-ransomware
27. https://securityintelligence.com/articles/what-has-changed-since-wannacry-ransomware-attack/

Zero Trust

Zero trust is not a product or a protocol; instead, it's an attitude and an architecture.[28] It's a way of looking at the problems of design and implementation of security to include the idea that no one should be trusted and everyone must be verified. Systems are treated as if they were already breached. All activity is suspect until proven otherwise. Traditionally, users would authenticate themselves once, and everything would assume that the associated activity was still that user. Zero trust removes that assumption, minimizing where trust credentials may be used.

See also "Færie Dust Can Make Old Ideas Magically Revolutionary" in Chapter 1, "What Is Cybersecurity?"

28. www.darkreading.com/perimeter/forrester-pushes-zero-trust-model-for-security

Acronyms

ABET Accreditation Board for Engineering and Technology

ACM Association for Computing Machinery

AI Artificial Intelligence

AML Adversarial Machine Learning

ANSI American National Standards Institute

APT Advanced Persistent Threat

APWG Anti-Phishing Working Group

AS Autonomous System

ASLR Address space layout randomization

AV Antivirus

AWS Amazon Web Services

BGP Border Gateway Protocol

CDT Center for Democracy and Technology

CEO Chief Executive Officer

CFAA U.S. Computer Fraud and Abuse Act of 1986

CIA Central Intelligence Agency

CIO Chief Information Officer

CISA Cybersecurity and Infrastructure Security Agency

CISO Chief Information Security Officer

CME Common Malware Enumeration

CMM Capability Maturity Model

CMS Content Management System

CNA CVE Numbering Authority

CTI Cyber Threat Intelligence

CVD Coordinated Vulnerability Disclosure

CVE Common Vulnerability Enumeration

CVSS Common Vulnerability Scoring System

CWE Common Weakness Enumeration

DaaS Desktop as a Service

DB Database

DDoS Distributed Denial of Service

DEP Data Execution Prevention

DFIR Digital Forensics and Incident Response

DHS Department of Homeland Security

DMCA Digital Millennium Copyright Act

DMZ Demilitarized Zone

DNS Domain Name System

DoS Denial of Service

DPRK Democratic People's Republic of Korea—North Korea

DRAM Dynamic Random Access Memory

EAR Export Administration Regulations

ECPA Electronic Communications Privacy Act

EDR Endpoint Detection and Response

EFF Electronic Frontier Foundation

EKG Electrocardiogram

EPIC Electronic Privacy Information Center

EPSS Exploit Prediction Scoring System

FACR Foreign Assets Control Regulations

FBI Federal Bureau of Investigation

FedRAMP U.S. Federal Risk and Authorization Management Program

FEMA Federal Emergency Management Agency

FFRDC Federally Funded Research and Development Center

FIRST Forum of Incident Response and Security Teams

FISMA Federal Information Security Management Act

FUD Fear, Uncertainty, and Doubt

GDPR General Data Protection Regulation

GUI Graphical User Interface

HIPAA Health Insurance Portability and Accountability Act

HR Human Resources

HTTPS Hypertext Transfer Protocol Secure

IaaS Infrastructure as a Service

IANA Internet Assigned Numbers Authority

IAU International Astronomical Union

ICS Industrial Control Systems

IDS Intrusion Detection System

IEEE Institute of Electrical and Electronics Engineers

IETF Internet Engineering Task Force

IMAP Internet Message Access Protocol

IoE Internet of Everything

IoT Internet of Things

IP Internet Protocol

IRB Institutional Review Board

ISO International Organization for Standardization

ISP Internet Service Provider

ISSA Information Systems Security Association

ITAR International Traffic in Arms Regulations

LOAC Law of Armed Conflict

MAC Media Access Control

MFA Multifactor Authentication

ML Machine Learning

NAT Network Address Translation

NATO North Atlantic Treaty Organization

NCSC National Computer Security Center

NFC Near-Field Communication

NFT Non-fungible Token

NICE National Initiative for Cybersecurity Education

NIST National Institute of Standards and Technology

NPPD National Protection and Programs Directorate

NSA National Security Agency

OPSEC Operational Security

OS Operating System

OSI Open Systems Interconnection

OSS Open Source Software

PaaS Platform as a Service

PCI DSS Payment Card Industry Data Security Standard

P2P Peer-to-Peer

PHI Protected Health Information

PII Personally Identifiable Information

POP Post Office Protocol

RAT Remote Access Trojan

RCE Remote Code Execution

RFC Request for Comments

ROP Return-Oriented Programming

SaaS Software as a Service

SBOM Software Bill of Materials

SCADA Supervisory Control And Data Acquisition

SHA Secure Hash Algorithm

SLA Service Level Agreement

SLO Service Level Objective

SMTP Simple Mail Transfer Protocol

SOC Security Operations Center

SSL Secure Socket Layer

TCP Transmission Control Protocol

TCSEC Trusted Computer System Evaluation Criteria

TLS Transport Layer Security

TOR The Onion Router

TPM Trusted Platform Module

TTP Tactics, Techniques, and Procedures

UDP User Datagram Protocol

UFO Unidentified Flying Object

VEP Vulnerabilities Equity Process

VPN Virtual Private Network

WWW World-Wide Web

XDR Extended Detection and Response

Index

A

B

C

D

E

F

G

H

J

K

L

M

N

O

P

Q

R

S

T

W

X

Y-Z